MAPPING REALITY

SUNY Series in the Philosophy of the Social Sciences

Lenore Langsdorf, Editor

MAPPING REALITY

AN EVOLUTIONARY REALIST METHODOLOGY
FOR THE NATURAL AND SOCIAL SCIENCES

JANE AZEVEDO

STATE UNIVERSITY OF NEW YORK PRESS

Published by
State University of New York Press, Albany

For information, address State University of New York Press,
State University Plaza, Albany, N.Y. 12246

Production by M. R. Mulholland
Marketing by Nancy Farrell

Library of Congress Cataloging-in-Publication Data

Azevedo, Jane, 1949-
    Mapping reality : an evolutionary realist methodology for the
natural social sciences / Jane Azevedo.
        p.   cm. — (SUNY series in the philosophy of the social
sciences)
    Includes bibliographical references and index.
    ISBN 0–7914–3207–6 (hb : alk. paper). — ISBN 0–7914–3208–4 (pb :
alk. paper)
    1. Sociology—Philosophy.   2. Knowledge, Theory of.   I. Title.
II. Series.
HM24.A94   1997   96-2367
301'.01—dc20   CIP

10 9 8 7 6 5 4 3 2 1

In memory of Denis Butler

CONTENTS

FIGURES

ACKNOWLEDGMENTS

I am grateful to the following individuals and organizations for permission to include their photographs, images, and maps in this book:

Figure 4.1   The Anastasia prospect. Photograph courtesy of Ross Jenkins.

Figure 4.2   Anastasia—oblique aerial photograph. Courtesy of John Nethery.

Figure 4.3   Anastasia—vertical aerial photograph. © Queensland Department of Lands.

Figure 4.4   Anastasia—2.2 micron wavelength image. ATM data acquisition and processing by CSIRO Exploration & Mining. Used with permission, after Fraser et al. 1986.

Figure 4.5   Anastasia—7762 Lyndhurst Edition 1.1:100 000 topographic map. This map is © Commonwealth Copyright, AUSLIG, Australia's National Mapping Agency. It has been reproduced with the permission of the General Manager, Australian Surveying and Land Information Group, Department of Administrative Services, Canberra, ACT.

Figure 4.6   Anastasia—Atherton 1:250 000 Geological Map, Sheet SE 55–5. © Queensland Department of Minerals and Energy.

Figure 7.1   Dorrigo Area B—East filter 5 × 5 Convolution Matrix. Landsat MSS image processing used with the permission of the Department of Geology, University of Newcastle.

Figure 7.2   Dorrigo Area B—Principle Component Analysis of Bands 1, 3, & 4—RGB. Landsat MSS image processing used with the permission of the Department of Geology, University of Newcastle.

Figure 7.3   Dorrigo Area B—Bands 7, 5, & 4—RGB. Landsat MSS image processing used with the permission of the Department of Geology, University of Newcastle.

Figure 7.4   Dorrigo Area D—East filter 3 × 3 Convolution Matrix. Landsat MSS image processing used with the permission of the Department of Geology, University of Newcastle.

Figure 7.5 Dorrigo Area F—East filter 3 × 3 Convolution Matrix. Landsat
           MSS image processing used with the permission of the Department
           of Geology, University of Newcastle.

INTRODUCTION

Sociology emerged as a discipline at the end of the nineteenth century. In the wake of the Industrial Revolution and the French Revolution, an entirely new form of society came into being, bringing enormous and rapid social dislocation and appalling living conditions to the new working class. Sociology arose with the recognition of the need for a systematic scientific approach to understanding these widespread problems.

But sociology has, from the start, been characterized by diversity. While this has always been seen as problematic,[1] crisis talk in sociology has been gathering momentum since the late 1970s.[2] The most likely reasons seem to be the downfall of the standard positivist/empiricist view of science; the changing nature of the world order, including the rise of postcolonialism and increasing globalization; and a pressing awareness of the environmental problems associated with capitalism. Whatever the reasons, the increase in crisis talk has given rise to renewed interest in the metatheory of sociology. Ritzer, for example, has devoted much effort to the establishment of metatheory as a respectable field of study within the discipline of sociology, and toward defining its terms of reference.[3]

But as we approach the end of the twentieth century, many doubt that the promise of a scientific understanding of society will ever be realized.[4] The Marxist base of critical (as opposed to mainstream) sociology in the West fell into disrepute—slowly at first with the realization of the excesses of Stalinism, then rapidly with the Polish Solidarity movement, the fall of the Berlin Wall, the massacre in Tiananmen Square, and the collapse of the Soviet Empire.

Postmodernism and poststructuralism, with their rejection of the Enlightenment values of universal humanism that historically led to both intellectual Marxism and liberalism, filled the gap. Instead of searching for universal solutions to the problems of the human condition, these perspectives encourage the recognition of difference, working piecemeal toward the betterment of the lives of the relatively powerless, be they defined by class, race, ethnicity, or gender, by providing them with a voice.

But in the same move, postmodernists and poststructuralists reject not only the positivist/empiricist models of science, but with this the Enlightenment values of truth and reason that gave rise to these models. Ironically, this leaves postmodernist and poststructuralist positions with nothing to underpin their defense of the powerless. The relativism entailed by their epistemology has no place for any perspective-neutral criteria of validity. How then can conflict between theories be resolved? With no intellectual means available, decisions revert to the will of the most powerful, leaving a sociology supportive of the status quo.

With no external criteria of validity, proponents of postmodernism and poststructuralism are themselves immune to criticism, often to the detriment of those whose voices they wish to be heard.[5] David Trigger illustrates this poignantly. Hodge and Mishra, he argues, while accusing much anthropology and history in Australia of silencing the authentic Aboriginal voice, are—by the nature and degree of their interpretive licence in an analysis of the art of Aboriginal artist, Peter Skipper, and by ignoring Skipper's own interpretation— guilty of the same.[6] By focussing on the texts of the less powerful, postmodernist and poststructuralist perspectives attempt to revive a critical and ethical social science, producing much good work. But their insistence on a relativist epistemology undermines their attempts and heightens the issue of ethics in social science.

The need for a critical and ethical science of society, then, has if anything increased, while the possibility of such a science has decreased. The pace of social and technological change and environmental degradation is increasingly threatening human existence, yet still we lack sufficient understanding not only of social processes, but of sociology itself, to be at all confident that such a threat can be avoided.

It was against this background that I decided to explore the nature of the diversity of sociology, identify any problems that might arise, and attempt to provide solutions to those problems. This book is the result. It will, I hope, contribute to the development of an adequate sociology.

The book is divided into four parts. Part I has two chapters. Chapter 1 is a study of the nature of sociology as a discipline and the problems to which its nature gives rise. Chapter 2 looks at the major metatheoretical attempts to come to grips with these problems—humanism, relativism, and naturalist realism— and argues that a naturalist realist metatheory is the only one that is in principle able to provide adequate solutions.

But Chapter 2 also raises a number of new problems that stand in the way of any naturalist realist metatheory of sociology as traditionally conceived. These problems depend for their solution on the development of a naturalist realist methodology of science. This is attempted in Part II. Chapter 3, in the naturalist tradition, explores the ways that human beings gain and validate knowledge of the world. Chapter 4 incorporates these insights into a model of scientific method.

Equipped now with a naturalist realist methodology of science, I attempt in Part III to develop a set of solutions to the budget of problems raised in Part I. Chapter 5 addresses the nature of mentalist explanations—a problem for any

naturalist account of the social sciences. Chapter 6 explains and applauds the
diversity of sociological theory, giving an account of both science and sociology that satisfies the relativist plea for a pluralist methodology. Chapter 7
shows how the knowledge acquired by a pluralist methodology can be unified,
showing the possibility of a naturalist realist methodology of science.

Chapter 8 is the only chapter in Part IV. It summarizes the arguments of
the earlier chapters and reflects on how together they provide solutions to the
problems raised in Part I.

My argument is necessarily wide-ranging and complex. While I have provided abstracts at the start of each part, a brief summary is presented here as a
preliminary guide.

The argument starts, in chapter 1, with an analysis of the nature of the diversity of sociological theory and method. Studies by Lodahl and Gordon[7] in
1972 and Gareau[8] in 1985 show that sociology is nationalistic, ethnocentric,
and sectarian. Furthermore, domination of sociology as a discipline parallels
economic domination, leaving sociology open to the charge of being mere ideology. Sociology as a whole is dominated by the major sects in the first and second worlds. Despite the breakdown of the Soviet Union, reports from the XIIth
World Congress of Sociology show the continuing influence of second world
sociology as late as 1990,[9] although its focus is changing rapidly. Recent analyses suggest that post-Soviet sociology is moving from its predominantly state-
dominated theoretical orientation to empirical studies and is in disarray,
precisely because of the current lack of a strong state.[10]

In the Western world, the most influential sociology stems from the major schools in the United States. C. Wright Mills's classic analysis of sociology
in the United States exposes both the philosophical underpinnings of the major
schools and the ideological consequences of the work they produce.[11] Mills's
analysis, which dates back to 1959, identifies the Parsonian "grand theorists"
as the dominant school, with what he calls "the abstracted empiricists," a school
based on a positivist philosophy of science, following hard on their heels. Today, the tables have turned. Recent analyses suggest that positivist sociology is
now dominant in the United States,[12] with Parsonian functionalism in decline.
The rising stars appear to be postmodernism and poststructuralism, perspectives that are rapidly increasing in influence throughout the humanities and social sciences in the West.[13]

I then turn to an analysis of the way various sociological perspectives can
be distinguished on the basis of the assumptions they make about the
social world, and illustrate these positions with various studies of deviance. The
chapter concludes with the identification of various epistemic and pragmatic
problems that arise for the discipline of sociology from the nature of its diversity. The epistemic problems center on the sectarian use of different perspectives whose underlying assumptions are conflicting. Sociology is

multi-paradigmatic, and there is at present no paradigm-neutral way to decide between the theories of opposing paradigms. The epistemic problems of sociology are often used to justify the claim that sociology is not scientific. This in turn diminishes the status of sociological research and leads, in these times, to a funding squeeze even more restrictive than that being applied to the natural sciences.

The nature of the problems faced by sociology as a discipline indicates that any solutions to these problems will be found in the metatheory of sociology. In chapter 2, I examine the major current metatheories of sociology—humanism, relativism, and naturalist realism—and argue that from a strategic point of view a naturalist realist solution is best. But the humanist and relativist positions themselves raise further methodological problems that a naturalist realist metatheory must deal with. Moreover, no adequate naturalist realist methodology of science has so far been developed.[14] So a naturalist realist solution to the problems outlined in chapter 1 will involve the development of a naturalist realist methodology of science that takes account of the problems that humanism and relativism raise for a naturalist realist position.

I make a start on this task in chapter 3, where I argue from an evolutionary naturalist realist perspective that despite the cultural and social influences on it, science, far from being *just* a social construction, does in fact give knowledge of reality. The biological nature of humans influences the nature of scientific knowledge. Scientific theories are necessarily partial abstractions from reality; the determination of validity is ultimately practical; and the objectivity of science depends on its social institutional nature and the norms of the scientific institution, which guarantee that reality is a factor in the selection of scientific theory. While a Rorty-type mirroring metaphor is adequate to modelling positivist science, these factors all suggest that a mapping metaphor is more appropriate for modelling non-positivist science. The use of the map as a model of the scientific theory takes account of both the social nature of science and its reliability.

Chapter 4 starts with the assumption that the successes of the natural sciences are to be explained by their methodology. I develop a methodology that adequately accounts for the determination of validity in the natural sciences while taking account of the contextual and culturally-bound nature of scientific theories. The mapping model of science proposed in the previous chapter is expanded to show the similarities between the nature of the validity of maps and the nature of the validity of theories. Major features of the methodology that I develop are (a) that all facts, concepts, theories, and laws are to be treated similarly as theories, the difference lying in their respective levels of abstraction, and (b) that all theories of whatever kind have a limited scope of valid application. The limits on the scope of valid application are a function of both the domain of a theory and its metatheory, and are thus a function of the problem the theory was intended to solve. It is in this sense that the methodology I develop is at least a partial answer to the issues raised by relativism.

In Chapter 5, I address the problems raised for the social sciences by humanism. There, I explore the nature of scientific explanation in general, and sociological explanation in particular, and address the question of whether reasons, motives, intentions, and so on, can have a place in a naturalist realist methodology. It is on the grounds that reasons are completely different from causes that the strongest arguments for humanism are based, but I show that, while different from causes, reasons do not have a separate ontological existence. Explanations in terms of reasons can be scientific. They are in fact a form of functional explanation. Functional explanations are common in the natural sciences, so under this interpretation there is no reason to believe that interpretive sociology requires a fundamentally different methodology from the natural sciences.

Chapter 6 is an argument for a pluralist methodology in sociology. I argue that sociology is among the most complex of sciences. I explore the way humans can know a complex reality and expand on the mapping model of science. Just as no single map can represent every feature of the geographic world, no single theory can represent a complex social reality. I draw the conclusion that a pluralist methodology is essential for such knowledge. Sociology, rather than being either unitary or eclectic, must necessarily be pluralist with respect to theory and method. The assumptions underlying the various sociological perspectives are best seen not as contradictory ontological assumptions, but as methodological devices for simplifying what is an extraordinarily complex reality.

While this view of sociology allows for multiple perspectives or world views, it results in parcels of unrelated knowledge, and is open to the charge of relativism. In chapter 7, I argue that the principles of validity that lie behind the mapping model of scientific knowledge developed in chapters 3 and 4 are adequate to the task of unifying sociological knowledge, and I develop a set of procedures by which unification of knowledge might be achieved. The theory of unification that I develop rests on the assumption of a unified reality, but is broadly anti-reductionist in nature.

Chapter 8 concludes the argument by drawing together the various threads. I show that a naturalist realist metatheory of sociology is possible; that the metatheory I develop provides adequate solutions to the problems raised by relativists and humanists; that it provides adequate criteria for testing the validity of sociological theory; and that it provides the solution to the ideological nature of much sociology.

I have written the book with three major audiences in mind, sociologists interested in methodological and foundational issues, philosophers of science generally, and philosophers of social science. The latter are the only group likely to be familiar with the issues from both sociological and philosophical viewpoints. So I have used examples from sociology, anthropology, and the natural sciences, in an attempt to make philosophical issues clear to sociologists and the nature of sociology clear to philosophers of science, many of whom—mistakenly, I believe—use physics as the exemplar of science.

Many people have helped with this book. It started life as a doctoral thesis, and I am deeply grateful to my supervisor, C. A. Hooker, who provided much stimulating conversation, constructive criticism, and, above all, encouragement when I most needed it.

I am indebted to a great many scholars, most known to me only through their work, who have influenced me over the years—perhaps most to Stephen Jay Gould, whose works provided many an interesting lead, and whose delightful prose, intellectual integrity, and insatiable curiosity were an inspiration.

Many friends and colleagues read some or all of the book at various stages. Their encouragement and criticism has been invaluable. I particularly thank Michael Carrithers, Bernd Baldus, Peter Quartermaine, Stephen Crook, John Bern, Geoffrey Samuel, and Kai Hahlweg, Steve Fuller, Peter Manicas, and Lenore Langsdorf. But their advice was not all heeded, and I alone take responsibility for flaws in the finished product.

My husband, Ross Jenkins, helped me to select and produce the photographs. I thank him. I also thank him, John Nethery, Steve Fraser (CSIRO Exploration & Mining), AUSLIG (Australia's National Mapping Agency), the Department of Geology, University of Newcastle, and the Queensland Department of Minerals and Energy for permission to use their photographs. Wal Murray produced the line drawings, and Kerry Delaney helped with the reproductions.

Much editing and proofreading of early drafts was done by my husband Ross, brother Simon, and friend Dorrit Nesmith. I cannot thank them enough. The job was to have been done by my journalist father Denis Butler, but sadly he died before I could give him more than the first chapter. I tried to apply to the rest what I learned from his comments, but I miss his savage pencil. This book is dedicated to his memory.

I

THE PROBLEMS

In Part I, I explore the nature of sociology as a discipline. Sociology exhibits a diversity of theory and method, and this diversity gives rise to a number of problems for the discipline. I go on to explore the ways that the dominant metatheoretical positions resolve those problems, and argue that a naturalist realist metatheory of sociology is the only one that is in principle capable of providing adequate solutions to the entire range of problems.

1

Sociology Today

Take all these tape recordings I make with fish. If I did it with people it would take ten times as long! First I'd have to get their consent and the permission of the top brass, then I'd have to work out what they really mean when they talk to each other, apart from what they say they mean. And then they'd only disagree with me! They'd argue with my findings! They'd say that wasn't what they meant at all! That I had it all wrong! They'd argue back! It's all too much! So I went into fish instead.

—Rosaleen Love, *Where Are They?*

1.1 The Diversity of Sociological Method

Sociology is characterized by a diversity of theories and methods. Kuhn's notion of a paradigm[1] has been used recently to analyze the nature of this diversity. The concept of a paradigm was developed by Kuhn as a part of his explanation for the progress of science. Sciences, according to Kuhn, develop through a number of stages. Before a scientific discipline is properly established, it is characterized by a number of schools with rival paradigms. Paradigms include the general theoretical assumptions, specific laws and theories, and the methods and techniques adopted by the scientific community. Paradigms set standards for legitimate work and coordinate and direct problem-solving activities. Normal science is characterized by a single paradigm, that is, by considerable consensus over theories and problems, methods and techniques. This facilitates efficient communication and decision making within the scientific community, and allows the accumulation of knowledge. Difficulties within the paradigm, for example, large numbers of unsolved problems, may lead to a crisis, which in turn may lead to a scientific revolution. This will be followed by a new period of normal science. The existence or otherwise of a single scientific paradigm marks the distinction between science and non-science for Kuhn, and it is on this basis that he labels sociology pre-scientific.

The lack of consensus in sociology was demonstrated by Lodahl and Gordon in a study of graduate schools in the United States, in which they compared the disciplines of physics, chemistry, sociology, and political science according to the level of agreement or conflict among university staff over theories, methods, and findings. Their study tested such features as the level of agreement over the content of survey courses and the ease of communications and decision making. They found that physics consistently ranked highest on consensus, whereas political science and sociology ranked lowest.[2]

While some, like Kuhn, argue that the multiplicity of theories and methods in sociology indicates its pre-scientific nature, and attribute its supposed lack of progress vis-a-vis the natural sciences to its lack of a paradigm, others argue that the diversity of theories and methods is itself paradigmatic for sociology, and is a result of the nature of its subject matter. From such a viewpoint, the diversity of theories and methods is itself not a problem for sociology. What is problematic is the apparently contradictory nature of the various assumptions underlying sociological methodology and theory. This, together with the existence of contradictory truth-claims, is a problem for all who believe that sociology should provide reliable knowledge of the social world.

These issues lie very close to the surface in sociology, and no student of sociology can remain unaware of them for long. Indeed, many introductory sociology texts devote space to raising the issues of theoretical and methodological diversity, and encourage students to look at some of the metatheoretical issues that lie behind them.[3] In this chapter, I explore the nature of the diversity of sociology in order to identify some of the associated problems. This discussion also provides a useful backdrop for my development, in later chapters, of a new metatheory of sociology.

1.2 The Patterns of Diversity

Despite the diversity within the discipline, sociology is far from chaotic, and can be analyzed in several ways, each of which illuminates one or more significant features of the discipline.

1.2.1 First, Second, and Third World Sociology

The first aspect of the diversity of sociology I shall discuss is its regional, national, and ethnocentric character. This feature of sociology is important because it indicates, at a gross level, the political and ideological influences on sociology.

In a global study of sociology, Gareau establishes that sociology has regional, national, and ethnocentric characteristics that go beyond the content of specific studies.[4] The various contemporary sociological perspectives, or "sects" as he calls them, are assumed by Gareau to be legitimate sociology. While acknowledging that sociology everywhere is characterized by diversity, Gareau is particularly interested in whether the patterns of diversity are different in the first, second, and third worlds.

Gareau finds that, just as the first world is dominated economically by the United States, first world sociology is dominated by North American sociology. There are considerable differences between North America and Western Europe, with the former tracing its philosophic ancestry to the analytic tradition and the latter to the more overtly normative and qualitative European philosophies. Despite this, Gareau is able to demonstrate United States dominance of Western sociology. In the United States, sociology was dominated throughout the 1950s and 1960s by the structural functionalist perspective and by a quantitative approach to methodology.[5] The influence of this perspective declined somewhat in the 1970s, but it is still influential.[6] Western European sociology is more openly normative and less quantitative in its approach.

Second world sociology was dominated, at the time of the study, by the U.S.S.R., although China was a major exception. The dominant perspective in Soviet sociology, at least until the mid-1980s, was Marxist historical materialism. While there is a strong tendency in North American social science to see sociology as value-free, Soviet social science argues that norms are an essential part of sociology. Soviet sociology tends to be more historical and less quantitative than North American sociology.

The differences between North American and Soviet sociology extend beyond the nature of sociology in general to the nature of society and sociological explanations. The dominant North American sects adopt a consensus view of society and have a tendency to prefer individualistic explanations of social phenomena. The dominant Soviet bloc sects[7] take a conflict perspective of society and prefer holistic explanations of social phenomena.[8] Gareau maintains that the differences between the dominant sects in the first and second worlds are such that sociology may be regarded as discontinuous, in much the same way that Kuhn regards successive paradigms in science as discontinuous.

Although some sociological perspectives may not be as dissimilar as these extremes, Gareau has shown that sociology today is multi-paradigmatic. And having shown how these dominant sects support the respective political ideologies in the regions concerned,[9] and are in turn supported by their respective ruling parties,[10] Gareau sees this discontinuity as almost guaranteed by the political power of the antagonists. This, in addition to developments in third world sociology to be discussed a little later, form the crux of Gareau's argument that if to be scientific is to be uni-paradigmatic, sociology will not become scientific in the foreseeable future.[11]

A major aspect of the discontinuity between first and second world sociology is that the dominant sects in each are supported by an ideology that serves to legitimize the sect as sociology. This is a further indication of the multi-paradigmatic nature of sociology, and illuminates the above distinction between sociology and the natural sciences. Sociology is legitimized at the sectarian (or perspective) level, whereas physics, for example, is legitimized at the disciplinary level.[12]

The ideologies of the dominant sects discussed so far work in much the same way as each other. They identify the sect concerned as a science (in Marxist formulations) or as a proto-science nearing maturity (in many non-Marxist formulations), often at the expense of competing sects, which may be deemed non-scientific or ideological.[13]

In a literature survey, Gareau identifies three myths related to the dominant sects: the Marxist myth (which excludes China), and the short and long forms of the non-Marxist myth. All three focus on methodological criteria as the basis for legitimacy. The Marxist myth legitimizes as science sociology based on the theory of historical materialism and the dialectic method.

The short form of the non-Marxist social science myth is rarely stated explicitly; more often it appears as an underlying assumption in books on the epistemology and methodology of the social sciences. The myth takes the form of acknowledging some progress in sociology (or, in some cases, the social sciences in general), locating it in the pre-scientific stage, and advising that further progress will be achieved if the methods of the natural sciences (particularly physics) are adopted. Thus, Reynolds identifies ambiguity in formulating statements and ignorance of the structure of scientific writing as the major impediments to sociology's attaining maturity.[14] And Popper, pointing out the limits of the historicist method, whereby prediction is based on historical studies designed to reveal patterns and trends in history, recommends its rejection and the adoption of the methods of physics. Interestingly, as Gareau points out, Popper comes precariously close to historicism himself when discussing the effects of Galileo and Newton on physics and Pasteur on biology. Popper continues, "But the social sciences do not as yet seem to have found their Galileo."[15] The implication is that they will, and that they will follow in the footsteps of physics and biology and reach maturity.[16]

The long form of the social science myth again assumes that each science develops through a pre-scientific stage. A precondition for the attainment of mature social science is a society characterized by rationalism, secularization, and respect for science in general. The transition to maturity, then, depends on two factors: the emergence of an autonomous field of study, and the application of the "scientific method."[17] This form of the myth can be seen in the works of Durkheim and Weber, two of the great founders of sociology. Both aimed to establish sociology as a separate and autonomous discipline, and both were keen to develop a scientific method of studying society.

The adoption of these myths enables the dominant sects of the first and second worlds to legitimize their own work as scientific (or very nearly so) and to write off, without too much consideration, the views of opposing sects as unscientific. This is in fact what has happened. Gareau refers to Gurney's study on the treatment of Marxist sociology in the United States. The study was based on an analysis of mainstream American sociological journals and books during the formative years of academic Marxism, from 1895 to 1920. Gurney's study found that on the whole, Marxism was ignored. But where references to the Marxist perspective were made, they were predominantly negative. Of the six major categories of criticism, the first was that Marxism was unscientific. The other categories were that Marxism is deterministic, and that it is wrong with respect to individualism, psychology, the class struggle, or private property.[18] On the other hand, Kassof's study reveals that Soviet sociology has criticized the sociology of the United States for not recognizing the universal validity of Marxist-Leninism. It is thus seen as reactionary and scientifically sterile, as being incapable of formulating general theory, and as being bogged down in insignificant and non-cumulative empirical studies. Moreover, it sees the dominant sect as functional for capitalism, hiding the exploitative nature of the system from the North American population.[19] Although far from being a comprehensive study of the various sociological perspectives, Gareau's study, then, makes it quite clear that sociology is characterized by at least two dominant and conflicting sects or paradigms.

In addition to showing that sociology in the first and second worlds is dominated by particular sects, Gareau argues that sociology is nationalist and ethnocentric in its focus. To support his argument, Gareau analyzed studies from two first world countries, the United States and France. The United States studies were designed to determine the great men (Gareau points out wryly that women are hardly ever found on these lists) in the discipline. The studies were based on the major journals and texts, and counted the numbers of citations of each person, excluding the classic sociologists such as Durkheim. Of the ten North American studies analyzed, eight found that North Americans comprised 100 percent of the modern scholars. In the other two studies, North American scholars comprised 95 percent and 95.7 percent. Gareau's argument is that unless sociology is seen as a nationalistic and ethnocentric enterprise, these results are disproportionate and hard to explain. To further support the contention that sociology is nationalistic, Gareau analyzes a series of seven French studies designed to show the best departments in the discipline for pursuing graduate studies. The studies asked French academics to nominate the universities, French or foreign, that they would recommend for doctoral studies, and were asked not to let location or residence influence their answers. French institutions were recommended overwhelmingly, capturing between 84.3 percent and 100 percent of the nominations. Although no comparable study has been done in the United States, a North American study did find that the most-cited authors were all at North American institutions.[20]

None of this is too surprising if one acknowledges that sociology is for the most part interested in solving particular problems in particular societies, and that empirical studies are carried out in particular societies. But problems do arise, if one fails (as Parsons, for example, does) to recognize the historical and cultural specificity of sociological theory.[21]

What is perhaps more surprising is the effect of nationality on truth-claims. In a study of the attitudes of social scientists to the Malvinas/Falklands War, Gareau surveyed political scientists and sociologists at the tri-annual conference of the International Political Science Association held in Rio de Janeiro in 1982, and at the quadri-annual World Congress of the International Sociological Association held in Mexico City in the same year. The respondents were mainly from the United States, Western Europe, and Latin America. Asia was poorly represented at the conferences, and Soviet bloc social scientists, with the exception of the Poles, refused to participate in the survey. Gareau hypothesized that the British and Argentine responses would represent extremes, that responses from United States and Western Europe would resemble the British responses, and that those from the rest of Latin America would resemble the Argentine response. The hypotheses were all confirmed.

Of greater interest than straightforward attitudes, though, were the conflicting truth-claims when respondents were asked to classify the war as either "colonial," "cold war," or "territorial"—83.3 percent of the Argentine respondents chose "colonial," whereas only 9.5 percent of the British chose this response. Of the respondents from the rest of Latin America, 61.3 percent agreed with the Argentine response, compared with only 36.1 percent of those from the United States and 31.9 percent of those from Western Europe.[22] Given the importance of such value-laden concepts to sociology, the implication is that the truth-claims of sociology are along nationalist lines, and are thus not verified or denied at a disciplinary level as are the truth claims of the natural sciences. This, as I pointed out in §1.1, is a problem for sociology.

Gareau continues his argument for the multi-paradigmatic nature of sociology by examining the major external influences on the development of sociology. He finds that the content and style of sociology are shaped by the discrete cultures and societies in which the discipline is found. Cultural differences in sociology often show up as national differences when a nation is dominated by one culture, but can be distinguished in studies of countries with two dominant cultures, such as Canada. Political factors, too, are a major influence on sociology. Governments and ruling elites may engage in censoring or prohibiting unwanted sects, as happened in the Soviet Union under Stalin, or may simply encourage favored approaches by influencing the institutional organization of social science and funding favored types of research, as happens in the United States and in Australia.

Economic factors (apart from direct government funding) are also influential in the first world. Gareau mentions that businesses, and in the United States, foundations, are involved in the production of sociological knowledge.

But the production of sociological knowledge anywhere requires journals, libraries, universities, and so on, in addition to researchers. Many third world countries are unwilling, and probably unable, to support the cost of social research. It is no accident that the great economic powers are the great social science powers.

The economic domination by the first and second worlds over the third world led Gareau to hypothesize that third world countries import sociology from the first world and second world, regardless (at least initially) of the cultural and historical specificity of sociology. A survey of studies of social scientific communications confirmed this. Incoming transactions to North American social science journals were overwhelmingly domestic in origin, and of those few that were not, all were from other first world countries, and the majority of these were from English-speaking countries. This contrasts sharply with incoming professional transactions in physics for the same country, where the majority of journals cited were foreign, and the majority of those were from the non-English-speaking first world. In physics, foreign, English-language journal citations ranked lower than citations from the second world, but in the social sciences, citations from the second world were virtually nonexistent. In the rest of the first world and most third world countries, incoming transactions in the social sciences are substantially North American.[23] Social science communications between the United States, the rest of the first world, and much of the third world, are characterized by unequal, vertical interactions. Gareau found indications that the same characteristics apply to the relations between the Soviet Union, the rest of the second world, and those parts of the third world under second world influence, but these indications were based on much thinner data than were available for the first world.

Third world sociology, then, is predominantly derivative from first and second world sociology. Social science communications in the third world are dominated by one-way flows from the United States, or perhaps the United States and the original colonial power. There is little return flow to the first world and little interaction among third world practitioners themselves, according to Gareau. However, this is changing. With the exception of China and other socialist countries, Roy has noted a trend among Asian social scientists towards indigenization, and a turning away from the dominant Western frameworks.[24] This development seems to have resulted in a deal of regional cooperation among Asian social scientists as they recognize the similarity of the problems they face. Gareau notes that Latin American sociology seems to be developing in a similar way. There is now a high level of regional interaction in Latin America, and Gareau sees the general framework of dependency theory as influential, and as being capable of providing an alternative paradigm to those of the dominant sects of the first and second worlds.

Gareau's global analysis of sociology not only establishes that sociology is multi-paradigmatic. His analysis of the trend in third world sociology also suggests the formation of a major new paradigm. If Kuhn's criterion for science is correct, sociology is far from approaching scientific status. It is instead becoming more diverse.

Gareau accepts Kuhn's definition of a mature science. But unlike Popper, he denies that sociology is waiting for its "Galileo." The global state of sociology is, according to Gareau, as good as can be expected. Sociology as a discipline produces much useful knowledge. But, Gareau argues, such knowledge is of a practical nature. Sociology can never aspire to scientific status. Rather, it is a craft, and a reasonably good one at that.

I shall not go into the distinctions that can be made between practical knowledge and theoretical knowledge. Gareau himself took this distinction for granted. But ultimately, as will become clear later in this book, such a distinction cannot be clear-cut. Nor, I believe, is it particularly useful in distinguishing scientific knowledge. However, I do agree with Gareau that much sociology is useful, and also with his characterization of sociology as multi-paradigmatic.

I disagree with his assumption that sociology as a discipline is as good as it can be. Sociology is diverse by nature, but, as I hope to show in chapters 6 and 7, sociology produces scientific knowledge as a result of its diversity, and the adoption of a consciously pluralistic methodology will improve sociology. And while it is diverse, sociology need not be multi-paradigmatic. Lack of communication between the various sects or perspectives can be overcome.

But Gareau's point that sociology today is multi-paradigmatic remains. I turn now to an analysis of the dominant sects or perspectives in the United States (which, recall, dominate first world sociology) to further illustrate the disparate nature of much sociology, and to identify more of the problems that this gives rise to.

1.2.2 Sociology in the United States of America

The multi-paradigmatic nature of contemporary sociology is apparent not only from the global pattern of diversity, but also from the patterns of diversity within the United States of America. C. Wright Mills's analysis of North American sociology,*The Sociological Imagination,* though dated, is still relevant. It has the advantage of bringing out some of the deeper conceptual and methodological problems associated with sociological sectarianism, so I use it as the basis of my discussion.[25]

Sociology as a discipline, according to Mills, is distinguished by the nature of the problems it seeks to solve and the questions it seeks to answer. These questions fall into three main groups. The first set is to do with the structure of particular societies; with their components, and how they are related to one another; with how a particular society differs from other varieties of social order; and with the importance of particular features of the society for its stability and for change. The second set of questions relates to the place of the society in human history; with the mechanics by which it changes; with how particular features affect and are affected by the historical period in which they move; and with the essential features of this period of history and how it differs from other periods. The third set of questions is concerned with the varieties of men and women that prevail in this society and this period; with what kinds of "human nature" are revealed in the conduct and character observed; and with the meaning for "human nature" of the features of society being examined. The skill that is required to answer these questions, to relate social structural issues to personal biography, is what Mills calls the "sociological imagination."[26] In the United States in the late 1950s, two dominant schools vied to be established as *the* way to do sociology. Mills named these schools the "grand theorists"[27] and the "abstracted empiricists," respectively. Both schools are open to criticism.

The "grand theorists."   Mills illustrates the position of the grand theorists with references to that archetypal grand theorist, Talcott Parsons. Parsons's main concern is with the problem of social order, with how societies maintain their integrity over time. He conceives of societies as social systems with certain functional prerequisites. According to Parsons, any society, if it is to survive, must meet the physical needs of its members, which means it must have systems of production and distribution. There must be some sort of common agreement among its members about their priorities and aims, which means it must have the institutional means for identifying, selecting, and achieving these collective aims. Any society has to ensure that its members are sufficiently motivated to play the roles required of them and have the necessary commitment to the values of that society. Members must also have ways of managing any interpersonal conflicts that may develop. And any society has to ensure the integration of the various parts of the system.[28] Grand theorists, then, are operating at a high level of abstraction. Their primary concern is conceptual analysis rather than empirical study.

The focus of Mills's criticisms of the grand theorists in general, and Parsons in particular, is directed at the way universal validity is claimed for their model of society. The simplifying assumptions of grand theory are effectively given the status of universal laws. But if they are treated as universal laws, they are false. The existence in most Western societies, and recently in the East as well, of large and well-organized groups of people with values opposing those of the dominant groups shows that far from being a universal feature of all societies, the assumption that societies must have a basic value consensus is false. And by ignoring the concept of power, and the fact that one form of power is the power to manage ideas, Parsons's framework precludes him from even posing the important empirical questions of how and to what extent the major institutions of any particular society are legitimized.[29] In fact, the way the grand theorists portray the normative order leads to the assumption that virtually all power is legitimized. To further illustrate this point, Mills quotes Parsons as saying that in the social system,

> . . . the maintenance of the complementarity of role-expectations, once established, is not problematical. . . . No special mechanisms are required for the explanation of the maintenance of complementary interaction-orientation.[30]

Within the framework of grand theory, the social system is seen as intrinsically stable and harmonious. The idea of conflict cannot be effectively formulated. Structural antagonisms, large-scale revolts, and revolutions cannot be considered. The idea of social change is unavailable to grand theorists and, according to Parsons, to sociology:

> When such a theory is available, the millennium for social science will have arrived. This will not come in our time and most probably never.[31]

This is not to say that grand theorists never use the concepts of conflict and change, but rather

> . . . that in so far as problems are dealt with realistically by grand theorists, they are dealt with in terms that find no place in grand theory, and are often contradictory to it.[32]

The error of the grand theorists is that they see the problem of social order as being simply a theoretical one, whereas in fact the question of what holds any particular society together is contingent. Different social structures differ in the degree of unity they have, and in the way that unity is achieved. Mills illustrates this point with brief analyses of the principles of integration of classical liberal society and Nazi Germany. The principle of integration of classical liberal society is the free ascendancy, within each order of institutions (for example, the economy, kinship, the military), of the free initiative of individuals in competition with each other. In Nazi Germany, the principle of integration was the coordination of society by an often uneasy alliance of the political, economic, and military elites, whose power within their respective institutional order was highly concentrated.[33] And it is hard to believe that, prior to democracy, contemporary South African society had a value consensus, or that such consensus was the basis of its social order. The point is that there is no one answer to the problem of social order, and that in studying social order in any particular society, historical and cross-cultural analyses are essential. These examples show the inadequacy of grand theory in treating the problem of social order. Mills's lesson is that conceptual analysis, although essential to sociology, cannot alone provide the answers to sociological problems. What ought to be a part of the sociological enterprise has become, in the hands of the grand theorists, the whole.[34]

The "abstracted empiricists." Of abstracted empiricism, Mills remarks that, "Like grand theory, [it] seizes upon one juncture in the process of work and allows it to dominate the mind."[35] Abstracted empiricism is recognizable by the types of problems that are researched and the way they are studied. Advertising and media research, public opinion, and voting behavior are characteristic areas of study, and the preferred methods are the set interview and the survey. The data obtained from these are subjected to statistical analysis in search of significant relations among them. The thinness of the results obtained is the focus of Mills's criticism.

He points to the school's studies of political life, most of which are concerned with voting behavior, primarily, Mills suggests, because of its amenability to statistical analysis. Mills questions the value of full-scale studies of voting that make no reference to the party machinery for electioneering or indeed to any political institution at all. He refers to an accredited and celebrated study carried out in Ohio that found that rich, rural, and Protestant persons tended to vote Republican, and that people of opposite type tended to vote Democrat. But there is precious little in the study about the dynamics of North American politics. The idea of legitimation is one of the central problems of political science, particularly so because the problems of this discipline bear on questions of opinion and ideology.[36] But these issues, and the answers to questions about the depth of understanding of political issues by North Americans, cannot even be raised in the framework of abstracted empiricism, as we shall see.

Before I discuss the reasons for the poverty of this approach, I shall look at another example of the type of work done by the abstracted empiricists, this time in the area of social stratification. Among the most fruitful ways of typifying and understanding social strata and in turn the structural features of a society are the sociological concepts of caste, estate, and class. Of these, class, usually defined in economic terms, is the concept most applicable to modern western societies. The concepts of class developed by Marx, who analyzed class in terms of relationship to capital and the means of production, and by Weber, who analyzed class according to economic differences of market capacity that produce different life chances, have been extraordinarily fruitful. The abstracted empiricists have not imported the key notions from either of these theories, yet neither has a new theory of class arisen from this school. Rather, its practitioners have been content to use "quite spongy 'indices' of 'socio-economic status'"[37] to produce rankings, for example, of jobs. Such a series of rankings can give no idea of such social structural features as power, let alone any understanding of it.

Abstracted empiricism, then, is characterized not only by the sort of problems it tackles and the way it tackles them, but also by a lack of substantive propositions and theories. A further characteristic of the school is the bureaucratic administrative apparatus it employs, and the type of workers it recruits—semi-skilled technicians rather than thinkers. Although critical of the latter, it is with the general lack of fruitfulness of the school that Mills is most concerned. Both can be traced to the main characteristics of the school—the positivist epistemology held by its practitioners, how they hold to it, and how they use it.

> It is this [positivist] philosophy that underlies both the type of substantive research undertaken and its administrative and personnel apparatus. Both the substantive thinness of the actual studies and the felt need for the apparatus find their major intellectual justification in this particular philosophy of science.[38]

A look at the major characteristics of positivism will show how adherence to it produces thin results. Positivism is a scientifically oriented form of empiricism first developed by the nineteenth-century French philosopher Auguste Comte. For the greater part of this century it was the dominant philosophy of science and it has been influential in sociology since the discipline first developed.[39] The natural sciences were regarded by the positivists as producing highly informative and certain knowledge of the world. The foundations of that certainty were sense experience and logic. Sensory experience was held to be incorrigible, and the logic of the scientific method truth-preserving. Beliefs about the world could be regarded as knowledge only if they could be put to the test of experience. The incorrigibility of observation combined with the logic of the scientific method to produce certain knowledge. Thus, the appropriate objects of scientific knowledge were phenomena and the general relations between phenomena.

The positivists regarded all phenomena as subject to invariable laws of nature. The task of science was to discover these laws, and scientific explanation consisted in showing the links between particular phenomena and these general laws of nature.[40] It was most definitely *not* the task of science to establish the underlying nature of phenomena, nor to search for generative/causal mechanisms. According to Comte, the search for these forms of knowledge belonged to the earlier "metaphysical" or pre-scientific stage in the development of knowledge. In the scientific or positivist stage, according to Comte,

> . . . the human mind, recognizing the impossibility of attaining to absolute concepts, gives up the search for the origin and destiny of the universe and the inner causes of phenomena, and confines itself to the discovery, through reason and observation combined, of the actual laws that govern the succession and similarity of phenomena. The explanation of facts, now reduced to its real terms, consists in the establishment of a

link between various particular phenomena and a few general facts, which diminish in numbers with the progress of science.[41]

For the positivists, then, scientific knowledge was characterized by several features. The objects of scientific knowledge were phenomena; such knowledge took the form of general laws that must be testable by experience; and explanation consisted in showing the logical links between specific phenomena and these laws. These tenets formed a general methodology for the acquisition of scientific knowledge. Such knowledge was certain and value-free, and only knowledge acquired via these general methodological principles had any claim to the term. It is these methodological principles that underlie the positivists' claim of the "unity of science."[42] The social sciences, then, were subject to the same broad methodological principles as the natural sciences. Insofar as they did not, or could not, comply, they were not producing knowledge at all.

The desire of the abstracted empiricists to be scientific and their belief that positivism provided *the* scientific method led them to follow its prescriptions in a way never seen in the natural sciences, even in physics, of which positivism was an attempted, if unsuccessful, model.[43] They allowed the "scientific method" to determine the sort of problems they took up and the ways in which they were formulated. To see how this happens, Mills turns to the work of Lazarsfeld, whom he regards as one of the more sophisticated exponents of abstracted empiricism.

Lazarsfeld regards sociology as a methodological speciality that stands between social philosophy and the mature social sciences (he mentions economics and demography as examples of the latter). The function of sociology is to turn the social analysis of the social philosopher (whom Lazarsfeld equates with the individual observer) into fully fledged social science.

Lazarsfeld identifies four steps in this process. "There is first the shift of emphasis from the history of institutions and ideas to the concrete behavior of people."[44] The point of this step seems to be to ensure that the data meet the positivist criterion of observability. In fact they do so only insofar as one believes in the veridicality of inner perception, for as Mills points out, the data are obtained from surveys and interviews, and the questions asked in these are put in terms of the psychological reactions of individuals.

The second step in the transition to a mature social science is, according to Lazarsfeld, "a tendency not to study one sector of human affairs alone but to relate it to other sectors."[45] Laudable if true, but Mills insists that it is not, except in the limited sense in which the meaning of "relate" is confined to statistical relations. Again this is consistent with the "scientific method," in which causal or generative relations in the world are held to be representable in some form of truth-preserving logic.

"There is third," Lazarsfeld continues, "a preference for studying social situations and problems which repeat themselves rather than those which occur only once."[46] Social structure is manifested in the regular patterns of social relations, but this is not, Mills points out, an attempt to introduce structural considerations, but rather a preference to study events (for example, elections) in which many people participate, and which recur and can thus be studied again.

This illustrates the way in which the positivist philosophy of science determines the sort of problem to be studied. For this version of positivism[47] uses induction as the logic of the scientific method. Induction cannot guarantee certainty. There is always a chance that one's next observation will falsify the generalization. But naive inductivists believe that generalization from a finite number of singular observation statements is legitimate, provided that certain conditions are satisfied. These conditions are: first, the number of observation statements forming the basis of the generalization must be large; second, the observation must be repeated under a wide variety of conditions; and third, no accepted observation statement should conflict with the universal law or generalization derived.[48] Lazarsfeld's third step for the transformation of social philosophy to a fully fledged social science can be seen as an attempt to ensure the first condition for legitimate induction.

The fourth step in the transition relates to the type of data required if sociology is to be a science. There will be "a greater emphasis on contemporary rather than on historical social events . . . ," and " . . . the sociologist will therefore have a tendency to deal mainly with contemporaneous events for which he is likely to get the kind of data he needs."[49] Lazarsfeld's prescriptions for sociology illustrate the way that the abstracted empiricist school allows the "scientific method" rather than the substantive problems of social science to be the orienting point for sociological work.[50]

The abstracted empiricists themselves have offered different explanations for the thinness of their results, the most convincing of which is that sociology, as practised by the abstracted empiricists, is a relatively new science, so many more studies are required before they can be added together to give a picture of the social structure. But as Mills points out, it is arguable that any number of studies could be added together without giving a picture of social structure, for the data collected by the abstracted empiricist school is in terms of individual attributes. No amount of data in terms of individual attributes or motivations can add up to a social structural view of society. People are often unaware of the structural features of society, and even if they are aware of them, their responses to the sorts of questions asked are unlikely to show such awareness.

These points are perhaps best illustrated by considering a study that I frequently run with my students, the aim of which is to give information about the structure of Australian society. The initial hypothesis is that there is gender inequality in Australian society. "Inequality" can be defined as unequal access to power and resources. To investigate "gender inequality" means to investigate whether inequality in a society is non-random, divided along gender lines, and due not to the biological characteristics of the sexes but rather to socially determined characteristics.

A simple, but not entirely trivial, example of how gender inequality might be instantiated is in the driving of motor cars. The driver of a car is in a position of power vis-a-vis any passengers. And both women and men in Australia drive well. In fact, on certain indices, for example, numbers of dangerous driving convictions and numbers of accidents, women seem to do rather better than men. A simple test of gender inequality in driving would be to establish whether significantly more men or women drive when adults of both sexes are present in a motor car.

Taking for granted the sampling issues that must be addressed in any statistical work of this kind, the test is simply a head-counting exercise. The results indicate that overall, in something approaching 85 percent of cars carrying adults of both sexes, a male is driving. Interestingly, between 10 p.m. and 1 a.m., these figures are reversed. This is a clear indication of power inequality along gender lines.

Now imagine the study is taken a little further. The relevant cars are pulled over and the occupants asked why that particular person is driving the car. The replies are varied. "It's my car." "Jessie gets nervous in traffic." "Bill is better at long distances." "It's her turn—we split the driving." "I know the way." And after 10 p.m.—"I always drive if we've been drinking," and "Bob's over the limit."

Note that none of the respondents' replies will be in terms of the social structure. They will be in terms of their personal motivations and their immediate milieu. The interesting question then becomes, what is the relationship between the social structural situation and individual motives and milieus. Do more men than women own cars? Why? Why is ownership linked with the right to drive (control)? Are women more nervous in traffic? Why? Or why are they said to be? Or are they just nervous with men? Do men drink more than women? Why? The list of questions is endless, and many of them end up in the territory of gender socialization and the social construction of masculinity and femininity, and thence back to the social structural situation in Australian society.

By considering this example, Mills's criticisms of abstracted empiricism can be made clearer. Theories of social structure are the starting point of the exercise. The study could not have been formulated without the concepts of social structure, power, and gender. These concepts guide the sort of data collected. One cannot simply gather data at random and hope that given enough of it, a picture of social structure will emerge. And one would never get a picture of social structure from the interview responses. The responses are in terms of individual characteristics, and the adding up of individual characteristics does not amount to a description of social structure. What Mills is saying of abstracted empiricism is that it provides no framework for the selection of research problems, putting it outside the framework of science. He is also saying that work within that school can never arrive at a social structural picture of society. But in good sociology, the selection of the milieu to be studied ought to be made in accordance with the problems of structural significance in society. And there should be a continuing two-way interaction between theory and empirical work. Although the specific methods used by abstracted empiricists, as distinct from their philosophy, are clearly suitable for the investigation of many problems (see the example above), the methodology of abstracted empiricism, besides being inoperable as method, eliminates the great social problems and issues of our time from inquiry.[51]

The appeal of abstracted empiricism, according to Mills, lies in its quest for certainty. Granted that certainty is unattainable, it remains to ask what level of verification is appropriate. If social scientists are too exacting in their demands, they will get nothing but a welter of very detailed exposition. If they are too unexacting they will end up with some very grand theories divorced from reality. Mills notes that the work of abstracted empiricism is often regarded as true but trivial, but he questions even its truth. It may be precise, but precision is not to be confused with truth. If one has been involved in the coding and processing of thousands of interviews, one sees just how malleable the realm of "fact" may be.[52] Precision, according to Mills, should not be the sole determinant of method.

> We should be as accurate as we are able to be in our work upon the problems that concern us. But no method, as such, should be used to delimit the problems we take up, if for no other reason than that the most interesting and difficult issues of *method* usually begin where established techniques do not apply.[53]

Mills's picture of American sociology is a picture of two dominant schools, the grand theorists and the abstracted empiricists. Both schools have major shortcomings. The abstracted empiricists are bound by a restrictive epistemology and cannot get beyond the collection and statistical sorting of data. The grand theorists have become stuck at a very high level of generalization and cannot get down to facts.

> Both of these tendencies or schools exist and flourish within what ought to be pauses in the working process of social science. But in them what ought to be a little pause has become, if I may put it so, the entrance into fruitlessness.[54]

In philosophic terms, Mills can be seen as criticizing, from a realist point of view, the grand theorists and the abstracted empiricists for their rationalism and empiricism respectively. Realism is the thesis that there is a real world existing independently of our attempts to know it; that we as humans can have knowledge of that world; and that the validity of our knowledge-claims is, at least in part, determined by the way the world is. Our knowledge of the world is not obtained simply from perceptions and a content-free logic, as the empiricists would have it; neither are its sources purely cognitive, as the rationalists would have it. Rather, such knowledge has both cognitive and empirical content.

Neither of these schools, then, is likely to produce good sociology. Neither is likely to add to the work of the classical theorists such as Marx, Weber, or Durkheim. For neither has what Mills regards as essential to good sociology, the "sociological imagination." There were always, even in the postwar America of which Mills was writing, good sociologists in what Mills calls the "classical tradition." Mills's point was they were not members of the dominant schools, and were consequently less influential.

The situation has changed since Mills's analysis, with, among other things, the fall from grace of the grand theorists (or structural functionalists), which leaves positivist social science dominant;[55] the rise of symbolic interactionism as a perspective; developments such as labelling theory in studies of deviance; the impact of feminism on sociology;and, most recently, the increasing dominance of postmodernist and poststructuralist perspectives.[56] So although these schools are both still influential, North American sociology, like world sociology, is becoming increasingly diverse. This returns us to the major theme of the chapter, the diversity of sociology.

1.2.3 Sociological Perspectives

Gareau's analysis of the diversity of sociology was a sociological analysis of the external[57] features maintaining the major divisions between sociological sects. Mills's analysis highlighted an internal dispute at the epistemological level between rationalism, empiricism, and realism. Another way of analyzing the diversity of sociology, popular in Britain but also apparent in Western Europe, the United States, and Australia, is according to the various assumptions about society used as starting points by various schools. This, too, is an internal analysis, but focussed at the level of methodology rather than epistemology. By looking at such methodological features as the assumptions made about the nature of society, the sorts of questions asked, the sorts of concepts used, and the sorts of answers or solutions or explanations that are given, one can roughly divide sociology into a number of perspectives.[58]

The divisions are rough in this sense: that although the perspectives identified by various analysts are all readily recognizable by sociologists, different analysts may identify different numbers of perspectives, depending on how broad they make the identifying assumptions about the nature of society, and on how important they regard a particular perspective for the purposes of their discussion. For example, some include Marxism in the conflict perspective, some treat it separately as a special case, and some simply identify the two or discuss Marxism at the expense of other conflict perspectives.[59]

Sociologists themselves may work entirely within one perspective, but they may also work with several, so the use of particular sociologists to illustrate one perspective or another should not be taken as an indication that they are confined to that perspective. Each perspective has its favored research methods, which is not surprising, as methods are a function of the problems being investigated.[60] But no perspective has exclusive rights over any method, and neither are perspectives confined to a single method.

The first distinction I should like to draw is between structuralist and agency (or action) approaches to society. The structuralist approach to society assumes that one's social environment—the way society is organized and structured—influences to a large extent, or even determines, one's values, attitudes, beliefs, and actions. It looks to the social structure of society to explain individual characteristics and actions. The agency approach assumes that society is simply the aggregate of individual social actions, and looks to the nature of those actions for an explanation of social structure.[61]

In this section, I will discuss the bases of each of these approaches, taking the structuralist perspective first, and illustrate the perspectives with examples from sociological studies. This will provide a glimpse of the diversity of sociology at the theoretical and methodological levels, besides providing a framework for the development of a naturalist realist metatheory of sociology.

The Structuralist Perspective

Within the structuralist perspective, a further distinction can be made between the consensus and conflict perspectives. Underlying the consensus perspective[62] is the assumption that societies are relatively stable and harmonious, and the major questions center on how that stability is maintained. Implicitly or explicitly an analogy is made between society and a living organism or society and a homeostatic system. Just as the different parts of an organism function to keep the whole intact and working, it is assumed that the various institutions and/or various features of society play a role in maintaining its stability.

The consensus perspective: Durkheim.   Emile Durkheim, one of the founders of sociology as a discipline, made a major contribution to the consensus perspective. His structuralist approach can be clearly illustrated in his definition of social phenomena, which he distinguishes from both physical and psychological phenomena. He recognized that there was

. . . a category of facts which present very special characteristics: they consist of manners of acting, thinking and feeling external to the individual, which are invested with a coercive power by virtue of which they exercise control over him. Consequently, since they consist of representations and actions, they cannot be confused with organic phenomena, nor with psychical phenomena, which have no existence save in and through the individual consciousness.[63]

Although the individual plays a part in their creation, several individuals at least must have interacted in order to give rise to new norms or to modify existing ones. These norms are crystallized, or institute themselves, outside the individual.

Social facts, though they are representations,[64] are not reducible to individual representations. They can be explained only in terms of other social facts. Against those who see individual consciousness as the only substratum of society, Durkheim points out that although society has no other active components than individual humans, there are integrating elements as well.[65] Durkheim's argument here is that the properties of a whole cannot be explained in terms of the properties of the individual parts.

> . . . what is so readily deemed unacceptable for social facts is freely admitted for other domains of nature. Whenever elements of any kind combine, by virtue of this combination they give rise to new phenomena. One is therefore forced to conceive of these phenomena as residing, not in the elements, but in the entity formed by the union of these elements.[66]

Durkheim, then, does not believe that social facts can be explained in terms of individual actions or representations. He argues that just as the living cell contains nothing but chemicals, so society contains nothing but individuals. But the characteristic phenomena of life do not reside in the atoms of hydrogen, oxygen, carbon, and nitrogen. Life cannot be split up in this way, but can be located only in the living substance in its entirety.[67]

As society is a set of institutionalized norms *external* to the individual and exercising constraint on the individual, the appropriate level of explanation for these social norms is to be found not in the individual but in other social phenomena. The individual is simply the means by which particular social phenomena are instantiated, not the focus of social explanation.

Durkheim, then, views society as a whole, or systemically, and as we might expect, stresses the importance of functional explanation in the process of scientific investigation. A functional analysis of a society may show what features of that society are required if it is to maintain its specific characteristics, and may point to what features may have to be changed if the society is to take a new direction.

Unlike Comte, Durkheim does not see functional analyses as automatically teleological. "We use the word 'function' in preference to 'end' or 'goal' precisely because social phenomena generally do not exist for the usefulness of the results they produce."[68] And unlike many later functionalists (for example, Parsons), Durkheim does not make the mistake of attributing a function to every social phenomenon. Just as in biology, where a normal feature of a creature, as a result of historic accident, may exist without serving any function, so the same can happen in society.[69]

Functionalists have often been criticized for assuming that the attribution of a function for society to a social institution or feature of society is sufficient for its explanation. Durkheim, despite his use of functional analyses, escapes this criticism. He believes that to intervene in nature, knowledge of the functions of social phenomena is not enough. One has to know how those particular phenomena arose, and how they can be manipulated. Durkheim insists that if sociology is to be of practical use, causal explanations are essential,[70] and he sees functional explanation and causal explanation as dual avenues of research. " . . . [W]hen one undertakes to explain a social phenomenon the efficient cause which produces it and the function it fulfils must be investigated separately."[71] The distinction between causal explanations and functional explanations turns out to be crucial to sociology, and will be taken up in depth in chapter 5.

Talcott Parsons played a leading part in the development of the consensus perspective, but the flavor of his approach came out in the discussions in §1.2.2. above. Instead, I shall discuss briefly Kai Erikson's approach to deviance, which starts from the consensus or functionalist approach.[72]

The consensus perspective: Erikson.   If one assumes that societies are entities in their own right, that they can be distinguished from other societies, then they must have some sort of boundary, some way of distinguishing members of a particular society from outsiders. When one considers the variety of societies or social groups that exist, not all of which are mutually exclusive, it becomes apparent that the boundaries of a society are normative rather than physical. A question that arises with respect to the stability of a society is how those normative boundaries are maintained and how they are changed, so that members of a society are aware of what they must do and what they cannot do in order to remain fully fledged members. A little reflection shows that norms retain their validity only if they are regularly used as a basis of judgment. Each time the community censures some act of deviance, then it can be expected that the authority of the violated norm is sharpened, re-establishing the boundaries of the group.

It is from within this framework that Erikson studied the Antinomian controversy of 1636. In Puritan New England before the 1630s, the church preached that grace was a condition bestowed upon chosen people by God, and that nothing that happened on earth could change one's state of grace. This was in contrast to the established church in Europe, which declared that grace could be obtained by prayer and good works.

But in the 1630s in New England, the clergy started to talk about the *covenant of grace* in a way that more resembled the *covenant of works.* They began to say of the state of grace that it was something for which one had to be prepared. And who better to prepare people for the state of grace than God's chosen ones, the clergy?

Now, according to the *covenant of grace* one could not know who were the chosen. Yet the clergy in Massachusetts were claiming that they themselves had been chosen, and that they could prepare others for the state of grace. This was radically at odds with the original covenant, and moreover had the effect of giving power to the clergy.

Mrs Anne Hutchinson, of Boston, challenged these new doctrines, and started to attract many of the faithful away from the church meetings to her own house, where she continued her criticisms of the clergy. The clergy were dismayed by her challenge to their authority and took action. Mrs Hutchinson had broken no law, nor had she committed heresy. Yet she was declared guilty of casting doubt on the authority of the church, excommunicated, and banished, being imprisoned until she was sent away. In the course of this incident the church had gained temporal, as well as spiritual, authority. The social boundaries of Puritan New England had been re-defined.

This institutionalization of the clergy's power may well have happened without the case of Mrs Hutchinson, but Erikson's point is that the labelling and public censure of her so-called deviant behavior helped to establish new social boundaries. By the same process, Erikson argues, the public censure of deviant behavior maintains a society's boundaries by reinforcing the norms involved. Deviance, at least in controlled quantities, can therefore be seen as functional for the stability of society.

This raises some important questions. As Erikson says:

> If we grant that deviant behavior often performs a valuable service in society, can we then assume that society as a whole actively tries to promote this resource? Can we assume, in other words, that some kind of active recruitment process is going on to assure society of a steady volume of deviance?[73]

Certainly one cannot assume that if an important function is served by some feature of society it must therefore exist. Still less can one assume that society can act in its own interest to maintain and promote such features. This would be functionalism at its worst. Nonetheless, there are empirical questions here to be answered, and this sort of approach to deviance has been very fruitful.

For example, it focuses attention on the agencies of social control in a society. In Western societies a number of agencies are set up explicitly to deal with social control; for example, the legal system, the police system, the prison system. One of the overt goals of the prison system in New South Wales, for example, is the reform of prisoners' behavior, acknowledged in the title of the department responsible, the Department of Corrective Services. Yet recidivism is high, and prisons provide a venue for socialization into criminal cultures. Prison systems often function to encourage crime.

And the implications of such functional analyses as Erikson's in fact go far beyond the functional or consensus perspective. For they lead to questions such as whether the agencies of social control are organized in such a way that they must encourage deviance, despite their stated goals, and how it is that the behavior of individuals committed to the stated goals of various institutions in fact has the opposite effect. This sort of question has led to some fine-grained studies of deviance from the social agency perspectives, which will be discussed later in this section.

The consensus perspective, then, can be a fruitful way of looking at society. Unfortunately, many of its proponents (for example, Parsons) insisted it was *the* way to look at society. Standing alone, the consensus perspective is at best limited, and at worst wrong. Indeed, the claims of any perspective, if taken to be the only way of seeing society, will probably be false, as I hope to show in chapter 7. And by concentrating on the mechanisms by which social stability is maintained at the expense of looking at how societies change, consensus sociology, if considered the only proper way to study societies, produces a body of knowledge with an inherently conservative bias.

The conflict perspective.   I shall now discuss the other major structuralist approach to society, the conflict perspective. The conflict perspective shares with the consensus perspective the assumption that the structure of society shapes individual behavior and attitudes. But rather than seeing societies as relatively stable and homogeneous, the conflict perspective points out that many societies, and certainly modern industrial societies, rather than being homogeneous, contain various groups of people in different material situations and with conflicting interests. These societies are organized in such a way that a certain group or groups of people have more power than other groups in certain respects. The conflict perspective sees change as ubiquitous, and instead of focussing on the problem of how societies remain stable over time, it focusses on the problem of how social change occurs, and the part played by conflict and coercion in such change.

The conflict perspective: Marxism and feminism.   Marxism is the best known of the conflict perspectives. Marx's theory of capitalism is an analysis of capitalist society aimed precisely at discovering the conditions necessary for its demise. Marx maintained that the root of all significant change in social development is class struggle. Classes were defined by the relationships of groups of people to the means of production, and shifts in class power constituted the motor of historical change.[74] The mode of production was the complex of the forces and relations of production with the emphasis on the ownership of the means of production. According to Marx, "the mode of production of material life conditions the social, political and intellectual life processes in general."[75]

Marx saw capitalism as a form of class society structured around a specific mode of production. The capitalist mode of production was based on private ownership of the means of production within which labor-power was itself a commodity, to be bought and sold like any other. The particular inequality of the classes in capitalism arose from the fact that ownership of the means of production lay in the hands of a few, while the majority had to depend on those few for work in order to subsist. Marx saw as fundamental to capitalist development its imperative need to accumulate capital.[76] Within the capitalist mode of production, this took the form of profit, acquired through extracting surplus value from labor. Basically, surplus value was any value produced by the worker over and above the cost of his production and reproduction. The latter had to be paid to the worker to ensure a continuation of the work force. The exploitation of labor, then, occurs in the sphere of production. But profit can also be accumulated in the sphere of circulation, via unequal exchange. Thus the accumulation of capital occurs both in the sphere of production and in the sphere of circulation.

Because the mode of production of material life conditions the social, political, and intellectual life processes in general, if the structure of class inequality in society is to change, according to Marx, the mode of production will have to be changed. Such change will be brought about as a result of the inherent conflict between the classes within the capitalist system.

Feminist theory, too, takes a conflict perspective of society. Patriarchal gender relations have existed in many forms of society throughout history, and still exist in most, if not all, societies today. Feminism aims at understanding the reasons for the continuing oppression of women in society, with a view to removing such oppression.

Both Marxism and feminism are overtly politically oriented, in that they focus on those aspects of society they would like to change. Marxism, particularly, has been criticized by consensus theorists as being merely politics masquerading as science. Such criticism is not sustainable. One may criticize studies for not adequately reflecting the nature of the world, or one may criticize the values underlying a particular branch of knowledge, but all knowledge is value-directed in some sense, even if the values are not made explicit.[77] Consensus theory, as we have seen, is inherently conservative, and if treated as the only way to view society, supports the status quo, whatever that may be. And empiricist-based perspectives such as abstracted empiricism have the same effect, by virtue of the sharp distinction that is drawn between value and fact. This allows value-selected partial views of the world to masquerade as value-free bodies of knowledge.

The conflict perspective: Pearce on deviance. Studies of society from the conflict perspective have been extremely fruitful. To illustrate, I shall look at one of the contributions of the conflict perspective to studies of deviance. The example I have chosen, Frank Pearce's study of corporate crime in North American society,[78] has the additional advantage that it illustrates the use of both the consensus and the conflict perspectives in the same study. The study starts from a conflict perspective, comparing the public perception of crime in the United States with the picture of crime found by the President's Commission on Law Enforcement. The public saw the crime problem as largely a matter of violent crime and the "index" crimes against property, that is, theft, burglary, and larceny. This picture was reflected in the policies and actions of law enforcement agencies. But Pearce's interest was in white collar and particularly corporate crime. He quotes the President's Commission:

> There is no knowing how much embezzlement, fraud, loan sharking, and other forms of thievery from individuals or commercial institutes there is, or how much price-rigging, tax evasion, bribery, graft, and other forms of thievery from the public at large there is. The Commission's studies indicate that the economic losses those crimes cause are far greater than those caused by the three Index Crimes against property.[79]

What interested Pearce was the small number of prosecutions under the antitrust legislation compared with the high incidence of violation of the legislation, and the openness with which it was violated by large corporations. Pearce inquired into whose interests were served by the antitrust laws; in whose interests were the particular number of prosecutions that did occur; and who had the power to administer these laws.

Then, changing to a consensus perspective, he investigated the comparative effects of corporate crime and the blue-collar crimes of violence, burglary, and so on, on the capitalist social order. His historical study of the enactment and administration of the antitrust laws showed that although the laws themselves appeared to be in the interests of the consumer and small business, big business was heavily involved in their administration. In addition, the particularly small number of prosecutions served to uphold "the imaginary social order." In other words, they helped people believe their interests vis-a-vis large corporations were being safeguarded by the authorities, when in fact they were not.

In searching for an explanation for the differential treatment of burglary and the other index crimes against property and corporate crime, Pearce turned again to the effects of the various crimes on the capitalist social order. He concluded that corporate crime was not only the norm, but upheld the capitalist imperative for increased accumulation, whereas the index crimes posed an ideological threat to the notion of private property required by capitalism, and the heavy prosecution of these crimes served to maintain that ideology and the ideology of individualism. Pearce's study served to show what was not obvious, particularly in the United States at that time: that the interests of capital were not the same as, and tended to override, the interests of democracy.

Other studies of deviance from the conflict perspective include the comparison of illegal drug use by various social classes and/or races with their conviction rates; comparisons of mental illness along gender lines; and many other comparative studies. Such studies point to inequalities in a society, and lead to a search for the mechanisms whereby such inequalities of treatment arise, often taking the researcher into one of the agency perspectives. Studies of deviance and crime from the conflict perspective are a fairly recent phenomenon, at least in Western sociology. Marxist sociologists ignored the area for some time, perhaps because Marx himself had little to say on the subject, and the feminist approach is itself a recent addition to sociology. But the last twenty years has seen a considerable increase in the understanding of deviance as a result of work from within the conflict perspective.

The Agency Perspective

In contrast to the structuralist perspectives of consensus and conflict, which have in common the notion that society exists in some sense independently of the actions of its individual members, agency or action perspectives hold the view that as society is comprised only of individuals, it is in terms of the understanding individuals have of society and their own actions that social structure is to be explained.

The agency perspective: Weber. Max Weber was largely responsible for the early development of the action perspective. Weber defined sociology thus:

Sociology . . . is a science concerning itself with the interpretive understanding of social action and thereby with a causal explanation of its course and consequences. We shall speak of "action" insofar as the acting individual attaches a subjective meaning to his behaviour—be it overt or covert, omission or acquiescence. Action is "social" insofar as its subjective meaning takes account of the behavior of others and is thereby oriented in its course.[80]

"Social actions," the objects of sociological study to Weber, are crucially different from Durkheim's "social facts." Durkheim's "social facts" are collective phenomena, existing externally to the individual, to be studied using the objective methods of science. The focus is on the social collectivity as existing *sui generis.* In contrast, Weber's "social actions" are individual actions, and interpretive sociology is the investigation of their subjective meanings. For such investigation, "collectivities must be treated as *solely* the resultants and modes of organisation of the particular acts of individual persons, since these alone can be treated as agents in a course of subjectively understandable action."[81] Durkheim and Weber, then, have different views of the nature of society, and consequently different views on how society should be studied.

This difference illustrates the difference between structuralist and action approaches to sociology. To Weber, to the extent that social institutions can be said to exist at all, they are the result of individual social actions, and the appropriate way to explain such institutions is in terms of the explanation of individual social actions. To support his methodological individualism against the attack that social institutions and social structures may actually affect the way people act and that therefore they cannot be completely explained by social action, Weber takes an instrumentalist view of social collectivities, saying that it is not the existence of social institutions, but people's belief in their existence, that affects their actions.

The agency perspective: Symbolic interactionism. One of the most productive of the action perspectives in terms of empirical research has been the symbolic interactionist approach. While not denying that individuals' beliefs and actions are influenced by the society in which they live, symbolic interactionists believe that structuralists overemphasise the extent to which this happens, ignoring the degree to which individuals are "free agents" involved in the construction of society. G. H. Mead conceptualised these two aspects of human individuals by regarding the "self" as a combination of the "I" and the "me."[82]

The "I" is the active element of the "self," acting on the social world; the "me" is the passive element of the "self," acted on or shaped by the social world. The "me" will include all of the social roles one performs when one behaves according to the norms one has learned, and is constructed by learning to see oneself as one thinks others see one. This grasp upon the attitudes and beliefs that others have toward one is only possible, according to the symbolic interactionists, because of a shared symbolic system.

To the symbolic interactionists, society is composed of the symbolic interactions of its members, and is constantly changing as the meanings of the symbols are negotiated and renegotiated (between the "I" and the "me") in the context of everyday life. This means that symbolic interactionists are interested in the way social situations are defined by the various participants. I will illustrate the use of this perspective with a study that, like the other illustrations I have used, throws some light on the problem of deviance.

Erving Goffman's *Asylums*[83] is a study of mental hospitals from the symbolic interactionist perspective. Mental hospitals are typical total institutions, organisations that encompass the total daily round of the lives of the inmates. Some other examples of total institutions are convents, military barracks and prisons. Total institutions are characterized by a physical barrier separating the institution from the outside world, and by a hierarchical social order with large numbers of inmates controlled by relatively small numbers of staff.

Control is often in the last instance by physical coercion, but is primarily achieved by assigning to each of the inmates a common role, set down in terms of the aims of the institution. On entering a total institution, the inmate is stripped of his or her former "self," by what Goffman calls mortification and stripping procedures. These may include restricting contact with the outside world, taking away inmates' personal clothing and issuing them with uniforms, issuing them with identification numbers to replace names, insisting on at least overt respect for the hierarchy, moving groups of people in blocks, and many other procedures, all of which are designed to strip away the old self and impose a new role, the role of inmate. One of the features of a total institution that interested Goffman is that for the inmate there is only one role, that laid down by the institution. Total institutions are regarded by Goffman as greatly simplified models of society for, in the latter, people have many roles.

Goffman's studies of mental hospitals revealed what he called "primary adjustment" on the part of the inmates. Primary adjustment occurs when inmates accept the role the institution has laid down for them, conforming to the behavior expected of them by the institution, becoming, in a sense, the person the institution requires them to be. But the concept of primary adjustment was not adequate to explain the range of behavior encountered by Goffman in the mental hospitals. Goffman discovered a wide range of what he called secondary adjustments.

Secondary adjustment is the unauthorized use of means or ends in order to get around the organization's assumptions of what one should do and hence of what one should be. Disruptive secondary adjustments are those that upset the smooth running of the organization. They will usually be met with punishment, and are rare. Contained secondary adjustments, on the other hand, fit in with the existing structures of the organization and so produce no pressure for change. They are endemic.

Secondary adjustments noted by Goffman in mental hospitals include "make do's," for example the use of radiators as clothes dryers, or even, in the closed wards, to piss on—access to the toilets often requiring the permission of staff; "working the system," for example going on sick call when one was not ill, getting assigned to jobs that had privileges attached, in the form of extra food, first choice of clothing, privacy, and so on; and the use of facilities in unauthorized ways, for example the use of handbags and pockets for personal storage space, or for the transport of illicit goods.

Because secondary adjustments involved getting around the institution's idea of what one should be, Goffman sees them as the constitution of the self in opposition to the institution. He notes that secondary adjustments involve a set of social interactions that are not part of the formal institutional structure. They constitute the "underlife" of the institution. And yet there is a sense in which many of these secondary adjustments are necessary to the smooth running of the institution. Assuming that the analogy between total institutions and society is valid, this study shows that the "I" as conceptualized by Mead can indeed play an active part in the smooth running of society, and also, as might be the case with disruptive secondary adjustments, as a force for change.

The interesting thing about Goffman's study from the point of view of theories of deviance, though, is the light it throws upon the nature of deviant behavior. For in mental hospitals, behavior regarded by staff as symptomatic of continuing mental illness, for example a tendency to carry all of one's possessions with one at all times, has been shown by Goffman to be a rational response to the conditions of the institution, in this particular case to the fact that there was little or no personal storage space in the institution. What little there was was subject to inspection by staff and was exposed to any who wished to rifle through its contents. Goffman's study showed that secondary adjustments, often regarded by staff as symptomatic of mental illness, could all in fact be seen as a rational response to the vicissitudes of life in the total institution. This view of deviant behavior has led to many cross-cultural and historic studies showing that there is no act that can be considered deviant in itself, and this in turn draws attention to the way particular acts are defined as deviant in particular societies.

The agency perspective: Ethnomethodology.   Another of the action or agency perspectives that has been fruitful in studies of deviance is ethnomethodology. Ethnomethodologists, like symbolic interactionists, are concerned with the study of social interactions, and they would agree with the latter that the meanings by which people understand the social world are variable, that the symbolic world must be interpreted. Unlike the symbolic interactionists, though, the ethnomethodologists are more interested in the processes or methods by which people make sense of the social world than in their interpretations of it.

Although most of the time people assume that they know the social world they live in more or less directly, and that they see it more or less as others do, ethnomethodologists point out that how one sees the social world is actually a function of who one is and what one is looking for as much as it is a function of the world itself. One's knowledge of the social world is essentially practical, and involves many shortcuts in reasoning, much invalid generalization. Whether or not one is actually aware of what is happening, one takes certain behaviors as indicative of an underlying pattern of behavior, and uses these supposed underlying patterns of behavior as justification for interpreting particular behaviors in a certain way.

According to H. Garfinkel, who first formulated ethnomethodology as a research program, people use the "documentary method" to make sense of events in the social world. The "documentary method"

> consists of treating an actual appearance as the "document of," as "pointing to," as "standing on behalf of" a presumed underlying pattern. Not only is the underlying pattern derived from its individual documentary evidences, but the individual documentary evidences, in their turn, are interpreted on the basis of "what is known" about the underlying pattern. Each is used to elaborate the other.[84]

Making sense of what people say and do in this way requires that one take the context of the actions or words into account, for words and actions can have quite different meanings in different circumstances. The work of ethnomethodologists, then, is distinguished by an emphasis on language and context. Ethnomethodologists argue that the production of social order is identical to the assignment of sense to events, and that to understand how social order is maintained is to understand the methods by which people make sense of the social world.

Aaron Cicourel's study[85] of juvenile delinquency and law enforcement agencies in California is an example of the use of the ethnomethodology perspective in the study of deviance. Cicourel's work is a fine-grained study of the way that a delinquent career is established in the course of the practical activity of the various agencies of social control. Cicourel follows the documentation of the deviant career of Smithfield Elston, through the many reports from teachers, probation officers, police, judges, and others concerned with Smithfield's case.

His study shows the very material effects on Smithfield's life of early stereotyping. For Smithfield was black, male, and from a broken home. When he was caught stealing a small amount of money from a purse that was found at school, he was charged. This was his first offense. Cicourel's study shows that others in the same town and even the same school were not charged for their first such offense, even when the amounts stolen were greater. The different treatment could be attributed to the different expectations officials had with respect to the future behavior of those concerned. These expectations were based on the assignment of different stereotypes to the individuals in question, that is, on the basis of color, gender, class, and family background, rather than on their previous behavior.

Cicourel's study is interesting because it ties in so well with the work on deviance from other perspectives. For example, it provides at least a partial answer to Erikson's question as to whether the agencies of social control are organized to produce deviance despite their overt aims. Cicourel shows that the methods used by the officials to understand their social world in order to do their jobs, along with the ways the various agencies of social control define success, are enough to explain, at least partially, Smithfield's adoption of a deviant career despite the overt aims of the probation officer to keep him out of trouble.

The study also shows the importance of stereotyping in deciding who will and who will not become a deviant, thus showing the importance ideologies can have in the differential treatment of people. This fits in well with studies from the conflict perspective, for example, that indicate that corporate crime is generally not perceived to be as great a problem as blue-collar crime. A consequence of this perception is that fewer resources and efforts are directed toward its punishment or prevention. The place of stereotyping in the creation of deviant careers also offers an explanation of how particular ethnic groups might be subject to differential treatment by agencies of social control, and indicates that this might be changed through conscious changing of stereotypes.

The various sociological perspectives I have discussed all start from different assumptions about the nature of society and of individuals, and are concerned with different problems. Proponents of each perspective often claim that their way is the only correct way to do sociology. Criticism of the various perspectives and of studies done from within the perspectives generally comes from outside the perspective in question. Nonetheless, I think I have shown through the examples given here that each of the perspectives, and indeed the interplay between them, has contributed to the sociological understanding of deviance, and that no single perspective can provide an adequate understanding of the phenomena.

There are many ways of studying deviance, not all of which fit easily into the perspectives I have outlined. This is in part because my discussion of sociological perspectives is not fine enough nor detailed enough to encompass all sociological work, and in part because sociologists do not always work within a single perspective, some preferring a pluralist approach. But this discussion has shown not only the diversity of sociology at the methodological and theoretical levels, but also the value of that diversity, the utility of a pluralist methodology in sociology.

Nonetheless, problems are created by the diversity of sociology at the theoretical and methodological levels, as well as at the epistemological level, and at the cultural and geo-political levels discussed earlier in this chapter. I shall summarize these problems in the next section.

1.3 The Problems of Diversity

In §1.2 I discussed the nature of the diversity in sociology. According to Gareau, the dominant sects of first and second world sociology are very different, both in theory and methodology, and third world sociology is developing its own distinctive style in opposition to first and second world sociology. Mills's discussion illuminated the differences between the two most prominent schools in the United States. Mills was critical of both schools for taking a small part of the task of sociological study and insisting that that part alone constituted the sociological method. The discussion of various methodologies according to each one's underlying assumptions about the nature of society and humans showed the value of looking at society from a variety of perspectives. But proponents of these perspectives, like the members of Gareau's sects and Mills's schools, often claim that theirs is the only way to do sociology.

This diversity of theory and method, and the conflicting claims of various groups to have access to the correct sociological method, raise a number of problems for sociology as a discipline. Some of these problems are more clearly conceptual, while others are of a more practical nature, though the two types of problem are interrelated.

Conceptual problems 1: Conflicting truth-claims. Perhaps the most obvious conceptual problem is the acceptance, albeit by different groups, of conflicting or apparently conflicting truth-claims. An example of conflicting truth-claims has already been mentioned in §1.2.1, where Gareau demonstrated a nationalistic bias in the description of the Falklands/Malvinas conflict. Some sociologists and political scientists described the conflict as a territorial war while others described it as a colonial war. There is a sense in which any war can be described as a war over territory, but nonetheless there is a distinction between territorial war and colonial war. Territorial war in this context is war to protect one's own territory or property. This is the way the British tended to see the Falklands/Malvinas conflict. Colonial war, on the other hand, is initiated specifically to gain control and ownership over other people's land and labor, and this is how the Argentine social scientists saw the conflict, as resisting a colonial power.

Another example of a conflicting truth-claim in sociology, this time perhaps more apparent than real, comes from studies in deviance. Under the assumptions of systems theorists such as Parsons, society is a stable and harmonious whole into which individuals are socialized. Such theorists, as we have seen, may see deviance as functional for social stability. But this sort of explanation is not a causal explanation. No matter how functional deviance may be for the stability of a society, it remains to be explained how individual people in that society come to be deviant. The explanations that systems theorists offer are often in terms of the personal characteristics of the individual, the fact that they do not accept the norms of society. And this is often explained in terms of faulty socialization processes leading to undersocialization. But Howard Becker's studies of marijuana smokers in the United States explain this

particular form of deviance at least partially in terms of socialization into marijuana smoking sub-cultures, rather than undersocialization with respect to society as a whole.[86]

The reason these claims may not necessarily be conflicting is that Becker
at least is offering only a partial explanation (in fact, a necessary condition) of marijuana smoking, and his explanation, socialization into a sub-culture, is not strictly
incompatible with undersocialization with respect to society as a whole. But the
case of the Falklands/Malvinas conflict illustrates incompatible truth-claims. The
war cannot be both primarily territorial and primarily colonial in nature.

Conceptual problems 2: Conflicting assumptions.   Another conceptual
problem for sociology relates to the seemingly conflicting nature of the assumptions underlying the various sociological perspectives. As we have seen,
there are two major conflicts regarding the nature of society in the perspectives
I have sketched. The first is the conflict between the structuralists and the
agency/action theorists over the nature of society and the proper way to explain
it. The structuralists give primacy to society as an entity in its own right and
use the structural features of society to explain the social behavior of individuals. The action theorists give primacy to the individual, explaining society in
terms of individual actions and relationships. If either of these assumptions
about society and individuals is treated as a complete description of the social
world, and the use of it seen as the only way to study that world, then each perspective is in direct conflict with the other. The definitions of the proper domain of sociology by Weber and Durkheim (§1.2.3) illustrate this conflict,
although Weber actually used structural concepts in his explanations—for
example, his concepts of class and status groups. And Durkheim certainly believed that individuals could be effective in changing the social structure—indeed, the motive behind his work was to find places where such intervention
would be effective.

If the foregoing assumptions about the relationship between society and
individuals are treated simply as aspects of the social world, no theoretical conflict need arise, although such treatment raises quantitative problems about the
relative importance, in any particular study, of both the structural limitations on
individual action and the effects of individual action on the social structure. It
also raises the whole issue, which C. Wright Mills regarded as the central issue
of sociology, of the relationship between the social structure and individuals.

Mills illustrated this issue with his distinction between the "public issues
of the social structure" and the "personal troubles of milieu."[87] Private troubles
occur within the character of an individual and within the range of that individual's personal milieu. Public issues transcend these local environments.
They have to do with the organization of many such milieus into the institutions
of society as a whole. But public issues cannot be reduced to private troubles.

If, in a city of 100,000 or so people, a few are chronically unemployed, their unemployment is a private trouble for those concerned, and an explanation of their unemployment would properly consider their personal characteristics. But if the rate of unemployment rises above that usually involved with people between work, say two percent, then unemployment has also become a public issue, and its explanation is not properly sought in the characteristics of the individuals involved, because there are not enough jobs for everyone anyway. The explanation must be sought instead in the structural features of society.

The second major conflict over the nature of society arises within the structuralist perspective. The consensus theorists see society as a harmonious and stable whole, while the conflict theorists see society composed of conflicting groups whose changing relations as a result of conflict bring about social change. Again, these assumptions about the nature of society are not necessarily incompatible, unless they claim to be complete descriptions of society rather than aspects of it. The extent to which any particular society at any time is harmonious and stable or comprises groups in conflict is a matter for empirical investigation. Nonetheless, practitioners of both perspectives have claimed that their view of society is the only basis from which to investigate the social world. Such sectarianism is often implicit, but is apparent, for example, in Marxist criticism of structural functionalist studies as being incapable of explaining social change, and in functionalist criticism of Marxist studies as failing to appreciate the extent of normative homogeneity in societies.

Conceptual problems, then, are endemic in sociology, and practitioners have a number of ways of dealing with them. One option for sociologists is to embrace a particular perspective as the correct way of looking at the social world and to work for the general acceptance of this view. Another option is to admit the inadequacy of all current approaches and to wait for the appearance of the "Galileo" or the "Newton" of sociology to come along with a new approach that will solve all problems. Increasingly more common is the strategy of accepting the different perspectives as ways of finding out about different aspects of a complex social world, the importance of which must be investigated in specific cultural and historic situations. What is clear, and is becoming increasingly prominent in sociology textbooks, is that all thinking sociologists must consider these conceptual problems, as there is no paradigmatic way of dealing with them.

Practical problems 1: Sociology is politics, not knowledge. The effect of these conceptual problems on the public image of sociology brings further problems, of a more practical nature, to the discipline. It has been claimed, for example, that sociology produces no knowledge of the social world, but merely reflects the dominant values of society. It would then follow that the reasons for the discipline's acknowledged successes have more to do with politics than

with rational epistemic choice. Quite generally, the lack of a single paradigm
for sociology is often considered an indication that sociology is not a science,
as we saw in §1.1. The importance of value judgments in sociology then suggests that as it is not science, it is pure ideology. More specifically, the mutually supporting links between the dominant social science sects in any country
and that country's politics, clearly demonstrated by Gareau, support this claim.
And both Mills and Andreski have pointed to the affinity between particular sociological perspectives or schools and particular political and economic values.

Mills, for example, notes that the ideological meaning of grand theory
tends to legitimize stable forms of domination. In other words it is inherently
conservative. But he also points out that as a matter of fact, grand theory is not
used in this way in the United States, as there is at present no need for this form
of legitimization of conservatism, and its lack of intelligibility limits any public favor it might come to have.[88] Mills does feel the obscurity of grand theory
may give it great ideological potential, and Andreski argues in detail that obscurity in social theory is a great political asset.[89] Abstracted empiricism, with
its ahistorical and non-comparative approach and its claims to objectivity, also
tends to support the status quo, by ignoring alternative ways of social organization and by masking the values that underlie any scientific enterprise. In addition, its individualistic approach to social explanation provides support for
the free market as a form of social organization, as the latter shares with abstracted empiricism the assumption that society can be explained solely in
terms of the actions of its members.

Any of the sociological perspectives, when taken as the only way to see
the social world, will support particular political ideologies, and will tend to become dominant where there is an affinity between the perspective and the dominant political values. This does not automatically invalidate the work done
from within the various perspectives. Good sociology has come from all of
them, as I illustrated in §1.2.3. Rather, it is the one-sided view produced by adhering to a single perspective that is supportive of particular political values.
And it is certainly the case that ideological issues are rather more important in
determining the success or failure of sociological theory than is the case with
natural scientific theory, although the natural sciences are not free of such concerns. This characteristic of the discipline means that at least in scientific cir-
cles sociology is often considered as ideology rather than science.

Practical problems 2: Funding sociological research. The implications
of not being granted the status of science are enormous in a society that not only
reveres science but assigns considerably more resources to the development of
science than to other areas of study such as the humanities. Disadvantageous
funding is of course an important personal issue for sociologists, although
scarcely good enough reason to fund the discipline more generously or to call

it a science. More serious is the effect of lack of funding on the growth of sociological knowledge, assuming always that the discipline can in fact produce worthwhile knowledge about the social world. To assume that sociology cannot produce such knowledge, is, I believe, demonstrably false, and also very frightening in a world in which the technological capabilities of humans have far outstripped their ability to make socially rational decisions, and in a social world that is changing rapidly in directions that cannot be foreseen, let alone directed in ways consistent with held values.

The Diversity of sociology; Concluding discussion.   The picture of sociology that has emerged from the discussion so far is of a discipline that is nationalistic, ethnocentric, and sectarian. Mills's criticism of the dominant schools in the United States of America shows that methodological sectarianism results in sociology that is bad, in the sense of being radically incomplete. He recommends the pluralistic use of both theory and method, for both moral and scientific reasons. The resulting, more comprehensive, sociology would be less supportive of any particular values, but would be of greater epistemic value. Andreski, more than a decade later, makes similar criticisms of the same schools, but with rather more emphasis on the abstracted empiricists, who had greater support by this time. He advocates a multi-perspective approach to sociological method, like Mills both in the interests of objective social science and morality. Andreski's point is that each sociological perspective influences the type of problems one studies, the sorts of concepts used, and the sorts of explanations or solutions that are acceptable. It is one's interest, or more broadly, one's sociological perspective, rather than the requirement of factual correctness alone, that tells one what to put into and what to leave out of any description of a situation.[90]

This can be illustrated simply if one considers possible maps of a city. One could draw a map that shows the location of art galleries, theatres, museums, and libraries. Another map of the same city could be drawn showing the location of brothels, opium dens, pubs, and night clubs. Both maps could be equally true or correct, but both are only partial. There is nothing wrong with this—indeed, any map or other description can only be partial. But each would be a false description of the city if it purported to show the only places of interest in that city. No description or theory should be allowed to masquerade as the only description or the only theory. This does not mean, as both Mills and Andreski point out, that we should give equal weight to any description or theory, for some may be just plain wrong. But the moral is that while the existence of multiple perspectives in sociology is good, the use of these perspectives to form sects is not.

The treatment of different sociological perspectives as sects, though common, and though encouraged by the various political and economic ideologies, is fortunately far from universal in sociology. The methods of the great "classic theorists," for example, Marx, Weber, Durkheim, and Spencer, described by Mills and Andreski and recognized by sociologists the world over, are eclectic or pluralist, often despite their own strictures on methodology.[91] Many sociologists today also work within a pluralist framework. Levine's studies of Ethiopian society, for example, are the richer for his use of multiple perspectives.[92]

But a sectarian approach to sociology leads to the production of radically incomplete, and hence bad, science. As I will argue at length in chapter 7, partial views of the world are false when regarded as complete. The sectarian nature of sociology, then, provides justification for the claims that sociology is mere ideology. Even if sectarianism can be avoided, sociology remains multiparadigmatic, and thus open to the Kuhnian charge of being merely pre-scientific. The problem then remains of showing how, with its multi-perspective nature and its base of conflicting assumptions about the social world, sociology can produce worthwhile, empirically based, and reliable—in other words, scientific—knowledge of the social world.

The rest of this book is devoted to showing that, to be scientific, sociology must be both pluralist and non-sectarian (and hence not multi-paradigmatic). I also hope to show that despite the application of multiple perspectives, the concept of validity can be applied to sociological theories, just as it can to other scientific theories, for all of science is multi-perspective by nature.

This program lies squarely in the area of the metatheory of science in general, and the metatheory of sociology in particular. Before starting to develop an adequate metatheory, I shall take a look, in chapter 2, at the most common metatheoretical perspectives currently available, both to see what light they throw on the problem, and to explore any further problems they might raise.

2

Issues in the Metatheory of Sociology

It just goes round again, said Hospital. Orpheus mourns, mopes about, won't go to parties any more, won't make love with the local women, they say he's queer, one thing leads to another, they tear him apart, and there's the head going down the river again, heading for Lesbos.
What does it all mean? said Kleinzeit.
How can there be meaning? said Hospital. Meaning is a limit. There are no limits.

—Russell Hoban, *Kleinzeit*

2.1 Can Sociology Be Scientific?

I have argued that the sectarian, multi-perspective, and multi-paradigmatic nature of sociology leads to a number of problems for the discipline, both conceptual and practical. The multi-paradigmatic nature of sociology means that there is no consensual way of arbitrating between conflicting truth-claims. It is such lack of consensus that lies behind Kuhn's claim that to be multi-paradigmatic is to be pre-scientific. The multi-perspective nature of sociology means that the discipline is operating with a variety of conflicting assumptions about the nature of the social world. This too can be interpreted as pre-scientific. And the sectarianism that characterizes sociology provides justification for the claim that sociology is at best pre-scientific, at worst, pure ideology. These issues cast doubt on whether sociology can be considered scientific, which in turn raises the pragmatic issues of the funding of sociological research and the seriousness with which its findings are taken. Thus the issue of whether sociology is, or can be, scientific, has great significance for the future well-being of the discipline.

The issue is not new. Whether sociology is, or can be, scientific, has been a major focus of discussion in the metatheory of sociology since the discipline began. Both Durkheim and Weber, the earliest holders of chairs in the discipline, were concerned to establish sociology as scientific, and devoted much discussion to the issue.

While the details of the discussion have changed over the years, its fundamental parameters have not. To determine whether sociology is, or can be, scientific, one must first know what it is to be scientific and what it is to be sociological, and then compare the two. On the assumption that if anything is scientific, the natural sciences are, the issue is usually resolved into a comparison of sociology (or the social sciences in general) with the natural sciences, to ascertain whether there are any fundamental differences between them.

There are two possible solutions to this issue. The naturalist position is that, while there may be, and indeed are, differences between sociology and the natural sciences, these differences are not fundamental. Sociology, provided it adheres to the methods of the natural sciences (I leave open for the moment what these might be), can indeed be scientific. The humanist position, on the other hand, is that the differences between sociology and the natural sciences are so fundamental as to require a quite different set of methodological principles. If the natural sciences are taken as paradigmatic for science, sociology must be considered non-scientific. The alternative is to add by definition to the notion of the scientific those specific methodological principles that are supposedly fundamentally different from those of the natural sciences.

It is to the debate between the naturalist and humanist positions that I turn in the next section. My aim is to familiarize the reader with the nature of the issues involved rather than to provide a comprehensive overview of the debate. Accordingly, I shall sketch what I regard as the most significant claims of both the naturalist and humanist positions by illustrating these positions with reference to those general positions and theorists likely to be most familiar to the sociologist. My treatment of the various theorists should not be regarded either as an exercise in scholarly interpretation or as being at all comprehensive, but simply as illustrative of the points I wish to make.[1] On the one hand, they are used because I can assume some familiarity on the part of the reader, which should help to clarify the issues. On the other hand, they show that the metatheoretical discussion that follows grows out of substantive sociological theorizing. Further, having sketched various positions here, I can refer back to them at will in later chapters, thus achieving some continuity in the examples I use.

It is not until the following section (§2.3) that I consider those other vexing questions for the metatheory of sociology, the question of how to arbitrate between competing truth claims and the question of whether good science can be distinguished from bad science.

2.2 The Status of the Social Sciences vis a vis the Natural Sciences: Naturalism versus Humanism

2.2.1 Naturalism

In the preceding section, naturalism was introduced as a response to an epistemological question, the question of whether sociology can be a science.

My starting point in this section, then, will be to discuss naturalism as an epistemological thesis. The importance of the epistemological thesis to the practising sociologist is that if sociology is, or can be, a science, it ought to be subject to the same criteria of objectivity and validity as the natural sciences. At least broadly speaking, it will be subject to the same methodologies. And as the status of knowledge produced by the natural sciences is high, reasons for the comparatively low status of sociological knowledge, and perhaps even guidelines for improvement, can be sought in the first instance by looking to the natural sciences as a model.

Common naturalism: Positivism, empiricism, and Popperianism   The archetypal naturalist epistemologies, if naturalism is regarded simply as an epistemological thesis (rather than, for example, an ontological thesis as well) are the major twentieth century forms of empiricism—early positivism, mainstream empiricism, and Popperianism. The most commonly used generic term for these positions in the social sciences is *positivism,* and I shall continue this usage except where it may cause confusion. To illustrate the naturalist epistemological thesis I shall look at the basic tenets of these positivist or empiricist positions and contrast them with the naturalist realist position to which I subscribe.

Positivism, as I outlined in chapter 1, has a characteristic view of scientific knowledge. For the positivist, the objects of scientific knowledge are phenomena; scientific knowledge takes the form of general laws that must be testable by experience; and explanation consists in showing the logical links between specific phenomena and these laws, i.e., explanation takes the form of logical subsumption under general laws. These basic tenets form a general methodology for the acquisition of scientific knowledge, which is believed to be certain and value-free. Only knowledge acquired via these general methodological principles has any claim to the term. It is in this sense that positivism is a naturalist epistemology. The social sciences either follow the positivist methodology and are hence fundamentally the same sort of enterprise as the natural sciences, or they do not, in which case they do not produce knowledge at all.

In the context of the development of a naturalist realist metatheory of sociology, it is vital to contrast naturalist realism with positivism, for two reasons. Firstly, while positivism is no longer dominant in philosophy of science, it still dominates sociology, at least in the United States.[2] And secondly, social scientists opposed to positivism often confuse it with realism.[3]

The best way to bring out the contrast between the positivist epistemologies and naturalist realism is to compare the positions systematically, both at the level of philosophy of science (which directly affects methodology) and at the level of metaphilosophy of science (to which any serious defense of the philosophic level must appeal).[4] Philosophy and metaphilosophy of science together form the core of a general world view—a general account of the nature of the world and our knowledge of it. As C. A. Hooker convincingly argues, each philosophy of science, if coherent, can be seen as embedded in a complete and systematic world view and ontology. These world views must be examined if the arguments between the positions are to be clearly understood and intelligently evaluated.[5]

Hooker's comparison of the various positivist philosophies and metaphilosophies of science with those of naturalist realism is worth exploring.[6] At the level of philosophy of science, he contrasts the theories of rationality, the semantics, the epistemologies, the psychological theories of humans, and the theories of the origin, scope, and significance of language that together support the theories of science held by each of the versions of positivism with those of naturalist realism. The metaphilosophies of the positivist positions, rarely explicitly acknowledged, are derived from this schema. In contrast, the naturalist realist metaphilosophy is not derivative in this simple sense, but arises from the interplay of theories at every level of philosophical and scientific discourse. Rather than dealing with Hooker's entire analysis here, I shall limit myself to a brief outline of the positivist theories of science and metatheories of science, to highlight the similarities of these positions. I then move on to a similar outline of Hooker's naturalist realist position that clarifies the extent of the difference between these two major positions.

Early positivism (or logical empiricism) was developed primarily in terms of a semantic theory, the theory that any meaningful statements about the world must be in terms of, or ultimately reducible to terms of, sensory experience. To the early positivists, the scientific language (L) consists only of cognitively meaningful sentences, which contain only those terms whose meaning and reference are acquired directly in sensory experience, together with truth-functional connections. Sensory experience is privileged in that it is held to be intersubjectively invariant. Scientific data consists of the class of immediate, honestly reported, logically simple sensory experience reports in L, and scientific theory is seen as a deductively axiomatized class of sentences in L. Theoretical terms are construed as generalizations of observation statements. The criterion for the scientific acceptability of a scientific theory is its truth, and a theory is regarded as true if and only if the scientific data entail the theory. Science can then be distinguished from non-science on the grounds that the sentences of empirical science consist of all and only the sentences of L. To the early positivists, the aim of science was to maximize the class of certain empirical truths. Thus, the appropriate methodology was to maximize scientific data and to accept all the true theories that result. Scientific knowledge was seen as cumulative, and the history of science was seen as the continuous expansion of scientific data and the acceptance of progressively more general and successively inclusive theories.[7]

One of the problems faced by early positivism was the realization that by excluding induction, this conception excluded most of science. Mainstream empiricism developed as a response to this problem, allowing the entry of more generalized (inductive and probabilistic) logics. For mainstream empiricism, the scientific language (L') consists of cognitively meaningful sentences, defined as generalized logical functions of basic observation sentences. The latter are sentences of the early positivist language, L. Observation, as with early positivism, remains intersubjectively invariant and is privileged; scientific data still comprises the class of basic sentences in the scientific language L'; and scientific theory is still seen as a deductively axiomatized class of sentences in L'. The criterion for the acceptability of scientific theory is adequate evidential support (as specified in the generalized logical theory). Science could be distinguished from non-science on the grounds that the sentences of empirical science consist of all and only the sentences of L'. To the mainstream empiricists, the aim of science was the maximization of empirical knowledge (maximally justified true belief). Thus the appropriate methodology was to maximize scientific data and to accept all theories that are adequately supported by the data. Just as for the early positivists, scientific knowledge was cumulative and the history of science was seen as the continuous expansion of scientific data and the acceptance of progressively more general and successively inclusive theories.[8] But mainstream empiricism too had its problems. The doctrine of the independence of observation from theory was roundly attacked on the basis of evidence from psychology, anthropology, sociology, and history showing clearly the theory-ladenness of observation.[9] The empiricist picture of the history of science as continuous accumulation was shown to be false.[10] And the notion that induction could guarantee even that a theory was probably true was questioned.[11]

Popperianism addressed the last criticism in particular, and sought to modify mainstream empiricism to deal with the problem by again restricting the use of logic to deductive logic. Popper rejected the notion that induction could either verify theories or even make them highly likely to be true and developed a new theory and methodology of science, based on deductive logic. While theories could not be proven true, they could be falsified by a basic statement that conflicted with the theory. Popperian science starts with a problem (a conflict between expectation and observation or just a question for which we have no answer). A theory is then invented to resolve the problem. The theory must be falsifiable, relevant, but not yet falsified. The reason it must be falsifiable is that if all possible states of affairs fit in with the theory, there is no observational difference between its being true and false, so it conveys no scientific information. A theory is testable only if some imaginable observation would falsify it.

The theory is then critically tested by observation (including experimentation). Ad hoc hypotheses to bolster the theory are not allowed, as such modification simply makes the theory invulnerable by reducing its content.

Successful criticism removes the theory and creates a new problem—the explanation of the old theory's successes and its failures. To resolve this, a new theory is required to explain the successes of the old one, deny its mistakes, and make additional predictions not made before. One proceeds by this kind of conjecture and refutation from less general to more general theories, and human knowledge is expanded.[12]

For a naive falsificationist, there are no grounds for accepting theories, only for falsifying them. A sophisticated falsificationist will accept theories on such grounds as increased content over rival theories, absence of ad hoc hypotheses, degree of coherence with other more established theories, and increased predictive ability. But acceptance is only tentative. Any theory can be falsified at any time, at least in principle.

While the logic of falsification is deductive rather than inductive, there are still many similarities with early positivism. For example, the Popperian notion of scientific language is similar to the other positivist positions in that it is defined in terms of basic observation statements and logic. The scientific language (L") consists of cognitively meaningful empirical sentences comprising empirically meaningful statements together with deductive logic. Every empirically meaningful statement has in its consequence class the negation of at least one basic existential assertion. Popper appears to differ from mainstream empiricism in that he denies the independence of observation from theory, and hence the incorrigibility of observation statements. But in practice basic statements (singular existential assertions or their conjunctions) seem privileged in the sense that they are potential falsifiers of theories.

Further, scientific data remains a class of basic sentences in L", and scientific theory is a deductively axiomatized class of sentences in L". The criteria for the acceptability of scientific theories are the degree of logical content combined with the severity of the tests actually applied and withstood. While different in structure to inductive support, these criteria are still designed to specify a purely formal relation between theory and evidence. The basis of the distinction between science and non-science remains that of belonging to L", that is, falsifiability. Only and all those sentences that are in principle falsifiable are to be admitted to science. Popper admits that his criterion for the demarcation of science from non-science is vague, but claims that it is "more than sharp enough to make a distinction between many physical theories on the one hand, and metaphysical[13] theories, such as psychoanalysis, or Marxism (in its present form), on the other."[14]

Popper's criticisms of Marx and Freud illustrate his use of the demarcation criteria. According to Popper, Marxism was once a science, but its predictions were refuted. Although Marxism continues, it is no longer a science, as it has ignored the methodological rule to accept falsification and has instead immunized itself against such falsification. The psychoanalysis of Freud never was a science, on these terms, as Freud's theory never excluded any particular person acting in any particular way. "The theory was compatible with everything that could happen—even without any special immunisation treatment."[15] The social sciences, then, are not dismissed in principle as non-science by Popperianism. Rather, each theory is evaluated as scientific or not according to the principles of falsifiability and falsification.

For Popperians, the aim of science is the maximization of the scope and depth of human understanding. The appropriate methodology is to maximize the creation of theories with the highest logical contents; to maximize the severity of the tests applied to these; and to provisionally accept those not eliminated. In contrast to the positivists and mainstream empiricists, the history of science is seen as proceeding by conjecture and refutation, and is a history of the rational evolution of scientific problems.[16]

Common naturalism: Metaphilosophy. Although Popperianism may seem on the surface to be quite different from early positivism and mainstream empiricism, it is quite firmly in the positivist tradition, and as such is subject to most of the criticisms that have been brought to bear against positivism in general. The extent of the similarities becomes apparent if we look at Hooker's analysis of the metaphilosophies of each position.

Hooker's analysis of the positivist metaphilosophies of science identifies, for each of the three variants of positivism under discussion, six metaphilosophic principles that are required for their defense. An examination of these principles shows just how alike the positions are. The first metatheoretical principle required for the support of early positivism is identified by Hooker as follows:

(M1) [M'1, M"1] There exists a First Philosophy which includes theories of epistemology, rationality and language. A First Philosophy is logically and epistemologically prior to, and hence normative for, all other statements in the admissible structure of human knowledge and (in some appropriate sense) constitutes a necessary framework for the expression of the content of human knowledge.[17]

The principle, (M1), is the exactly the same as this for both mainstream empiricism (M'1) and Popperianism(M"1). Likewise, the second metaphilosophical principle of early positivism holds for both more recent forms.

(M2)[M'2, M"2] All acceptable sentences, whether philosophical or empirical, are expressible in a language $\sim$ L [$\sim$ L," $\sim$ L"], where $\sim$ L [$\sim$ L," $\sim$ L"] is a logically and semantically clear and precise language.

Theories of epistemology, rationality, semantics and of science itself are to be characterized in terms of logical structures in ∼ L [∼ L," ∼ L"].[18]

The third metaphilosophical principle of early positivism is shared only by mainstream empiricism.

(M3)[M'3] The theory of epistemology is the analysis of the foundations of human knowledge; an epistemological foundation is adequate if and only if it provides grounds for epistemic certainty. In the construction of epistemology it may be assumed that the mind is epistemically transparent to introspection.[19]

The Popperian position differs here, reflecting the notion that theories can never be proven true but only falsified.

(M"3) The aim of epistemology is to explain how science is possible; in particular to explain how an evolving, improving science is possible.[20]

The fourth metaphilosophical principle deals with the scope of rationality, and it too is the same for all the variants of positivism under discussion.

(M4)[M'4, M"4] The scope of the theory of rationality is confined within the domain of the empirically meaningful; that part of the theory of rationality pertaining to the pursuit of truth is logically independent of any other component of the theory (if any).[21]

The fifth metaphilosophical principle concerns the nature of philosophy and metaphilosophy. It too can be formulated in the same way for all three positivist positions, but Hooker allows that mainstream empiricism and Popperianism can each consistently substitute an alternative with a Kantian flavor. I shall quote the common version first, followed by the alternatives—mainstream empiricist, followed by Popperian.

(M5)[M'5, M"5] The doctrines of philosophy and metaphilosophy must be logically consistent; hence it follows in particular that both sets of doctrines are conventions, devoid of empirical content, which in some sense constitute successive logical frameworks for the construction of empirical knowledge.[22]

(M'5*) The doctrines of philosophy and metaphilosophy are necessarily universally descriptive of intellectual structure.[23]

(M"5*) The doctrines of philosophy and metaphilosophy are descriptive of intellectual structure.[24]

From the five metaphilosophical principles that underlie positivism, it follows that for all of the variants discussed:

(M6)[M'6, M''6] First Philosophy (and of course metaphilosophy) is logically and epistemologically prior to, independent of, and normative for theory of science.[25]

Naturalist realism: Metaphilosophy. Positivism has been thoroughly criticized on all levels, with the result that it no longer dominates the philosophy of science.[26] Unfortunately, as I have already mentioned, naturalist realism, as an alternative epistemology and theory of science, has been dismissed by many social scientists as "neo-positivist." This myth can be dispelled by looking at Hooker's parallel analysis of the naturalist realist metaphilosophy of science, itself a critique of positivism.

One of the distinctive features of naturalist realism is that it takes the findings of science into account in its philosophy, including scientific theories about the nature of the world and the nature of humans. But nature has an evolutionary history, and humans evolved, both biologically and socially, in interaction with a changing universe, and human knowledge and rationality evolved along with them. From this point of view, the notion, made explicit in the positivist metaphilosophies of science, that philosophy is normative in the sense of necessarily applying to any rational creature and for all time, must be regarded as unsatisfactory. A naturalist realist, in contrast, sees philosophy in dynamic interplay with science. This becomes clear in Hooker's discussion of the naturalist realist metaphilosophy of science. Hooker's first naturalist realist (NR) principle states, in contrast with all variants of positivism, that:

(MNR1) There is no First Philosophy (in the traditional sense).[27]

If one admits that human rationality, language, and knowledge have an evolutionary history (or even that they have changed through time by some other process), one cannot know a priori of any foundation for science, or admit any transcendental normative principles. A different account of the nature of the normativeness of philosophy must be given. Hooker gives such an account in (MNR2).

(MNR2) The normativeness of philosophical doctrines consists in this: they stand in the same relation to the theories of science as theories of science do to their own data fields.[28]

All theories, at all levels of generality, and not just philosophical theories, are the carriers of normative force, in that any theory can be used as a

framework for the criticism of the data in its domain. Philosophical theories differ from scientific theories in terms of their level of generality but are normative in just the same way. They too constitute a framework for criticizing,
evaluating, and even rejecting scientific theories and procedures.[29] A corollary
of this is that philosophical theories, like scientific theories, are confronted by
the data in their domain, and it is partly on this basis that they are themselves
evaluated. Thus there is a continual interaction between the descriptive and the
normative, for ". . . it is precisely a theory's *descriptive* (explanatory) success
that justifies its use as *normative* . . "[30] With normative theories developing in
interaction with scientific theories, it should be apparent that naturalist realism
recognises no transcendental values.

From (MNR1) and (MNR2) it follows that a naturalist realist epistemology will not be foundational, at least in the transcendental sense that positivism
is foundational. The third NR principle developed by Hooker reflects this.

(MNR3) The aim of epistemology is to offer a general theory which will
explain how science is possible (in particular, explain how an evolving,
improving science is possible), what the scope of scientific knowledge is,
how that knowledge is acquired and what the relative epistemic status of
various components of that knowledge is.[31]

A naturalist realist epistemology will be based on the best scientific
knowledge available about the epistemic nature of humans. Thus, it will take
into account the physical, psychological, and sociological nature of humans. It
will also take into account the nature of language, as the theory of language will
affect the epistemic status of some classes of assertions.[32]

(MNR4) The theory of language is founded on the scientific account of
Homo sapiens; the use of symbolic forms, in particular formal or natural
languages or fragments of them, for certain purposes is to be justified on
the basis of this latter account. In particular, there is no pre-determined
preference for formal languages, nor any initial assumption concerning
either their greater adequacy in all or any particular respects, or their universal applicability—their specific use is to be justified as above—and
conversely for natural languages also.[33]

Hooker points out that such a view becomes necessary once an evolutionary view of humans is taken seriously, for an evolutionary account does not
see language as given, but as something that has developed socially for certain
purposes. Current scientific accounts of the nature of language give rise to a
point of general epistemic significance. Language is thought by many to indicate a much richer reality that cannot be expressed linguistically.[34] In this sense,

all assertions must be seen as distorting reality by being radically partial, and should be epistemically qualified as such.

(MNR5) The concern of a theory of rationality is the construction of the most adequate theory of the well-functioning mind, where "well-functioning" is a term whose content is informed by scientific theory.[35]

Hooker's "well-functioning mind" needs modifying to "well-functioning mind or other decision-maker," for not all decision-makers are minds, and it would be premature to exclude any decision-maker from a general theory of rationality. By "other decision-makers" I do not mean merely computers and the like, which can be seen as modelling certain aspects of human thought and might thus be included anyway. I am referring to social institutions that have decision-making procedures in which the decisions of those institutions cannot be reduced to the decisions of the individuals who participate in the decision-making procedures.[36] But I agree with the main feature of Hooker's notion of theories of rationality, that with the breakdown of the normative/descriptive distinction, rationality can be seen as dynamic. Normative notions of rationality will be based on historical evidence of the evolutionary success and survival of the human species and of scientific methods over time, and will change accordingly. And interestingly, normative theories of rationality cannot be tied to language if language is indeed a reflection of more complex information processing, as science suggests. As Hooker points out, "[w]e can hardly expect . . . that either in ourselves or in any other intelligent species will a linguistic form provide the most significant characterization of rational processes."[37]

(MNR6) The content of a philosophy of science comprises a theory. This theory is of the same kind as those of science in every philosophically relevant respect except logical role, insofar as the subject matter of the philosophy is science itself.[38]

The import of this metaphilosophical principle is that the elements of a naturalist realist philosophy of science are subject to modification and even rejection like any scientific theory. And the criteria for their acceptance will be the same as for scientific theories too. Thus, it is to be expected that philosophy of science will change along with the development of science and of humans. As Hooker points out, this means that the doctrines of philosophy of science may be "less precise, more programmatic, certainly less final, than is customary in philosophy, and of a distinctive content."[39]

Philosophy of science, then, is built on the basis of scientific theories about rationality, language, and the epistemic nature of humans, and the theory of science turns out to be dependent on the fleshing out of these theories. To do this adequately enough to justify a specific theory of science (or even to show how Hooker's version is derived) would take me too far afield here, and I leave it to the interested reader to follow the enormous field this opens up. For my purpose, that of distinguishing clearly positivist philosophies from a naturalist realist philosophy, it is sufficient to point out the differences at the metaphilosophic level, where the naturalist realist position can be sharply stated. A comparison of the naturalist realist metaphilosophy of science with the positivist metaphilosophies of science shows that the naturalist realist principles directly oppose all of those of early positivists and mainstream empiricists, and most of the Popperian ones. The exception is the Popperian theory of epistemology (M3"), which is thoroughly evolutionary, and to which the naturalist realist epistemology owes credit.[40]

It should be obvious from the discussion of the naturalist realist metaphilosophy of science that there will be no a priori distinction between the natural sciences and the social sciences. Indeed, the fleshing out of the naturalist realist position owes much to the social sciences. As with the positivist positions, any distinction between science and non-science will refer to methodology. But methodology to the naturalist realist is something to be investigated rather than something given. And it might well include the operation of institutional decision-making procedures as well as those of individuals.

Naturalist realism: world view. So far, in this section, I have discussed naturalism as an epistemological thesis that has bearing on the status of the social sciences vis-a-vis the natural sciences. Naturalism as an epistemological thesis in this sense will make no fundamental distinction between the natural and the social sciences. I have outlined two kinds of naturalist, yet contrasting, epistemologies: positivism and naturalist realism. Positivism is peculiarly focused on epistemological security, and positivist positions limit themselves, at least overtly, to epistemology. But the discussion of naturalist realism should have given enough of the flavor of the position to show that it is not limited to epistemology. A thoroughgoing naturalism, unlike positivism, will have an ontological component too.

Naturalism as an ontological thesis is the thesis that despite its complex nature, every aspect of the world is capable of causal interaction with every other aspect of the world. Naturalism sees humans as continuous with nature rather than as fundamentally different types of being existing apart from nature. This view of humans need not be a priori, for it is a consequence of accepting from the natural sciences a picture of humans as part of the evolutionary nature of life on earth. The connection with epistemology is that for all those who see humans as continuous with nature, there will be no a priori reason for studying humans and human systems in a fundamentally different way from the study of natural systems.

The obvious naturalist ontology is materialism. To the naturalist, if the natural world is seen as material in nature, humans will be seen as material beings as well. Note that although naturalists are usually materialists, there is no inconsistency in the notion of an idealist naturalist.[41] Indeed, phenomenological sociologists such as Berger and Luckmann[42] verge on an idealist naturalism, as we shall see in the next section. But I shall not discuss idealist naturalisms here. My purpose is limited to showing that ontology has implications for sociological methodology and theory, and I shall simply sketch two contrasting forms of materialism common in sociology, reductionist materialism and historical materialism.

Reductionist materialism (not a position I defend) gives explanatory priority to the causal relationships and properties of the basic components of a system rather than to the system as a whole in the explanation of the system's behavior. Reductionists believe that a collectivity or whole is nothing more that the sum of its parts, or the units that comprise it, and these are regarded as ontologically prior to the properties of the whole. The properties of the whole are explicable solely in terms of the properties of its parts and their interrelations. The causal chain is one way, running from the units to the whole. When a reductionist view is taken of human society, we have the position known as biological determinism. The properties of society are seen as no more than the sums of the individual behaviors and tendencies of the individual humans comprising it. These individual behaviors and tendencies in their turn are determined by the biochemical composition of humans, and this depends on their genetic constitution. Human nature, according to this view, is fixed by our genes. Thus, the causes of social phenomena are ultimately located in our genes. Sociobiology is the latest in the line of reductionist social sciences, which date back at least to Hobbes.

In contrast, the historical materialism developed by Karl Marx recognizes causal interaction as taking place at various levels. Marx was concerned particularly with social change, and at a societal level of analysis gave causal priority to economic factors (the forces and relations of production) in explaining social change. But Marx saw individuals as not only shaped by society but shaping it, and thus as causally active. In the following extract from his *Theses on Feuerbach*, Marx attacks those materialists who see humans as simply the products of external natural (including social) circumstances.

The materialist doctrine that men are products of circumstances and upbringing, and that, therefore, changed men are products of other circumstances and changed upbringing, forgets that it is men who change circumstances. . . . The coincidence of the changing of circumstances and of human activity can be conceived and rationally understood only as revolutionizing practice.[43]

Historical materialism, far from being reductionist, sees causal relations occurring at various levels of analysis, and even between levels, as, for example, when events at a macro level affect circumstances at a micro level, and vice versa.

This brief discussion of some naturalist ontological positions familiar to sociologists was intended to give an intuitive idea of the links that exist between ontology on the one hand and epistemology, methodology, and theory on the other, in a systematic naturalism. This brings me to the end of my discussion of the naturalist position on the question of whether sociology is, or can be, scientific. To the naturalist, there are no a priori grounds, either epistemological or ontological, for making a fundamental distinction between the natural and the social sciences. The naturalist positions I have discussed are able to distinguish science from non-science on general methodological grounds. To the positivist, scientific methodology is tightly prescribed, whereas to the naturalist realist, scientific methodology consists of the best known ways humans have of finding out about the world. As far as both of these positions are concerned, sociology is or can be scientific insofar as it follows a scientific methodology. Hence, sociology can—and in the case of positivism, must—draw on the methods of the indubitably successful natural sciences in its search for a successful methodology.

Historically, naturalism in one form or another has had broad support in sociology. Of the three great early sociological theorists, Marx, Weber, and Durkheim, both Marx and Durkheim were committed naturalists.[44] But humanism has a strong tradition in sociology as well, where its formulation owes much to Weber, although there has been considerable debate both over whether Weber saw himself as a humanist, and over whether he should be interpreted as a humanist.[45]

2.2.2 Humanism

As we have seen, during the formative years of sociology in the late nineteenth and early twentieth centuries, positivism was the generally accepted model of science. The humanists of the time generally accepted positivism as an adequate model of the natural sciences, but argued that it provided a totally inadequate methodology for the social sciences. As Gadamer points out, "The logical self-reflection which accompanied the development of the human sciences in the nineteenth century is wholly dominated by the model of the natural sciences."[46] As a result, early sociological theorists were, on the whole, limited to three positions.

The first position was to accept positivism as an adequate methodology for the social sciences and try to develop sociology within its constraints. The second was to deny positivism's adequacy as a model of the social sciences and accept as a consequence that sociology was not a science. The third position was to insist both that sociology had its own fundamentally different methods and that it could be scientific. The second position is a weak form of humanism, in that while it makes a fundamental distinction between the natural and the social sciences, it is also consistent with positivism. The third position is a stronger form of humanism, in that it insists that knowledge in the social science is to be obtained by fundamentally different methods from that in the natural sciences, and yet is still to be considered knowledge. The strong form of humanism is in fact a challenge to positivism, which holds that there is only one scientific method and dismisses as non-science any attempts at knowledge-seeking that fail to adhere to it. As it is not at all clear that even the strong versions of humanism that developed need be in opposition to the naturalist realist position that I outlined above, it is best to consider humanist positions as they actually developed, that is, in opposition to positivism, rather than in opposition to all forms of naturalism.[47]

Max Weber.   Of the early sociological theorists, Max Weber best exemplifies the strong humanist position. Weber was interested in establishing sociology as a science but at the same time was insistent that the nature of sociology required the development of its own methodology, a methodology that could not be reconciled with positivism. Recall his definition of sociology.

> Sociology . . . is a science concerning itself with the interpretive understanding of social action and thereby with a causal explanation of its course and consequences. We shall speak of "action" insofar as the acting individual attaches a subjective meaning to his behavior—be it overt or covert, omission or acquiescence. Action is "social" insofar as its subjective meaning takes account of the behavior of others and is thereby oriented in its course.[48]

Weber's definition of the subject matter of sociology illustrates one of the classic distinctions thought to exist between the natural and the social sciences, the non-observability of the objects of sociological study. Weber distinguishes "action" from "behavior" in terms of the subjective meaning that attaches to the former. "Behavior" can be seen in purely physiological terms, and can be explained causally from a physiological point of view. "Actions," on the other hand, are "meaningful."[49] But "meaning," the feature that distinguishes "behavior" from "action," is not observable. Simply to distinguish the subject matter of sociology requires interpretive understanding.[50] Social action, the object of sociological knowledge, cannot be distinguished from behavior by observation alone.

Sociological explanation, then, according to Weber, differed from natural scientific explanation in that the latter explained an observable subject matter by subsumption under the laws of nature, whereas the former explained a non-observable subject matter by interpretive understanding. Interpretation involves understanding the meaning of a particular action, or placing it in a wider contextual setting. Thus, sociology required the development of a fundamentally different methodology, the nature of which leads to criteria of objectivity and standards of validity quite different from those of a positivist natural science. Weber's methodological position in fact illustrates most of the major distinctions thought to exist between the natural sciences and sociology, so I shall examine it in some detail.

While realizing that sociology could not be approached in the same way as positivist natural science, Weber was concerned to bring to sociology the clarity and precision associated with the natural sciences. In order to achieve such clarity and precision in the interpretive understanding of social action, Weber developed the use of the "ideal type." Ideal types are clearly-defined constructs or models that emphasize particular aspects of the institutions, actions, persons, and so on that are being studied. The "ideal" here is not normative, but refers to the abstract and generalizing nature of the concept. Ideal types are rarely, if at all, encountered in real life. Rather, the ideal type is a comparative tool, a yardstick against which to compare particular instances, enabling one to work out what is unique to each case. Ideal types are constructed according to the purpose of the research, and are to be assessed according to their usefulness.[51]

To help achieve precision in the interpretive understanding of social action, Weber developed four ideal types of behavior: traditional behavior, affectual behavior, rational value-oriented action, and rational goal-oriented action. Traditional behavior, behavior in conformity with custom, is not necessarily behavior with a motive, for it is often undertaken unconsciously. If this is so, then it is not amenable to interpretive understanding as Weber defines it, as the behavior has no meaning to the individual. Such behavior can only be explained causally. But traditional behavior may be open to interpretive understanding if it is undertaken because of a positive valuing of tradition. Affectual behavior similarly lies on the borderline of what can be explained purely by causal sociology and what is open to interpretive understanding, in that it may be a totally automatic response to stimuli on the one hand, or may involve planning for delayed gratification on the other.

Weber defines value-oriented action as action in which the means take precedence over the ends. The value-oriented individual is guided by some behavioral ethic that is pursued without concern for the consequences of any actions. Its rationality lies in the coherence of the action with the individual's ethical convictions about behavior. Goal-oriented conduct is the pursuit of chosen goals by the most rational means available, the latter being determined by experience and involving a rational projection of future possibilities.[52]

The closer the action under consideration is to an available model of rationality, according to Weber, the more confident one can be of understanding its motivation. Thus, in the case of rational goal-oriented action, one can be reasonably sure of achieving the correct interpretation, but this certainty decreases as one moves to value-oriented action, and further to affective and traditional action. Weber illustrates this point in his discussion of understanding.

Weber identifies two sorts of understanding, "direct understanding" and "explanatory understanding." Direct understanding is the recognition of the meaning of a proposition or action by "direct observation." For example, we understand directly the meaning of an arithmetic proposition like $2 \times 2 = 4$. Weber calls this direct rational understanding. We may also have direct understanding of irrational (emotive) actions. For example, we may directly understand certain facial expressions as manifesting anger.[53]

Explanatory understanding involves putting the action in an intelligible and more inclusive context. Explanatory understanding of the action of a person chopping wood is achieved when we know that that person chops wood for a living. Thus, explanatory understanding involves the attribution of motives, or the placing of the act in "an intelligible and more inclusive context of meaning."[54]

For an explanation to be valid, the particular subjective interpretations or understanding of the action in question have to be justified. To Weber, "the basis for certainty in understanding can be either rational, or it can be of an emotionally empathic or artistically appreciative quality."[55] These notions can best be explained by looking at some of Weber's examples of direct understanding. When someone is carrying out an arithmetic or logical argument, for example multiplying 2 by 2 to get 4, it can be seen that the conclusion follows logically from the premises. This is "rational understanding" of the action. When someone sets about mending a roof and is going about it in the most efficient way, we have rational understanding of that person's actions in terms of means/ends rationality. Rational understanding is, according to Weber, the most certain. Slightly less certain, but still adequate for most purposes, is the understanding of rational action involving error.[56] The justification of the understanding of an action on the basis of the logic or rationality of the action seems to be based on the availability of clear models of rationality.

"Empathic understanding" is involved in cases where the action is not rational. Ultimate ends or values cannot be rationally determined, according to Weber. Likewise, emotions are not rationally understandable. In such cases, we rely on empathic understanding. Empathic understanding cannot be regarded as certain, and in the case of values, is reliable only to the extent that we share the culture in which the values are embedded. Sometimes empathic understanding may be impossible, although it may be possible to grasp the values involved intellectually. Sometimes values must simply be accepted as data of which there is no understanding. But even so, it may still be possible to understand the course of action as motivated by the value in question. The extent to which empathic understanding of emotional reactions may be achieved depends on the extent to which the sociologist is susceptible to such emotions. The validity of empathic understanding, then, depends to some degree on the extent to which the culture and experiences of the investigator match those of the person or people being studied.[57] It is for this reason that less confidence can be placed in the interpretive understanding of affectual and traditional behavior.

An adequate interpretive understanding is what Weber calls "adequate at the level of meaning." But at this stage it is no more than a plausible hypothesis. To be "adequate at the level of cause," such hypotheses must be empirically tested.

> . . . even the most perfect adequacy on the level of meaning has causal significance from a sociological point of view only insofar as there is some kind of proof for the existence of a probability that action in fact normally takes the course which has been held to be meaningful.[58]

Weber regards the empirical verification of subjective interpretations of social action as indispensable if sociology is to be scientific. It is this insistence on the necessity of causal explanation in addition to interpretive understanding that raises the issue of whether Weber should be considered a humanist—an issue I take up in chapter 5. But certain verification is rarely possible in sociology. Controlled experiments are usually not possible, and one has to resort to comparative methods, finding cases that differ from the event or action in question only in the absence of the hypothetical cause. Even the comparative method is not always available, and often, according to Weber, the only method possible is the use of thought experiments.

The uncertainty of these less rigorous methods, along with the uncertainty inherent in much interpretive understanding, points to another of the distinctions Weber made between the natural sciences and sociology. Causal propositions in the natural sciences took the form of "laws," whereas in sociology they are best considered "rules." Weber reserves the term "law" for "general causal propositions of unconditional strictness," and uses "rule" for those empirical propositions incapable of this degree of strictness, and also for those propositions for which no exceptions have been found but where we lack insight into the decisive causal determinants.[59] Sociology, unlike the natural sciences, would never be in a position to formulate laws in this sense. It could not, therefore, be subjected to the same standards of validity (that is, certain truth) as the positive sciences.

Another of the ways in which Weberian sociology differed from positivist natural science was in the inevitable intrusion of values. Recall the fact that Weber's sociology was concerned with the interpretive understanding of social action, which was to be achieved by comparison with ideal types. The ideal types are constructed by the researcher according to the purposes of the research, rather than having objective reality, and are therefore imbued with the values of the researcher. While the intrusion of values in Weberian sociology was inevitable, this did not, according to Weber, make it less scientific, because the theories that were constructed as a result of applying the interpretive methodology could be assessed as true or false independently of the fact that values played a part in their construction. What could make sociology unscientific was the use of value judgments, that is, either condemning or praising particular actions or practices under investigation.

For Weber, then, sociology differed from the positive natural sciences in a number of ways. Sociology, being concerned with the subjective interpretation of social action, required a different methodology and form of explanation from the natural sciences. Values intruded inevitably into sociological method. And Weber's concept of an adequate sociological explanation was markedly different from the positivist model of explanation as subsumption under general laws. Weber regarded sociological explanation as requiring both interpretive understanding and causal explanation, rather than simply the latter, and he saw no parallel in the natural sciences for interpretive understanding as a part of explanation. So for Weber, sociology was in many ways different from the natural sciences. But rather than deny that it was scientific, he constructed a separate methodology for the interpretive aspect of sociology, with its own standards of validity.

Humanist arguments.   While it may be unclear whether Weber was a humanist in the sense of proposing a *fundamental* distinction between the natural and the social sciences, the methodological issues of causality, meaning, and values that interested him are those on which humanists tend to base their case for a fundamental distinction.[60] Runciman points out that the relationships between these issues are controversial, and that the various humanist positions that have been put forward are based on often incompatible interpretations of these issues. Nonetheless, at a general level, humanist positions are usually based on one or more of the following premises:

. . . first, that human actions cannot be explained in terms of law-like relations of cause and effect; secondly, that to grasp the meaning which human actions have to those performing them requires a different method from any known to, or required by, practitioners of natural science; and thirdly, that the social scientist's moral, political and/or aesthetic values necessarily enter into his conclusions in a way that those of the natural scientist do not.[61]

I shall look briefly at some of the arguments in support of these propositions, as they are issues that any naturalist metatheory of sociology must address. The first proposition is perhaps best seen as an ontological one, that the objects of study of the social sciences are very different from the objects of natural scientific study. Humans are regarded as distinctive in that they are free agents, engage in meaningful activity, and construct the social world they live in. They act because they have reasons, or motives, rather than because of physical causes. These reasons and motives cannot be reduced to causes, as reasons and motives, unlike causes, have no precise spatiotemporal location. They can be localized no more closely than in the person as a whole. Human action, then, cannot be explained causally, and interpretive understanding must be substituted for causal explanation in the social sciences.

This position is taken, for example, by William Dilthey, the leading exponent of hermeneutics as the proper methodology for the social sciences, and also by later hermeneutic social scientists.[62] It presents a challenge to naturalism, because if human action is not amenable to causal explanation, the naturalist ontology and unity of science theses fail. It is for this reason that naturalists have devoted much attention to the question of whether reasons can be treated as causes. I return to this issue in chapter 5.

The second proposition, that understanding the meaning of human action requires a different method from any required in the natural sciences, can be related to the first, but must be considered separately. Although there might be what Weber would have called an "elective affinity" between humanist epistemologies and the mind/body dualism assumed in the first proposition, humanism is more usually an epistemological rather than an ontological thesis, and the only form of dualism that the epistemological thesis is committed to is explanatory dualism. Explanatory dualism is not necessarily committed to the existence of *irreducible* reasons and motives. It is quite conceivable to hold that intentions are the sort of thing that can somehow be physically instantiated in the brain, that is, that reasons and motives can be instantiated as causes, but at the same time to hold that reasons and motives require interpretive understanding rather than, or as well as, causal explanation. This is because, although it might be possible to explain meaningful action causally, it is seen as more relevant or useful to explain it in the terms in which people themselves see it, as part of a shared understanding or cognitive framework for interacting with the world. This is Weber's position.

The second proposition challenges the naturalist to show that the methods of interpretive sociology, while different from those of the natural sciences (and perhaps even from the other social sciences), are not so fundamentally different as to require completely different criteria of assessment. What is at issue here is the proposition that the theories produced by interpretive sociology are fundamentally closed to empirical investigation. This position is often supported by the ontological claims of the first proposition,[63] and accompanied either by the claim that interpretive sociology therefore has no claim to validity and is thus not scientific,[64] or by the claim that the interpretive social sciences are ultimately to be justified by appeal to some universal principle of rationality.[65] Weber meets the first part of this challenge by insisting that the theories of interpretive sociology are just so many plausible hypotheses unless they can be verified by a causal account. But he remains convinced that the methods of interpretive sociology have no parallels in natural science. These issues too are taken up in chapter 5, where I show both that interpretive sociology is not fundamentally closed to empirical investigation and that the methods of interpretive sociology do have parallels in the natural sciences.

The third proposition on which arguments for humanism are based is the notion that social scientists' moral, political, and/or aesthetic values enter into their conclusions in a way that those of natural scientists do not. We have already seen that Weber realizes that the values of the social scientist are involved in the selection of features to be included in the construction of the ideal types that are an essential feature of his interpretive methodology. He arrives at this conclusion because he correctly believes that the features considered relevant to historical explanation change over time and vary from culture to culture.

But in the light of studies in the history of science that show how the meanings of natural scientific concepts change over time, it is no longer necessary to see this feature of interpretive sociology as distinguishing it from the natural sciences. Ideal types are still constructed with a view to examining those features of a complex total situation likely to prove relevant in the causal explanation of an event or process; and while Weber regards decisions about relevance as value-oriented and as such not scientifically justifiable, such decisions of relevance have to be made in the natural sciences too, as we shall see in chapter 4. While not scientifically justifiable within the positivist framework, the place of such decisions on relevance is assured in the naturalist realist framework.

Another humanist argument centering on the issue of values distinguishes the natural sciences from the human sciences in terms of the consequences that research has for social and moral practice. It is argued that natural science is possible without an ethics if one presupposes only knowledge values, whereas this is not the case with the human sciences, where study presupposes relevance for moral and social practice.[66] It is certainly the case that social scientific research has implications for moral, political, and social practice. Despite the diversity of their methodological and substantive works, this point was not only recognized by the great early sociologists, Marx, Durkheim, and Weber, but can be seen as guiding their work. Marx believed that the emergence of capitalism brought with it new forms of exploitation, and his work was directed at understanding social change and the structure and dynamics of capitalist society with a view to ending such exploitation. Durkheim saw the distressing social conditions that accompanied rapid industrial development as in part the result of the inability of traditional institutions to produce social cohesion, and much of his work was directed at discovering new modes of socialization that might overcome this problem. Weber was concerned that the developing modern nation-states required a new political ethos of responsibility, and believed that the insights of sociological analysis could help with the political reconstruction of post–World War II Germany.[67]

But natural science is surely in the same position. While it is conceivable that, in the early days of the gentleman scientist working alone, natural science was possible without an ethics if one presupposed only knowledge values, this is not possible today. In the natural sciences, most activities are now both cognitively and economically beyond the resources of the individual. Even large institutions and nations must make choices as to which areas of research they will pursue. These choices are surely based on values and ethics, overt or not, and in their turn will affect future values and ethics. Current research choices depend not only on the current state of knowledge in a field, but on the availability of appropriate technology. The development of technology is clearly dependent on moral and political values. One has only to consider the technological developments that have arisen as a direct result of policies of aggression and defense in the twentieth century to realize this. And it has long been realized (at least since Marx) that the technology used by a society has a profound effect on the economic, social, and political structures of that society as well as vice versa. Direct political intervention in the development of science aside, then, the relationship between science and technology precludes any neat separation between cognitive and other values.[68]

I have not come across any further and substantially different arguments for distinguishing the natural sciences and the social sciences on the basis of value issues, and upon investigation, none of the above arguments for humanism stand up. While they were valid on the assumption that positivism was an accurate model of the natural sciences, when held against the actual practices of science or against the more realistic naturalist realist model of science, they fail. I have, however, come across some further arguments for humanism that are not immediately concerned with the issues of causality, meaning, or values, but rather with the lack of reliability of social scientific research and/or the status of social scientific generalizations, and I now discuss these.

Radnitsky, for one, believes one of the grounds for a distinction between the natural and social sciences is that the very act of studying in the human sciences produces effects on the objects of study, and that this may have unpredictable and unintended consequences.[69] It seems to me, though, that this will not stand up as a distinction between the natural and the social sciences. It is surely also the case in some areas of the physical sciences, for example, in biology in the area of recombinant DNA research, and in certain nuclear experiments in physics, that the act of study produces effects on the objects of study with sometimes unpredictable and unintended consequences. That the act of sociological study affects the people and human systems being studied is of importance, but more because it may render such studies unrepeatable, as often what is being studied are features unique to a people. This in turn affects the certainty with which such studies can be accepted. But with respect to the certainty with which theories are held, this points only to a difference of degree with the natural sciences. No method can guarantee certainty, and moreover, some experiments are more repeatable than others. The cost and availability of experimental equipment often prohibits the replication of experiments in physics, for example. The period of proximity of astronomical bodies, such as a comet on an elliptical "escape" orbit, precludes repetition of many astronomical experiments. And much of the substance of historical natural sciences such as biology and geology involves the explanation of events that clearly can never be repeated.

Another and related reason for distinguishing the natural sciences from sociology is that the objects of sociological study may react to the results of the study (as opposed to simply being affected by the study itself). Andreski points out that this feature of sociology has two major consequences.[70] The first is that predictions arising from a social scientific theory may become self-fulfilling prophecies. This has been forcefully demonstrated by Rosenthal and Jacobson, who found that teachers' expectations of children could affect the children's performance.[71] Non-verbal IQ tests were administered to school children with the purported aim of predicting "bloomers." Twenty per cent of the children were picked arbitrarily by the experimenters, and the teachers were told that they had been identified as "bloomers." Tests four months later and a year later showed that the children who had been identified as "bloomers" had improved IQ scores while those not so labelled had not improved. The point I wish to make here is neither a sociological one about the effects of labelling, nor an ethical one about about the morality of such studies, but rather the epistemological point that the creation of a self-fulfilling prophecy from a sociological theory means that the theory itself is self-validating. It actually creates the empirical evidence needed to verify its predictions. But rather than distinguishing the social sciences from the natural sciences in any fundamental way, this merely points to another reason for not attributing the same degree of certainty to such studies as one would if independent verification were available.

There is a second consequence of the fact that the objects of social scientific study may react to the results of that study: the influence it may have on the publication of results, the funding of researchers, and consequently on the disciplinary hierarchy. Findings that are critical of the political status quo or oppose the dominant sect in sociology will not always have a favorable reception. But this feature of the sociology of science will not serve to distinguish the social sciences from the natural sciences either, except in degree, for similar considerations come into play when one compares research into nuclear energy with research into solar energy. It does mean that non-empirical factors may be more important in the selection of the disciplinary hierarchy than is the case in the natural sciences, with all the implications that has for the credibility of the social sciences, but such factors are present in the natural sciences as well.

Weber, as we have seen, considered the relative unreliability of social scientific research one of the features that meant that sociology could not produce universal generalizations (or laws) as could the physical sciences. The other reason that sociology could not produce universal generalizations was that the concepts used in sociological explanation were culturally and historically specific. To this can be added the fact that the results of social scientific research are also, for the most part, culturally and historically specific. What holds for modern capitalist societies generally does not hold, say, for traditional Australian Aboriginal societies.[72]

The lack of universal generalizations comparable to, say, those in physics, is considered by some to be reason for distinguishing the social sciences from the natural sciences, and even for regarding the former as non-scientific. Philip Converse cites Gergen as maintaining that the social sciences "cannot be science like the others (i.e., . . . real science) because [they] cannot truly generalize."[73] But Converse argues that such comments stem from an inappropriate model of the scientific enterprise, one based on an idealized notion of physics. He argues that the sciences exhibit many "textures." "Texture" includes the methods, criteria of validity, accuracy of prediction, scope of generalization, and so on, that are peculiar to any field of study as a result of the variety in the nature of the subject matter or domain of fields of inquiry.

Differences in texture depend on differences in the subject matter from science to science, and even within specific sciences. For example, the texture of the social sciences will be more akin to that of the biological sciences than that of physics, because the former two deal with living things. Converse shows that many generalizations in the biological sciences are as historically and geographically contingent as generalizations in the social sciences.

Converse argues that rather than regarding this as a basis for making a fundamental distinction between the physical sciences and the biological sciences, the model of science that requires all real or mature sciences to produce universal generalizations after the manner of physics should be abandoned. He also challenges the common notion that universal laws are "precise assertions that, with ridiculously few specified conditions, none of which is a sheer limitation in time or space (such as the next universe over), we are convinced will hold," suggesting it should be modified.[74] Instead, he argues that all generalizations are spatially and temporally qualified, and that the greater the scope of the generalization, the more it approaches the ideal concept of a natural law. This means that the relative inability of the social sciences to produce universal laws cannot be used to distinguish them from the natural sciences, as all generalizations have a limited scope, although some are broader than others. Converse's argument supports the view that while scientific inquiry has basically the same nature across the disciplines, it is inappropriate to judge the social sciences by precisely the same standards as the natural sciences, which anyway are themselves not all judged by the same specific criteria.

2.2.3 Naturalist Realism and Sociology as Science

I have been considering the status of the social sciences vis-a-vis the natural sciences. The issue is one that has to be resolved in order to decide whether sociology is, or can be, scientific. As I argued earlier, if it can, this might help to solve the problems that have arisen as a result of the current nature of sociology as a discipline, both by allowing sociology to model its methodology on that of the obviously successful natural sciences, and by taking advantage of the prestige associated with science in modern society.

The naturalist holds that sociology can be scientific. But the dominant naturalist models of science throughout most of the development of sociology, and indeed until at least the 1960s, were positivist. While positivist models of science no longer dominate within the philosophy of science, they are still influential in sociology, and are often regarded as synonymous with naturalism. Humanism, the position that the social sciences are fundamentally different from the natural sciences, developed against a backdrop of positivist models of science, and realized that the social sciences could not operate according to the methodology specified by positivism, nor meet its rigorous standards.

But positivism is not the only naturalist model of science. The recently developing naturalist realist model presents a radically different view of science. I illustrated the radical nature of the differences with a metaphilosophical comparison of the two. While humanism showed that the social sciences could not conform to the positivist models of science, it is not clear that humanist arguments can fundamentally distinguish the social sciences within a naturalist realist model of science. From a naturalist realist point of view, the arguments about the relative lack of reliability of social scientific research serve only as a distinction of degree, for the naturalist realist accepts the fallibility of all theories. Likewise, the relative lack of ability of the social sciences to produce universal generalizations will not serve to distinguish the social sciences in kind from the natural sciences. For one thing, if Converse is correct (this point is argued in chapter 4), all generalizations are limited to some extent in scope. And for another, the naturalist realist model of science does not specify universal generalizations as a criterion of science. Finally, the natural sciences face the same issues as the social sciences with respect to the place of values in science.

But the humanist-naturalist debate does raise issues of concern for the naturalist realist. Any adequate naturalist realist account of the social sciences must be able to link explanations in terms of reasons and motives to a causal account of the social world. And it must be able to show that whatever the best methodology for acquiring an interpretive understanding of the meaning of human action, that methodology does not lie outside of any generalized methodology of science.

These issues can, I think, be adequately solved within a naturalist realist framework, and I attempt a solution in chapter 5. If this attempt is successful, then there is no doubt that sociology can in principle be incorporated in a naturalist realist model of science—that it can be scientific. However, to say that sociology *can* be scientific is not to say that all of the problems identified in chapter 1 disappear automatically. Certainly, the problem of the status of sociology, if its methodology could be shown to be scientific, should be resolvable. But to show whether or not the methodology of sociology is scientific requires some sort of specification of a generalized scientific methodology against which sociology can be compared. This raises the question of whether such a specification is indeed possible. It is to this question that I turn in the next section.

2.3 Scientific Knowledge and Validity

2.3.1 Naturalist Realism and General Methodology

Recall that sociology as it is actually practiced has some problem features that make it seem rather unscientific. Its multi-paradigmatic nature means that there is no consensual way of arbitrating between competing truth-claims. And its multi-perspective nature means that the discipline is operating with a variety of conflicting assumptions about the nature of the social world. This, combined with the sectarianism that haunts sociology, means that it is often considered ideology rather than science.

Whether attaching the label of "scientific" to sociology will help resolve these issues is going to depend very much on whether scientific methodology can provide perspective-neutral mechanisms for arbitrating contradictory truth claims and for either choosing between, or somehow unifying, conflicting assumptions about the nature of the world. The positivist models of science discussed in §2.2 guaranteed such mechanisms. But internal difficulties with the positivist philosophies of science, in addition to studies in the history and sociology of science, have shown that none of the positivist models of science is an adequate description of the scientific process. Not only are the positivist models inadequate as descriptions of the scientific process, they are inadequate as normative models. Feyerabend has argued convincingly that had any of the positivist models actually been followed by scientists, science could not have progressed, as it obviously has.[75] Moreover, the historical and sociological studies have pointed to the inevitable existence of many external[76] factors in the scientific process, raising serious doubts about the ability of science to provide any such perspective-neutral mechanisms.

Positivism's fall from grace came with the realizations that (a) observation was theory-laden, and (b) there was more to the rational acceptance of theories than logic (either inductive or deductive). Epistemic values such as simplicity, internal consistency, and the potential to lead to further research, among others, may all be involved. But if theory choice involves values, and observation is theory-laden, the distinction between fact and value can no longer be seen as clear-cut. Observation and formal logic, then, cannot be seen as the foundation of a certain and objective science.

But realism,[77] historically one of the major opponents of empiricism, offers promise of a different notion of objectivity, and has gained currency among philosophers of science since the recent downfall of positivism. Realism, recall, is the thesis that there is a real world existing independently of our attempts to know it; that we as humans can have knowledge of that world; and that the validity of our knowledge claims is, at least in part, determined by the way the world is. Our knowledge of the world is not obtained simply from incorrigible perceptions and a content-free logic, as the positivists would have it; neither are its sources purely cognitive, as the rationalists would have it.[78] Rather, such knowledge has both cognitive and empirical content.

In §2.2, I contrasted Hooker's naturalist realism with positivism, primarily to bring out the epistemological differences between them, as they are both naturalist positions from a purely epistemological point of view. Indeed, because modern versions of realism were developed against the background of the recent debate with positivism and realists were tackling the empiricists on their own ground, realism is most often developed as an epistemology.[79] But from the definition of realism given above, it is clear that realism has an important ontological component, too, and one that is appealed to in justifying its notions of objectivity, for the realist claim is that the world itself is a perspective-neutral arbiter between competing truth-claims and theories. As realist ontology is important epistemically, I shall briefly discuss the ontological aspects of the naturalist realist thesis I support.

The basic ontological position of realism is that a world exists independently of our knowledge of it, and that the nature of that world is such that we can have knowledge of it. Beyond that, the nature of the world is a matter for empirical investigation. Realism, then, is not committed a priori to any account of the specific nature of the world.

Nevertheless, realism is monistic in the sense that it holds that the nature of the world is such that it is, in principle, open to empirical investigation. So it is committed to an ontological unity of nature thesis in that it does not recognize ontologies that are in principle closed to empirical investigation. This unity of knowledge thesis can be seen as a special case of the naturalist unity of nature thesis. The naturalist thesis maintains that everything in the world is of such a nature that it can in principle interact with everything else. While causal isolations are possible, they are contingent, and the naturalist imposes no ontological distinctions for semantic or epistemic reasons. The realist thesis maintains that everything knowable in the world can interact with humans, because humans know the world via their interactions with it.

The notion of cause plays a vital role in naturalist realist accounts of science. The realist view of science holds that scientific theories aim to discover the real nature of the world, appearances notwithstanding. The realist is interested in discovering the generative/causal mechanisms underlying phenomena. A further ontological thesis of realism, then, is that the theoretical entities of a valid causal theory actually exist.[80] This is in marked contrast to instrumentalism, the thesis that scientific theories are merely heuristic devices and/or are simply a convenient way of expressing the relations existing between phenomena. But more importantly, causal interactions between humans and the world form the basis of naturalist realist notions of validity.

This brief sketch of the naturalist realist ontological thesis, along with the discussion of the naturalist realist metaphilosophy of science in the previous section, makes sense of the realist response to the failure of positivism to provide criteria for the validity of theories. In response to the theory-ladenness of facts and the failure of logic to guarantee certainty, the realist adopts a fallibilist approach to science and denies that it is rational to accept only what one is forced to. The process of acquiring knowledge involves taking risks—going beyond the evidence.[81] Nonetheless, the realist wishes to maintain appropriate objective criteria for deciding whether a theory is good or bad. The realist, then, has to develop a quite different notion of rationality from the logic of the positivists, and a quite different notion of objectivity from the incorrigibility of observation. In other words, the realist has to develop a new methodology for science.

Although facing the challenge of developing non-positivist criteria for determining the validity of scientific theories, the realist has a major gain in the general recognition of the theory-ladenness of observation, for this removes the strongest argument for limiting science to the study of phenomena. The positivist notion of the incorrigibility of observation and the ideal of certain knowledge were the main arguments against the study of the nature of the world underlying the phenomena. The failure of these arguments opens the way for a much broader notion of explanation than was possible under positivism. The positivist notion of explanation, recall, consisted in showing the formal logical links between specific phenomena and the general laws of nature. But now the way is open for the realist to specify a more powerful form of explanation, one that throws light on the causal mechanisms involved in the production of the phenomenon in question.

While many natural and social scientists have explicitly used a naturalist realist methodology,[82] there has so far been no generalized model of such a methodology to serve as a guide or heuristic. If one can be developed, naturalist realism has the potential to provide perspective-neutral criteria for deciding between competing truth claims and theories.

2.3.2 Relativism

But realism has not been alone in the field since the downfall of positivism. Relativism is another, and purely epistemological, thesis that has made ground in the recent debate. Relativism takes as its starting points the theory-ladenness of observation, and, following Kuhn and Feyerabend,[83] the paradigm and/or cultural specificity of methodology. As a consequence, relativism, like naturalist realism, embraces fallibilism. But for the relativist, unlike the realist, once the incorrigibility of observation is denied and the inadequacy of formal logics to account for scientific methodology is recognized, there are no grounds for objectivity. Contemporary relativists do not usually take this to entail a retreat to solipsism, but rather to cultural frames of reference. Different cultures have been found to have different sets of values, and different ways of categorizing the world. Within each culture, it is held, common values and theories as to the nature of the world may ensure objective knowledge, but there can be no way of judging between the theories of different cultures. The point at issue, then, is the relativist claim that even if there is no fundamental difference between the social sciences and the natural sciences, the natural sciences themselves are not able to provide the perspective-neutral criteria necessary to solve the problems of sociology. In what follows, I critically examine that claim, and argue from a realist perspective that science can indeed arbitrate between competing theories, on the basis that reality does impose constraints on the content of scientific theory.

Within the metatheory of sociology many theorists[84] have held a relativist view of the social sciences while maintaining some kind of empiricist view of the natural sciences and the objective nature of natural scientific knowledge. Gareau, for example, in the light of his findings that sociology is nationalistic and sectarian and supports contradictory truth-claims, concludes that sociology is not a science, but what he calls a "craft;" i.e., it provides only local knowledge of a practical nature as opposed to universal, theoretical knowledge. Gareau retains from positivism the idea that science comprises universal laws or generalizations, and distinguishes science from non-science using this criterion, in addition to Kuhn's criterion for distinguishing the pre-scientific stage from mature science, i.e., the existence in the latter of a single paradigm. Gareau does not address specifically the question of the validity of practical knowledge, nor does he mention any uses sociological knowledge may have apart from its ideological use. His point is simply that at present the process of accepting or rejecting sociological knowledge takes place within sectarian and nationalistic boundaries, and so sociological knowledge is relative. But in the light of my discussion of humanism in the previous section, Gareau's position is no threat to the naturalist realism, for it does not imply that sociology *cannot* be objective, but merely that it *is* not.

Of those contemporary relativists who maintain that knowledge is necessarily relative (rather than simply that some particular body of knowledge is, as a matter of fact, relative), few make any distinction between the natural and the social sciences, seeing the production and content of all knowledge as relative to the values and the social and cultural backgrounds of the knowledge producers. I want to distinguish two forms of such relativism here, radical relativism and benign relativism. Radical relativism is the position that because the production and content of knowledge is always relative to the values and sociocultural situation of its producers, there are no objective criteria, no culture- or paradigm-neutral ways, of determining the validity of scientific theories.[85] If this is the case, then the problems listed at the start of this section may have no solution, and indeed may be indicative of a more general problem faced by contemporary science when compared with the knowledge systems of different cultures. Benign relativism, on the other hand, while acknowledging the part played by values and sociocultural situation in the production of knowledge, still allows that there may be some objective criteria for determining the validity of theories, in the sense that the validity of theories may be in part determined by the way the world is. Benign relativism is no threat to realism.[86]

To illustrate relativism with the works of theorists likely to be familiar to sociologists, I turn now to several contemporary sociologists of knowledge, for many of them appear to take a strong relativist position and argue against a realistic interpretation of science. The aim of Bloor and Barnes and other proponents of what is called the "strong program" of the sociology of knowledge, for example, is to provide an account of the production of scientific knowledge in terms of supposedly arational social causes. In following this program they have met with considerable opposition from contemporary philosophers of a more rationalist bent, such as Larry Laudan.[87]

The crux of the debate seems to be that the critical rationalists[88] prefer to explain the progress of science in terms of its supposedly inherent rationality, while the proponents of the strong program prefer to explain the history of science, which is not necessarily seen as progress, in terms of supposedly arational social causes. The critical rationalist position here is reminiscent of Weber, in that both the critical rationalists and Weber attempt to explain certain actions or events in terms of their rationality. Inasmuch as an action conforms to our ideas of what is rational under the circumstances, then, according to both Weber and the critical rationalists, no further explanation is needed to understand the action in question. Inasmuch as any action deviates from commonly held conceptions of what is rational, such action needs to be explained. Both Weber, and, for example, Laudan, admit that all actions are caused. But actions, like any event, are caused by a complex set of prior circumstances and events. The explanatorily significant causes are those which, had they not been present, would have changed the action or event in question. And for both Weber and Laudan, it is its very rationality that is the significant cause of rational action. As long as one allows that in some sense reasons can act as causes, the critical rationalists are not disputing the notion that rational actions must have causes, but rather the notion that causes other than rational ones are significant. The proponents of the strong program, on the other hand, insist that social causes are relevant in the explanation of all social events, rational or not, science included.

Both parties to the dispute agree that observation is theory-laden—that what one perceives is influenced by, among other things, one's social and cultural background. The thrust of the strong program seems to be that the processes of scientific discovery, and, perhaps more importantly,[89] the acceptance of scientific theories, are also dependent on social and cultural factors. Even in science, that paradigm of rational behaviour, there is no context-free way of deciding between rival theories. Barnes, for example, points out that the inductive practices used by scientists vary.

> . . . inductive inferences are never determined by "the rules of inductive logic" or anything comparable; this indeed is why crude inductivism is not widely accepted as a satisfactory epistemology. The analogies relied upon, the level of generality moved to, the scope claimed, are all endlessly problematic features of inductive inference. When inductive inference within a community takes on a stable and uniform character, it is never because the "rules of induction" have satisfactorily imposed themselves; rather it is because a particular pattern of inductive practices has been agreed upon or institutionalized.[90]

Such variation requires explanation. Barnes continues:

> Wherever (collectively accepted) inductive practices are actually encountered, they raise empirical (sociological) problems: the specific form and scope of inductive inference requires empirical explanation.

The intrusion of such supposedly arational factors into science raises the question of whether science can transcend the society that produced it and forms the basis of the Edinburgh school's claim to relativism, for they believe that theorizing can never be justified. But the relativism implied by the Edinburgh school, if it can be called relativism, is rather innocuous. As Nicholas points out, it is at most "descriptive relativism," simply asserting that individuals and groups do as a matter of fact have different opinions over matters of empirical fact.[91] That there is a diversity of beliefs, that the social circumstances of the parties concerned affects which of the contrary beliefs on a topic is held in a given context, and that all beliefs may have social causes, says nothing about whether those beliefs can be judged valid or invalid. Likewise, the variety of specific forms of inductive inference and the intrusion into these of social factors scarcely shows that inductive processes are not appropriate ways of knowing the world. Radical relativism is the position that the social origins of categories of perception and forms of reasoning render them wholly arbitrary with respect to their application to nature,[92] and this is not being claimed by the Edinburgh school.

It is, however, possible to interpret other sociologists of knowledge as espousing radical relativism. Bruno Latour and Steve Woolgar, in their study, *Laboratory Life*,[93] can be seen in this light. *Laboratory Life* is a fine-grained study of the social microprocesses involved in the establishment of thyrotropin releasing factor (hormone) (TRF) as a fact. Following Latour and Woolgar, I use the word "fact" rather than "entity'—indeed it is this distinction that is the locus of the dispute between Latour and Woolgar (and phenomenologists in general) and realism. Latour and Woolgar are clear about their hopes for the study.

> TRF(H) is now an object with a well-defined molecular structure, which at first sight would hardly seem amenable to sociological analysis. If the process of social construction can be demonstrated for a fact of such apparent solidity, we feel this would provide a telling argument for the feasibility of the strong program in the sociology of science.[94]

Latour and Woolgar, using the methods of discourse analysis,[96] do indeed show the social processes involved in the many stages of research, from access to initial funding and facilities, through the design of instruments and experiments, the disputes over results and interpretations in settings as diverse as the tea room and the leading journals in neuroendocrinology, to the appearance of TRF as an objective fact in textbooks.

I have no quarrel with the empirical findings of the study, but I do question the conclusions Latour and Woolgar draw. For Latour and Woolgar argue that their study shows that the way the world is has no bearing on the establishment of the validity of scientific theory, and this is in direct conflict with the realist view. Latour and Woolgar chart the changing status of TRF(H). For quite some time there was dispute over whether TRF(H) was a fact or merely an artifact of the instrumentation.[96] But quite suddenly its status stabilized as a fact. Latour and Woolgar argue that this shows that reality, or the way the world is, cannot be used to explain why a scientific statement becomes a fact, "since it is only after it has become a fact that the effect of reality is obtained."[97] In other words, reality cannot be the ground of objectivity because there is no knowledge of what reality is in any particular case until *after* the facts have stabilized.

But this is to mistake the part that the realist would have reality play in the establishing the existence of an entity (or even just a fact). For the realist will hold that there are good inductive reasons, supported by our knowledge of evolution and the biological nature of humans and by the psychology of perception and cognition, for believing that *in general* the stability of a fact about a theoretical entity across a variety of situations is a good indicator of its existence.[98] The facts about stability in general can be used as a guide to the reality of any particular putative entity. The realist will be able to say, in advance and based on known facts about stability, that if an entity turns out to be stable then it is real.

Despite their claim that reality plays no part in the establishment of scientific facts, Latour and Woolgar do not see themselves as relativists.

> We do not wish to say that facts do not exist nor that there is no such thing as reality. In this simple sense our position is not relativist. Our point is that "out-there-ness" is the *consequence* of scientific work rather than its *cause*.[99]

But it is hard to see in what way Latour and Woolgar can be other than radically relativist, intentions notwithstanding. Admitting the existence of reality is alone not enough to avoid relativism—reality must play some part in arbitrating competing claims. But the "reality" of Latour and Woolgar cannot play that part, for it is not the reality of the realist, existing independently of our knowledge of it, but a socially constructed "reality" that the realist would call *knowledge* of reality. Latour and Woolgar argue for this notion of "reality" on the basis of their research. Their laboratory studies included observing the initial indications to the scientist that a new and discrete object had been isolated. In keeping with their methodological approach, Latour and Woolgar see the discovery simply as the difference between two inscriptions.

> An object can be said to exist solely in terms of the difference between two inscriptions. In other words, an object is simply a signal distinct from the background of the field and the noise of the instruments. Most importantly, the extraction of the signal and the recognition of its distinctiveness

themselves depended on the costly and cumbersome procedure for ob-taining a steady baseline. This, in turn, was made possible by laboratory routine and by the iron hand of the scientist who organised the laboratory work and took all precautions available within the laboratory context. Once again, to say that TRF is constructed is not to deny its solidity as a fact. Rather it is to emphasize how, where, and why it was created.[100]

The argument seems to be that because the inscription devices and tech-niques were (socially) constructed, so too were the inscriptions, as a product of the devices and techniques. Thus TRF (reality) is constructed. But this argu-ment only works on the assumption that the sign is the same as what is signi-fied—that the object simply is the signal. Woolgar readily acknowledges that this assumption underlies his work.[101] But this assumption leads automatically to equating "reality" with claimed knowledge of reality, without the interven-tion of any empirical work. This is simply the phenomenalist assumption that only appearances can be known and that there is not only no need to postulate the existence of an unknowable reality beyond those appearances, but no basis on which to do so. Thus, this particular dispute between Latour and Woolgar and realism has its source at the philosophic level.

But this does not mean that the empirical data that Latour and Woolgar present are equally compatible with both positions, for what they cannot ex-plain and the realist can is what causes the *difference* between any two inscrip-tions, which presumably are both constructed in the same way. Or if one wants to argue that the experimental control is in some (perhaps social) sense con-structed differently from the column in which the presence (or fact) of TRF is indicated, the realist can explain why this reading rather than that appears in any column.

This point is made very clearly in Radford's critique[102] of Berger and Luckmann's *The Social Construction of Reality*.[103] Berger and Luckmann take the same phenomenological stance as Latour and Woolgar, but are perhaps more familiar to generalist sociologists as their work is intended as a contribu-tion to social theory as well as to the sociology of knowledge.[104] Radford's crit-icism is aimed against Berger and Luckmann's claim that all knowledge is socially constructed, that all the determinants of belief and/or knowledge are social factors.[105]

Radford's argument is particularly forceful because he uses cricketing examples to illustrate his points, and cricket is so obviously a socially con-structed game governed by socially constructed rules. Radford asks why a so-cial constructivist should avoid bowling slow long hops down the leg side. The constructivist answer (consistent with what Berger and Luckmann say) is be-cause he has been taught not to and his team mates would would be most unim-pressed if he did. These long hops and any attempts to defend them have been "nihilated," in Berger and Luckmann's terms.[107] But, Radford asks, weren't they "nihilated" because the batsmen "annihilated" them? Not according to the social constructivists. To them, it is as if

> the institutionalized beliefs about long hops found in the sub-culture of cricket (and in [their] own beliefs about bowling long hops) had the same source and were maintained by the same factors as produce and maintain the view commonly held among cricketers about the desirability of wearing whites.[107]

But, counters Radford, the bowler's having his long hops hit for six is not socially constructed in this way, despite its taking place in a highly conventionalized situation. Rather, it is an immediate response on the part of the batsman to a physical event, and moreover, to one that is usually unintended. These long hops are more frequently hit for six and easier to hit than others, and this is a natural phenomenon. That it is natural rather than social can be seen by the fact that it is so even for untutored and inexperienced batsmen, that is, those who have not been socialized into the subculture of cricket.[108] Radford makes the additional point that the bowler's attempts to avoid bowling long hops and the batsman's wish to hit them are rational, given the rules of the game. Yet this is at odds with the social constructivist point (shared by proponents of the strong program of the sociology of knowledge) that social factors produce beliefs, attitudes, and behavior non-rationally.

Radford argues that the claim that beliefs about things that exist and happen are always and only produced and maintained socially, and never produced by things acting on the believers and maintained by their remembering this, is just not plausible. As Radford points out, he knows that Gary Sobers hit six sixes off one six-ball over because he, along with several million other people, saw it, albeit on television. The fact that someone from a completely different culture unexposed to cricket could not have recognized the actions for what they were does not mean that Radford's belief is produced and maintained by the fact that many other people hold and maintain their belief. "All it shows it that *perhaps* a propensity to notice what Sobers did and *certainly* our capacity to identify what he did at one level . . . as scoring six sixes, depends on our familiarity with an understanding of the game of cricket."[109] Radford could have added that what the realist can explain, and the social constructivist cannot, is that he saw Sobers hit six sixes as opposed to four sixes, say, or being bowled by the second ball. The strong thesis of social constructivism is both false and inadequate.

Radford argues that not only is the strong thesis false, it is incoherent. The strong thesis states that beliefs are determined only by social factors and forces. But one cannot coherently argue that socialized persons are totally unaffected by natural phenomena. If they were, they would also be unaffected by social phenomena, since the transmission of the latter relies on natural phenomena, for example, sounds and movements, and their perception.[110] Radford's argument for the incoherence of the strong thesis can, of course, be denied, for it depends on the realist assumptions that there is a reality independent of our knowledge of it, and that we can know that reality by means of our interactions with it. But the cost of rejecting those assumptions is high, even for the committed social constructivist, for it means rejecting all knowledge about perception, and entails a retreat to super-idealism. How one can allow the reality of the social from this position, thus avoiding solipsism, remains a mystery.[111]

The same sort of incoherence is apparent in Harry Collins's work, notably in his book, *Changing Order,* which argues for social constructivism.[112] Collins argues that not only are any stable rules of induction used by a community negotiated social conventions, but that all such rules are necessarily underspecified to the extent that they can be infinitely reinterpreted. This point is then applied to the replicability of observations and experiments, which Collins sees as the criterion of the scientific. Collins argues that in fact it is not replication itself, but what scientists can be gotten to accept as replication, that is what actually demarcates "objective knowledge." Taking Popper's assertion that with a little ingenuity any two things can be found similar in some respect, so similarity is not an objective relation between things, Collins argues that replication is in fact a matter of social negotiation, and hence that "[i]t is not the regularity of the world that imposes itself on our senses but the regularity of our institutionalized beliefs that imposes itself on the world."[113]

There are several problems with Collins's argument. As I have already pointed out, replicability is not a good criterion for demarcating science. A great deal of science, particularly in the historical sciences such as biology and geology, but also in the so-called "hard" sciences, is just not replicable. Moreover, to assume that the replicability of a single experiment is the only criterion of the objectivity of its findings is to ignore the wider institutional context of science, in which the coherence of the findings with the entire network of scientific knowledge is a vital part of the acceptability of new facts.

But even if replicability were the only criterion of objective knowledge, it simply is not the case that social negotiation is the only constraint on replicability. As Hesse points out, "our habitual perceptions do discriminate *degrees* of similarity and dissimilarity between things, both in respect of overall similarity of all their properties, and of the degrees in which any single property (for example, a color) exhibits itself."[114] Collins seems to take these discriminations as wholly a matter of social convention. But the works on which he bases his arguments (for example, those on the extent of cultural differences in color recognition) are still controversial. Moreover, Hesse argues, to make all recognitions entirely a matter of social consensus "shows extraordinary neglect of the *biological* basis of perception, which must for reasons of survival relate to real regularities in the world."[115] This neglect sits uneasily with Collins's view of science, for he claims that "[f]or all its fallibility, science is the best institution for generating knowledge about the natural world that we have,"[116] and indeed (selectively) uses the findings of science to support his claims. This sort of incoherence makes one wonder how Collins's own work should be interpreted.

Despite these problems, it is not clear to me whether Collins is forced into the phenomenological and radically relativist position of Berger and Luckmann, or whether the appearance of radical relativism is simply a result of the methodological device he uses to establish the social factors involved in the production of scientific knowledge. For Collins is quite clear that he uses skepticism about reality as a methodological device, and never claims it as a transcendental proposition. I argue in chapter 6 that conflicting or apparently conflicting assumptions about the nature of the social world are best seen as methodological devices for simplifying a complex reality, rather than as conflicting ontological assumptions. The same point could be made to reconcile Collins's methodological skepticism with an ontological realism.

Despite their claims to relativism it is by no means clear that the proponents of the "strong program" in the sociology of knowledge present a challenge to realism. Those who adopt a phenomenological approach as methodology (such as Collins and, I believe, Latour and Woolgar) can be reconciled with a realist ontology and epistemology. The social constructivism of those for whom phenomenology is first philosophy (such as Berger and Luckmann and many postmodernists) is, I have argued, both false and incoherent. But most sociologists of knowledge have a great respect for science and for their own work, and seem concerned not so much to show that it is mere fiction constructed entirely from social conventions as to dispel the positivist and common sense notions of science that hold science to be infallible and even "sacred."

The debate between the critical rationalists and the Edinburgh School of the sociology of knowledge centers on the rationality of scientific practices. The sociologists of knowledge deny that theories can be justified because they have shown (correctly) that the positivist ideals of incorrigible observation and value-free logic are not achievable. Certainty, therefore, is not attainable. On the assumption that it is only rational to accept what one is forced to accept,[117] all that can be done, according to the Edinburgh school, is to provide a causal (or descriptive) account of the history of science in terms of the arational factors affecting the acceptance of scientific theory. The critical rationalists, on the other hand, insist (also correctly) that normative accounts of the rationality of science are vital in the process of deciding the validity of scientific theories, and are concerned to produce models of scientific rationality to replace the inadequate positivist models.

But the critical rationalists go further than this, in assuming that if one has a valid theory then rational factors must have been the primary factors responsible for that theory. There is considerable disagreement and confusion in the debate over what is to count as a "rational" or a "social" factor, most of which equates the "rational" with the "internal," and the "social" with the "external,"[118] but no matter how these terms are defined it seems to me a contingent matter what combination of factors led to the adoption of any particular belief, whether valid or invalid, by the scientific community. We have already seen that the importance of social factors in the acceptance of theories varies considerably between the natural and the social sciences.[119] The point is also illustrated by the fact that we can look back and determine good and bad science by criteria other than whether it was at the time or is now accepted.[120] So the critical rationalists' argument that rational factors always play a part in the acceptance of scientific theory is not sustainable. Nonetheless, that rational factors may, and indeed should, play a part in the acceptance of scientific theory need not be denied by the sociologists of knowledge, provided that they accept a much broader notion of rationality than the positivists held.

Whether or not the problem of rationality is resolved, it remains the case that according to the realist, the validity of a theory can be determined separately from whatever factors influenced its creation and acceptance. And the "strong program" entails a radical relativism only if it can be shown that there *can be* no objective way of assessing the validity of scientific theories, rather than that such a way was not in fact the sole cause of the acceptance of such theories. In other words, the "strong program" entails radical relativism only if the realist program fails to provide adequate normative criteria of the validity of scientific theories.

Relativists are correct to point out that any set of norms that are held on a priori grounds to transcend cultural differences should be questioned, for they may simply be the preferences of one group (or *in extremis* an individual). But the naturalist realist position I have sketched has no such a priori epistemological foundations. Rather, it accepts on the basis of experience that, however it actually happens to work, the institution of modern science does in fact provide reliable knowledge of the world, facilitating enormous control over nature.[121] Scientific knowledge, then, can be examined retrospectively to see if it can provide a model for the assessment of validity, and if found, such a normative model may actually become a causal factor in the production of future science, irrespective of whether it was actually used (and if so to what extent) in the past. Such a normative model of science, based on adequate descriptions of science, would of course be subject to revision as science itself changes.[122] There would be nothing sacred about it. Such a model should take account of the findings of the sociologists of knowledge that social values are embedded in scientific theory. The possibility of such a model, based on an adequate description of science that takes account of the way values are embedded in theories, has not been successfully refuted by the sociology of knowledge, and its provision could see an end to the disputes between realists and relativists by removing the need for radical relativism.[123]

2.4 The Naturalist Realist Strategy

In §2.1 I argued that a resolution of the problems that sociology faces as a discipline could be found if it could be shown that sociology could be scientific. For if sociology could be scientific, not only might this give it access to the status and funding of the natural sciences, it might also be able to solve some of its methodological problems by turning to the natural sciences for a methodology. In §2.2 I argued the naturalist case against the humanist position that there is a fundamental difference between the natural sciences and the social sciences that might thwart this strategy. In §2.3 I tackled the relativist claim that even if there were no fundamental difference between the social sciences and the natural sciences, the natural sciences themselves were not able to provide the paradigm-neutral criteria necessary to solve the problems of sociology. I argued from a realist perspective that science could indeed arbitrate between competing theories, on the basis that reality does impose constraints on the content of scientific theory. In the course of these discussions, then, I have shown the possibility of resolving the problems of sociology from a naturalist realist perspective.

The appeal of a naturalist realism is not new. Durkheim, for example, although commonly known as a positivist, developed his methodology of sociology from within a naturalist, realist framework. To illustrate, it is quite clear that Durkheim is a realist with respect to the nature of theoretical entities. While seeing social facts[124] as representations of a normative nature, he insists on their reality. Social facts *may* be directly observable, in the sense that they may be codified. But even if they are not directly observable they can be known objectively by their effects, that is, by the constraint they exercise or by their generality. For example, certain norms may exist in a society with respect to fatherhood. These norms exist outside the individual in the sense that while a father may or may not conform to them, the norms nonetheless remain. They can be known by the constraint to conform that is exerted on fathers and felt by them if they resist them. If there is no resistance to norms, they may also be known by their generality. For example, if all Australians in the tropics in midsummer wear clothing even inside their homes, where external constraints can be avoided, the wearing of clothes might be taken as normative. Durkheim, then, is committed to a causal account of social phenomena and of society. And as social facts can be known by observation, either directly or by observing their effects, they are in this sense no different from natural phenomena. Durkheim finds no reason why sociology, despite the nature of its subject matter, should not in principle be studied in the same way as the natural sciences. He is, in fact, a committed naturalist.

But he is no reductionist. Durkheim takes from Comte the idea that the domain of every science is irreducible to that of any other. Sociology, to be a science, has to have its own distinctive subject matter and principles of explanation. Nonetheless, being naturalist, he believes that while *every* scientific discipline, natural or social, has its own subject matter and principles of explanation, for a discipline to qualify as science at all, certain general methodological principles must be adhered to. These principles are basically that all science should be based on observation and inductive logic, and it is in this sense that Durkheim can be seen as positivist.

Durkheim sees science as primarily concerned with the rational and methodological establishment of relations of cause and effect.[125] It was the extension of this notion of science to the study of human behavior that led, according to Durkheim, to what has been termed his "positivism." Durkheim is sympathetic to positivism in the sense that it is naturalist, studying social phenomena in the same scientific and objective manner as that used in the study of nature. Indeed, he often uses the term "positivist" in the same sense as "scientific." But despite his frequent use of the word "positive" to describe his own work, he insists it must not be confused with the positive metaphysics of Comte and Spencer.[126] We have already seen that from a metaphysical or ontological point of view at least, Durkheim is a realist. So whatever his ideas of science and scientific method, his use of the term "positive" brings out his commitment to naturalism rather than a commitment to the positivist philosophy of science.

That Durkheim is committed to naturalism, and is aware of some of the difficulties he was likely to encounter in putting forward such a thesis, becomes apparent in this extract from his introduction to Marcel Mauss's *Socialism.*

> To add a science to the list of sciences is always a very laborious operation, but more productive than the annexation of a new continent to old continents. And it is at once much more fruitful when science has man for its object. It almost had to do violence to the human spirit and to triumph over the keenest resistance to make it understood that in order to act upon things it was first necessary to put them to trial. The resistance has been particularly stubborn when the material to be examined was ourselves, due to our tendency to place ourselves outside of things, to demand a place apart in the universe.[127]

Durkheim, then, despite his own reluctance to use the term, can be seen as a committed naturalist. The natural sciences and the social sciences are fundamentally the same sort of enterprise. And Durkheim implicitly supports the naturalist thesis that there is a fundamental unity of nature, when he argues that in the sense that he would accept that the term "naturalistic" could be applied to sociology (i.e., "that it regards social facts as explicable naturally"), it is "somewhat useless, since it merely means that the sociologist is engaged in scientific work and is not a mystic." His rejection of the term altogether where it is "assigned a doctrinal meaning relating to the essence of social things—if, for instance, it is meant that they are reducible to other cosmic forces," is a rejection of the reductionist thesis rather than a rejection of naturalism.[128]

Durkheim's methodology of sociology rests entirely on naturalist and realist presuppositions. I shall not discuss the details of that methodology here, partly because to do so would take me too far afield, and partly because anyway it related only to that small part of the discipline that Durkheim regards as sociology, the study of social facts. Enough here to say that sociology as a science could not begin, according to Durkheim, until the doctrine of metaphysical dualism, "which made humanity a world apart, exempt, by some mysterious privilege, from that determinism whose presence the natural sciences affirm everywhere else in the universe," was denied, and replaced by a "bold assertion of the unity of nature."[129] This assertion, according to Durkheim, is a result of the synthesis of knowledge from the sciences. In the terms I defined earlier, realism includes the doctrine of the unity of knowledge, and advances in scientific knowledge lead to the naturalist thesis.

But sociology requires, in addition to acceptance of the unity of nature and knowledge, a recognition of the natural heterogeneity of things, if it is to be distinguishable from the other social sciences. Durkheim, following Comte, believes that "the different fundamental sciences are irreducible to one another, although as a whole they form a homogeneous system. The unity of the positive method is no bar to their specificity."[130]

Despite describing himself as a positivist, then, Durkheim distances himself explicitly from many of the doctrines of positivism. Positivism does share some presuppositions with naturalism and realism, but they are not synonymous. Perhaps Durkheim's description of himself as positivist, and the undoubtedly positivist traditions that developed from his work, is what leads many sociologists today to confuse positivism with a naturalist realism and to assume that the damning criticisms of positivism apply to naturalism and realism as well. They do not. And there is no doubt of the fruitfulness of Durkheim's conception of sociological method, despite the fact that it does not encompass much of what was, and continues to be, valuable sociological research.[131]

Durkheim is, of course, not the only sociologist to have worked within a naturalist realist framework, and I include him here merely to illustrate how the framework may have a general influence on methodology. Marx, and many later Marxists, also worked from a naturalist realist perspective,[132] and contemporary naturalist realist sociologists are too numerous to mention.[133]

But although a naturalist realist metatheory of sociology seems a good strategy for resolving the problems of sociology as a discipline, and although there are individual naturalist realist sociologists, and indeed have been throughout the history of the discipline, the fact remains that there is not as yet any generalized naturalist realist methodology of science. Naturalist realism is now well developed and defended at the level of the philosophy and metaphilosophy of science. But whether that is of any use in resolving the problems of sociology depends on whether an adequate naturalist realist methodology of science and metatheory of sociology can be developed.

While discussions in this chapter have shown that a naturalist realist position is likely to be able to resolve the problems of sociology, that humanism is unlikely to be able to do so, and that radical relativism is incapable of doing so, these discussions also raise some further issues that an adequate naturalist realist methodology of science and metatheory of sociology must deal with. From the discussion of humanism, it became apparent that any adequate metatheory of sociology must be able to incorporate explanations in terms of reasons and motives into a causal account of the social world. And from the discussion of relativism, particularly as portrayed by proponents of the strong program in the sociology of knowledge, it became apparent that any adequate methodology of science must take full account of the social implications of the underdetermination of theory by data and of the impossibility of formalizing any precise rules and logical definitions of the scientific method. In general, as Hesse remarks, " . . . science need not be supposed to exhibit one-to-one correspondence with objects and regularities in the world independently of human categories and classification."[134]

The rest of this work is devoted to the problem of developing a naturalist realist methodology of science and a metatheory of sociology that takes account of these factors. It is hoped that this will in turn go some way toward solving the problems, analyzed in chapter 1, that sociology faces as a discipline.

II

TOOLS FOR A SOLUTION

The diverse nature of sociology gave rise to a set of conceptual and pragmatic problems for the discipline. In the last part, I identified these problems, and looked to the dominant metatheoretical perspectives to see if they could provide solutions to those problems. I argued that, in principle, only a naturalist realist metatheory of sociology could provide solutions to all of the problems that sociology faces. For this promise to be fulfilled, a generalized naturalist realist methodology of science had to be developed. My examination of the humanist and relativist metatheoretical positions brought to light a further set of problems that any adequate naturalist realist methodology of science must address. In this section, I attempt to develop a naturalist realist methodology of science that takes account of these metatheoretical problems and that has the potential to provide solutions for the problems that sociology faces as a discipline.

3

Theories as Maps of the World

Maps of towns and plains he sold, and other maps made to order. He would sell a young man a map that showed where a particular girl might be found at different hours of the day. He sold maps to poets that showed where thoughts of power and clarity had come to other poets. He sold well-digging maps. He sold vision-and-miracle maps to holy men, sickness-and-accident maps to physicians, money-and-jewel maps to thieves, and thief maps to the police.

—Russell Hoban, *The Lion of Boaz-Jachin and Jachin-Boaz*

3.1 Sciencing as a Human Activity

The metatheoretical discussion in chapter 2 showed that perhaps the most important barrier to the adoption of a naturalist realist approach to sociology, and indeed to science in general, is the lack of a generalized naturalist realist methodology of science. Such a methodology would in principle be able to determine the validity of theories in a perspective-neutral way, because the naturalist realist metaphilosophy insists that the validity of theories is determinable, perhaps only partially, but in some significant way, by reality.

But there are problems in the way of developing a methodology of this kind. Studies in the psychology of perception have shown that perception is theory-laden. Perception may vary significantly from person to person, and in particular across cultures. And research within the sociology of knowledge has shown clearly that social factors are involved in both the creation and the assessment of scientific theories, affecting not only scientific procedures, but the content of scientific theories. Discussion in the previous chapter showed that it is not at all obvious how these supposedly arational factors can be reconciled with the notion that the products of science, scientific theories, in any sense reflect the world.

The fallibility of science is grounded in the biological and cultural nature of humans as knowers, so I start the search for an adequate naturalist realist methodology of science by looking at the extent to which biological and social processes shape the nature of human knowledge. These issues are discussed under the umbrella of evolutionary epistemology.

Evolutionary epistemology is the field that explores the relationship between evolutionary theory (usually neo-Darwinism) and epistemology. It looks at the implications of evolution for epistemology, and also examines ways in which evolutionary theory might be put to use in the development of an adequate epistemology. Now a flourishing field within the philosophy of science, it starts from the insight, pushed home by psychologists of perception, historians of science and sociologists of knowledge, that science is a human activity. As such, it has to be something that humans, as creatures of biological evolution on earth, can do.

Evolutionary epistemology is a diverse field, exploring the relationship that obtains between the development of science and the biological evolutionary process.[1] Minimally, evolutionary epistemologies hold that biological evolution explains the structure of perceptual and cognitive mechanisms.

From a biological point of view, perception can be seen as a mechanism for vicariously exploring the environment. A well-equipped ship at sea provides a good example of vicarious exploration. The ocean holds many hazards for shipping—islands, rocks, other ships, storms, and so on. Particularly in light of the time and distance a large ship requires to avoid obstacles, direct exploration of the ocean by locomotion is an expensive way to locate hazards—one that will frequently result in the damage or destruction of the ship. The use of devices such as radar and sonar constitute the vicarious exploration of the ocean. Such devices are fallible, have a limited range, and are unable to locate all hazards in time for them to be avoided. Nonetheless, they greatly enhance the ship's chances of survival.[2]

Evolutionary epistemologies, then, stress the fallibility of human perception, but at the same time give an account of its general reliability. The argument here parallels that of Descartes, who argued that God would not have left us with eyes that regularly deceive us. The evolutionary version is that natural selection wouldn't have left us with eyes that regularly deceive us, at least not grossly. Otherwise we would not have survived as a species to be deceived by them. So despite its theory-ladenness, which is a biological phenomenon, there is reason to believe that human perception is reliable. But on its own, this position, while it can accommodate the psychological evidence against the incorrigibility of observation, is still compatible with a scarcely modified positivism. In other words, it can be used as the basis of a perceptual foundationalism that differs from positivist formulations only in granting that perception, and hence scientific knowledge, are fallible. It does not address the problems raised by the sociology of knowledge, particularly the intrusion of non-logical social processes into the creation and acceptance of scientific theory and the impossibility of completely formalizing scientific method.

These problems can partially, at least in principle, be dealt with by the position that biological evolution can explain not only the structure of perceptual mechanisms, but also the structure of cognitive (and perhaps epistemic cultural) mechanisms. The notion that evolution explains cognitive mechanisms is common enough. But some neo-Kantians go further, holding that the Kantian categories are themselves the products of natural selection. Konrad Lorenz puts it thus:

> One familiar with the innate modes of reaction of subhuman organisms can readily hypothesize that the a priori is due to hereditary differentiations of the nervous system which have become characteristic of the species, producing hereditary dispositions to think in certain forms.[3]

The neo-Kantian position is controversial, because anthropological research makes questionable the notion that the Kantian categories are species specific, suggesting instead that at least the categories of time and space may vary cross-culturally. Both the non-Kantian and neo-Kantian versions raise the question of whether (other things being equal) it is the most rational humans who survive and reproduce. This is clearly not the case (irrespective of what notion of individual rationality one holds). Many societies, for example, intervene to ensure the survival and dignity of those quite clearly mentally handicapped. In the light of this fact, one must at least consider whether it is social rationality rather than (or perhaps as well as) individual rationality that counts in the evolutionary stakes.

This raises the question of whether biological evolution can explain culture—an important issue anyway, given the sociocultural factors that form part of the process of sciencing.[4] It is generally accepted that evolution can account for the emergence of culture. More controversial is the notion that evolution can account for the variety of human cultures. For while the emergence of culture can be explained in terms of the biology of human beings (for example, sociality could be an individual characteristic, and one that has been selected for),[5] if the variety of cultures is to be explained in evolutionary fashion, societies and not individuals must be the unit of selection.[6]

The fact that human cognitive structures have evolved is compatible with positivism, for the positivist can argue that while human cognitive structures have evolved, they may still use some a prioristically derived logic. But it is also open to a naturalistic interpretation. While naturalistic accounts of perception are well known, having played a large part in the downfall of positivism, naturalistic models of cognition are perhaps less well known.

In order to show how naturalist accounts of cognition can account for the production of valid beliefs in a non-positivistic way, I turn to a discussion of

Rubinstein, Laughlin, and McManus's account of science as an active cognitive process.[7] This approach takes account of the criticisms of positivism already outlined. Given that observation is theory-laden, knowledge fallible, and so on, Rubinstein, Laughlin, and McManus focus "on discovering the processes people use to keep their views and understandings of how the world is in some passably accurate relationship to how the world actually is."[8]

Rubinstein, Laughlin, and McManus employ a functional (or systems) analysis of cognition that starts from the premise that there is a real world existing independently of our knowledge or perceptions of it, and that the major function of the brain is to model that reality. The ability to model reality confers an additional biological advantage over direct perception. While perceptual mechanisms allow vicarious exploration of the environment, the ability to model reality allows for exploration of a vicarious environment, further increasing the chances of survival provided that the models adequately represent reality in relevant ways.

Thus, the distinction between the models of the world in our brains and the real world, which is modelable, and the relationship between these, is fundamental in any attempt to understand how we know what we know. It is with this in mind that Rubinstein, Laughlin, and McManus distinguish between the cognized environment (Ec) and the operational environment (Eo). The operational environment is the real world, which is modelable, although not necessarily modelled, by the individual. The cognized environment, on the other hand, "consists of all the information modelled in an individual's nervous system through the operation of which the individual recognizes, processes information about, and responds to the operational environment (Eo)."[9]

Following Piaget and others working in the field of developmental psychology, Rubinstein, Laughlin, and McManus note both that the cognized environment changes and develops in interaction with the operational environment, and that cognitive principles place constraints on the completeness and accuracy of the individual's cognitive representation of the environment. Further, they note that there are many Ec models that have little or no correspondence with reality, for example, the gods that many people believe in and entirely fictitious characters such as the Easter Bunny. This raises the question of to what extent the interaction between the Ec and the Eo constrains the construction of false beliefs, which in turn raises the question of whether, given the nature of human perceptual and cognitive processes, knowledge claims are able to be validated.

While veridicality and illusion may be combined in some models in adaptation to the operational environment, Rubinstein, Laughlin, and McManus argue from an evolutionary perspective that, at least to some extent, the structure and content of an individual's cognized environment will model the elements and relations among elements in the operational environment. The question is, to what extent?

Complete isomorphism, which occurs when the elements and relations between the elements of one system completely map the elements and relations between the elements of another system, is rare, and Rubinstein, Laughlin, and McManus note that the cognized environment is never more than partially isomorphic with the operational environment. Cognitive modelling is always selective, is importantly interest or value driven, and presumably involves idiosyncratic conceptual modelling structures that may be species or culture specific.

Nonetheless, there is a constraint on this modelling process, because, as Rubinstein, Laughlin, and McManus point out, the construction of knowledge is a biological phenomenon, and is thus open to selection. So any old partial isomorphism will not do. What is required is *adaptive isomorphism*." . . . the cognized environment is adaptively isomorphic with the operational environment when the degree of "fit" between the cognized environment and the operational environment leads to the individual's survival and production of offspring."[10] This formulation shows how it might be argued that such positions could support a modified positivism, in that they are able to support a perceptual/conceptual foundationalism. The point here is that natural selection would not have left us with grossly misleading cognitive mechanisms.

But the examples of the many false and fictitious beliefs that have been held throughout history show that outside of the narrow range of beliefs that directly affect survival and reproduction there are no biological guarantees that the Ec will in any way correspond with reality. Indeed, as Peter Munz has argued, humans live in societies, and false beliefs may, under certain circumstances, be functional for the survival of societies and hence the holding of those beliefs may be functional for the survival of individuals in those societies. In these circumstances, the holding of false beliefs—precisely a lack of correspondence between the Ec and the Eo—may be selected for.[11] I shall take up this point later. Meanwhile, I return to Rubinstein, Laughlin, and McManus's analysis and show that for a quite different reason it cannot support positivism. The reason is that, according to their argument, human cognitive mechanisms, while reliable, are not strictly truth-preserving, although some models of those mechanisms may be. Let us examine the argument.

Rubinstein, Laughlin, and McManus point out that the operational environment is subject to change, raising the problem of how the cognized environment can maintain adaptive isomorphism. They identify three general types of change in the operational environment: those caused by unique events, those that result from ongoing and relatively stable process (such as increase in population density), and cyclical changes with a more or less predictable range of frequency and amplitude (such as seasonal rainfall and temperature variations). While these changes in the Eo can be accommodated directly by the Ec, there is another strategy for adapting to changes of the cyclical kind, and that is to model the cycle itself, resulting in greater complexity of the Ec. The more complex an organism's cognized environment, the more adaptable it can be; that is, the more flexible or responsive to a changing environment it can be.

This occurs, paradoxically, because the cognized environment, in modelling the operational environment, abstracts from it, necessarily losing content, and that loss of content facilitates application to a wider range of operational environments. Not only do models necessarily lose content as a result of interest-driven selection of features from the modelled environment, but this is precisely their function—to simplify the modelled environment to cognitively manageable proportions. The extraction of selective but generalizable relations from the modelled environment is a prime example of this process.

In complex cognitive systems, the cognized environment can model itself. But each successive model will be only partially isomorphic with the first. Therefore, as increasingly abstract models are constructed, there will be further loss of content, but these models will be applicable in a wider variety of environments. Recognition of this point serves to emphasize the extremely partial nature of abstract theories such as those of physics, which in turn indicates that no matter how general a theory is, it will not be able to explain all the data that can be explained by less general theories. But this is to preempt a point that I take up in more detail in chapter 4, and which becomes a major theme of this book. The point I take up here is that in some circumstances, the maintenance of the stability of the cognitive system is in conflict with accurate representation of the environment, and that the stability requirements of the cognitive system may take precedence.

The cognized environment may be, as it is in humans, a highly complex, hierarchically organized structure. The stability of the structure of the cognized environment relates to how much it is directly affected by changes in the operational environment. A totally flexible cognitive structure will not be able to store information at all, whereas a totally rigid one will be unable to respond to a changing environment. Responses of the cognized environment to change in the operational environment may vary from those of very flexible structures, in which representation is maximally responsive to the environment and minimally specified by the selective values of the cognizer, through to those of very rigid structures, in which representation is minimally responsive to the operational environment and maximally specified by the selective values of the cognizer. The motility of bacteria—quick and flexible behavioral reaction—is an example of the former type of response. The mason wasp, with its hard-wired rule for breaking out of its larval chambers, provides an example of the latter type of response. The adult female digs a tunnel into the pith of a tree. She then lays a series of eggs in the tunnel, starting at the bottom. Each egg is sealed off with its own food supply from the next by a mud partition. The partitions are rough and convex on the daylight side of the cells, and smooth and concave on the inward side. When the young adults emerge, they chew their way through the rough convex side of the cells to gain access to the outside world. But this rule is hard-wired. If the partitions are experimentally reversed, the young adults still chew through the rough side, pile up at the end of the tunnel and die.[12]

Drawing on empirical research in developmental psychology and cultural anthropology, Rubinstein, Laughlin, and McManus argue that the human cognized environment operates as a system which, when faced with anomalous inputs from the operational environment, will function to maintain the integrity of its structure for as long as possible. This is achieved in various ways, including distorting information to fit it into the system, rejecting certain information, and storing certain information in the memory without assimilating it.[13]

Such a view of the cognized environment allows both for an explanation of the theory-ladenness of observation and for the possibility of error. Humans not only select which features of the operational environment they model, they also process information from the operational environment in conformity with their current, fallible, cognitive model. They even reject information if it doesn't fit the model, at least until such time as it is obviously beyond repair. But despite this, the human cognized environment is open to information input and action output with respect to the operational environment.

> This occurs through a feedback-feedforward system involving sensory input and motor systems in complex tests of the goodness of fit between the cognized environment models and the operational environment.[14]

This testing, evaluating, and modifying of the models can, argue Rubinstein, Laughlin, and McManus, maintain their adaptive isomorphism. But the cognitive model that has been described, while it may maintain adaptive isomorphism, is not capable of winnowing out false models or theories unless they relate directly to the survival of the individual holding them. This means that the notion of adaptive isomorphism cannot account for the general reliability of science. Moreover, when this model is applied to the cognitive processes themselves, it shows that truth-preserving logics are too restrictive to account for the reliability of scientific theories. Let me explain.

When complex cognitive systems model themselves, they can only produce partial models of the cognitive processes available, although these models are not necessarily the less adaptive for being partial. Language, for example, models cognition in much the same way as the cognized environment models the operational environment, with the necessary attendant loss of content. Language, then, is more abstract than cognition. But it is not on this account less adaptive—in fact, the opposite. The facilitation of memory is just one advantage that accrues from its greater abstraction, as Kinsbourne points out:

> Whereas speaking out loud communicates your thoughts, speaking covertly to oneself encodes them for better remembering . . . formulating one's thoughts in words lightens the load on immediate memory.[15]

So language is advantageous in individual cognition as well as providing humans with a highly sophisticated means of communication that allows them to share their cognitive contents and to participate in collaborative epistemic development.[16]

But, just as language only partially models the cognized environment, so too do truth-preserving logics. Because the cognized environment can model itself at different levels of abstraction, every cognitive theory can itself be seen as an abstraction from the full set of cognitive processes. Formalized logics, then, can never be complete accounts of rationality. Parallel to their distinction between the cognized environment and the operational environment, and the notion that the cognized environment models the operational environment, Rubinstein, Laughlin, and McManus distinguish cognized logic from operational logic.[17] Symbolic logic, for example, models rational information processing but abstracts from it, losing content. The use of such a logic alone can thus stifle research. Symbolic logic, while truth-preserving, tells us nothing about the truth of the original premises, or which items of the operational environment are significant, for example.

More importantly, deductive symbolic logic does not encompass many of the reasoning processes vital to science, for example, reasoning involving risk and probability, induction, choosing relevant constraints for theory inference, and so on. Thus Rubinstein, Laughlin, and McManus's cognitive model of knowing, based as it is on both psychological and anthropological research, argues that the empiricist model of scientific knowledge as produced by organizing incorrigible facts with logic cannot be an adequate descriptive account of the process of sciencing. Moreover, any model of sciencing that is based on a single model of rationality is likely to be radically incomplete, as all models of rationality are partial abstractions from the operational logic, and there can be many such models, each focussing on a different feature of rationality.

Rubinstein, Laughlin, and McManus have provided a plausible naturalist model of sciencing as a human activity. But their model, like all of those restricted to a discussion of perceptual and/or cognitive mechanisms, makes no contribution to the question of how scientific theories are selected, or whether, and if so how, they can be known to be valid. Such positions can do no more than argue that human perceptual and cognitive mechanisms are generally reliable within the range of the environmental interactions that selected them. The cross-cultural variation of belief systems, the persistence of false beliefs, and the fact that in some circumstances, false beliefs may be functional for survival and reproduction, all show that the nature of human perceptual and cognitive systems, while accounting for the fallibility of science, is insufficient to account for the reliability of science. Any account of the reliability of science must move beyond the nature of human perceptual and cognitive mechanisms to examine the ways in which beliefs are selected and justified.

To examine this question, I turn to the work of Donald Campbell. Campbell provides a general model for inductive gains that takes full account of the social nature of scientific knowledge.[18] For this reason, I will discuss his work in some detail. Campbell argues that there is an analogy between biological evolution and scientific progress. Both evolve via a process of blind variation and selective retention. Science, seen as a problem-solving activity, is continuous with the problem-solving activity of all organisms. The paramecium, for example, exhibits blind variation of locomotor activity until a nourishing or nonnoxious setting is found. This solution is then retained as cessation of movement. In a world of only benign or neutral states, such organisms can operate without exteroceptors. Wherever it is, the organism is trying to ingest the environment, and when starvation approaches, blind locomotor activity takes place until more food is found. But even at this level, Campbell points out, an interoceptor sense organ is required to monitor the organism's nutritional states. This organ monitors nutritional level and substitutes for the whole organism's death. "Only indirectly, through selecting the selectors, does life-and-death relevance select the response."[19]

Vicarious locomotor devices such as vision constitute an epistomological advance, but are less direct. Although enhancing the chances of an organism's survival, such devices, because less direct, are in an absolute sense more prone to error. This is because the penalty for error is decreased—it is less likely to result in the death of the organism—which is precisely why it constitutes an advantage in the first place. The exploration of a vicarious environment that occurs in sophisticated cognitive modelling and particularly in science, as Rubinstein, Laughlin, and McManus argue, is still less direct, more advantageous, yet more prone to error.

Campbell's problem, then, is to explain how it is that scientific beliefs increasingly improve their fit with the world. It cannot be just because humans have the perceptual and cognitive mechanisms that they do. As he and Paller remark: "In the evolutionary epistemology movement, there is too much uncritical passing-the-buck to an omnipotent 'Dear Old Mother Natural Selection.'"[20] At the level of perception, Campbell and Paller argue, natural selection has validated the general operation of the visual system for middle-sized physical objects. But this does not of itself justify a visual-perceptual foundationalism because the mechanisms that produce compelling experiential objectivity in the conscious mind are the same whether the perceptions are valid or illusory. This is the basis of the argument from illusion.

Campbell approaches the problem by considering the ways in which humans select and revise their perceptions. Illusory perceptions *can* be revised. Given a Muller-Lyer illusion and a ruler, we can convince ourselves that our eyes are deceiving us. But Campbell and Paller point out that when this happens, the perceptual belief is revised, not just by one other perception, but by trusting "the great bulk of other perceptions plus some constancy conditions that are only approximately true."[21] Humans have a coherence strategy of belief revision rather than one based on perceptual correspondence. Moreover, anthropological and sociological evidence to the effect that perceptual and cognitive frameworks are socially learned and vary from culture to culture indicates that the reliability of the human perceptual system comes not so much from the perceptual mechanisms of the individual as from the social cross-validation of beliefs.

Nonetheless, this does not lead, as some sociologists of knowledge have argued, to a cultural solipsism. Campbell argues convincingly that reality plays a part in editing beliefs, particularly in the sort of environment in which the organism's perceptual mechanisms evolved. Thus, for humans there is general cross-cultural agreement over middle-sized objects and boundary acts. Campbell's argument for this thesis relies on an analogy with language. He argues, again in opposition to the assumptions of many sociologists of knowledge,[22] that language is subsequent to, rather than prior to, cognition. While linguistic concepts may to a certain extent limit or constrain cognition, they are not all entirely conventional. At the common level of middle-distance objects, reality edits every language. This can be shown by the way language "will cut nature at her joints."[23] Not all languages, for example, will have words for pieces of trees (for example stems and leaves), but none that do will have a word for a twig plus the first centimeter or so of a leaf.

The point can be further illustrated by considering in detail the different ways that different cultures divide up the natural world. While species are the largest natural kind recognized by biology, the Linnæan system of classifying organisms is a hierarchical system that divides species further into genera and family groupings. Studies in folk taxonomy have shown that all known folk systems of classification are likewise hierarchical, assigning species into more general groups.[24] The principles that form the basis of folk classifications, particularly at a level equivalent to the Linnæan species, i.e., the folk genera, seem to be based primarily on the recognition of gross morphological similarities and differences. It is rare, at this level, for classification to be based on the functional attributes of the organism for the people concerned.

Brent Berlin, in a study of the folk taxonomy of the Tzeltal people of Mexico, compared the Tzeltal system of classification with the Linnæan system.[25] Linnæan species were compared with folk genera. The folk genus consists of the smallest recognized class of organisms. The comparison showed three sorts of relationship to exist between the folk genus and the species. One-to-one correspondence occurs when the folk generic taxon refers to one and only one Linnæan species. Overdifferentiation occurs when two or more folk generic taxa refer to the one species. And underdifferentiation occurs when a single folk generic taxon refers to two or more species. Berlin, Breedlove, and Raven show that of a total of 471 Tzeltal generic taxa for plants, 61 percent are in one-to-one correspondence with botanical species. Although 36 percent are underdifferentiated, more than two-thirds of these are further differentiated by the Tzeltal into folk specifics that correspond to Linnæan species. Only 3 percent are overdifferentiated. Berlin notes that in most of these cases, the plants are culturally significant and have marked morphological differences that give them different utility.[26] The bottle gourd *Lagenaria siceraria,* for example, has three Tzeltal generics, *bohch, tsu,* and *ch'ahko'.* The *bohch* has large round fruits used for containers for tortillas and drinking water. The *tsu* bears long necked gourds used mainly to carry liquids. The *ch'ahko'* has no known use.[27]

While functional attributes play little part in folk taxonomy at the folk generic level, appearing, when they do, as overdetermination, the higher levels of classification reflect not natural kinds but rather human decisions as to how species should be grouped. One would expect, then, that higher level groupings in folk taxonomies would be based more on utility and cultural significance. This is just what Bulmer and Tyler found in their studies of the folk taxonomy of the Karam of the New Guinea Highlands.[28]

Bulmer and Tyler studied Karam classification of frogs, which are highly significant both as a subsidiary food source and culturally. They conclude that the Karam have a good appreciation of natural species and that this is a significant factor underlying their zoological classification. Many Linnæan species have a one-to-one correspondence with Karam folk generic taxa. Where they underdifferentiate species, the Karam are usually well aware of what they are doing, while in cases of overdifferentiation they assert that the units they distinguish are in fact natural kinds, and in at least one case this has since been granted by biologists.[29]

At the level of the primary taxon, the Karam divide four-footed vertebrates into three groups: frogs are classified collectively as *as,* along with small mammals, in contrast to *kopyak,* rats of genus Rattus, and *kmn,* a collection consisting mainly of assorted larger marsupials and rodents. The grouping together of frogs and small mammals seems strange, yet the Karam insist that they really are to be grouped together. Inquiries as to why these (very different to us) classes should be placed together elicited the response that *as* were collected by women, whereas *kmn* were collected by men. This explanation seemed unsatisfactory to Bulmer and Tyler, as men were often seen collecting *as,* and women *kmn.* Further investigation revealed that the *as, kopyak* and *kmn* appeared to

represent categories with contrasting status in terms of Karam food prohibi-
tions, and to reflect underlying principles of opposition in Karam cosmology.[30]

The groups represented both by scientific genera and families and by the
higher levels of folk classification illustrate the different cognitive frameworks
of different cultural groups. The frameworks reflect the significance of the items
in the various groups to the culture concerned and have no objective reality. But
the correspondence between (even different) folk generic taxa and Linnæan
species shows that at this level, nature edits classification and language.

Language, then, is not purely conventional. Moreover, language learning
depends on shared perceptual reifications, which thus become "socially 'foundational' in achieving linguistic transfer of valid beliefs from person to person."[31] As Campbell points out, language cannot be taught by telephone.
Shared reference through language presupposes that reality has edited ostensi-
bly transmitted vocabulary.

Valid beliefs, therefore, are achieved as a result of social processes rather
than despite them. As with positivism, the basis of objectivity lies in intersubjective, and even cross-cultural, agreement, at the level of middle-distance objects and boundary acts. Campbell, then, supports a fallible social perceptual
foundationalism. But "foundationalism" in Campbell's sense differs from the a
priori foundationalism of the positivists. Campbell's foundationalism is not of
the First Philosophy type. Rather, it is descriptive of the processes by which beliefs are tested for validity.

Reliable as perception may be at this level, it remains a puzzle how scientific beliefs, the social products of an elaborate social system, increasingly
improve their fit with reality. For science extends far beyond middle-distance
objects. Campbell argues that an abstract blind variation and selective retention algorithm is applicable to all examples of increased fit between one system and another.[32]

> Such a general selection theory can be regarded as the all-purpose phys-
> icalist (a.k.a. materialist, mechanist, naturalist) solution to puzzles of
> "design." For Darwin, the perceived fit between animal form and envi-
> ronmental opportunity was the design puzzle. For the epistemologist of
> scientific belief, the design puzzle is the presumed fit between scientific
> belief and the invisible world to which such belief refers.[33]

Invisible theoretical entities lie outside the validity range of human perceptual mechanisms. And as anthropologists and sociologists are well aware,
there are many social institutions whose business includes the production and
maintenance of beliefs that palpably do not fit with reality. The question becomes, at this juncture, what is it that distinguishes the selection of scientific
beliefs from those of other social belief-producing institutions.

All knowledge is physically embodied, and by the same token, all knowledge is subject to constraints and biases due to the nature of the system that embodies it. For example, a mosaic representation of some part of the countryside is necessarily incomplete, inaccurate, and distorted, as a result of the characteristics of the medium, for example, the size, shape and color of the pebbles available, the change from three dimensions to two dimensions, and the change of scale. So the validity of knowledge is constrained by the characteristics of the medium or vehicle of that knowledge.[34] It is also constrained by the structure of the vehicle. If the mosaic were attempted with colored drops of water rather than colored pebbles, the transferred information could not be retained. As Campbell points out, " . . . if the vehicle is completely flexible, it lacks the rigidity to hold together the picture it carries."[35] The carrier of scientific knowledge is the scientific community, so it is in the nature of the scientific community, and, in a broader sense, the institution of science itself, that the answer to the great reliability of scientific knowledge will be found.

Science, according to Campbell, differs from other social belief production and maintenance systems in two respects. The first is that its methods provide a narrow window through which "Nature" can speak. It shares this feature with several other social systems. The second is that "science's social norms are specifically designed to channel consensus in science in a manner maximizing the opportunity for "physical reality" to optimally influence the new consensus."[36] It is this that distinguishes science from all other social institutions. Together, these two features can account for the success of science in producing increasingly valid knowledge of reality.

The part played by reality, as opposed to other factors, in the selection of scientific beliefs, is illustrated by Campbell in his discussion of "divination rituals." We saw in chapter 2 that some sociologists of knowledge treat scientific facts as though they had been completely fabricated by a series of social processes. It was this sort of treatment that led Campbell to compare the "creation" of facts with divination rituals.

Divination rituals are of two major types. The first type can be illustrated by the Norwegian fishermen, who, when their fishing grounds were exhausted, used a system that involved building a shoreline and island map of sand, filling it with water and watching for the place where bubbles first rose. Functionally, such rituals were adaptive in that they justified the search for food in new and unexpected places; no one person in the group could be blamed if the expedition were unsuccessful; and they provided the subtle advantage of making the hunters' behavior unpredictable to the prey. This wisdom was not explicit in the belief systems of the communities, whose manifest justifications for the practices centered on belief in potentially helpful but often perverse supernatural beings.[37]

The second type of divination ritual is designed to provide supernatural authority for the human wisdom of a shaman or priest. Deception may be involved, as in the ancient Egyptian hidden voice tubes and mechanisms for getting statues to move. But just as often there is no deception, the ritual being designed to prevent the shaman from determining the answer.[38] The Azande use of the poison oracle to determine the truth of the matter in cases as varied as the determination of witchcraft or trials for infidelity is a good example of this type.

Campbell argues that science can be seen as a divination ritual, but that it is of the first type rather than the second. The distinction is crucial, for the first type is, where the second is not, "designed to put questions to 'Nature Itself' in such a way that neither questioners nor their colleagues nor their superiors can affect the answer."[39] For even though no deception is involved, the actions of the Azande shaman can affect the nature of the result. Certainly, the language provided for "Nature" to answer is socially created. Laboratory scientists, as Latour and Woolgar have demonstrated, construct the apparatus, interpret the readings, and so on.[40] But they do not control the particular readings that appear. And those readings are precisely within the middle-distance range over which human perception can be cross-validated. "A narrow window has been provided through which 'Nature' can speak, free from the scientist's control,"[41] and this knowledge can be socially validated.

But what distinguishes science from the first type of divination ritual? The institution of science is a relatively autonomous self-perpetuating social system, existing outside of any individual scientist. It is a "social fact," in Durkheim's terms. As such, it has certain structural requirements that must be met if it is to carry out its functions of belief production, and the selection and retention of valid beliefs. At first sight, these structural requirements may seem inimical to the production of valid knowledge.

Take the requirement of vehicle maintenance. Campbell argues that:

> . . . before a scientific community can be a self-perpetuating social vehicle for ever-improving a set of beliefs about the physical world, it must first meet the social structural requirements of being a self-perpetuating social system. The requirements of achieving this "tribal" continuity come first, even if they compete and interfere with the cognitive task of increasing the validity of the image of the physical world carried by the "tribe."[42]

The structural requirements of a scientific community include such features as the recruitment of new members and the rewarding of old members; the publication and reading of journals; the provision of jobs for loyal followers; funding for research; and social processes that facilitate group cohesiveness (leadership, for example). These requirements are often tangential, or even inimical, to improved competence of reference, for theories may be selected to maximize these structural requirements at the expense of validity requirements. These features of science have led sociologists of knowledge to characterize scientific communities as tribal, and as being the same as any social superstition preservation system.[43]

But there are differences, and important ones, and these lie in the content of the norms and procedures of the institution of science. As Campbell argues, "... [S]cience has different specific values, myths, rituals, and commandments. These differences are related to what I presume to be science's superiority in the improving validity of the model of the physical world which it carries."[44] Let us take a look at some of these normative differences, and the implications they might have for the selection and retention of increasingly valid beliefs.

All self-perpetuating belief communities, scientific communities included, are to some extent ridden with tradition, viewing the present through the eyes of the past. Many such communities (for example, religious institutions) explicitly venerate traditional ways and beliefs as belonging to a truth revealed in some way in the past. But for science, truth does not lie in the past. Rather, it is something to be continually sought—an ideal that orients science toward a future with increasingly better knowledge through better methods. Tradition is something to be questioned and often decried as a source of error. Such an approach makes science less tradition-ridden and more open to innovation (and hence variation) than the more traditionally oriented belief maintenance institutions.[45]

Scientific communities share with other "tribes" a geriarchical and authoritarian bias. Scientific administrators and leaders have greater power to promote their favored research programs, and often persist in power beyond their declining abilities and their increasing rigidity. But the military and many churches officially support such practices, whereas science explicitly decries it. Campbell argues that this normative difference is sufficient to make science less authoritarian, and more open to challenge and change, than more rigid hierarchies. As evidence, science more frequently rewards young rebels and more frequently passes over the favorite disciples of "the old man" than other institutions.[46]

Finally, the notion that contribution to truth should be the only criterion of status in science does have the effect of insulating science at least partially from the values and politics of the external social system. No social system can completely insulate itself from such influence, and science is not exempt. As Campbell points out:

> Science is influenced by the external social system in many ways counter to optimizing scientific truth. Thus, the status systems of the larger society, based on political and economic power and social class, contaminate the internal status system of science. Given equal ability, it helps a young scientist's appointment, promotion, grant-getting, and publication to be well connected in the extrascientific world. It helps if one has good manners and is cultured. It helps, too, if one's ideas support rather than

oppose the dominant interest groups of the larger society. Likewise, it helps if one comes from a high-prestige university.[47]

Race and gender are obviously issues, too.

But the positive valuing of contribution to truth in science does have testable insulating effects. Campbell suggests that one such test would be to compare the external social status and connections of humanities with science faculty members of Harvard and Yale over the last century. Campbell hypothesizes that there will be a higher correlation between external status and humanities members than with science members.[48] Studies by Hull into the frequency of scientific fraud also support the efficacy of the truth-seeking norm for the scientific community, for he shows clearly that fraud is far less frequent in the scientific community than in any comparable institution.[49] That this reflects on the norm of truth-seeking, rather than honesty more generally, is shown by the fact that the scientific community punishes fraud with much greater severity than literary theft. The norms of science are not only preached. They are enshrined in the institutional practices of science, where not only are the penalties for fraud very high, but the chances of detection are great. This is (a) because competitive replication forms a major part of scientific method, and (b) because applied science and technology feed back into the system.

So while science may be in many respects indistinguishable from other belief production and maintenance communities that open a window on the world, Campbell believes that the particular norms of science in fact favor greater selection and retention of valid knowledge about the world. This is because those norms demand an openness that encourages a greater variety in the production of beliefs, and insist that the nature of the world itself is included among the factors that play a part in the selection of scientific belief. And while there is always some inconsistency, and often a great deal, between the values of science and the practices of scientists, this is not sufficient reason to conclude that science is therefore no different from other social belief maintenance systems and should abandon its norms as hypocritical, as some relativists have suggested. Rather, it is reason to encourage more positive adherence to those norms.[50]

Science, then, Campbell argues, differs from other social belief production and maintenance systems in two respects. The first, that its methods provide a narrow window through which "Nature" can speak, it shares with those other systems whose "divination rituals" ask questions directly of "Nature." The second is that "science's social norms are specifically designed to channel consensus in science in a manner maximizing the opportunity for 'physical reality' to optimally influence the new consensus."[51] It is this that distinguishes science from all other social institutions, for it is not the specific methods of science, but its norms, that are reinforced by the scientific community. Together, and at a general level, these two features can account for the success of science in producing increasingly valid knowledge of reality.

In this section, I have looked at the implications for science of its being a human activity. I argued that the biological nature of human perceptual and cognitive mechanisms accounts for both their fallibility and their reliability within the range of middle-distance objects and boundary acts. I argued that humans adopt a coherence strategy of belief revision, and that inter-subjective agreement overrides individual judgement, and I adopted Campbell's model of fallible, socially-validated perceptual foundationalism. But according to Campbell's model, It is the norms of science rather than its methods that distinguish science from other belief production and maintenance systems.

It may seem, then, that I am no closer to my goal of developing a generalized naturalist realist methodology of science that can provide criteria for establishing the validity of theories. But this is not the case. The generality of those norms suggest that they will lead to the continual production of better methods in the quest for more reliable knowledge. These methods are themselves part of human knowledge. Taking account of the nature of sciencing as a human activity has a profound effect on how one can conceptualize theories as the products of this process, and this in turn affects one's conceptualization of the validity of theories.

To illustrate: under positivism, theories were regarded as true, standing in a correspondence relationship with the world. The correspondence relationship was thought to be determinable by the epistemically transparent or secure intersubjective verification of observations, and by the correctness of the logical procedures applied to them. Those theories that corresponded to reality in this way were held to be valid. But the view of sciencing presented above means that validity cannot be determined by correspondence with the world in the positivist sense. Cross-validation is achieved socially and through practice, rather than by virtue of incorrigible observation and truth-preserving logic. This does not mean that the correspondence theory of truth must be abandoned as a semantic thesis.[52] It does mean that logically determined correspondence with the world cannot be used as the criterion of validity. In the next section, then, I look for a model of scientific theories that admits of quite different criteria for the establishment of validity.

3.2 A Naturalist Realist Model of Scientific Theory

The task in this section is to search for a model of scientific theory that takes account of the fact that sciencing is a human activity. Such a model must take into account the means available to humans to validate beliefs about the world. I start the search with a brief characterization of scientific theory as it appeared under positivism. This is not because positivism provides an adequate account of sciencing or an adequate account of theory—I have argued that it does not. Nonetheless, as Campbell has shown, positivism has certain features in common with a naturalist realism.

Positivism stresses the intersubjectivity of observation as the criterion of its veridicality, and the necessity of truth-preserving logics in theory construction. These requirements have considerably loosened correlates in naturalist realist positions. The latter still insist on the importance of intersubjectively agreed perceptions and of cognition in the construction and validation of scientific theory. The major differences arise from the fact that the naturalist realist account, while normative, is also descriptive and does not have the status of First Philosophy. Perceptions are seen as fallible; the range within which they are able to be intersubjectively validated is limited; and validation is intrinsically social. The rational cognitive processes involved in science are not limited to formalizable logics. Neither are they truth-preserving. The modelling process often involves the distortion of features, and truth-preserving logics are themselves selective models of thought processes that need not be truth-preserving.[53] So there is a sense in which a naturalist realist account of sciencing can be seen as a loosening of the requirements of positivist sciencing.

It therefore makes sense to look at a positivist model of scientific theory to see if and how it can be loosened in an appropriate way to provide an adequate naturalist realist model. By doing this, I hope to retain the simplicity and precision of the positivist model that made it so readily applicable as a normative heuristic. While many scientists, including notable social scientists such as Marx, have in fact used a naturalist realist methodology, that methodology has not been characterized in a cognitively simple way, hence reducing its potential for use.

So in the search for an alternative model of knowledge, I start by asking what the positivist model of knowledge is like. According to positivism, science produces certain objective knowledge of the world. Objective facts are collected and organized by logic to produce general laws of nature. It is not part of science to look for the underlying nature of, or causal or generative mechanisms behind, the phenomena.

The image that comes to mind is that positivist knowledge mirrors reality. This thesis has been argued in detail by Richard Rorty.[54] Here I give just a brief account of the analogy. A mirror reflection has no human input. It simply reflects the phenomena. Similarly, according to positivism, science deals with incorrigible facts organized via an incontrovertible logic. There is no place in such an account for human interests. Further, a mirror reflects just the visible surfaces. Likewise, positivist science maps just the phenomena, disregarding their underlying nature or any causal mechanisms responsible for the phenomena.

Mirrors do not abstract from the phenomena in that they do not select particular phenomena of interest and reflect only those. But they do map three dimensions onto two, losing information in the process. Further, mirror images are not subject to revision in the light of information from other images. These features together mean that it is conceivable to have a simple accumulation of mirror images, because mirror images do not exclude or interfere with one another. In theory, then, it is possible to provide a complete mirror image of reality. Likewise, the positivist account of knowledge has no place for selection from the available phenomena. Rather, positivist knowledge objectively generalizes over the phenomena in a domain. And because knowledge obtained by the positivist scientific method is seen as true, it is not subject to revision. All partial scientific theories are compatible. Positivist knowledge, like a set of mirror images, can be seen as cumulative, and can in theory be complete.

Without carrying the analogy further, I think it is clear that positivist science can in many respects be seen in terms of the mirroring metaphor. Indeed, Rorty argues that positivist science *must* be seen in this way, in the light of its underlying assumptions.[55] But it is clear that for precisely the same reasons that positivist science can be seen as mirroring reality, it cannot be seen as an adequate model of science. Observation is not incorrigible; science is not value-free; and scientific knowledge is fallible and subject to revision, and hence not cumulative. The mirror metaphor is not an adequate metaphor for scientific knowledge.

But in view of the fact that I wish to retain some of the empiricist insights about science, I suggest that some generalization of the mirror metaphor might prove a good source for an alternative model of scientific knowledge. Maps are just such a generalization. Mirrors are a special case of maps but are subject to such tight constraints that to use the mirror metaphor as a model for scientific knowledge obscures the cognitive and social processes involved. But it might well be possible to use maps as the source of a new, more general, and more adequate model of knowledge. Rubinstein, Laughlin, and McManus's cognitive model of sciencing is in fact suggestive in this respect, in that it talks in terms of models that are partially isomorphic with the environment.

The use of the mapping metaphor for scientific theories is quite common. One finds references to *this* theory mapping *that* aspect of reality scattered throughout scientific literature, although such use is rarely conscious. But the notion that sciencing is a mapping process and that scientific theories are analogous to maps has been consciously taken up and explored by several theorists.[56] J. M. Ziman's model is of particular interest, because his approach takes full account of the psychological and social factors involved in the production and validation of scientific knowledge. By using it, I am able to make explicit the connections between Rubinstein, Laughlin, and McManus's cognitive model of sciencing, Campbell's model of science as a social process, and the mapping metaphor for scientific theories.

Ziman's model of the scientific process, like Campbell's, considers a number of individual scientists linked by various means of communication. These scientists have their own stores of personal knowledge. Scientific knowledge, though, or candidates for it, must be included in the content of the messages between scientists. These messages accumulate and are available in the public domain. Ziman distinguishes scientific knowledge from other intellectual domains by the fact that its contents are consensible, i.e., they are capable either of receiving wholehearted consent or of attracting well-founded objections. The goal of science, according to Ziman's model, is to achieve maximum consensuality, i.e., to maximize the amount of consensible knowledge that is widely accepted without serious doubt by an overwhelming majority of competent and well-informed scientists.[57] Ziman's model of sciencing, then, contains three elements—a community of interchangeable knowers, a set of consensible beliefs, and a body of scientific knowledge comprising consensible beliefs on which consensus has actually been achieved and maintained.

I have already discussed briefly the place of the scientific community and the institutional organization of science in the production, selection, and maintenance of scientific knowledge, and shall not discuss it further here, although the issue will reappear in the course of this work. In this section, I am interested primarily in the adequacy of the mapping metaphor as a model for scientific knowledge. Hence, I concentrate on the second element of Ziman's model, that knowledge comprises part of a set of consensible beliefs. I leave examination of the third element of Ziman's model to the next chapter, where I explore the notion of the validity of scientific theories.

Consensible theories, according to Ziman, are models of some aspect of reality. By definition, models are not complete and faithful renderings of reality in the sense that mirror images are. Nonetheless they are consensible, and this consensibility depends on intersubjective pattern recognition, which is something that humans do well by virtue of being the sort of biological and social creatures they are.

> . . . adequate consensus may be achieved in the realm of theory—i.e. in the generalized, abstracted representation of a body of detailed observational information—in the form of a "pattern" which may be accepted, recognized and assimilated intellectually without necessarily being capable of complete definition and analysis in formal mathematical or logical language.[58]

These representations often take the form of maps, in that they are presented visually rather than linguistically. Ziman claims that humans are adapted both neurologically and psychologically to comprehend information in map form. Although the claim is not supported with particular references to neurophysiology or psychology, this is unnecessary, because Ziman is able to show that much human knowledge, both scientific and practical, is actually presented in map form. He illustrates his point by listing many examples of scientific knowledge from the fields of geology, chemistry, and physics that is presented visually rather than linguistically. Having shown that much human knowledge is represented in map form, Ziman proceeds to make the stronger claim that all of our scientific theories can be seen, metaphorically, as maps of reality. This claim is made on the basis of the many similarities that exist between scientific knowledge and maps, and I shall explore some of these similarities here.

There are many kinds of map: color maps, institutional maps, authority maps, mathematical maps, and maps of processes, to name but a few. In exploring the similarities between scientific theories and maps, I simplify the discussion by confining myself to an analogy with geographic maps. This should not prove too restrictive as there is great variety even among geographic maps. These range from finely detailed survey-type maps to topographical maps (such as that of the London Underground system) that merely represent the relationships between recognizable geographical features without being metrically accurate. My procedure in discussing the analogy will be to point to various features of maps and show how they apply also to the view of scientific theories when these are seen as the products of human activity.

An important feature of maps in establishing their suitability as a model of scientific knowledge is that there is no single or uniquely correct map of a particular territory. For example, there are many maps of Australia's Hunter region: railway maps, road maps, geological maps, maps depicting population density, and so on. These are all different, partial, but equally correct, maps of the region. Likewise, it is a myth that any scientific theory, no matter how comprehensive, is able to give a complete description of a set of phenomena. Against the micro-reductionist thesis that the properties of a composite entity can be completely explained in terms of the properties of its parts, for example, Putnam has pointed out that one cannot explain why a square peg won't fit into a round hole in terms of the microscopic composition of both. And gravitational theory, general as it is, while it may enable the prediction of tides in an estuary, will be unable to predict which fish one might expect to catch on the rising tide.[59]

Another similarity between scientific theories and maps is that the methods used to produce both ensure that they can only be partial, fallible representations. A map has to be drawn to fit the data. Obviously the data will vary according to the sort of map being produced, but as Toulmin has pointed out, one doesn't need many measurements in cartography (or many experiments in physics).[60] The data used to draw the map is incomplete and subject to error. Although generally reliable, in many details the map may be no more dependable than a shrewd guess. Likewise, scientific theories are underdetermined by the data, contain conjectural elements, and are subject to error.[61]

A further similarity between maps and theories is that more can be read off a map than was needed to construct it. A cartographer can use projection theory to construct a map from a few precise and well-chosen measurements and observations. From this map one can read off an unlimited number of geographic facts of equal or almost equal precision. There is no hard and fast rule as to how many such observations and measurements are needed to make a map of a particular scale. This will vary according to the regularity of the terrain and what is to be mapped. Just how many measurements must be made in any particular terrain to produce an adequate map of some set of features is something the practising cartographer must judge.[62]

Scientific theories, too, are formulated on the basis of a limited number of observations, and yet an unlimited number of predictions can be made from them. To use an example of Toulmin's that will be discussed in more detail in chapter 4, the principle of the rectilinear propagation of light explains a regularity noticed in patterns of light and shade, but can be used to predict phenomena that would happen given certain (not necessarily existing) conditions. It could be used, for example, to predict by how much the sunlight falling on a particular park would be reduced if a building of a certain height were built on its western boundary. Theories in this sense contain extra content in that they go beyond the data that was used to produce them. This, as I discussed in § 3.1, is the paradoxical result of theories being abstractions from a particular domain, and hence applicable over a wider variety of environments than those in which they were produced. The fact that theories, like maps, are multiply connected, is another source of the new information that theories can generate, because a theory generated from a particular set of relationships may lead to the discovery of further relationships not specified in the original data.

A map is not just an accumulation of data. Rather, it is a necessarily abstract representation. It selects certain features and represents them in a schematic form that is generally quite unlike the original except in terms of the mutual relationships between the elements. For example, towns on railway maps are generally represented as colored dots on a piece of paper. Likewise, scientific knowledge cannot just be the total of accumulated observations. As such it would be totally incomprehensible. Rather, scientific theories abstract regularities from the world and produce explanations of them in terms of the relationships between entities and/or phenomena. Scientific theories, like maps, are necessarily abstractions, and are quite unlike the world they map except in terms of the relationships that they represent.

Maps and theories also share the fact that their content is directly related to the interests of their producers, or the purposes for which they are constructed. As I have already pointed out, there can be many different types of map for any single territory. Maps of the same territory can also be on different scales. For example, Newcastle will appear as a dot on a road map of New South Wales, yet will fill a book if a detailed street directory is required. The types of map produced and the scale used are selected with the interests of the users in mind. The same applies to scientific theories. The aspects of reality to be described, and in what detail, are selected with the interests of users in mind.[63] An example of this would be the decision to encourage research into nuclear physics during World War II, and in particular research aimed at harnessing atomic energy for possible use in a weapon. This point also emphasizes the fact that maps, while describing reality, have human input. They are not merely there for the taking, like mirror images. Rather they are human artifacts. Scientific theories, too, are human artifacts, not merely discoveries.

Another important analogy can be drawn between scientific theories and maps. When a cartographer or surveyor sets out to make a map of some particular territory, she starts with the purposes of the prospective map in mind, a body of theory about projections, and so on. She then has to choose a baseline, orientation, scale, method of projection, and system of signs.[64] These choices will relate both to the purposes of the map and to the body of background theory, and will determine the sort of map produced. But the fact that these choices must be made does not make the map less correct relative to the purposes for which it was constructed. Indeed, there is no way that a map can be made without such choices. Map making requires a body of prior theory, and interest-related decisions must be made over the choice of appropriate construction tools.

The situation is similar with scientific theorizing. The scientist starts with a reasonably clear objective (for example, what entities or processes are to be the object of his study, and what it is he wishes to find out about them) and a body of background theories and assumptions, both scientific and metascientific. The metascientific theories and assumptions include the working tools of science—language, mathematics, logical systems, and methods. The choice of tools is interest-related and will affect the sort of theory produced. But scientific theories are no less reliable on this account, and indeed could not be produced without such choices being made.

This chapter marked the start of a search for a generalized naturalist realist methodology of science that would be capable of providing solutions to the problems that sociology faces as a discipline. A methodology that is adequate to this task would have to take account of the fallible, interest-related, socially constructed nature of science. At the same time it would have to account for its reliability, and provide perspective-neutral criteria for the establishment of validity—in other words, it would have to show that reality itself plays a part in the selection and retention of scientific theories.

In attempting this task, I turned first to the field of evolutionary epistemology. A good part of the agenda for evolutionary epistemology is the production of models of sciencing that take full account of the biological nature of humans as knowers. I argued that evolutionary theory, while it accounts for the general reliability of human perceptual and cognitive mechanisms in the range of middle-distance objects and boundary acts, gives no guarantees of certainty. But my discussion of Rubinstein, Laughlin, and McManus's cognitive model of sciencing gives considerable insight into the nature of the production of beliefs about the world, and of how those beliefs achieve some passable fit with reality. Beliefs about the world are at best partially isomorphic with reality, and at worst false. But within their validity range, they are able to acquire a passable fit with reality through feedback-feedforward mechanisms in interaction with the environment.

To explain the reliability of scientific beliefs that go beyond the validity range of middle-distance objects and boundary acts, I turned to Campbell's model of science as a social institution. Campbell argued, consistently with Rubinstein, Laughlin, and McManus, that humans adopt a social coherence strategy of belief revision. Scientific knowledge is based on a socially validated perceptual foundationalism. To explain the reliability of science outside the perceptual range, Campbell compared science with other belief production and maintenance systems. He argued that the reliability of science depended crucially on two features of the institution of science. The first was that science opens a window on nature, by asking questions that, however indirectly, can be answered by distinctions within the perceptual validity range. The second, and what distinguishes science from all other belief production and maintenance systems, is that the institutionalized norms of science are designed to ensure at least some degree of objectivity and openness.

The insights obtained from my excursion into evolutionary epistemology were still too general to serve as a methodology. My next strategy was to incorporate those insights into a model of scientific theory that might be developed for this purpose. According to the model of scientific knowledge developed here, scientific theories are necessarily incomplete in that they are abstractions from the phenomena to be accounted for. No unique theory will describe all aspects of reality. Scientific theories are human artifacts, subject to error. They are sought with particular interests in mind and are built upon a foundation of equally fallible but accepted theory, which may itself be questioned should circumstances warrant it. In these respects at least, scientific theories resemble maps.[65]

But positivist knowledge was able to be represented as mirroring the world, and mirrors are simply a special class of maps. And I argued that the naturalist realist model of knowledge that I have developed can be seen as a generalization of positivism, a loosening of its too restrictive constraints. On these grounds, there is hope that by using mapping as a model of sciencing, and maps as a model of scientific theories, I will be able to develop a methodology that takes account of the social (and often arational) processes that influence the construction and selection of scientific theories, and at the same time establishes perspective-neutral criteria for assessing the validity of scientific theories. I take up this task in chapter 4, where I explore further the analogy between maps and scientific theories, with a view to showing how the validity of both can be determined.

4

The Nature of Validity

Miss Lovell displayed the depth of the indentation, and the shape of the toes. Toes? Talons? Claws? There was an element of each. All it needed to see them was a little imagination, as all theory and its relationship to practice must require.

—Rosaleen Love, *The Sea-Serpent of Sandy Cape*

4.1 The Adequacy of Maps

While I have argued that scientific theories are in some respects analogous to geographic maps, so far this analogy has provided no methodological guidelines for the establishment of the validity of scientific theories. In this chapter, I explore the nature of the relationship between scientific theories and the world in order to establish the nature of the validity of scientific theories. It turns out that scientific theories and geographic maps share the same general criteria of validity. My strategy is to turn my attention first to maps, for maps have the advantage of being so familiar that the points I make can be grasped almost intuitively. They need not be argued in detail and should not be seen as particularly controversial. In §4.2 I go on to show that the nature of the validity of scientific theories is essentially the same as that of maps. But before I do either of these things, the notion of validity I am using needs some clarification.

The word "valid," when used in the philosophy of science, is often taken in the narrow logistic sense of "truth-preserving." But consistently with my aim to produce a model of scientific knowledge that loosens the constraints imposed by positivism, I use the word "valid" in its more general sense of "well-founded." This needs some explanation. One of the major functions of science is to model reality.[1] The problem faced in this chapter is whether it in fact does so—whether its beliefs are justified, whether they are in any way distinguishable from the beliefs produced by other institutions, and if so, how this could be known. With the naturalist realist rejection of the sorts of solution provided by First Philosophies, the answer must be in terms of the connection between knowledge and human action. Scientific knowledge cannot be known to be true in any absolute sense of the word, but it can be known to be reliable. So the concept of validity I use refers to the connection between knowledge and action. If a scientific theory proves a reliable guide to action, then it is valid.

To see scientific theories in this way, as guides to decision making and action, and to see validity as a measure of their reliability as such guides, explains the importance of the confirmation of novel predictions in the establishment of the validity of scientific theories. While this is not the only way that validity can be established, as I emphasize later in the chapter, it is perhaps the most exciting, for it extends into new areas the power of science to extrapolate the future, thus widening the basis of decision making.[2] The fact that not all scientific research is undertaken with the specific aim of providing beliefs to form the bases of decision making, or that some research is not immediately applicable, does not detract from the fact that the ultimate criteria of validity is practice. It is because maps and scientific theories share the function of being guides to action and decision making that the ultimate tests of both are practical. This in turn, as I argue in §4.2.6, means that they share certain other general criteria of validity.

I shall now explore the nature of maps as guides to action and decision making to find out just how this affects the relationship between maps and the world, and the question of their validity.

4.1.1 The Content and Form of Maps

Maps, as I pointed out in §3.2, are constructed with interests in mind. At base, our judgment of how good a map is will relate to how well it enables us to carry out the task we have in mind. No matter how good in other respects, for example, detailed topographical maps[3] will not be particularly useful to the prospector looking for gold-bearing quartz deposits. Such features are just not shown on topographical maps. The prospector's aim is to find gold, and the sort of map that will enable him to predict where gold is likely to be found is a geological map. Such a map will be good to the extent that it enables the prospector to find, if not gold, at least the type of geological structure in which gold is known to be found. Maps are selective representations of the world, and the contents of maps are selected according to their relevance to the problems they are intended to solve. And because the usefulness of the map can only be assessed by how well it helps to solve the problems of the user, not only is the content of a map interest-related, its validity is interest-related as well.

Just as the content of a map is interest-related, so too is its form. Indeed, content and form are intimately related. Topologic maps (say, the simple sketch maps that one might draw showing how one's house is linked to major approach routes) differ in form, for example, from topographic maps. They can convey reliable and significant information without being metrically accurate. Such maps represent the topology of the relationships between recognized geographic features. But if they are not metrically accurate, on what basis can such maps be considered valid? Ultimately, a map is good insofar as it enables us to successfully complete the activity we have in mind. In many cases, topological maps (an example is the justly famous London Underground map) and other highly selective maps such as highway maps, may be better than highly detailed and accurate maps, by virtue of the very fact that they leave out irrelevant detail, thus making the task of following them easier. As Phillip Anderson, in his 1977 Nobel Prize Lecture, remarked, "the art of model-building is the exclusion of real but irrelevant parts of the problem." Topologic maps differ in form from topographic maps, and this difference in form is related both to a difference in content and to the different interests of the users. Thus, the form a map takes, like its content, is interest-related.

4.1.2 Mapping Methods

Not only are the form and the content of maps interest-related, so too are the methods used to produce each map. These methods are also affected by background assumptions about the nature of the area being mapped. A map is a formal representation of selected features and relations in the world that preserves those relationships of particular interest. Each map, then, can be seen as a model. Models have a relationship not only to their subject (the territory, in the case of geographic maps) but to their source. The source for a three-dimensional replica of the Earth is a sphere. The selection of this source means that the use of such a replica to determine, say, the distance between two cities, relies on a particular set of inferring techniques—those associated with the geometry of curved surfaces. The distance between the two cities will be represented by the shortest surface difference between two points on the globe. Which particular source is selected for a map is a function of beliefs about the nature of the Earth. A flat-earther, for example, would insist that a two-dimensional plane be used as the source for a replica of the Earth. The use of this source to determine the distance between two cities relies on a different set of inferring techniques—the techniques of plane geometry, where the distance between two cities is represented by the shortest distance between two points on the plane.

Given that the sphere is considered an appropriate three-dimensional model of Earth, the only easy way to preserve the areas of the land masses, the shapes of the land masses, and the lengths of the various coastlines of earth would be on a three-dimensional replica. These features cannot all be preserved on the same two-dimensional map. If, as is most often the case for practical reasons, a two-dimensional representation of some area is required rather than a three-dimensional one, the preservation of at least one of the above features must be sacrificed.

But this affects the choice of method, for which of these features we are most interested in will determine the method of projection used to construct the map. The maps of the Arctic and Antarctic polar masses, for example, are constructed by the use of *zenithal equidistant projections* because of the special interest attaching to the distances from the poles. Aitoff's projection represents a *zenithal equal area projection* of a hemisphere, and is often used for air routes. *Conical orthomorphic projections* are used for large-scale maps, because the projection is one that is everywhere free from local distortion in shape, although the scale may vary slightly in different parts of the map.[4] In determining the distances between two cities on a two-dimensional representation of a three-dimensional source, the particular method of projection used to construct the representation becomes part of the calculation. One cannot assume, as one could with a two-dimensional source, that the distance is represented by the shortest distance between two points on the representation. Mapping methods vary, then, and are quite explicitly related to the purposes for which the map is intended.

4.1.3 The Relationship between Map and Data

Each of the projection methods described above gives a high degree of accuracy in a particular feature of interest (such as shape) at the expense of accuracy in a feature of less interest (such as scale). This is interesting because it shows how judgments based on values are an intrinsic part of map making, rather than something to be avoided.

To construct a good, appropriate map, then, requires more than just a set of data and a simple truth-preserving mechanism by which to represent it. The cognitive processes involved in map making cannot be restricted to any simple formal logic. Given the interests of the user, a theory of what data is appropriate is needed. The construction of a map for the gold prospector, for example, will be informed by a background theory of the geological occurrence of gold deposits. Given the purposes for which the map is to be used, there must be a theory of what relationships an appropriate map for that purpose is required to represent, to what degree of accuracy, and in what form. Where there are multiple interests, judgments must be made as to which is of prior importance, as they may not all be able to be represented with equal accuracy. In the example of the large-scale maps in the Oxford Atlas, a judgment had to be made to trade off accuracy of shape against accuracy of scale. Such judgments, although rational, cannot be said to be logical in the narrow sense of the word.

The concepts of what data are appropriate to a particular map, and of what an appropriate map might be, belong to the *metatheory* of map making. This is in contrast with, say, a particular projection theory, which belongs to the *theory* of some particular type of map making, and is itself determined by the metatheory. The metatheoretic level will include notions such as the sort of background theories applicable, concepts of what an appropriate map for a particular purpose will consist in, the standards of accuracy required of any particular map, and other standards that may apply to the validity of maps in general.

Each map will be a representation of data, selected and organized by the principles of the metatheory of mapping. This metatheory cannot be arrived at deductively,[5] and many of the judgments made at this level are not purely matters of logic in the narrow sense either, as I have already shown. The map, then, can be said to have greater content than the data in some respects, despite the fact that (as we saw in chapter 3) it is an abstraction. Moreover, the construction relationship between the map and the data cannot be seen merely as a relationship-preserving mechanism. That is, the validity of a geographic map cannot be determined solely by reference to the territory it maps and a particular projection theory. The data selected for mapping, the form and scale of the map, the degree of accuracy required, and even the projection theory itself, are directed by the fact that the value of the map lies in its ability to guide actions relevant to purposes in the area of interest. These metatheoretical features of a map are as important in determining its validity as is the relationship between a map and its domain.

4.1.4 The Public Nature of Validity and the Consensibility of Maps

The fact that these interest-related metatheoretical features enter into the determination of validity means that the objectivity of mapping cannot lie in the use of any simple truth-preserving mechanism relating a map with its domain. Nonetheless, valid maps are objective, and in this section I try to give some account of the objective nature of the determination of the validity of maps. While individuals may make maps simply for their own use and judge them according to how well they guide their own actions, I am not interested in such maps here, limiting my attention to consensible maps. This is because one of the criteria of scientific theories is that they are consensible, and I cannot expect the analogy to hold if I discuss idiosyncratic maps.

Consensible maps are for public use, even if that public is limited in some way (geological maps containing dips and strikes, for example, are not easily interpreted without some training). Hence, given a commonality of interest and purpose, and equal competence in map reading, a particular map should be as good (or bad) for one person as for another. The validity of a map, then, is a matter for public assessment. Any competent map reader should be able, in theory, to check the validity of a map, bearing in mind the purposes for which it was made, by predicting from the map that certain features and the relationships between them are a certain way, and then checking this with the domain itself.

Our prospector, for example, should be able to predict from an appropriate geological map that a particular mountain will contain the quartz in which gold is likely to be found, and perhaps even its likely depth from the surface. His consequent action, to look for the quartz in that place, constitutes a check of the validity of the map. The discovery of the quartz would validate at least that part of the map. Whether he actually found gold would be irrelevant, although should he do so the information that that particular quartz was gold-bearing could be included in future (more detailed) maps. Any discovery of gold may also feed back into the background theory about the likelihood of gold occurring in such quartz. That is, a discovery in the domain may feed back into the metatheoretical level. If the quartz was not found in the place suggested by the map, the map would have to be modified in the light of this information.

This example emphasizes the point made in the previous section, that cognitive hierarchies are involved in mapping. The process of mapping involves at least three cognitive levels:[6] the data to be mapped, the map itself, and the metatheory of mapping. These form a reiteration loop. The map is a function of both the data and the metatheory. The data selected is a function of the metatheory. Both the map and the metatheory may have to be modified in the light of the data. Finally, the map may itself bring about change in the metatheory. All levels of the hierarchy are subject to modification in interaction with the other levels.

Normal map making involves refining and extending maps in the light of changes in the other levels. For example, topographic maps are constantly updated as a result of changes at the level of data, including such things as the construction of new roads and dams, the appearance of new islands or changes to a river delta. They are also changed, or new ones are constructed, because of changes at the metalevels. These might include new mapping techniques, and even such things as a change in the value of gold. A large increase in the price of gold may lead to the inclusion in maps of formations, previously of little interest, that might be expected to contain gold only in minute proportions. A change in mining techniques could also bring about some such change. Occasionally, radical changes may occur in these levels, resulting in revolutionary map making. The change in the metalevel from regarding the earth as flat to regarding it as spherical, for example, revolutionized map making.

The fact that the prospector can use the map, and even amend it, does not mean that he can construct it. He may be trained in map reading, but need not have either the expertise to make the judgments required at the metalevel, or even the ability to follow the methods of map-making directed by the metalevel. Should he wish to be assured of the validity of the map in question before he uses it, he will have to rely on experts in map construction to make the appropriate judgements, and on people already familiar with the territory in question who can certify that the map is a good one for the purposes of the prospector. But the fact that the experts in question will be fewer than the competent map readers does not make the issue of validity any less a public affair. It is the fact that the validity of maps can be and is checked by the actions of non–map makers as well as map makers—that map makers are responsible in this way to map users—that is one of the features distinguishing map-making from other types of belief-creating institution.

It is the consensibility of maps, then, that underlies their objectivity[7] and makes them the sort of thing that can be validated or invalidated, as the case may be. But what is it about maps that makes them consensible? Ziman argues that it is part of the intrinsic nature of maps as abstractions that makes consensus on the validity of maps possible. The argument is that, paradoxically, the agreement of experts that a map is a good representation of the territory in question is easier to obtain than would be the case with a picture of the territory.[8] This is because despite the fact that maps are made with an interest in mind, they are not subjective in the way pictures are. Pictures are representations of what is seen by a particular person in a particular place at some time. They are far more detailed than maps, and it is unlikely that general agreement will be reached that the picture actually represents the territory in every detail. Maps can be seen as abstracting from pictures (or directly from the territory) what can actually be agreed upon. According to Ziman, it is the possibility of obtaining this intersubjective agreement that constitutes the objectivity of maps as opposed to the subjectivity of pictures.[9]

These points can be seen by looking at Figures 4.1 to 4.6. These are all representations of the Anastasia exploration area, approximately 200 km west of Cairns and at the base of the Cape York Peninsula. Figure 4.1 is the least abstract and most subjective, being simply a photograph of the landscape. The photographer is certain that the photograph does indeed represent Anastasia, and rightly so, for he can trace the causal chain that produced it, he remembers taking the photograph, and it recalls the landscape to him. But it is unlikely that the photograph would represent Anastasia to anyone else, even others who have been there, although the clues provided by the type of vegetation and rock formation may help some of those familiar with the area to hazard an educated guess.

Figure 4.2, an oblique aerial photograph, is slightly more abstract. The details of rock and vegetation of Figure 4.1 are replaced by a picture of the ground formation and the pattern of vegetation. It is likely that several people could reach agreement that this is a photograph of Anastasia, but the group concerned would still be very small, comprising those who had seen the formation as a whole from perhaps one or more perspectives, either personally or vicariously.[10] Figure 4.3, a vertical aerial photograph, is still more abstract and yet more consensible. There is little detail, and the perspective and distance make the landscape look like nothing most of us have ever seen. But the picture places the Anastasia formation in a wider context and includes those features that can be represented in map form, for example, hills and valleys.

Figure 4.4, an aerial thematic mapping (ATM) image, is even more abstract and yet if anything more distinctive. The greater abstraction is not only a result of the greater distance from the ground of the point of data collection, but also because particular information has been selected for while other information has been discarded. These images and, for example, Landsat images, are virtual maps, at least in the context of this discussion. But they are specialized maps, and as such, while major features such as watercourses could be verified by any map-literate traveller, much of the information can only be verified by experts, say, in the fields of geology or biology. But note that these experts are not those who construct the aerial thematic images.

Mapping Reality

FIGURE 4.1

The Anastasia prospect.

Photograph courtesy of Ross Jenkins.

FIGURE 4.2

Anastasia—oblique aerial photograph.

Photograph courtesy of John Nethery.

Mapping Reality

FIGURE 4.3

Anastasia—vertical aerial photograph.

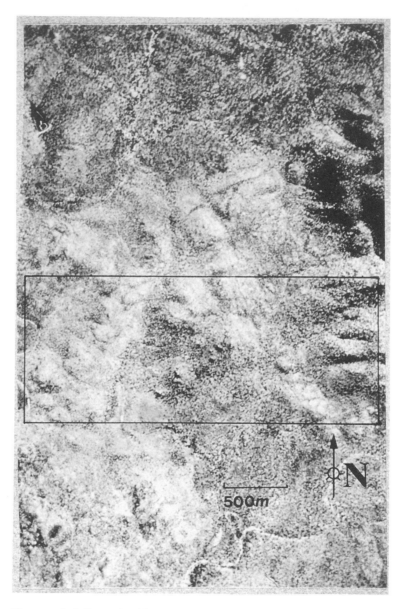

Photograph © Queensland Department of Lands.

FIGURE 4.4

Anastasia—2.2 micron wavelength image.

ATM data acquisition and processing by CSIRO Exploration & Mining. Used with permission, after Fraser et al. 1986.

Mapping Reality

FIGURE 4.5

Anastasia—7762 Lyndhurst Edition 1. 1:100 000 topographic map.

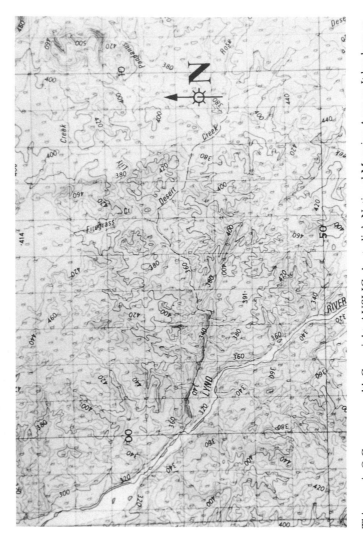

FIGURE 4.6

Anastasia—Atherton 1:250 000 Geological Map, Sheet SE 55-5.

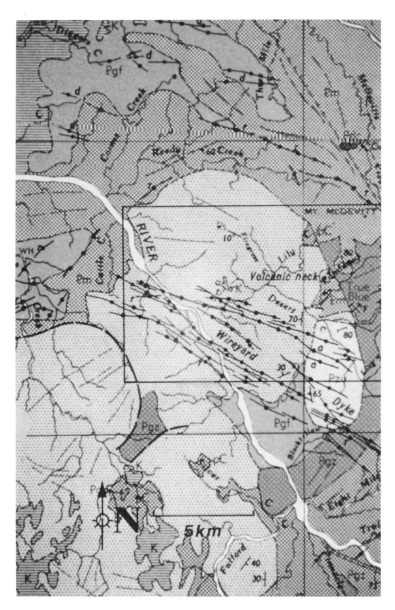

© Queensland Department of Minerals and Energy.

Figure 4.5 is a 1:100 000 topographic map of Anastasia, with an ontology that includes contours, waterways, roads, and buildings, among other things. But it excludes most vegetation distinctions, rock types, fauna patterns, and much other information. Figure 4.6 is a geologic map with an ontology that includes dip and strike data, dikes, and intrusive contacts. Note that such specialist maps are likely to be both made and verified by those in the same broad institutional setting. But they are also verifiable by, for example, those non-geologists who actually extract the ore and put it into production.

Maps, then, are the sort of thing about which agreement may be reached. The fact that they are abstractions makes them more objective than pictures, and hence more consensible. Consensus on validity is reached by a public institutional process in which both mapping experts and map users (who may, but need not, be expert in other fields) may criticize and check the selection of data, the projection method, and the degree of "fit" between the map and the domain, according to the purposes for which the map was constructed.

4.1.5 Criteria of validity

Maps may be tested via prediction, as I have already shown. But there are further features of maps themselves that can also be used to assess their validity. Maps are multiply connected. A map cannot be significantly altered at one point without affecting neighboring relations. This means that a surveyor can, and does, collect redundant data. The coordinates of a particular feature may be determined with reference to a variety of other features, which means that its position can be double-checked by means of the relations it holds to features other than those used originally to determine it. In a good map, features are cross-situationally invariant under multiple determination. So a good map must be internally consistent or coherent, and the "fit" of any particular feature of the map with the territory may be checked with reference to its place in the map as a whole.

Moreover, maps of the same territory are deeply compatible. This is obviously so among maps that differ only in scale. But it is also the case among maps that abstract different features of the territory, such as road maps and railway maps, and also with topologic maps which abstract only the most general relationships. We can combine maps of different features of the same territory, for example a railway map and a road map, into a more general map which includes both features. A mapping relationship exists between any two maps of the same territory. This is illustrated in Figure 4.7.

D is the domain, or the territory to be mapped. R_1 and R_2 are the different ranges or maps. M_1 and M_2 represent the mapping relationships between D and R_1 and R_2 respectively, and M_R represents the relationship between R_1 and R_2. $M_2 \ 0 \ M_R = M1$. Transposing this, we get $M_R = M_1 \ 0 \ M_{2-1}$. That is, M_R exists if M_2 has an inverse (and M_{R-1} exists if M_{1-1} does). That M_2 *does* have an in-

FIGURE 4.7

Mapping relations.

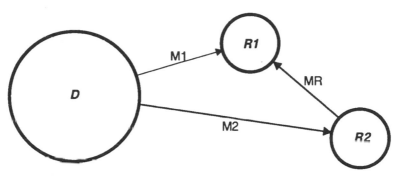

verse for geographical maps seems obvious; such maps would be useless otherwise. Given that we can correctly identify our position in the territory and thus locate ourselves on the map, we can use the map to identify other objects and relations in the territory.[11] Thus, whether a particular map is compatible with other maps of the same territory will be a further guide to validity. Maps should ideally be externally coherent, and at least externally consistent, to be valid.

Maps, then, are valid insofar as they enable us to act successfully in pursuit of our interests. Explanation is no less a feature here than prediction and coherence, for maps enable us to explain general connections among the data. For example, a topographic map (combined with background theories of the nature of water) will enable us to explain the positions of the water courses by reference to the contours. Some of these watercourses may be marked with a dotted line indicating they are not permanently flowing. This feature may itself be explicable in terms of the terrain as represented on the topographical map, combined with information from a general rainfall map of the territory in question.

4.1.6 Maps and the Limits on Their Scope of Valid Application

Validity, then, can be assessed in a number of ways; empirically, and by internal and external consistency and coherency checks because maps are multiply connected and maps of the same territory are deeply compatible. But because maps are abstractions constructed with an interest in mind, there are limitations on the valid use to which even an excellent map can be put. Consider, for example, a street directory of a city. It would not be valid to assume that because all of the streets along both sides of a blank strip were indicated as dead ends, the strip marked a railway line. One might be able to guess that there was some blockage there, but it could as easily be a stormwater gully as a railway line. Indeed, there might not be any blockage at all. Planners might have left the area free for a proposed motorway. It would be invalid to move beyond the scope of the map to arrive at such a conclusion. Of course, the presence of the strip might well prompt further investigation, but the map itself would not provide an explanation of the strip.

This limitation on the valid use of a map is directly related to the interest that guided its construction, the sort of problem it was intended to solve for the user. This is what is used to select the data that is mapped. That maps of the same territory are deeply compatible means that any single map may indicate the existence of other areas to be mapped, and requires that the other maps be consistent with it. The more general the map, the wider its scope. Nonetheless, every map, no matter how wide its scope, has a limited range of valid applicability. No single map can encompass every feature of the reality in question.

4.2 The Adequacy of Theories

In §4.1, I derived a notion of the validity of maps from the fact that maps are primarily guides to purposive action. But scientific theories, too, are constructed with interests in mind, and are used to guide decision making and action. Science aims to increase our understanding of, and control over, phenomena of interest,[12] and as such can be seen as a problem-solving activity.[13] Some of the problems that science addresses may be quite specifically oriented toward a particular practical problem such as the harnessing of nuclear power and are consequently analogous to the prospector looking for gold. But a great part of science is oriented more generally toward finding out about reality, and has no specific end in mind. Such science is in this sense more analogous to the general topological maps intended for multiple purposes. So when I talk of the problems that a theory is intended to solve, I am not necessarily talking of specific and immediate practical problems, but of epistemic problems in general.[14]

An implication of treating science as a guide to decision making and action and as a problem-solving activity is that it is to be assessed at base in terms of such pragmatic criteria as effectiveness or success.[15] The pragmatic nature of assessment makes causal explanation the basis of the naturalist realist criteria of validity. This does not mean that causal explanation is the only sort of scientific explanation. Explanations in terms of composition, structure, and function are just as much part of science. But as I argue in chapter 5, the validity of these types of explanation depends on their being shown to be instantiated in a causal explanation. In §4.2, I explore the nature of the validity of scientific theories with these pragmatic features of science in mind.

4.2.1 The Nature of Theories

Scientific theories can be roughly divided into the descriptive and the explanatory, although no absolute distinction can be made between these two, and most branches of science involve both. Descriptive science, for example botany, is concerned with seeking and classifying what are essentially surface patterns in nature. This activity is so like geographic mapping (indeed in many cases it *is* a form of geographic mapping, as when vegetation is mapped) that the analogy between the nature of the validity of maps and descriptive science does not have to be argued. But control over nature requires not just the recognition of classes of phenomena but also an understanding of the causal mechanisms involved in their production. A good part of explanatory science is devoted to investigating the underlying causes of regularities whose existence has already been recognized. In the rest of this chapter, I concentrate on showing that the analogy between explanatory science and geographic maps also extends to the nature of the validity.

Although most branches of science involve both descriptive and explanatory theories, physics is more explanatory than descriptive, for many of its descriptions are not of surface regularities. The properties of the theoretical entities of physics, such as electrons, can be described only in relation to the theory in which they are embedded. So in what sense do the theories and descriptions of explanatory science resemble maps? Maps, as we saw in §4.1, are formal representations of selected features and relations in the world that preserve those relationships of particular interest. Can explanatory theories be seen in the same way? To answer this question requires a look at how the structures underlying the phenomena of the explanatory sciences are represented, and what sort of relationship holds between the representation and the phenomena.

In the physical sciences, underlying structures are often represented diagrammatically. The ray diagrams of geometric optics are an example. But a visualizable model, although it may be preferable in that it enables one to *see* the force of an explanation in a particularly convincing way, is not necessary. In most of physics today, for example, the role that is played by ray diagrams in geometric optics is taken over by more complex forms of mathematics. Nonetheless, Toulmin argues that some representational device comparable in function to the ray diagram of geometric optics is logically indispensable in the representation of underlying structures.[16] Theories contain models. In causal theories, the models posit mechanisms that can be used to explain the phenomena in question. But geographic maps are just a special kind of model. So it is in the nature of explanatory theories as models that the analogy with maps seems likely to hold. Rom Harré has long treated scientific theories as models,[17] and in the rest of this chapter I frequently draw on his insights into the implications of seeing them thus. His work illustrates the incredible richness of the metatheoretic features of scientific explanation, in contrast to the relative poverty of this level in the positivist schema.

4.2.2 The Content and Form of Theories

Theories, like maps, are selective representations of reality, and the domain of a theory is selected according to its relevance to the problem the theory is intended to solve.[18] But because many theories are intended to solve general epistemic problems rather than particular practical ones, the notion of how the domain of a theory is selected becomes problematic. Domains cannot be specific to branches of science, because, as Dudley Shapere points out, there is no one-to-one correspondence between branches of science and the domains they study. Sometimes several domains will be studied under a single branch of science, and sometimes a single domain will be relevant to several branches of science. Shapere illustrates this by pointing out that initially the branches of science studying electricity and magnetism had separate domains. Maxwell's theory then explained the phenomena of both electricity and magnetism, unifying their domains. This new domain became associated with chemistry, and potentially fruitful research began, to unify the domains of electromagnetism and chemistry.[19]

Shapere has investigated the way that domains come to be constituted in science, and concludes that items of information come to be associated together as domains when the association is based on some relationship between the items and there is something problematic about the body so related. But as Shapere notes, it is possible to establish some sort of relationship between any two sets of information. The relationship needs to be specified further as being well-grounded and significant. For example, the nineteenth-century attempts by Paul Broca and others to correlate average brain sizes in human races with intelligence was well-grounded in the sense that in general, the relative average brain sizes of different species of mammals increases with intelligence. Its significance lay in the concern to provide scientific evidence that would support the racist social order of the day.[20] These additional qualifications on the constitution of a domain show that the selection of the items of information constituting a domain is related to interests and purposes.

But this is not the only way in which the content of a theory is affected by the problem in question. When theories are seen as models, the content of a theory is affected by the source of the model (what the model is based on) as well as by its subject (the domain the model represents). No object or process, either real or imagined, is a model in itself. It functions as a model only when it is seen as being in a certain relationship to other things or processes. The solar system becomes a model for the atom only when it is specified in what respects it is supposedly like and unlike an atom.

Not only must the source and subject be similar, the similarities must be adequate for the purposes for which the model is to be used. To use one of Harré's illustrations, a toy replica of the 1963 Buick Riviera, despite having the similarities that all toy cars have, cannot be used as a model of the 1963 Mini Cooper that won at Le Mans that year. To do so would be misleading, as a Buick Riviera was in the same race and didn't win.

Both the domain of a theory, then, and the source of any explanatory model, are selected with reference to the problem the theory is intended to solve. And because the usefulness of the theory can only be assessed by how well it helps to solve the problems of the user, not only is the content of the theory interest-related, the determination of its validity is interest-related as well.

The discussion of the role that models play in relation to theories shows that the construction of theories involves much more than a simple truth-preserving mechanism and the phenomena the theory is to explain. The selection of the model depends to a certain extent on the purposes for which the theory is designed. This will also affect the form the theory takes. Many theories, particularly in physics, are expressed mathematically. Such theories require a certain amount of numerical fit between the theory and the data. The principle of the rectilinear propagation of light requires such fit. Mathematically expressed theories can be likened to topographic maps that preserve accurately the numerical relationships between the features of greatest interest. But much knowledge, and particularly much social science, is qualitative rather than quantitative. The anthropologist studying rites of passage, for example, is interested in the changes of role and status that such rites bring about. Quantifiable knowledge, such as the number of people who pass through such rites, is irrelevant, and the question of numerical fit with a model does not arise. Rather, the question is whether the model correctly represents the significant relationships between identifiable entities within that field of knowledge. Qualitative knowledge can be likened to topological maps in this respect.[21] The difference in form between quantitative and qualitative knowledge relates both to the subject matter of the theory and the purpose for which the theory is constructed. Thus the form that a theory takes, like its content, is interest-related.

4.2.3 Scientific Methods

Not only are the form and the content of theories interest-related, so too are the methods used to construct them. These methods are also affected by any background assumptions about the nature of the feature of reality being modelled. These points can be explained by expanding on the notion that scientific theories are models of reality. Just as theories can be seen as models, theory construction can be seen as model building. And just as there are many types of map, each requiring its own methods of construction, so too are there many different types of model, each requiring different methods of constrution.

This can be seen by looking at Harré's taxonomy of models.[22] As the taxonomy is complex, I outline the relationship between the various types of model in Figure 4.8. Harré's classification is based on the various ways that a model can relate to its subject and its source. The main division is between those models whose subject is the same as the source, *homoeomorphs*, and those whose subject and source are different, *paramorphs*. A toy car is an example of a homoeomorph, as the subject of the toy car is a real car, and a real car is also the source of the model. The use of a computer (source) as a model of human cognitive processes (subject) is an example of a paramorph.

Harré distinguishes three kinds of homoeomorphs. The first comprises *micro* and *megamorphs*. These are scale models of the subject, and the method of construction is either enlargement or reduction. But note that except for simple cases, such as the reduction of a line drawing, features other than scale may have to be changed. A working miniature model of a Spitfire will likely have to use different construction materials and a completely different sort of power and control system, such as a radio-controlled electric motor. The sort of changes other than scale that will be made will depend on the use to which the model is to be put. If appearance is more important than flight, the Spitfire may have a non-working engine that externally resembles the Rolls-Royce engines of the subject-source.

The second kind of homoeomorph is the *teleiomorph*. Harré defines these as in some respect or respects "improvements" on the subject. Teleiomorphs are of two kinds. Both kinds can be seen as modelling an object which has properties p1 . . . pn, relevant to the enquiry for task. Both are *abstractions*, having the properties pj . . . pk $(1 < j < k < n)$, that is, fewer than the source-subject, and the method involves selecting the properties to be abstracted. But *idealizations* are a special kind of abstraction in which each selected property of the source is matched by a property in the model, but the model properties are considered (according to some set of values) more perfect than the source-subject's properties. The method in this case includes the creation of such idealizations. Weber's ideal type of rational action is a good example of an idealization in this sense, as is the ideal gas of thermodynamics.

The third kind of homoeomorph is the *metriomorph*. Metriomorphs model "conceptual" objects rather than real ones and the subject-source is always a class. An example would be "the average family". The methods used in the construction of metriomorphs may include the methods of abstraction and idealization already mentioned, but they also involve other techniques. The modelling of the average family, for example, requires statistical analysis.

As well as showing that the various types of homoeomorph involve different methods of construction, the above discussion illustrates the notion that

FIGURE 4.8

Harré's Taxonomy of Models.

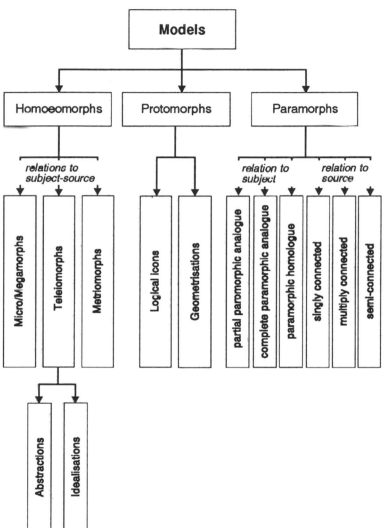

models are created with purposes in mind, because all models are selective abstractions. The properties not modelled are those that are considered irrelevant, and relevance and irrelevance are relative to purposes.

To continue with Harré's taxonomy of models, paramorphs are usually constructed with the aim of modelling processes. Paramorphs model a subject, but the form of a paramorph and its mode of operation are drawn from a source quite different from the subject. Paramorphs are needed in cases where difficulties of various sorts are encountered with the study of the subject. For example, genetic factors were introduced as a model for the then unknown process of the inheritance of Mendelian characters. The source of the model in this case was roughly the geometry of two sets of strung colored beads from which the beads could be separated, and then put together again to form different linear patterns. The taxonomy of paramorphs is thus more complex than that of homoeomorphs as they include both the relation between a model and its subject, and that between the model and its source.

A *partial paramorphic analogue* occurs when the processes in the model and the subject are different. Functional models are of this type.[23] The input and output of the subject and the model are exactly alike, but the causal processes of the model and the subject differ. The computer simulation of a mathematical calculation by a person is a partial paramorphic analogue. The sort of method involved in this case includes a functional analysis of the subject process and the discovery or design of a model that can also carry out the functions analyzed. A *complete paramorphic analogue* occurs when the model process and the model input and output are analogues of the subject process and the subject input and output respectively. Wind tunnel models are of this sort. The method involved in this case is causal analysis of the relevant features of the subject and their replication in a simplified (often scaled) model. A *paramorphic homologue* occurs when the input and output are analogous but the process is identical. Harré suggests that the use of living nerve cells for building computers illustrates the idea of a paramorphic homologue, "since the input and output would be only analogous to giving information and receiving reports, but the process by which the cellular computer and the brain found the answer would be the same, whatever that is . . . ".[24] The method here is a functional analysis of the input and output processes rather than of the calculating process itself.

Harré also distinguishes three sorts of relation between a paramorph and its source. *Singly connected paramorphs* are those in which the principles of only one science[25] supply the definition of the entities and laws of the processes which constitute the model. The corpuscular theory of gases, for example, draws only on mechanics. *Multiply connected paramorphs* draw on two or more sciences, the principles of which are not explicable in terms of one another. Bohr's atom draws on electrodynamics and mechanics. *Semi-connected paramorphs* include models such as Freud's psychic energy model of the mind, which draws on principles of energetics from physics, and also introduces principles unknown to any other source. The methods used to construct these relationships between model and source are the same as those described in the discussion of homoeomorphs.

For completion, I add the third family of models that Harré distinguishes, *protomorphs*, although I have no methodological point to make about these. Harré describes protomorphs as being related to homoeomorphs and paramorphs roughly as lampreys are related to fish.[26] Protomorphs can be divided into logical icons, which are diagrams concretely representing logical relations, but in such a way that they can be reinterpreted (or misunderstood) as teleiomorphs; and geometrizations, which represent possible geometric relations.[27] The point about protomorphs is that they can develop into proper models that postulate hypothetical mechanisms for the process in question.

The preceding discussion of the variety of methods involved in the construction of models shows clearly that the general methods used in the construction of scientific theories or models are interest-related. Different types of model are required to solve different types of problem, and each type of model involves a different set of construction methods. But scientific knowledge includes not just the models themselves, but the way the models function. This point is illustrated by Toulmin when he points out how mystifying it is when popularizers of science speak of a scientific discovery in terms of the model alone. To be told, for example, that there is not only a common-sense solid table but also a scientific one consisting mostly of empty space is not particularly helpful in understanding the atomic theory of matter. The point of atomic theory is that it helps to explain things that could not be explained before, and to do this, one has to know how the model functions.[28] This means that one has to know what particular set of inferring techniques is required by the specific model in question.

In illustrating this point with reference to the principle of the rectilinear propagation of light, Toulmin points out that the discovery of this principle was not the literal discovery that something ("light") moved in a certain way (straight lines). It was, rather, an extension of the notion of *travelling* to do a new job in physics. The phenomena (light and shadow patches) were in no sense new but the discovery involved new ways of thinking of them. In drawing inferences from the principle, the ray diagram has a logically indispensable role. Just as the use of the sphere as the source for the three-dimensional replica of the earth means that the use of such a replica relies on a particular set of inferring techniques (those associated with the geometry of curved surfaces), so the use of the model of straight line travel means that it relies on the set of inferring techniques associated with the geometry of straight lines. The model comes hand in hand with a new set of inferring techniques and itself explains the phenomena.

Viewing theories as models brings out not only the variety of methods that are involved in their construction and use, but also the way in which these methods are directly related to the kind of model employed. This is in turn directly related to the interests of the user. The methods of sciencing, like the methods of mapping, are related both to the nature of the reality being theorized and to the interests of the user. There is no single scientific method.

4.2.4 The Relationship between Theory and Data

The variety of methods involved in the construction and use of scientific theories raises the question of the relationship between theory and data. As we saw in chapter 2, positivists saw the relationship as a logical one, either truth-preserving or probabilistic. It was by virtue of this logical relationship that theories were held to be explanatory. The paradigmatic account of explanation within the positivist tradition is Hempel's deductive-nomological (DN) account of explanation.[29] Basically, under the DN model of explanation, a theory T explains a fact or set of facts when, along with certain initial conditions, it entails those facts. According to this model, the logics of explanation and prediction are the same.

This notion of explanation is problematic in a number of respects. One of the major problems is that "explanation" in this model need have nothing to do with understanding. Hooker illustrates this by pointing out that from a symptomatic account of the course of a certain disease (an example of an indicator law) and from the fact that a certain person has just contracted that disease, one can predict that he will be in a certain condition, say, in a few days. But because the logics of explanation and prediction are the same under this model, the description of the course of the disease counts as an explanation of the sufferer's condition, despite the fact that it adds not at all to the understanding of the cause of that condition.

While far from espousing the empiricist view of science, as we saw in chapter 2, Hooker has investigated ways in which the DN model might be altered so that it captures the idea of increased understanding. He argues that to be an adequate account of explanation, the DN model would have to be supplemented by some such condition as, "D: the premises (explanans) of an acceptable DN explanation constitute an increase in depth of understanding over that provided by the conclusion (explanandum)."[30] Hooker argues that empiricism has no account to offer of this requirement, and that Popper's version is also inadequate. If "increased depth of understanding" is cashed out in terms of increase of Popperian content, and D is added to the criteria for an adequate DN explanation, the explanation will be acceptable "only if the theory to which its premises belong has more content than does the theory to which its conclusion belongs."[31] But this reformulation is still unsatisfactory, as it does not exclude the indicator laws. Hooker's own proposal for cashing out "increased depth of understanding" is "C: A theory T1 provides an increase in depth of understanding over a theory T2 if and only if the ontologies of T1 and T2 are each systematic and the ontology T2 can be reconstructed as derivative in that of T1 but not vice versa."[32] Hooker notes that C needs to be extended to be used in the context of explanation, to include partial use of theories in the explanans, and facts in the explananda. The former could be accomplished by referring to the embedding theories, and the latter by regarding facts as belonging to phenomenological theories. C also needs extending to account for the fact that the explanans often contain sentences from more than one theory. With these extensions to C, it can be used as the criterion of depth of understanding in D, and a DN explanation supplemented by D will now rule out the indicator laws.

The requirement that an adequate explanation satisfy some such condition as D reflects the fact discussed in the last section that explanatory theories are not simply constructed from (even selected) data from the domain and a truth-preserving logic. They include models that function to provide a causal explanation of the data, and in this sense have greater content than the data. Moreover, theory construction requires a variety of methods, all of which include many extra-logical judgments such as judgments of similarity and relevance, and this argues for a far richer concept of explanation than that theory be related to facts in a narrowly logical way.

Another problem with the DN model of explanation is that scientific laws, with the exception of phenomenological laws (which are made to "fit"), rarely, if ever, agree with the facts in their domain. While the normal test of a theory is that it yields results that "fit" the experimental data, this fit may range all the way from remarkable quantitative accuracy to simple qualitative patterning.[33] Often, as Ziman points out, the numerical fit between theory and observation lies within the instrumental uncertainty of the experimental technique, and

[i]n practice, the theoretical physicist may have no better evidence for his model than that it gives the correct qualitative pattern of results for a variety of data, some of which are closely fitted.[34]

Ziman illustrates the lack of fit between observational data and theory with a graph taken from his own work in the thermal conductivity of sodium. The graph plots the values predicted by his new theory, a previous theory, and the experimental data. Each had a distinctive curve, but although they were similar in many respects, Ziman was able to claim that the new theory fitted better with the experimental data than the old one. This sort of judgment of fit, say between different curves, or the patterns that arise out of different wavelengths and frequencies, are required frequently in science.

Examples such as this show how validity assessment cannot be formalized in any narrowly logistic manner. To make the required sort of judgments
of better fit means that one has to have a theory of what a "best fit" is. There
are such theories. Least squares regression, for example, allows one to pick
which particular curve from a certain class of curves provides the best fit, and
there are other such theories. But the use of a theory of fit requires the use of
judgments other than those concerning logical relations. First, judgments have
to be made as to which theory of fit to use; for example, whether the method of
least squares or another theory of fit uses the best criterion of fit for the case in
question. Second, each specific method requires its own non-logical judgments. When using the method of least squares, for example, a judgment must
be made as to the appropriate class of curves to be used.

Although the fundamental laws of physics are rarely, if ever, precisely
confirmed by the data, they can be (and often are) adjusted to "fit the facts".
But then, as Nancy Cartwright points out, they are no longer fundamental laws,
but have been transformed into phenomenological laws. Because of the way
these phenomenological laws have been adjusted, they are not entailed by the
fundamental laws. Thus, although the relationship between phenomenological
laws and the known experimental facts is deductive, that between the fundamental laws of physics and the facts is not.[35]

This is another reflection of the nature of theories and the methods that
are used to construct them. As with maps, projective conventions are involved
in the construction of models. This means, as we have seen, that tradeoffs
have to be made when deciding which aspects of the subject are to be modelled accurately. The reason that A is a model of, or for, B is that it was constructed to be similar to B in certain respects. But it must be dissimilar in
certain respects, too, or it would just be a replica, and as such would not be
explanatory.

Let me explain. A model can start as an analogue for a real, unknown
mechanism of nature. It may become (by a change of attitude in its users) a hypothetical mechanism. For example, as I have already mentioned, genetic factors were introduced as a model for the then unknown process of the inheritance
of Mendelian characters. When the model was first introduced it was regarded
merely as an analogy for the real processes by which inheritance occurred. Further investigation suggested the model could be seen as a hypothetical mechanism, that is, genetic features were considered to be a plausible suggestion as
to how the real mechanism operated. Further investigation (the discovery of
chromosomes and DNA) then confirmed the hypothesis.

As hypothetical mechanisms, models bear hypothetically to their subject
matter exactly the relations that real mechanisms bear to the phenomena for
which they are responsible.[36] These relations can be of two kinds. In the first,
the state of the mechanism is causally responsible for some state of things

which can be observed. The model states are linked to the phenomena by hypothetical generative relations. In this case, Harré refers to the relationships between the sentences used to describe the model and the sentences used to describe the phenomena as causal transforms. Where there is a causal relation the cause and effect have independent existence and the mechanism by which they are related can fruitfully be asked for. In the other kind of transform, the modal transform, the relation between the states of the model and the phenomena is not such as would give them independent existence. Harré's example here is that the reflection of light of a certain wavelength and being colored a certain hue are identical states of the world.[37] While causal explanations (those that offer increased depth of understanding as Hooker defined it) are more significant in that they offer increased control, theories with only modal transforms, such as the wave model of light (at least, as illustrated here) may still advance science.[38]

Harré sees the total theory as a statement-picture complex.[39] If only the sentences of the theory are considered, then the form of explanation resembles DN explanation. Where there is a causal transform, the sentences expressing this relation will appear as conditionals, asserting that if the model state obtains then the phenomenal effect of that state will come to be. Where there is a modal transform, the sentences will take the form of bi-conditionals, asserting that if and only if the model state obtains will the phenomenal aspect of that state come to be.

Harré's analysis of Darwin's theory of natural selection provides a further illustration of the explanatory powers of models and illustrates how his taxonomy of models might be used. Darwin was interested in the mechanisms of the transmutation of species. The model of an unknown mechanism must be paramorphic with respect to that mechanism, since in the absence of knowledge all that can be hoped for is some kind of parallelism of behavior. But the model will be homoeomorphic with respect to each of the sources on which it is based. With respect to Darwin's theory, this can easily be seen by looking at the schematic diagram Harré provides (see Figure 4.9).

Darwin's model is a paramorphic model (a partial analogue multiply connected) with respect to the unknown mechanism of change, and is a homoeomorphic model (a teleiomorphic abstraction) both with respect to domestic variation and selection and with respect to Malthus's theory of the competitive struggle for existence in human populations via competition for resources. This model illustrates a feature already noted with respect to Toulmin's example of the principle of the rectilinear propagation of light. What Darwin postulated was a novel kind of process, for when we use the word "competition" with reference to species of grass competing in a particular environment, we are using the word in a new way, just as we took the word "travelling" into physics to do a new job in explaining various phenomena related to light.

FIGURE 4.9

Sources for Darwin's theory of natural selection.

Phenomena	Tranforms	Model of unknown mechanism	Sources
Natural variations	The cause of natural variation is natural selection	Natural selection by the struggle for existence	The causal structure of domestic variation as selection. *Malthus's theory*

After Harré (1970).

A good causal theory, then, is explanatory, and the explanation lies in the fact that the phenomena are seen in a new way—as effects of the mechanism hypothesized in the model. A good model also leads beyond the phenomena, to further questions. An obvious one in the case of the principle of the rectilinear propagation of light is "what sort of thing is this light, which travels?"[40] The answering of this kind of question should lead to increased depth of understanding, and theories that pose such further questions may be regarded as more fruitful than those that do not.[41]

The construction of a good, appropriate theory, then, requires more than just a set of data and a simple truth-preserving mechanism by which to represent it. The complexity and variety of the cognitive processes involved in theory construction cannot be restricted to any simple formal logic, hence neither can the relationship between theory and data be adequately represented in this way. Theory construction is informed by background theories as to the nature of the rest of the world. Given the purposes for which the theory is designed, or the problem that it aims to solve, there must be a theory of what relationships an appropriate theory for that purpose is required to represent, to what degree of accuracy, and in what form. Where there are multiple interests, judgments must be made as to which is of prior importance, as they may not all be able to be represented with equal accuracy. Such judgments, though rational, cannot be said to be logical in the narrow sense of the word.

Analogously to maps, the concepts of which items of information belong to a domain, and of what an appropriate explanation might be, belong to the metatheory of science. The metatheoretic level will include notions such as the sorts of background theories applicable, concepts of what an appropriate solution to a particular problem might consist in, the standards of accuracy required of any particular theory, and other standards that might apply to the validity of theories in general.

Each theory will be a representation of a domain, selected and organized by the principles of the metatheory. This metatheory itself cannot be arrived at deductively, and many of the judgments made at this level are not narrowly logical. A theory, then, can be said to have greater content than the domain it represents, despite the fact that it is an abstraction. The construction relationship between the theory and its domain cannot be seen merely as a truth-preserving mechanism. The validity of a theory, therefore, cannot be determined solely by reference to the domain and deductive logic. The selection of a domain, the form the theory takes, the degree of accuracy required,[42] and the method of theory construction itself are directed by the fact that the value of the theory lies in its ability to solve problems, that is, to guide our actions relevant to our purposes in an area of interest. These metatheoretical features are as important in determining the validity of a theory as is the relationship between the theory and its domain.

4.2.5 The Public Nature of Validity and the Consensibility of Theories

The fact that these interest-related metatheoretical features enter into the determination of validity means that the objectivity of science cannot lie in the use of any simple truth-preserving mechanism relating a theory with its domain. Nonetheless, valid science is objective, and in this section I try to give some account of the objective nature of the determination of the validity of scientific theories.

Scientific knowledge is, by definition, consensible. One of the features of scientific knowledge, as we saw from Ziman's model in chapter 3, is that its contents must be framed in such a way that they are capable of either receiving wholehearted consent or attracting well-founded objections. Like consensible maps, scientific knowledge is for public use, even if that public is limited in some way.[43] Hence, given a commonality of interests and equal literacy in the area of science in question, a particular theory should be as good (or bad) for one person as for another. The validity of a theory is a matter for public assessment. Anyone competent in the applications of the relevant area of science should be able, in theory, to check the validity of a scientific theory. This is because, as I have shown, a theory can be looked upon as a solution to a problem or problems. A theory can be tested experimentally by setting up a practical problem of control which the theory is intended to solve, and, using the theory for guidance, seeing if that control is achieved.

For example, if I wished to confirm the principle of the rectilinear propagation of light, I could predict that if I placed a wall of a certain size and shape in a specific place, it would cast a shadow of such and such a shape and size at various times of the day. This could be tested by erecting the wall and measuring the shadow it casts. Should this measurement conflict with the theory, the theory might have to be revised.

This example emphasizes the point made in the previous section, that cognitive hierarchies are involved in sciencing. The process of science, like that of mapping, involves at least three cognitive levels: the information constituting the domain, the theory itself, and the metatheoretic level of science.[44] These form a reiteration loop. The theory constructed is a function both of the domain and the metatheory. The domain selected is a function of the metatheory. Both the theory and the metatheory may have to be modified in the light of fresh information from the domain, and the theory itself may bring about a change in the metatheoretic level.

Normal science involves refining and extending theories in the light of changes in the other two levels. Occasionally, radical changes may occur in these levels, resulting in revolutionary science. For example, the discovery that energy is quantized forced the consideration of radical and wide-ranging changes in the metatheoretic level of science. Bohr's quantum postulate calls into question basic notions of identity by suggesting that electrons have no continuous space-time trajectory, and his theory of complementarity challenges the classical realist notion of what constitutes an adequate theory of explanation, as the Einstein-Bohr debate shows.

Despite the public nature of theories, scientific theories cannot be constructed by everyone, just as our prospector could not make a map. The specialized nature of science and the lengthy education required to achieve competence in even a single speciality ensure that. Even a competent user of scientific knowledge need not have the expertise to make the sort of judgements required at the metatheoretic level, or the ability to apply particular scientific methods. Should a prospective user wish to be assured of the validity of a theory, she will have to rely on experts in the field in question, who acquire such skills via training and experience, and on people already familiar with the practical applications of the theory.

This does not make science any less public or objective. The institutional organization of science ensures not only that science is public but, via such avenues as journals, seminars, and so on, ensures that such theories as are considered important by the scientific community are subjected to the most rigorous criticism by other experts in the field. Moreover, the assessment of science, no matter how specialized, is not a matter for experts alone. The links between science and technology, or knowledge and action, ensure that eventually, scientific theory is validated by a much wider community. For example, I am not a physical scientist and have very little knowledge of electronics. But I am a competent user of many of the end products of electronic theory, not the least of which is the computer I now use. And I can tell as well any theorist when it is not doing the job it is supposed to be able to do. In this sense, the validity of science as a whole can be and is assessed by non-experts as well as by experts, and it is this feature that distinguishes science from those belief-creating institutions in which beliefs can be verified only by experts.

It is the consensibility of theories, then, that underlies the objectivity of science and that makes scientific theories the sort of thing that can be validated or invalidated, as the case may be. But what is it about theories that makes them consensible? Ziman's argument is that intersubjective agreement by the scientific community on the validity or otherwise of theories is possible, in principle, for the same reason that agreement on the validity of maps is possible.

Maps and theories are functionally similar. Indeed, if one removes the geographic restriction on the mapping analogy, to which I have remained faithful simply for its heuristic power, maps and theories are functionally equivalent. Theories, like maps, abstract from the phenomena in question, in order to provide a useful and consensible representation. And if one agrees with Toulmin and Harré that explanatory theories always contain some functional equivalent of the ray diagram in geometric optics, that is, that they make some use of a model, then maps and theories are not only functionally equivalent at the level of input and output, they operate in a functionally equivalent way too. While it may be very difficult (if not impossible) to gain agreement on precise empirical data, theories abstract from the data precisely what can actually be agreed upon.[45]

The congruence between this social model of scientific knowledge, the cognitive model of sciencing developed by Rubinstein, Laughlin, and McManus, and Campbell's model of socially validated perceptual foundationalism should now be apparent. The key to the congruence lies in the fact that in all three models, scientific knowledge is an abstraction from reality, based upon a socially validated perceptual foundation. Consensus on validity is reached by a public institutional process in which both experts in the field and users may criticize the selection of data, the methods used, and the degree of fit between the theory and its domain, according to the purposes for which the theory was constructed.

4.2.6 Criteria of Validity

I now turn to the means by which validity may actually be determined. I have discussed the fact that theories should be explanatory and that the empirical adequacy of theories may be tested via prediction. While the logical structure of explanation and prediction differ, both have to do (if not entirely) with the relationship between the theory and its domain. While there are various kinds of explanation, all have to do with the relation between the model that forms the basis of a theory and its subject. Causal explanations are especially significant because of the practical nature of assessment, and in the final analysis, other kinds of explanation depend for their validity on being linked with causal theories.[46] In a causal explanation, the model provides a hypothetical mechanism that explains the phenomena. A good model will in this case contain a causal transform and will be more than just a metaphor. Before the discovery of the principle of the rectilinear propagation of light, the phenomena in question, patches of light and shade, were unexplained primitives, to be accepted for what they were. After the discovery, they were seen as the effects of something, "light" in a new sense, travelling from the sun, or a lamp, to the illuminated objects.[47] The principle of the rectilinear propagation of light explains the phenomena. But also, and by virtue of that explanation, it enables the prediction of phenomena, such as the shadow that will be cast by a not-yet erected building. In this way, the principle acts as a guide to decision making in areas where light and shade are of importance, and it can be assessed by how well it does that job.

But as with maps, there are further features of theories themselves that can be used to assess their validity. The multiply-connected nature of maps, recall, meant that maps had to meet criteria of internal consistency and coherence. Scientific theories, like maps, are multiply-connected. An error in the determination of one relationship will, if not corrected, lead to error throughout the theory. A theory that is internally inconsistent will generate conflicting statements about its domain, making it both useless and untestable.[48] A good theory, then, should be internally consistent.

Moreover, scientific theories, like maps, should at least be deeply compatible. As they are representations of a single reality, at some deep level a mapping relationship exists between any two theories, and consistency is a minimal requirement. Such consistency is not necessarily easily established,[49] and as Feyerabend argued, theories should not be rejected simply because they appear inconsistent with other accepted theories.[50] Nonetheless, external consistency is ultimately a requirement of good theory and can be used as a criterion of validity.

Ideally, theories should not only be externally consistent with the body of accepted knowledge, they should be coherent, just as the pages of a street directory are expected to make a coherent whole. The consistency requirement is just the requirement of non-contradiction, but the coherency requirement is the requirement to establish links between theories. Just as coherency is one of the strengths of a street directory, so too is it one of the strengths of science as a whole. As Ziman puts it,

> . . . scientific knowledge eventually becomes a web or network of laws,
> models, theoretical principles, formulae, hypotheses, interpretations etc.,

which are so closely woven together that the whole assembly is much stronger than any single element.[51]

Ziman points out that although initially a theory may be "one-dimensional", like an itinerary, with no more authority than a single causal chain, the researcher seeks alternative corroboration routes from various starting points until the theory has been incorporated unequivocally into the knowledge of the field in question. This double-checking is an intrinsic part of the research strategy and the source of the extraordinary reliability that scientific knowledge can obtain in practice.[52]

The lack of external consistency and/or coherence can create problems for theories at all levels of the cognitive hierarchy [53] Larry Laudan illustrates from the history of science some of the problems that can arise at three levels, the intrascientific level, the normative level, and the level of world views. Intrascientific difficulties result from inconsistency or incompatibility between scientific theories. Laudan cites as an example the problems raised in the late nineteenth century by Kelvin's argument from thermodynamics that the earth could not be as old as the assumptions of uniformitarian geology and evolutionary biology required. The argument caused much concern, particularly for geology and biology, for thermodynamics was better established at the time, and the argument presented by Kelvin meant that the time scales of uniformitarian geology and evolutionary biology would have to be so radically altered as to reduce or destroy their explanatory potential. Kelvin's argument was logically valid, but as it turned out, his premises were incorrect. He had assumed that the earth had no internal source of energy and had calculated its age on the basis of the second law of thermodynamics, whereas it is now assumed that nuclear energy is produced within the earth's crust. The assumption of an internal source of energy allowed all three theories to be retained, but had radioactivity not been discovered, all three theories would have remained under question. This illustrates a point I made earlier, that science is as concerned with epistemic problems as it is with more obviously pragmatic ones.

Normative conceptual problems occur when a new theory is not compatible with the current methodological norms. Laudan illustrates this by claiming that Newton's theories could not be seen as compatible with the inductivist norm of the time. In this case, the hypothetical-deductive methodology replaced the inductivist methodology. This example illustrates the point that accepted methodology may itself change, in response to a new theory or set of theories; and it reinforces the point made earlier that the scientific process involves a reiteration loop in which the acceptance of a new theory may demand a change at the metatheoretic level.

External conceptual problems at a higher level occur when scientific theory is inconsistent with the accepted world view. Newtonian science in the eighteenth century, with its ontology of forces, was in conflict with the prevailing mechanical world view of physical scientists, which saw properties located with material objects. Laudan sees much of the philosophy and science of the time as directed towards making sense of the idea of action at a distance.[54]

Such illustrations, along with Laudan's more detailed discussion, show that while external inconsistencies can be and have been tolerated by science, they are always taken seriously as indications that something is amiss. They cast doubt on the offending theories and lead to work aimed at removing the problem. Analogously with maps, then, theories of the same reality should ideally be externally consistent and coherent. If a theory is not externally consistent, it will generate statements that conflict with those generated by other theories. And if it is not externally coherent, its scope will be limited like that of an itinerary map, and it will receive no support from the further body of accepted knowledge. Thus, the external consistency and coherence of a theory are a further guide to its validity.

I started this section looking for ways in which the validity of theories could be determined. It turns out that theories, like maps, are valid insofar as they are reliable guides to action and decision making, and that explanatory and predictive success and the criteria of internal and external consistency and coherence are guides to their reliability and hence to their validity.

4.2.7 Theories—Limits on Their Scope of Valid Application

Scientific theories, as I have shown, are valid insofar as they provide solutions to problems within a certain domain, that is, insofar as they increase understanding of and control over the domain in question. This validity can be assessed (as can that of maps) empirically directly, and via internal and external consistency and coherency checks. It now remains to explore whether, like maps, they have limits on the scope of their valid application.

To do this, I return to Toulmin's example of the principle of the rectilinear propagation of light. The importance of this principle is that over a wide range of circumstances it is an adequate representation of light. But on a naive interpretation of the principle, it is patently false. The phenomena of refraction and diffraction show that light does not always travel in straight lines. These phenomena do not destroy the value of the principle, but they do limit the use of the techniques that come along with the principle, or require them to be supplemented in some way. Toulmin points out that every branch of science, and more particularly every theory, has a limited scope. Each theory can explain only a limited range of phenomena. In science, argues Toulmin, law-like statements in ordinary language are always subject to qualification. For example, the statement, "This is made of wood, so it must float," must be qualified by something like, "—unless it is lignum vitæ, or is waterlogged," if it is to be true. These limitations are not written into the theories, as it is a matter for research to discover them and they may often have to be modified. As Toulmin points out, "The physicist seeks the form and scope of regularities which are found to happen, not universally, but at most on the whole."[55] A great deal of the training of a scientist is concerned with the scopes of different laws and theories.[56]

In the case of refraction, the techniques of geometrical optics made possible by the discovery of the principle of the rectilinear propagation of light were modified by Snell's Law. This states that "whenever any ray of light is incident at the surface which separates two media, it is bent in such a way that the ratio of the sine of the angle of incidence to the sine of the angle of refraction is always a constant quantity for those two media."[57] But let us imagine what we might have to do to test Snell's Law. We have to get light to travel in sufficiently straight and narrow beams, and in sufficiently precise directions. This cannot be done simply by placing a screen with a narrow slit in it in front of a light source, because, as the source will be at least a millimeter or two across, we will get a fan of light diverging from the slit. But if we place another slit screen beyond the first one and let the slit in the first act as a source for the beam that hits the slit in the second screen, then in principle, according to geometrical optics, we can make the beam as narrow as we please by progressively narrowing the slits. This works, up to a point, but beyond that point, the beam, instead of getting narrower, just blurs, or appears spread out and fuzzy. The phenomenon of diffraction sets a limit on the scope of geometrical optics.

As with maps, this limitation on the valid use of theories is directly related to the interests that guided its construction, the sorts of problem it was intended to solve for the user, because it is these problems that guide the selection of the domain. The principle of the rectilinear propagation of light is valid within the scope of the problem it was intended to solve—the explanation and prediction of areas of light and shade.

The fact that theories are deeply compatible means that the limitations of any single theory may lead to the construction of further theories. The phenomenon of diffraction indicated a further problem about light, requiring another theory to solve it. Such a theory should be consistent with the theory that raised the problem (at least to the point, in the above example, of allowing that under certain limiting conditions light can be regarded as travelling in straight lines), and ultimately more general theories with wider scope may unify the theories in question. Nonetheless, each theory, no matter how wide its scope, will have a limited range of valid applicability related to the purpose for which it was constructed. As Cartwright has shown, we have to make a tradeoff between the level of generality of a theory and the degree to which it is accurate in detail. No single theory can encompass every feature of reality.

In this chapter, I set out to explore the extension of the model of scientific theories as maps to include the nature of validity. The nature of the validity of both maps and theories hinges on the fact that both can guide action and decision making, and are valid to the extent that they reliably do just that. This notion of validity led me to explore whether the content and the form of maps and theories were related to the purposes for which they were constructed. The fact that they were so related led to the further belief that any assessment of their validity must be related to the purposes for which they were constructed, rather than being simply a matter of the relationship between theory and data, as the positivists thought. An analysis of the methods of mapping and of sciencing pointed to greater complexity and variety than was apparent in the positivist accounts of the scientific method, and methods, too, were found to relate to the purposes for which the maps and theories were constructed.

The complexity and variety of the methods of both mapping and sciencing led to the suspicion that the relationship between maps/theories and data could not be the simple logistic one of positivism. Yet it was in just such a relationship between theory and (incorrigible) data that the positivist notions of validity as a truth-preserving relationship and the objectivity of science lay.

I turned then to look at the ways in which validity was actually established and the nature of the objectivity of science. As I showed in chapter 3, while observation is by no means incorrigible, a perceptual foundationalism does underlie scientific belief. And in this chapter, I argued that the establishment of validity was a public affair. This raised the question of what made maps and scientific theories the sorts of thing on which public agreement could be reached. Ziman's argument, which I elaborated, was that maps and theories are consensible by virtue of the fact that they are limited to abstracting from the domain the sort of thing that can be agreed upon.

This notion, that theories and maps are consensible because they are a special kind of abstraction from reality, has profound implications for the notion of validity. For while the validity of both maps and theories can be established on the basis of explanatory and predictive success and the criteria of internal and external consistency and coherence, the fact that they are abstractions from reality means that they have a limited scope of valid application that is related to the purposes for which they were constructed.

4.3 The Mapping Model of Knowledge

In chapter 1, I argued that sociology as a discipline faced serious methodological and pragmatic problems. The nature of these problems was such that any solutions to be had were to be found in the metatheory of sociology. In chapter 2, I explored the major metatheoretical positions that had some bearing on the problems faced by sociology in particular and by the social sciences in general. I argued that a naturalist realist position was the only position with any chance of providing an adequate set of solutions. But while naturalist realism is healthy and developing rapidly at the metaphilosophical and philosophical levels, there was as yet no adequate naturalist realist methodology of science. And a discussion of the humanist and relativist positions raised further problems that an adequate naturalist realist methodology would have to take into account.

The task I set myself in chapters 3 and 4 was to develop an adequate naturalist realist methodology of science. Such a methodology would in principle be able to determine the validity of theories in a perspective-neutral way, because the naturalist realist metaphilosophy insists that the validity of theories is determinable, perhaps only partially, but in some significant way, by reality. But an adequate methodology would also have to take account of both the theory-ladenness of perception and the involvement of social factors in both the creation and the assessment of scientific theories, affecting not only scientific procedures, but the content of scientific theories.

The mapping model of knowledge (MMK) that I have developed in chapters 3 and 4, does, I believe, take adequate account of these factors. Both the theory-ladenness of perception and the existence of perspective-neutral criteria for the assessment of validity are accounted for by using Campbell's evolutionary model of socially validated perceptual foundationalism. This model proposes that within the range for which human perceptual capabilities evolved it is possible for perceptual beliefs to be socially validated, even cross-culturally. For social validation to be extended to the institution of science, which in many cases deals with objects, events, and processes outside that perceptual range, two conditions must be met. The first is that the beliefs of the institution are open to rigorous criticism from both within and without the institution. The second is that the methods of science are such that they allow reality to play a part in the selection of beliefs. It is to the extent that science satisfies these criteria that it can be considered reliable.

Ziman's social model of science, which consists of a body of scientists, a set of consensible beliefs, and a set of consensual beliefs, and which sees scientific theories as maps, takes account of both of these factors. I extended this model, using insights from Harré and Toulmin, to develop a generalized methodology of science that explores the way in which the validity of theories is both relative to the interests that guide theory creation and a function of the reality that they represent. The fact that theories are relative to guiding interests has the effect of limiting their scope of valid application, but does not mean that they cannot be assessed in a perspective-neutral way, given those interests. Indeed, it is the very fact that science is ultimately a guide to action and decision making, and is guided by interests, that allows it to be assessed pragmatically by how well it facilitates understanding of and control over nature. It is in precisely this way that science "opens a window on Nature, allowing her to speak".

The mapping model of knowledge, then, is not only descriptive, in the sense that it is based on how humans in their social setting can and do know—it is prescriptive in that it provides criteria for the perspective-neutral assessment of validity. And more, it has the advantage, as did the positivist model of science, of being easy to apply, for mapping is so nearly intuitive. The fact that the nature and the criteria of the determination of validity are the same for maps and scientific theories means that the mapping model of knowledge can act as a powerful heuristic.

The naturalist realist methodology developed in this chapter does, then, address the problems raised by relativism. In the next chapter, I apply the naturalist realist philosophy and the mapping model of knowledge to addressing the problems raised for a naturalist realism by humanism. In following chapters, I apply these same tools to the solution of the specific problems faced by the discipline of sociology.

III

THE TOOLS APPLIED

In Part II, I developed an evolutionary naturalist realist methodology of science that allowed relativism the point that the validity of theories must be assessed relative to the problems they were intended to solve. But I also argued that it was because of this, rather than despite it, that reality itself is able to play a part in the assessment of scientific theory, thus providing perspective-neutral criteria for the assessment of scientific theories. In Part III, I apply the tools developed in Part II to develop a metatheory of sociology. In chapter 5, I address the outstanding problems that humanism raises against the possibility of a naturalist realist metatheory of sociology. In chapter 6, I look at the implications of the complexity of sociology for an adequate methodology. In chapter 7, I take up the problem of the fragmentation or sectarianism of sociological knowledge.

5

Validity and Reality in the Social Sciences

Scratch the world of appearances and out leaps the hidden reality All is revealed once the right question is asked.

—Rosaleen Love, *Where Are They?*

The mapping model of knowledge (MMK), the model of scientific knowledge developed from the natural sciences in the last chapter, takes account of the many critiques of empiricism and goes beyond them to establish a more complex notion of the validity of scientific theories. Within the MMK the validity of any theory is socially determined, and is always relative to the problem being addressed. In this way, the MMK models both the theory-ladenness of observation and the fact that the social processes involved in the construction of scientific knowledge affect both the content and the methods of science.

Despite this, the MMK is essentially both naturalist and realist. This is because validity is determined not solely in relation to a problem or set of problems, but also in relation to a unified reality. While the problem-relatedness of a theory is the major determinant of its scope of valid application and in addition determines the nature of the essentially pragmatic empirical tests, it is the relationship to a unified reality that underlies the internal and external consistency and coherence checks and makes possible a unified science.

The methodology developed in the MMK shows how the validity of a theory can, given the problem that it was intended to solve, be established in a perspective-neutral way by appeal to a unified reality. It therefore constitutes a response to the relativist challenge to realism discussed in §2.3. But it leaves untouched, at least so far, the humanist challenge to a naturalist realism. Recall that in my discussion of humanism in §2.2, I answered several of the humanist challenges to a naturalist realist position. But two were deferred. These were the propositions that interpretive sociology was fundamentally closed to empirical investigation, and that the methods of interpretive sociology have no parallels in the natural sciences. In this chapter, I aim to develop a response to these challenges to a naturalist realism.

Interpretive sociology, recall, was the explanation of social actions in terms of reasons, motives, or intentions. Reasons, motives, and intentions, the humanists argued, have no precise spatiotemporal location, and therefore are not the sorts of things that can be incorporated into a causal explanation of an action. They have a distinct and immaterial nature. It was further argued that even if reasons, motives, and intentions could be given a causal explanation, interpretive understanding was still required, and that the methods of interpretive understanding were unique to the social sciences.

My approach to these challenges involves an examination of the nature of the causal explanations that, because of the essentially pragmatic nature of validity, form the basis of the naturalist realist criteria of validity. But causal explanation is not the only sort of scientific explanation. Explanations in terms of composition, structure, and function are just as much part of science. The validity of these types of explanation depends on their being shown to be instantiated in a causal explanation.

I examine the nature of these types of explanation and explore the nature of their relationship to causal explanation. It turns out that functional explanations are quite distinct from causal explanations, and have their own methodology. While they can be shown to be valid by being instantiated in causal explanations, the nature of the instantiation relationship between functional and causal analyses of a system is far from straightforward. Nonetheless, it can be specified.

A detailed analysis of functional explanation shows that the mentalist explanations of interpretive sociology are best interpreted as functional accounts of the person. The validity of interpretive sociology therefore depends upon showing that these functional accounts are causally instantiated. While the instantiation relationship does not involve a type-type reduction of reasons to causes, I show that a valid functional account is nonetheless constrained by empirical evidence. Interpretive sociology is not completely closed to empirical investigation, nor are its methods fundamentally different from those of the natural sciences, for interpretive sociology shares a general methodology with all functional explanations, whether natural or social.

5.1 Cause and Reality

The naturalist realist thesis assumes that everything that exists can in principle interact, either directly or indirectly, with everything else that exists. Knowledge can be obtained only via interactions with the environment. The naturalist realist thesis, then, assumes that knowable reality is unified by interactions. These interactions are commonly called causal connections. Causal connections are therefore processes, and causal explanations explain changes in the state of a system by establishing the causal connections that bring about that change of state. The reality of any process or entity can be established if it can be shown to have a valid causal explanation.

Causal explanations have long been recognized as an essential part of science, but they are pivotal to a unified science, and hence to the notion of validity developed in the MMK. It is therefore important to be able to distinguish causal explanations from other types of explanation and description.

A brief discussion of Aristotle's notion of cause is as good a place to start as any, for although the concept of cause has narrowed considerably since Aristotle explored it, his broader conception of cause includes the other major types of scientific explanation recognized today. Aristotle argued that, for a complete explanation of anything, one might have to invoke four distinct kinds of cause.[1] These causes are those factors without which a particular state of affairs would not have existed or come about, or would at least have been very different from its actual state. Aristotle illustrates the nature of these four types of cause by showing how they contribute to the making of a statue.

To carve a statue, one must have the material (a block of marble in Aristotle's example) from which to make it. The marble is the *material* cause of the statue. The activity of the sculptor then transforms the marble block into the statue. The sculptor who carves the statue is the *efficient* cause. But the sculptor cannot carve the statue without an idea of the form the statue is to take— without a blueprint or design of the finished product. The geometrical form of the finished statue is its *formal* cause. Finally, the statue would not have been carved at all if its carving was to serve no purpose or function for either the sculptor or whoever ordered it. The purpose of the statue Aristotle called its *final* cause. While the example given here illustrates Aristotle's causal principles with reference to a purposely produced artifact, Aristotle intended the principles to apply to any object, event, or process.

The notion of efficient cause is all that is retained in current usage of the word "cause", and it is in this sense that causal interaction is to be interpreted. But approximations of Aristotle's notions of material, formal, and final causes still have their place in modern scientific explanation. I shall discuss them briefly here, so that they can be distinguished from causal explanations.

Causal interactions occur between entities, be they objects, processes, or whatever. Descriptions of such entities in terms of their material composition, an approximation of Aristotle's notion of material cause, are an important part of science. They can be distinguished from causal explanations because material composition and causal explanation are appropriate answers to quite different sorts of questions. A description of the material composition of an entity is a response to a question about what something is made of, whereas a causal explanation is an appropriate response to a question about how a state of affairs came to be.

Aristotle's formal and final causes, or approximations of them, also still play a part in scientific explanation, and they too can be distinguished by the sort of question they answer. The word "structure" is commonly used now to indicate the form or arrangement of an entity or entities, and takes the place of formal cause. A structural description is an appropriate response to a question about how the components of something are organized or arranged. The distinctly teleological notion of final cause is now seen as a special case of "function", one reserved for artifacts. The final cause of an object is the purpose it is intended to serve or the function it is intended to perform. But the concept of function is not necessarily teleological, for it is perfectly possible for something to serve a purpose without having been designed specifically for it. A sparrow's wings, for example, are functional for flight, but were not *designed* at all, let alone for that purpose.

Functional explanations, like causal explanations, apply to state changes in a system, but unlike causal explanations, functional explanations are not applicable to all systems. A fundamental distinction can be made between open systems and closed systems. Closed systems have no energy exchange across their boundaries. They are completely isolated from their environment. Although completely closed systems may theoretically exist, they could not be known, and are assumed not to exist, with the exception of the universe as a whole. In practice, talk of closed systems refers to systems that are so insulated from the environment that the exchange of energy across their boundaries is small enough compared to within-system exchanges to be ignored for the purposes of the study.[2] Closed systems tend towards thermodynamic equilibrium, a state of maximum entropy. The physical structures that may result from interactions within closed systems (for example, the crystals that precipitate from a solution) are equilibrium structures. Such structures can be explained by applying the (causal) laws of thermodynamics to the behavior of the closed system.[3]

Open systems, on the other hand, have non-equilibrium structures. Living systems are the paradigm open system. Such systems are called dissipative structures because they constantly convert structural energy to thermal energy and dissipate it into the environment. Nonetheless, they are stable structures, maintaining their organization by "feeding" on negentropy from the environment. Because of this, and unlike those of non-dissipative equilibrium structures, the components of dissipative structures can be characterized both causally and functionally. They can be characterized in terms of thermodynamic processes and explained as the result of those processes. But they can also be characterized and explained in terms of their function as members of a coherent and interrelated organization that maintains a non-equilibrium dissipative structure. This is because as long as the system exists in relative autonomy from its environment, "feeding" on negentropy, the stability of the system constitutes a constraint on the variety of possible configurations of the components. Each component can therefore be seen in relation to how it functions for the stability of the whole.[4] A functional explanation is a response to a question about the role a component plays for the system as a whole.

Causal explanations, then, are explanations in terms of causal or generative mechanisms, and are distinct from descriptions in terms of material composition, structural descriptions, and functional explanations. Note that the concept of "causation" here is defined minimally as "connectedness." The nature of any specific cause or connection is contingent, a matter for empirical investigation. This is because the realist model of knowledge I develop assumes no more than that there is a real world existing independently of us as knowers and that we can know the world only via our interactions with it. The nature both of the world and its connections are a matter for investigation. And in the light of the radical ontology implied by the MMK (developed further in chapter 6), the specification of the nature of causation is as theory-dependent as the specification of any other entity or process.

But in the light of modern science, causal interactions of whatever kind are understood to involve energy exchange and to take place in space-time. Furthermore, any entities included in a purely causal explanation have a reasonably precise set of spatiotemporal coordinates.[5] For any putative entity, then, an indicator of its reality is that it is in fact instantiated in a causal explanation, and hence that it has a reasonably precise set of spatiotemporal coordinates. I refer to entities that are instantiated in space-time in this way as *actual* entities.

None of this is to say that the material composition and structure of an entity, or the fact that an entity has a function, are irrelevant to causal interaction. It is only to say that the existence of structural descriptions or functional explanations in the absence of causal specifications are not sufficient to establish the reality of anything, because they can apply equally to imaginary objects. The ultimate test of reality is whether the entity, property, or process in question is causal, where causality is defined in terms of energy exchange and is located in space-time. And to the naturalist realist it is the establishment of causal relations so defined that unifies science.

The significance of assigning efficient causality this role can be illustrated by looking at Rupert Sheldrake's hypothesis of formative causation, which has been widely criticized as being unscientific.[6] In *The Presence of the Past,* Sheldrake takes a grab bag of anomalies, problems, and unexplained or partially explained features of science and interprets them in the light of his new and radical theory. Among other things, he deals with the varied phenomena of atavism, apprenticeship-type learning in humans, group behavior in humans and other animals, the transmission of societal forms of organization and cultural belief systems, and the formation of crystals. Many, though not all, of these areas and the others dealt with by Sheldrake, pose fundamental problems for science, and Sheldrake's theory of formative causation aims to give a materialist, unified, and indeed unitary, explanation of all of them.

Sheldrake proposes the existence of a new type of field, the morphic field. Morphic fields are non-material fields of influence that shape the form and behavior of natural objects and systems. These fields are localized round the system in question, and yet are non-local in the sense that they do not disappear if and when the system itself ceases to exist. There is a sense in which they transcend space and time. Natural systems "tune in" to their appropriate morphic fields, and it is in this sense that all natural systems, according to Sheldrake, have a "memory".

Information is acquired by a morphic field via a kind of resonance, morphic resonance, which involves non-energetic transfer of information. The more a particular sort of behavior is repeated, the stronger the morphic field becomes, and the greater the ease with with such behavior is accomplished in the future. Thus, according to Sheldrake, the more often that a new molecule or crystal is synthesized, the more that people learn to windsurf, the more that rats learn to solve a new problem, the greater the ease with which these tasks will be accomplished by their successors in the attempt.

Sheldrake's motivation for developing such a radical theory becomes apparent in his discussion of the laws of nature. There is order in nature. Sugar crystals, for example, have a distinct structure, and scientists have more or less precisely discovered the laws governing their formation. But what sort of things are these laws? Sheldrake points out that according to traditional ways of thinking, these laws are eternal and unchanging. Sugar crystals formed perfectly well before scientists discovered the laws governing their formation. In this sense, the laws existed even before the first sugar crystal was formed. Sheldrake challenges this idealist view of the laws of nature, as he rejects both the dualist view of reality it implies, and the assumption, in an evolutionary world, that these laws are unchanging. The laws of nature, he suggests, may be more like habits. As every new piece of behavior, from the bonding of atoms to the learning of a new skill, is repeated, a morphic field is set up by the process of morphic resonance. When the activity is repeated yet again, the object or system involved in some way "tunes in" to the existing morphic field, getting information from it, and at the same time strengthening it.

Sheldrake, then, is able to explain a diverse range of phenomena by invoking morphic fields. For example, atavism, whereby an individual animal adopts a form or structure of an evolutionary ancestor, is accounted for by the notion that morphic fields do not disappear when the system with which they are associated disappears. An animal may therefore "tune in" to an ancestral morphic field, allowing development of the ancestral form.

But Sheldrake's presentation of the hypothesis of formative causation is problematic in a number of ways. He presents the reader with numerous false dichotomies; he provides no evidence for his theory in terms of, for example, the confirmation of novel predictions; and the experiments that he suggests might provide such evidence could not in fact do so.[7] And Sheldrake's treatment of the problem areas of science is incredibly shallow. To illustrate, atavism can be explained by seeing genetic systems as hierarchical arrangements. Small changes in the timing of action by controller genes can lead to major changes in form. Horses, though descended from five-toed mammals, now have only one toe. But a small mutation in a controller gene can lead horses to seemingly revert to an earlier, three-toed form. Although science does not yet have all of the details, there is no apparent need for Sheldrake's theory here. The horse always did carry the genetic information necessary for the formation of multiple toes. A small mutation of a controller gene is not only enough to explain the development of three toes, but also shows the phenomenon is not actually a reversion, because the genes were always there. This possibility was not discussed by Sheldrake.

The problem of learning skills illustrates one of the many inconsistencies in Sheldrake's theory. Morphic fields must transcend both space and time in order to make it possible, as Sheldrake claims that it is, for rats in New Zealand to find learning a puzzle quicker and easier by virtue of the fact that rats in England have already mastered it. But if this is so, why does Sheldrake explain the need for a teacher in sensory-motor skills by the fact that proximity to the teacher's morphic field is what makes the learning easier?

Criticisms of Sheldrake have been primarily directed at the sort of problems already mentioned. In his own defense, Sheldrake cites the history of science, pointing out that radical new theories have never been well received initially, and must be given time to develop. But while this is true, and there is an outside chance that Sheldrake might be right, there is a further and more serious reason for considering this unlikely.

The theory's most serious problem is the fact that Sheldrake radically redefines causation. Sheldrake's aim was to produce a naturalist realist theory, and further, a materialist one. Consequently, he explicitly rejects platonic dualism in favor of a causally unified view of the universe. Sheldrake's morphic fields interact causally with the material world. But if morphic fields also transcend time and space, and are involved in non-energetic transfer of information, as Sheldrake claims, then not only is his notion of causality radically different from the scientific view, but his self-claimed materialism becomes impossible to sustain. Sheldrake realizes the importance of causal interaction for a unified science, but by divorcing the notion of causality from materiality, albeit unconsciously, he has either produced an empty theory or is committed to a radical Cartesian dualism. This is the strongest case for regarding the theory of formative causation as unscientific.

Causal explanations and descriptions, then, are essential to a unified science. This is not to say that the notions of structure and function are not also an important part of scientific inquiry. They are, for example, absolutely pivotal to much evolutionary biology, and also to sociology, as I show in the next section. But they cannot be used to determine the reality of any entity or process, as can instantiation in a causal analysis.

5.2 Structure, Function, and Cause in Sociology

As we have seen, causal explanation carries the weight of unifying science, and a unified science is essential for the establishment of the validity of scientific theories. The specification of the actual entities that take part in a causal explanation (i.e., the material components of the system in question) is likewise essential. It is thus important to be able to recognize the difference between causal, structural, and functional explanations, and to establish the nature of any relationship between them. All are commonly used across the range of disciplines, but because the focus of this thesis is the metatheory of sociology, I shall return to the examples of theories of deviance outlined in §1.2.3 to illustrate their use.

The structuralist approach to sociology, recall, was based on the assumptions that (1) societies exist *sui generis,* (2) they have a structure (i.e., they are not just an undifferentiated mass of people or institutions), and (3) their structure affects the people who live in the society, both materially and in terms of the values, attitudes, and beliefs they hold. Thus, a fundamental part of the structuralist approach to society is to identify the components of society and describe the social structure. The structuralist approach involves both compositional and structural analyses. Parsons, for example, saw society as composed primarily of institutions such as the family and the education system. The various institutions of society acted together to produce a stable whole. Marx saw society as composed of people, and essentially structured along class lines, where a person's class was determined by the nature of her relationship to the means of production. In a capitalist society, the capitalists own the means of production, and by virtue of that fact hold more power than the working class. Feminists see society structured along gender lines, with males dominating females. A structural analysis of a society, then, is simply a description of the components of that society and their relationships to one another.

While based on structural analyses, structural explanations may have to do with how the structure came about (causal explanation); the effects of the structure (again, causal explanation); how a particular part of the structure functions to maintain the whole (functional explanation); or how a particular aspect of the structure serves the interests of a particular group (functional explanation). Thus, structural explanations may turn out to be either functional explanations or causal explanations.

Functional explanations in sociology usually derive from a structuralist approach, from either the consensus perspective or the conflict perspective. While sharing the general structuralist assumption, these perspectives differ in that the consensus perspective sees societies as relatively stable and homogeneous, whereas the conflict perspective insists that societies contain various groups of people with differing interests, some of these groups having more power than others.

As we saw in §1.2.3, Erikson's study of deviance is quite clearly from the consensus perspective. Erikson argues that the public censure of deviant behavior maintains a society's boundaries by reinforcing the norms involved, and hence that deviance is functional for the stability of society. While having no pretensions to being a causal theory, Erikson's study is very important, raising, as we saw, such questions as whether the correctional institutions of society are actually organized to produce deviant behavior despite their overt purposes.

Functional explanations have fallen from favor in sociology of late. The reason seems to be that functional explanations are conflated with the functionalist perspective. Typified by Talcott Parsons,[8] the functionalist perspective attempts to account for a social activity by referring to its function for another social activity, institution, or society as a whole. A functionalist, for example, would hold that deviance exists *because* it is functional for society. This is to confuse cause and function, is teleological, and is rightly condemned. Functionalism has been criticized on a number of other counts,[9] but these criticisms apply not to functional explanations considered as a *part* of sociology, but to the limitations of a functionalist approach as the *only* approach to sociology.

Causal explanations are quite different from functional ones. Rather than showing how something functions for a system, causal explanations attempt to show the mechanisms involved in producing any state of affairs, or what previous state of affairs led to a consequent state of affairs. Cicourel's detailed study of juvenile offenders, for example, explores the social factors relevant to the production of the deviant *qua* deviant.[10] Causal explanations of deviance of a structural type are offered, for example, by Marxist sociologists such as Chambliss and Gordon.[11] Chambliss argues that the structure of capitalism as it is instantiated in modern capitalist societies creates both the desire to consume, and, in a considerable proportion of the population, the inability to earn sufficient money to cater for their (largely manufactured) needs. Many try to satisfy these needs illegally. Thus, the capitalist economic system directly affects the sort of crime committed in capitalist countries. Gordon argues that while the crime rate is spread evenly across socioeconomic classes, the type of crime committed by members of each class differs. Middle-class people are more inclined toward white-collar crime, while the working class contribute more crimes of violence. Gordon attributes this difference to different opportunities, showing that the class structure affects the type of crime committed. The last two examples show how the structure of society can have causal effects.

In this section, I have gone some way toward distinguishing structural, functional, and causal explanation in sociology. Functional and causal explanations are distinct types, distinguishable in terms of their content. They answer different sorts of questions about the systems they are concerned with. Structural explanations also answer a distinctive sort of question, about the composition and organization of a system. But these questions refer either to the

functional composition and organization of a system or to the causally instantiated composition and organization of the system. Structural explanations,
then, may be either functional or causal.

The examples I have used here are very straightforward. It is not always
easy, as I shall argue in §5.3, to distinguish functional and causal explanations.
Yet the task is vital, because, as I argue in §5.5, it is by distinguishing causal and
functional explanations and showing the relationship between the two that the
dichotomy between mind and body that underlies humanism is to be resolved.

5.3 Distinguishing Causal and Functional Explanations

In the last section, I distinguished four types of explanation: compositional, structural, causal, and functional. Descriptions of composition and structure may form part of either causal or functional explanations, but the latter are
distinct. It is important to be able to distinguish causal and functional explanations and to show the relationship between them. If no such relationship can be
found, we face the possibility of a radical cause/function dualism, because it is
through causal explanation and the unique instantiation of components in the
space-time framework that the unification of science is achieved. The examples
of causal and functional explanation given in the last section were easy to distinguish and gave an intuitive idea of the difference between these types of explanation. But they are not always easy to distinguish.

Robert Cummins provides a careful analysis of the various types of scientific explanation and a detailed discussion of the distinction between causal
and functional explanation.[12] Cummins argues that scientific explanation can
be divided into two major kinds, *causal subsumption* and *analysis*. Causal subsumption explains change from one state of affairs to another by subsumption
under transition theories. Transition theories are designed to explain changes as
effects, and are thus explanatory only if they are causal.[13] Transition theories,
then, appeal to causal laws, i.e., to "laws that subsume cause-effect pairs".[14]

But causal laws are not necessarily immediately recognizable. The equational form of many physical laws obscures their causal nature. Cummins illustrates with the pendulum law, which tells us that the period of a pendulum's
swing varies in proportion to the length of the pendulum.

$$(1) \quad T = 2\pi \sqrt{l/g}$$

The law as it stands contains no obvious reference to events. The period of a
pendulum of length 0.5m is usually explained like this:

$$(2) \quad T = 2\pi \sqrt{l/g}$$
$$\underline{l = 0.5m}$$
$$T = 1.419 \text{ sec.}$$

There is still no mention here of causation, or explicit reference to the cause-effect pair. Here the explanation is tacitly but commonly considered to take the form of DN explanation. Because of this, the fact that an explanation is in DN form is not sufficient to distinguish causal explanations.[15] This can be illustrated by the following formula for calculating the length of a pendulum where its period is known. Although of the same form as (2), this is not a causal explanation. The length of a pendulum is said to determine its period, but not vice versa.

$$(3) \quad T = 2\pi \sqrt{l/g}$$
$$T = 1.419 \text{ sec.}$$
$$l = 0.5m$$

In fact, Cummins points out, neither (2) nor (3) is an adequate causal explanation. An adequate causal explanation must be of a form that takes account of our intuitions that length determines period but not vice versa. He suggests an alternative form:

(4) (i)   A change of u to v in l
           causes a change of
           $2\pi (\sqrt{v}/g - \sqrt{u}/g)$ in T;
     (ii) l increased from 0.25 to 0.5m
     (iii) T increased from 1.003 sec to 1.419 sec.

This is clearly a case of causal subsumption, whereas (3) put in this form is simply wrong. Formulae like (2) are useful abstractions from the causal law, but their equational form obscures the causal elements of the transition laws.[16]

The methodology of causal subsumption has been widely discussed by both philosophers and scientists. Cummins briefly surveys these discussions, and abstracts from them three commonly accepted canons of scientific method: *causality*, *determinism*, and *justification*. The canon of *causality* is the requirement that only genuine causes, as opposed, say, to mere correlations, are to be invoked in transition theories. The use of shared needles may strongly correlate with the contraction of AIDS, and as such may be a good predictor for AIDS, but unless one can control the spread of AIDS by controlling the sharing of needles, or has sufficient understanding of the causal mechanisms involved in the transmission of AIDS to show that sharing needles could be part of the causal chain, no causal claim can be made.

The canon of *determinism* is the requirement that no uncaused or idle events be allowed. Since the aim of causal theories is to explain events as the effects of causes, a theory is considered problematic if it allows uncaused events. Quantum theory, while a highly successful predictor, is controversial for this reason.[17]

The canon of *justification* refers to the requirement that causes and effects must be independently observable or measurable. Cummins's example of a common use of the principle of justification here is illuminating. Anxiety is often defined operationally in terms of galvanic skin responses (gsr) because it cannot be measured except by such external manifestations. The application of the canon of justification to this situation means that gsr cannot be explained by anxiety, because anxiety and gsr cannot be measured independently. Any appeal to anxiety as the cause of gsr is therefore considered unjustified. While not particularly sound, this sort of reasoning is nonetheless commonplace. Cummins's point in using this example is to show that it makes sense only on the assumption that gsr is to be explained *only* causally.[18] If anxiety were regarded as a dispositional property of a system, physically instantiated in gsr, then gsr would be best explained by an instantiation law rather than by a transition theory.

Transition theories, of which 4 (i) is an example, specify the properties of a system—in the pendulum example, the property that the period of the pendulum varies with its length. Properties are defined as dispositional or non-dispositional. Cummins defines dispositions as follows:

> To attribute a disposition d to an object x is to assert that the behavior of x is subject to (exhibits or would exhibit) a certain lawlike regularity: to say x has d is to say that x would manifest d (dissolve, shatter) were any of a certain range of events to occur (x is put in water, x is struck sharply).[19]

But while transition theories may specify dispositions, they do not explain them. This is not surprising. The role of transition theories is to explain events or event-types, and dispositions are not events. Yet a great deal of scientific explanation is concerned with the explanation of dispositions—with showing how they occur.[20] Cummins's point here is that, contrary to widespread belief, much of science is not in fact concerned with the strategy of causal subsumption, but rather with what he calls analysis.

Cummins regards the overemphasis on causal explanation in analyses of scientific explanation as due in part to the predominance of the DN form of explanation. But it is only for subsumptive explanations that the DN model is even initially plausible, and only in the case of causal subsumption that it provides as much as a hint of the nature of the explanation.[21] Although analytical explanations can be expressed as subsumption, this form completely obscures their nature, allowing them to be regarded, if they are considered at all, as causal. But whatever the reasons, the concentration of analyses of scientific methodology and explanation on the methods of causal subsumption has led to the conflation of analysis with subsumption, and a lot of ignorance with respect to the methodology of analysis.

While the strategy of causal subsumption results in transition theories that explain state changes in systems, analysis is the appropriate strategy for explaining the properties of those systems. Property theories explain what it is for a system to have a particular property. Ideally, the explanation will show the components of the system and their properties, and show that when the components are organized in a particular way, the system property to be explained must exist Typically, the first step in such explanations is the analysis of the system into its components and a specification of their mode of organization, which Cummins calls *compositional* analysis. Next comes the analysis of the properties of the components. Property analyses of either the system or its components or subsystems are divided into the analysis of dispositional properties, which Cummins calls *functional* analysis, and the analysis of non-dispositional properties, which he calls *property* analysis.

According to Cummins, the analytical methodology is subject to methodological principles that differ from, but run parallel to, those of causal subsumption (see Figure 5.1).[22] The first requirement is that instantiation laws be derivable from nomic attributions specifying the properties of the components of a system. If they are not, then there is no reason to believe one is analyzing the property that is actually instantiated in the system to be analyzed.[23] The second requirement is that the analyzed property should not reappear in the analysis, as this is to reintroduce the thing that is to be explained. The third requirement is that the analyzing properties should be confirmable independently of the property being analyzed.[24]

So far, through a discussion of Cummins's analysis of scientific explanation, I have shown that while causal subsumption and analysis have different aims and produce different sorts of explanations, they may easily be confused. This is partly because causal explanation has been widely regarded as the only kind of scientific explanation, and thus every scientific explanation has been regarded as causal, and partly because the structure of scientific explanation has been regarded as DN. The DN explanatory structure cannot distinguish causal from other types of explanation, and yet as a model of explanation it makes sense initially only if explanation is assumed to be causal. Functional theories are analytic and therefore differ from causal theories in both their aims and the details of their methodology, but have often been mistaken for causal theories, and then criticized for not meeting the principles of causal explanation. Functional theories can be distinguished from causal theories, but this distinction will be in terms of the aims of the theories (the questions they are intended to answer), their methodologies, and their content, rather than their structure.

FIGURE 5.1

Cummins's analysis of the types of possible explanation using common premises

TYPE OF EXPLANATION

Subsumption	Analysis (includes functional, compositional and structural explanation)

WHAT IS EXPLAINED

System S makes a transition from State S1 to State S2	System S exhibits (possesses) property P

CONSTRAINTS ON EXPLANATION

• Only genuine casual laws to be invoked • No uncaused events (transitions) • Causes and effects independently testable and confirmable	• Only instantiation laws genuinely derivable from basic nomic attributions to be invoked • No analysed properties reappear in the analysis • Nomic attributions and analyses independently testable and confirmable

5.4 The Relationship between Causal and Functional Theories

In the previous section, I argued that functional explanations are easily confused with causal explanations, and showed the grounds on which they are distinguishable. But I have still not shown the sort of relationship that exists between causal and functional theories. To do this, I continue initially with Cummins's analysis, as it not only shows the relationship between the two kinds of theory but also demonstrates the significance of functional analysis to the social sciences.

I start with Cummins's formal definition of functional analysis:

> In the context of science, to ascribe a function to something is to ascribe a capacity to it that is singled out by its role in an analysis of some capacity of a containing system. When a capacity of a containing system is appropriately explained by analysis, the analyzing capacities emerge as functions.
>
> Functional analysis consists in analyzing a disposition into a number of less problematic dispositions such that a programmed manifestation of these analyzing dispositions amounts to a manifestation of the analyzed disposition.[25]

The schematic diagrams in electronics and the flow charts of manufacturing processes are typical functional analyses. In these examples, the symbols represent any physical object whatever that has a certain capacity. This need not always be the case. In physiological analyses, the symbols usually represent the particular organ having the capacity. But these could be replaced by symbols signifying general capacities. The heart symbol, for example, could be replaced by a more general symbol for a pump.[26]

The analysis of dispositions often parallels the compositional analysis of a system, particularly with artifacts. For example, in the flow chart of a power station, the generator or generators pictured usually do represent actual generators in the power station. Nonetheless, the concepts of structure and function must be kept distinct, as this correlation is often absent, particularly in natural systems, but in some artifacts as well. Complex human mental capacities, for example, can be broken down into other less complex capacities, but none of these are capacities of localized components of the brain. The same thing applies to sophisticated computers.[27]

This point shows that functional analyses in general are only indirectly constrained by the composition of the system, and that the sort of constraint that operates will vary according to the type of functional analysis. The system and/or its parts must have the analyzed capacities, that is, the capacities must be instantiated, either in the system as a whole or its parts, or we would have

Mapping Reality

FIGURE 5.2

Varieties of functional analysis

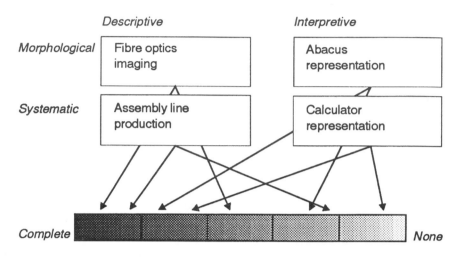

no reason to suppose that we have analyzed the capacity as it is instantiated in the system. The validity of the functional analysis depends on its actually being instantiated in the system analyzed. But the type of relationship between the functional organization of the system and its physical structure varies according to the type of functional analysis.[28]

More detailed exploration of the relationship between functional and causal theories, then, depends on a further classification of functional analysis. In providing this finer classification, Cummins first distinguishes *morphological* from *systematic* analysis. The explanatory force of morphological analyses derives from the fact that the physical composition and structure/organization of the sub-systems itself guarantees the transformation of a given input into a given output. No theoretically significant interaction between the sub-systems occurs. A bundle of fiber-optic tubes transforms information in this way and could be given a morphological analysis, as could number representation in an abacus. The explanatory force of systematic analysis, on the other hand, derives from a specification of how the analyzing functions interact in a systematic way to transform inputs. Assembly line production requires systematic analysis, and so does arithmetic computation in a calculator.[29]

The next distinction Cummins makes is between *interpretive* and *descriptive* analysis. Descriptive analysis is appropriate when the analyzing capacities are individually instantiated in the system components, as they are in the assembly line, for example, or a fiber-optic bundle. Interpretive analysis refers to the analysis of systems in which the inputs and outputs are symbolic interpretations rather than physical descriptions.[30] Analyses of both number representation in an abacus and arithmetic calculation in a calculator are examples of interpretive analysis.

Neither the morphological/systematic nor the descriptive/interpretive distinctions are clear-cut. Analyses can be more or less morphological or systematic, more or less descriptive or interpretive. But the categories crosscut one another and are distinct enough to produce a four-way classification of functional analysis (see Figure 5.2). The significance of this classification is that each category has a different sort of relationship to the physical structure—that is, the constraints on instantiation are different in each case.

Functional theories, to be complete and valid, must not only analyze the disposition in question but show how it is instantiated physically in the system. It is the instantiation step that differs according to the type of functional analysis. Morphological analysis is not concerned with interactions (if indeed there are any) between the various sub-capacities. The sub-capacities of a morphological analysis may therefore be instantiated directly and independently in the physical system, and there will be detailed correlations between the sub-capacities and structure displayed in the functional analysis and the components and structure of the physical system. With systematic analyses, what has to be explained is how the interactions between the analyzing capacities are instantiated. Systematic functional analyses, then, will show less detailed correlation with structural features of the physical system.

The same point applies to descriptive and interpretive analyses. By using symbolic inputs, outputs, and function analyses, interpretive functional analyses, particularly systematic ones, need have very little coherence with the instantiating system. The components of an interpretive analysis need have no one-to-one correspondence with the physical components of the system, and the sub-capacities of a systematic analysis may be organized quite differently from the way the components of the physical system are organized. The only constraint that the physical system places on a systematic interpretive functional analysis is that the system as a whole be capable of transforming inputs into outputs consistently with the inputs and outputs specified by the functional analysis.[31]

Cummins's analysis of functional explanation raises an issue that I have not yet dealt with explicitly, the reality or otherwise of any components of a functional analysis. It should by now be clear that the properties analyzed in a functional system can be instantiated in innumerable ways. There is no possibility of a type-type reduction between the states of the physical system and the states of the functional system. But this is not required for the validity of the functional analysis. All that is required is that the functional analysis explain the properties of the physical system. To do that it must at least be compatible with the physical system at the level of input and output. A greater degree of coherence with the physical system may be required in the case of a morphological or descriptive analysis. But the analyzing properties of the system, irrespective of the type of functional analysis, have no independent ontological existence, no unique spatiotemporal location. Rather, they are instantiated in the system as a whole.

Hooker illustrates this point with a discussion of the "virtual governor", a term sometimes used in engineering in functional descriptions of power-generating systems.[32] While agreeing that type-type reduction is out of the question as a means of specifying the relationship between functional and causal entities, Hooker shows that a token-token reduction can be accomplished for each specified case. That is, while the virtual governor is a functional entity that can be instantiated in innumerable ways, in any particular power-generating system with the property of having a virtual governor, it can be shown how the virtual governor is instantiated. And such reduction explains why the two theories in question are empirically equivalent at the input/output level of the system in question. Hooker outlines the situation thus:

> Consider a set of electric generators G, each of which produces alternating current electrical power at 60Hz but with fluctuations in frequency of 10% around some average value. Taken singly the frequency variability of the generators is 10%. Taken joined together in a suitable network, their collective frequency variability is only a fraction of that figure because, statistically, generators momentarily fluctuating behind the average output in phase are compensated for by the remaining generators and conversely generators momentarily ahead in phase have their energy absorbed by the remainder. The entire system functions, from an input/output point of view, as a single generator with a greatly increased frequency reliability, or, as control engineers express it, with a single, more powerful, "virtual governor".[33]

The point here is that the property of "having a virtual governor" is a functional property of the system as a whole, but not a property of any of its parts. It can be instantiated physically in any number of ways, and has no spatiotemporal location that can be localized more closely than the system as a whole. Nonetheless, the property of having a virtual governor is entailed by the properties of the individual generators plus a specification of the structure of the system. "The virtual governor enters discussion only at the level of input/output theory; at the level of component, structure and mechanism it has disappeared."[34]

The point I wish to make here is that the ontological status of functional components is distinctive. The properties of a functional analysis have no spatiotemporal location that can be analyzed more closely than the system as a whole. Physical properties, on the other hand, can be given precise spatiotemporal locations.

Cummins's analysis of explanation is highly significant for the social sciences. Besides showing the necessity for both causal subsumption and analysis in any complete account of explanation, and defining the relationship between them, Cummins's analysis provides an illuminating account of explanations in terms of meanings as a species of functional explanation, namely systematic interpretive analysis. This falls out of Cummins's analysis under the following conditions: firstly that, as Hilary Putnam among others has argued, mental states (reasons, intentions, dispositions) are functional states, relatively high-order properties of the organization of a system;[35] and secondly, that reasons and intentions are, while plain dispositions are not, linguistic by nature. These being so, Cummins can argue that:

> Interpretive analysis is the proper strategy for explaining a sophisticated capacity whose inputs (precipitating conditions) and outputs (manifestations) are specified via their semantic interpretations.[36]

All theories of the mind, then, even the connectionist theories currently being developed as alternatives to the more traditional computational theories of the mind, can be seen as functional analyses. Cummins illustrates this point in a detailed analysis of several well-known psychological theories, showing that none of them ought to be seen as a causal theory of the mind.

But interpretive sociology shares with cognitive psychology the fact that actions are explained in terms of reasons, motives, and intentions. While it may be reasonably sharply distinguished from simple behaviorist psychologies of the stimulus-response variety, Weber, for example, was able to distinguish interpretive sociology from cognitive psychology only on the grounds that the actions that were the subject of explanation in the former were oriented toward the actions of others, while those of psychology were not. And Durkheim actually called interpretive sociology "social psychology".

The importance of Cummins's distinction between causal explanation and functional analysis to the metatheory of sociology will be taken up in the rest of this chapter. In §5.5, I discuss the relationship between reasons and causes, and in §5.6 and §5.7, I extend the discussion to the reality of symbolic systems and the status of reason explanations.

But before I proceed, it will be worthwhile to make a short detour to contrast the position being developed here on the nature of causal explanations with that of Roy Bhaskar,[37] perhaps the best-known contemporary realist philosopher of social science. While Bhaskar's transcendental approach differs from mine, at base there are few fundamental differences between our positions, although as far as I know, Bhaskar has not developed a methodology for science. But ultimately, as I hope to show in the rest of this chapter, my position on the nature of causal explanation is both more defensible and more fruitful.

Briefly, Bhaskar insists, as I do, on the fundamental nature of causal explanation in science, and on the ontological poverty of DN type explanations. Like Cummins, he insists that adequate scientific explanation should invoke underlying causal mechanisms and the structures that produce them. But Bhaskar's analysis is not fine enough to distinguish the range of scientific explanations and the ways that they relate to one another. This leads to terminological differences between Cummins's analysis and Bhaskar's. Bhaskar refers to the theories covering causal mechanisms and their structures as causal laws, whereas to Cummins, these are property theories. Causal laws are simply cause-effect pairs. Recall that property theories explain what it is for a system to have a particular property. Ideally, the explanation will show the components of a system and their properties, and show that when organized in a particular way, the system property to be explained will exist.

This difference leads Bhaskar to argue that causal laws specify tendencies rather than actualities. Actualities can only be realized in closed systems. Closed systems can be approximated experimentally in the natural sciences, meaning that prediction can act as a criterion of the validity of natural scientific theories. But in the social sciences, closed systems cannot be achieved, meaning that accurate prediction cannot be applied as a criterion of an adequate social scientific explanation—hence Bhaskar's "qualified" naturalism.[38] Social scientific theories can only be assessed according to their explanatory value, i.e., in terms of causal mechanisms and the structures that produce them. Just how explanatory value gets cashed out empirically is left a mystery, but the MMK can help here. Recall that the MMK allows for internal and external consistency and coherence to be used as criteria of validity, as well as a theory's pragmatic value as a guide to action.

The problem with Bhaskar's analysis is that unless reasons can be shown to be causes, much of the social sciences seems closed to empirical investigation. Bhaskar certainly claims that reasons are causes, but I have found no sustainable argument for this in his work. So what appears initially as a mere terminological distinction between Cummins and Bhaskar points ultimately to a major flaw in Bhaskar's analysis.

5.5 Reasons and Causes

So far in this chapter, I have shown that the basis of validity in the MMK is the existence of a unified (i.e., connected) reality, and that the unification of science is achieved by showing the causal connections that exist. But while causal explanation is essential to science, it is not the only form of explanation. Explanations in terms of composition, structure, and function are very important to science, although to be valid they must be grounded in causal explanation. Little attention has been paid to these other forms of explanation by philosophers of science, but Cummins has provided a long-overdue analysis of them.

We can bring this analysis to bear on the problem of the relationship between causal explanations in the social sciences and explanations in terms of meanings, intentions, motives, and reasons. This relationship is of importance to the metatheory of sociology, because much sociological explanation is in terms of the meanings things have for people and the reasons people have for acting as they do.

Weber's interpretive sociology provides a classic example of sociological explanation in terms of meanings. This is perhaps best illustrated by his study of the rise of modern capitalism [39] Capitalism is a social and economic structure, and is, according to Weber, to be explained in terms of individual social actions, and thus in terms of the values and motives of individuals. Weber constructed an ideal type[40] of the sorts of values and motives required for the emergence of modern capitalism. These included the idea of a worldly calling to engage in economic activity as an end in itself rather than a means to satisfy other ends, and the justification of the virtues of other characteristics such as hard work in terms of the acquisition of wealth. Weber called this ideal type "the spirit of capitalism", and sought an explanation of its development. Empirical studies had shown that there was a tendency for the new business entrepreneurs to come from a Protestant rather than a Catholic background, so he looked at the doctrines of Protestantism to see if there was anything in them that could explain the emergence of the spirit of capitalism. While the ethics of Catholicism valued monastic life and a traditional or organic model of society stressing the importance of the social group, Weber found that the ethics of Calvinism valued a methodological, this-worldly, and individualistic approach to life. There was a congruence of meaning between the ethics of Calvinism and the spirit of capitalism. But the theological doctrines of Calvinism showed no such congruence with the Protestant ethic, so Weber had to show how these doctrines could lead to the adoption of the Protestant ethic.

Weber identifies three Calvinist doctrines he thought were relevant to the development of the Protestant ethic: the doctrine of predestination, the doctrine that God created humans to labor for his glory in establishing the kingdom of God on earth, and the notion that human nature led inevitably to sin and death unless one was blessed with the gift of grace. The first of these doctrines, the doctrine of predestination, Weber believed was too terrible for humans to cope with, and that this led to the adoption of an ethic logically incompatible with the doctrine. Weber believed that the thought of living in the knowledge that one may not be chosen for salvation was so terrifying that Calvinists were intent on looking for outward signs that one was chosen. And where better to look for the chosen than among those who worked for God's glory on this earth, and who denied themselves the pleasures of the flesh? Thus, Weber established to his satisfaction the motivational link between Calvinist doctrine and the Protestant ethic, which he had already shown was sufficient for the spirit of capitalism. As the link was not a logical link, empathic understanding rather than rational understanding was involved. Though less certain than rational understanding, it nonetheless provides a motivational explanation for the rise of the spirit of capitalism.

Weber set about testing his hypothesis by examining the writings of Calvinists for evidence of the change from a traditional ethic to the Protestant ethic. Adequate evidence of the change was found, and in finding it, Weber had shown that the Protestant ethic actually did act as a guide to action. The ethic was instantiated as a set of motives in a particular set of people. As further evidence for the link between the Protestant ethic and the spirit of capitalism, Weber undertook cross-cultural studies, examining societies, in particular China and India, that had achieved the kind of material and organizational bases necessary for the development of modern capitalism, but where the religious ethic would be contrary to such development. This is simply an application of the principles of comparison and control that are used to establish cause/effect pairs. India and China, while similar to industrial Europe in other respects considered relevant to the rise of capitalism, differed both in respect of the dominant religious ethic and in the fact that there were no signs that modern capitalism would develop. On this basis, Weber argued that the Protestant ethic was a necessary precondition for the development of capitalism. Weber's procedure incorporated both interpretive understanding and the methods of causal instantiation and causal explanation, showing how meanings and reasons, as long as they can be shown to be instantiated, can be incorporated in a causal account of events.

Symbolic interactionism also provides a good illustration of the importance of reasons in sociological explanations. One of the major features of Goffman's work, as we saw in §1.3, was to show that in mental hospitals, much of the inmate behavior that was used by staff as signifying continuing mental ill health was in fact better seen as a rational response by inmates to the vicissitudes of institutional life.

Much of the study of human behavior, then, involves explanations in terms of intentions, motives, or reasons. But reasons, as we saw in §2.2, are not the sort of thing that can unproblematically be regarded as causes. Moreover, it is notoriously difficult to relate explanations of an action in terms of reasons to causal explanations of that action. This is traditionally the strongest case for holding that the social sciences are fundamentally different from the natural sciences. So it is essential that a naturalist realist metatheory of sociology be able to specify the relationship between explanations in terms of reasons, motives, and intentions (in other words, mentalist explanations) on the one hand, and causal explanations on the other. To a naturalist realist, the determination of the validity of mentalist explanations depends on the specification of some such relationship. If the relationship between mentalist explanations and causal explanations cannot be specified, then the naturalist realist must reject much of what passes for social science, and the humanist cause is strengthened.

Traditionally, the issue of the relationship between the two types of explanation has been approached via a discussion of whether or not reasons themselves are in fact causes. The question arises because we want to say, for example, in certain cases, that it is not an event itself (or a sentence, or a symbol), but what it means to a person, that determines the person's response to it. Now if meanings, reasons, motives, and so on, are in fact causes, the naturalist realist has no problem. Indeed, the thesis that reasons are not causes has fallen from favor of late, simply because it is clear that reasons do indeed explain actions. The unstated assumption of this position is that such explanations are causal.[41]

But arguments have been advanced that suggest that reasons are not causes. For example, if we trace the causal chain that produces (physical) human behavior, we end up with physical and neurophysiological phenomena. No mentalist entities appear in the transition theories. Now, if reasons are in fact causes, one argument runs, we ought to be able to reduce them to neurophysiological states. Meanings, though, are specifiable independently of causal relations, in terms of the semantic content of sentences, i.e., in terms of their logical relationships to other meanings. For example, the meaning of the proposition that "x believes the grass needs mowing" is said to be determinable only with reference to the belief states of x, not to whether the grass is or is not long, or, presumably, the electrochemical conditions of the speaker's neurons.

And as Gergen points out, intentions, motives, and reasons have no precise spatiotemporal location.[42] This is just another reflection of the fact that semantic content is specifiable without reference to any causal relations. Further, mentalist entities can be instantiated causally in any number of ways. And to complicate matters, no disposition, reason, or motive can be unequivocally defined in terms of behavior. Any reduction of reasons, motives, intentions, and so on to causes seems impossible.

On the face of it, then, mentalist explanations bear no causal relationships to anything, having no empirical reference to the outside world. To many, it seems as though the social sciences, insofar as they deal with meanings, float free of the natural sciences, carrying with them their own methodology and criteria of validity. Such validity as they may have can only be in terms of the internal relationships between meanings.

These, and other arguments like them, are often cited as reasons for adopting a rationalist position vis-a-vis the science of human action and/or a humanist position vis-a-vis the status of the social sciences.

Gergen, for example, in his discussion of the relationship between theory and evidence, argues for the necessity of a humanist approach to the social sciences. Gergen makes the familiar point that much study of human behavior is concerned not so much with the behavior itself as with the underlying meaning of the behavior to the person. He distinguishes human behavior (bodily movement over which the person has no control) from human action, which is intentional. To understand the latter, one must take into account the reasons that precipitated it. Thus, the appropriate language for describing human actions is intentional.[43]

This, Gergen argues, has profound implications for social science, for the language of personal descriptions has no spatiotemporal referents. Rather, the referents of intentional language are psychological conditions (intentions, motives, reasons, and so on). As Gergen puts it, "When we speak of a person being aggressive, helpful, obedient, conforming, and the like, we are speaking, not of the overt movements of the body, but of psychic dispositions."[44] Moreover, these dispositions can themselves be explained or clarified only in terms of other dispositions, motives, intentions, and so on. They cannot be unequivocally defined by behavior, because it is not the behavior itself but what it means to the person that counts. According to Gergen, "By and large, the language of human action simply has no recognizable spatiotemporal coordinates. . . . Theoretical description and explanation may thus proceed in relative independence of behavioral observation."[45]

It is this, Gergen argues, that demarcates the natural from the social sciences, for it is possible to link the language of theory and the language of observation in the natural sciences in a way that is not possible in the social sciences. " . . . [I]n the case of human action, we confront the possibility that theory is fundamentally closed to empirical evaluation."[46] It is claims such as this that have contributed to the view that the social sciences are unreliable and that social scientists are writers of fiction.[47]

Michael Carrithers provides a direct response to the claim that the language of observation in the natural sciences and the language of human action are so different in nature that the latter cannot be verified empirically.[48] He is concerned with how knowledge claims are warranted in ethnology. And since valid cross-cultural interpretation is traditionally regarded as extremely difficult, if not impossible, his argument is particularly relevant. Carrithers adopts Ziman's social model of science, which, as we saw in §3.2, consists of a community of interchangeable knowers, a set of consensible beliefs, and a body of scientific knowledge comprising those consensible beliefs on which consensus has actually been achieved. The basis of the validity of science lies in the intersubjective agreement that can be reached on consensible beliefs. All perception is to some extent interpreted, but the reliability of science does not depend on uninterpreted facts or "pure" observations. Rather, it depends on the consensibility of candidates for scientific knowledge. This in turn is based on the common human ability to recognize patterns.

Carrithers argues that just as intersubjective pattern recognition forms the empirical basis of the natural sciences, so too it forms the empirical basis of ethnography. The patterns of ethnography are the patterns of human action and interaction. To illustrate the nature of pattern recognition in ethnography, Carrithers quotes a passage by Raymond Firth, who, during his fieldwork among the Tikopia, received a message that his friend, Pa Rangifuri, son of the local chief, was angry and upset.

> When we got to his house we found him highly agitated. He and I greeted each other with the usual pressing of noses, as publicly recognized friends, but for him this was an unusually perfunctory gesture, and he paid me little attention. He was uttering brief incoherent statements: "I'm going off to sea" ... "They said their axe should cut first" ... "But was it for a dirge, no! It was for a dance!" Men were trying to soothe him down by respectful gestures, and to enquire the reason for his agitation. Tears were streaming down his cheeks, his voice was high and broken, his body quivering from time to time.[49]

Carrithers points out that his students and colleagues grasp this passage immediately. This, he argues, is because the passage evokes discrete patterns of human action and interaction. For example, the phrase "highly agitated" reminds us of "other occasions on which we have met such a pattern, through personal experience or through representations of emotion in conversation, literature, film, or even ethnography."[50] Likewise, "Pa Rangifuri's tears, the incoherence of his words, and his general demeanor are distinct, vivid, and discriminable from other patterns such as, say, 'riotous jollity.'"[51] Despite the fact that the patterns evoked by the passage are not just perceptual but include constitutively social ones, and the fact that some of the actions and indeed the entire social context are culturally specific, the pattern as a whole is intelligible. It is certainly the case that many such patterns may be totally obscure to the field worker newly arrived in a community. There may, for example, be some difficulty in distinguishing ceremonies from less formal social gatherings, or even such things as when a particular ceremony starts and finishes. But as Carrithers points out: "The idea of consensibility does not . . . require that patterns be immediately and easily elicited. The only requisite is that once patterns are elicited they be intersubjectively intelligible."[52]

The reader still remains puzzled as to the reasons for Pa Rangifuri's outburst, but then so were the participants at the time. They needed to link the consensibly recognized pattern with a larger explanation, in order that they could know how to act appropriately themselves. The explanation was forthcoming after Pa Rangifuri had been persuaded to apologize to his father. Firth's account continues:

The background to his [Pa Rangifuri's] outburst then became clear to us
[all those present before the chief]. My friend's son had been lost at sea
some months before [as I knew] and he had wanted to make preparations
for a celebratory mortuary rite. . . . But when he had gone to ask his
father for an axe to begin to cut down trees to make barkcloth for the
graveclothes the old chief had temporized, and he had thought his father
was refusing him, so threw himself out of the house. [As it emerged later,
in private, he had put this down to manipulations by his brothers whom
he had suspected of wanting a dance festival to precede the mourning ritual, so making their drain on family resources a priority.] His father now
explained that he had not refused the request for the axe, that he had had
something else on his mind, and that if his son had only waited, permission to go ahead with the funeral preparations would have been given to
him. After this, the axe was handed over, and the way to the funeral rites
was now open.[53]

    This passage, although complex and representing a unique situation, is
nonetheless explanatory, and it is explanatory by virtue of the fact that it places
the events intelligibly in a broader temporal context or flow of human events.
Carrithers argues that just as the capacity for visual intersubjective pattern
recognition is common to all humans (even though it must be activated or
formed by training and experience), humans have a common capacity to comprehend a flow of events, the capacity for narrativity. Human beings understand
both characters and plots. They "perceive any current action within a large temporal envelope, and within that envelope they perceive any given action not
only as a response to the immediate circumstances or current imputed mental
state of an interlocutor or of oneself but also as part of an unfolding story."[54]
The temporal dimension is crucial to an understanding of human action.
    To return to the example of the Pa Rangifuri incident, the only sort of ex-
planation that could remove the puzzlement of the participants over Pa Rangifuri's outburst is a story that places the incident intelligibly in a larger flow of
events. What is more, the story that Firth presents is not just his personal explanation, because it arose out events and utterances that occurred in front of a
group of people. While there may have been idiosyncratic interpretations of
particular events at the time or afterwards, "in order to act relevantly the participants had to fasten on some minimal shared understanding . . . "[55] The capacity for narrativity, Carrithers agues, presupposes an intersubjective account
of emotions, intentions, motives, and so on, and the yardstick of the correct attribution of these is success in responding appropriately to the social situation.
Ethnographic knowledge is, like natural scientific knowledge, to be judged not
by any absolute standard, but according to how well it guides action and decision making.

Carrithers's response to such claims as Gergen's, then, is to argue that the opposition that is depicted between observation in the natural sciences and interpretation in the social sciences is false. Both are grounded empirically in the human capacity for intersubjective pattern recognition, and the theories of both are to be assessed pragmatically, according to how well they guide action and decision making.

While this sort of response shows that the interpretive social sciences are not fundamentally closed to empirical evidence, and that reasons, emotions, intentions, and so on can be intersubjectively recognized, it does not throw much light on the philosophical question of how explanations in terms of these mentalist entitles can be reconciled with causal explanations. For it remains that reasons, intentions, and the like have no spatiotemporal location more closely located than the person as a whole. And they have logical relations among them different from the relations among causes. They cannot, therefore, be causes.

In his argument that mentalist theories should be understood as empirical theories, Paul Churchland provides the basis for a naturalist answer to the nature of such mentalist entities as reasons and intentions.[56] Churchland asks us to conceive of an isolated society of humans whose physiology differs in no way from our own. Their language is indistinguishable from ordinary English, except that when we speak of bodies as being "hot" or "cold", they speak of them as being of "high caloric pressure" or "low caloric pressure". Their observation terms for heat are in terms of caloric, that is, in terms of a now defunct theory of heat.

By exploring this thought experiment, Churchland argues that the caloric perceptual framework must be evaluated as any other theory, by comparing its virtues with alternative theories. The fact that a people are accustomed to thinking and perceiving in the terms of the theory is historically accidental, culturally idiosyncratic, and epistemologically irrelevant. Their commonsense theoretical framework has been superseded by a superior theory to which caloric is reducible only grossly, if at all.[57] Folk psychology, Churchland argues, is in exactly the same position. It is an empirical theory, to be evaluated like any other.

As further support for his argument, Churchland argues that there are deep similarities between the structure of folk psychology and the structure of paradigmatically physical theories.[58] Folk psychology displays propositional attitudes, and mathematical physics displays numerical attitudes. Take the propositional attitude, " . . . believes that P", and the numerical attitude, " . . . has a length of n." Churchland notes a structural parallel here, in that in both cases what makes the predicate determinate is the substitution of specific terms in place of P and n. And just as the relations between numbers (e.g., twice as long as n) can characterise the relations between numerical attitudes (e.g., my weight is twice your weight), so also do the relations between propositions characterize the relationship between propositional attitudes.[59] Churchland argues that these parallels underlie the most important parallel of all.

> Where the relation between certain kinds of propositional attitudes, or between certain kinds of numerical attitudes, holds universally, we can state *laws,* laws that exploit the abstract relations holding between the attitudes they relate. Many of the laws of folk psychology display precisely this pattern.[60]

This structural similarity between folk psychology and physical theories is another reason for considering folk psychology to be like any empirical theory. But this means that folk psychology, like caloric theory or our own perceptual framework, is open to falsification, and may just turn out to be false. And if folk psychology does turn out to be false, then there will be no better reason to believe in the existence of the mentalist entities, such as reasons and motives, than there is now to believe in the existence of caloric. With such uncertainty over their existence, mentalist entities cannot be seen as privileged.

Churchland's argument, from similarities between folk psychology and theoretical perceptual frameworks on the one hand, and between the structure of folk psychology and the structure of physical theories on the other, is that folk psychology is indistinguishable (except in terms of specific content) from other empirical theories, and that it should be evaluated as such.[61] Mentalist entities, according to this argument, should be treated as hypothetical causes. That they do not have precise spatiotemporal locations and can be instantiated in innumerable ways, is, according to this view, an indication of the inadequacy of folk psychology as an empirical theory rather than a function of any special (immaterial) ontological nature. The reason that reasons cannot be reduced to causes might simply be that the theory of folk psychology is wrong, and the theoretical entities it proposes do not exist.

Churchland's conclusion is a potent argument against rationalist solutions to the problem. These see the validity of mentalist theories to be a matter of the internal, logical, relationships between meanings. Since logic is held by rationalists to be a priori, such solutions completely divorce the validity of mentalist theories from empirical evaluation.

But there are problems with Churchland's approach. While it establishes that mentalist theories are indistinguishable in structure from empirical theories, and are best treated as such, no distinction is made between different types of empirical (i.e., scientific) theories. It is assumed that empirical theories are causal theories. But Cummins's analysis of explanation shows that a good deal of science comes under the category of analysis rather than causal subsumption. Moreover, Cummins shows that causal theories are indistinguishable by structure (or at least, by DN structure) alone from functional explanations. The possibility remains, therefore, that mentalist theories, while empirical, are not causal but functional explanations.

Recall that functional theories can be distinguished from causal theories in terms of their aims, their methods, and their ontology. Functional theories aim to explain dispositions, whereas causal theories aim to explain transitions. The method of causal explanation is subsumption, whereas the method of functional explanation is systems analysis followed by instantiation. The entities of causal theories have specific spatiotemporal coordinates, whereas the entities of functional theories have no spatiotemporal location that can be defined closer than the system as a whole. On these counts, mentalist theories are clearly functional theories. They aim, as Gergen and Putnam have argued, to explain dispositions rather than transitions; they use the methods of analysis and instantiation, as the analysis of Weber's *Protestant Ethic* illustrated; and the entities of mentalist theories (reasons, motives, and intentions) have no spatiotemporal location other than the person as a whole.

Recall that mental states have no spatiotemporal location, and may be instantiated in innumerable neurophysiological states. A type-type reduction between mental states and neurophysiological states is therefore impossible. But the solution that Hooker provides for the reduction of functional entities applies equally to reasons, motives, and intentions.[62] On this account, mental states, like virtual governors, have no independent ontological existence. Reasons, motives, and intentions are not causes. Rather, they are part of a functional specification of a person.

Let us return to the example of the virtual governor. Assume for the moment that, as is the case with brains, we have no easy access to the internal workings of the generating system as a whole. Although the virtual governor has no independent ontological existence, no spatiotemporal location more closely localizable than the system as a whole, we can still tell if there is something wrong with it by reference to the output of the system, for example, if the system shows marked fluctuations in frequency. Not only is there a relationship between the functional and causal specifications of the system, there is a relationship between the functional specification and the causally specified input/output relation. Functional systems need not be regarded as fundamentally closed to empirical evidence, as subject only to internal validity requirements. What is required is that, to be valid, functional theories be compatible with related causal theories and with the empirical evidence. More specifically, they should satisfy the specific constraints on instantiation that Cummins identified, according to the type of functional system being discussed. Once these instantiation requirements have been met, the theory is valid to the extent that it is a reliable guide to action.

According to this account, there will be no uniquely correct attribution of intentions, just as there is no uniquely correct functional analysis of any system. The attribution of intentions need only be adequate to account usefully for the stream of action. Indeed, as Carrithers points out:

> . . . it is difficult to see how such attributions could go beyond what is revealed in the stream of action. We cannot seek an absolutely correct, unequivocal, "scientific" understanding of such mental states apart from interaction, for it is only interaction that gives them sense and makes them available to consensible representation.[63]

The entities of functional theories, and particularly the entities of interpretive systematic functional theories, which include all mentalist theories, need have no correspondence to the entities within the causal system being explained. In this sense, functional theories must be considered not only partial, as all theories are, but as human constructs whose point is not to map a causal reality reasonably accurately but to make it intelligible in a way that facilitates appropriate action. It was the fact that Firth's account of the Pa Rangifuri incident is a construct in this sense that led Carrithers to analyze it for those characteristics that make it satisfactory. He isolates five characteristics that inspire confidence in Firth's account. I list them here to show how they fit into the account I have developed of mentalist explanations and their requirements.

The first characteristic of the chronicle is that "[i]t accounts for the flow of events".[64] This is the aim of the story, and as I have already shown, the validity of a theory must be assessed relative to the problem it was intended to solve. In accounting for the flow of events intelligibly, the story is able to act as a guide to action for those present, and vicariously for those who are not. The second point that Carrithers makes about the story is that "[t]he attributions of attitude and motive are closely and intelligibly tied to the people's interactions."[65] This characteristic speaks to the requirement that must be frequently applied in the complex course of human events, that the functional (intentional) explanation must be equivalent to the causal explanation at the level of input and output.

The third characteristic of Firth's account is that "[t]he attributions are those disclosed by the participants in the course of events."[66] This simply reflects the requirement that the various elements of the functional (intentional) analysis can be shown to be instantiated in the physical system. The fourth characteristic of Firth's story is that the "action is unequivocally and vividly related to the particular circumstances of life among the Tikopia."[67] This reflects the requirement that any theory, whether causal or functional, exhibit external coherence. The fifth characteristic is that the "episode as told has a robustness and independence from its use by Firth".[68] In other words, the account could be used by others to illustrate a variety of features, for example, fraternal rivalry. It has the character of evidence rather than of inference from evidence. The characteristic of robustness is, I believe, a reflection of the other characteristics, or of the validity of the explanation as a whole.[69]

Carrithers's analysis of the specific characteristics that make Firth's account of the Pa Rangifuri incident warranted, then, illuminate the validity requirements of interpretive explanations that I argue for, at the same time showing that the interpretive social sciences, while relatively independent from empirical evidence compared with causal explanations, are far from closed to it.

In this section, I have argued that explanations of human action in terms of reasons, intentions, motives, and dispositions are best conceived, not only as empirical or scientific theories, as Churchland would have it, but also as functional explanations. As interpretive functional analyses, intentional explanations do have a specifiable relationship with the physical structure of the system. This not only saves us from the radical dualism of the rationalists. The fact that functional descriptions of a system bear a relation to the input-output relation also saves us from the possibility that such descriptions are fundamentally closed to empirical investigations, leaving open the possibility of a naturalist, realist approach to the social sciences.

5.6 The Status of Rational Explanations

The preceding analysis of mentalist explanations of human behavior shows that they can, and indeed should, play an important part in a naturalist realist social science, but that there are conditions attached to their valid application. The fact that reasons are not causes does not of itself invalidate mentalist explanations, nor does it require humanism. But the fact that reasons are entities in functional explanations means that if they are to be invoked to explain human behavior they must be shown to be instantiated in the person or persons concerned.

Weber, the founder of interpretive sociology, was well aware of the necessity of explaining human actions causally as well as placing them in a wider context of meaning. He gave great emphasis to the fact that a valid explanation of human action must be adequate at the level of cause as well as at the level of meaning. As Weber argued:

> . . . no matter how clear an interpretation as such appears to be from the point of view of meaning, it cannot on this account claim to be the causally valid interpretation. On this level it must remain only a peculiarly plausible hypothesis.[70]

Thus, Weber placed great emphasis in his substantive studies on showing that the set of meanings, motives, and reasons hypothesized to explain any action were in fact causally instantiated. As we have already seen, in his study of the rise of capitalism, Weber examined Calvinist writings for evidence that the change from a traditional ethic to the Protestant ethic had in fact occurred. And as evidence for the link between the Protestant ethic and the spirit of capitalism, Weber used cross-cultural studies to show that the Protestant ethic was a decisive feature in the rise of capitalism.

The social sciences, even insofar as they deal with the interpretive understanding of social actions in terms of meanings, motives, and intentions, do not float free of the natural sciences. As Weber long ago realized, the key to assessing the validity of interpretive explanations lies in showing that the interpretation was in fact instantiated in the actor or actors concerned, and that it led to the action or event in question.

So far, in keeping with the traditional way in which humanist/rationalist debate has been framed, I have concentrated on the ontological status of mentalist entities, showing that they are best seen as entities in a functional explanation. Any explanation that appeals to them must show that they are in fact instantiated in a causal explanation. But it is not actually the mentalist entities of an intentional explanation that have to be shown to be instantiated, but the entire functional organization, including the deliberation process. Recall that in Cummins's analysis of explanation, functional explanation depended on an analysis of the components of the system and the ways in which those components were organized. Indeed, it was the nature of the structural relationships between the components that determined the degree of coherence required between the functional analysis of a system and its causal description.

This point has been picked up by Barry Hindess in his examination of the portfolio model of the actor that underlies both structuralist and agency explanations of social change.[71] The portfolio model of the actor defines the actor as the locus of decision-making, and adds the further assumption " . . . that an actor's decision is the rational product of states of mind that characterize that actor at the time of the decision".[72] Action results from intentions that themselves result from the actor's portfolio of beliefs and desires. The structuralist view of the actor differs from the agency view only in that it sees the actor's portfolio of beliefs and desires as determined by the social structure.

Hindess argues that the portfolio model of the actor is seriously incomplete in that it treats the actor's deliberation as unproblematic. The action of a rational agent is said to result from beliefs and desires in much the same way that the conclusion of an argument follows from its premises. Agents are assumed to be rational in the same way.[73] But this ignores the fact that there are many different forms of deliberation.

In an extended discussion, Hindess provides many examples of the ways rational deliberation may vary from actor to actor. Simon's principle of bounded rationality, for example, asserts that humans are generally faced with problems of such complexity that they cannot solve them accurately but must resort to various simplifying and approximating techniques. Different interests and/or cultural perspectives lead to the use of different techniques. And, as we saw in the discussion of Weber's *Protestant Ethic*, particular values may override even accepted forms of reasoning. It was the fact that humans found the doctrine of predestination too terrible to live with that led to the adoption of an ethic that was logically incompatible with the doctrine.

Hindess points out as well that various specialized cognitive techniques have been developed to solve problems in specialized areas. Moreover, he argues, human individuals are not the only actors. Institutions may also be (social) actors in that they are decision makers. And institutional methods or procedures for decision making vary from institution to institution and are quite different from individual forms of decision making.

Hindess's discussion shows that actions do not arise unproblematically from beliefs and desires but are also a function of the deliberation process used. These deliberation processes may themselves be rational or irrational, appropriate to the problem or not, and correctly or incorrectly used.[74] The point is that unless one can identify the form of deliberation actually used as well as the beliefs, desires, motives, and so on, one cannot explain the action. As systematic interpretive functional explanations, valid mentalist explanations must show how the symbolic entities and the form of deliberation used interact to produce the action, given the initial state of the system.

The fact that there are different methods or techniques of deliberation shows that one should be wary of any attempt to construct standards of validity for mentalist explanations independently of empirical considerations. For without resort to how well these methods of deliberation help the actor actually achieve goals, one could not choose between them. The problem of choosing between the *I Ching* and cost-benefit analysis as decision-making techniques in any situation must surely be based on the sort of results achieved by each, and hence be empirical rather than a priori.

5.7 Conclusion

I started this chapter by showing how the notion of validity developed in the MMK is based on the assumption of a unified reality. While the problem-relatedness of a theory is the major determinant of its scope of valid application and in addition determines the nature of the essentially pragmatic empirical tests, it is the relationship to a unified reality that underlies the internal and external consistency and coherence checks and makes possible a unified science. Reality is unified by causal interactions. Thus, causal explanations form the basis of a unified science, and instantiation in a causal process becomes the criterion of reality.

But causal explanations themselves are not sufficient for science. I showed how structural, functional, and compositional explanations all form an important part of sociology. And Cummins's analysis of scientific explanation in general pointed to the limited explanatory role of causal explanation and stressed the importance of the other forms of explanation, which he included under the term "analysis".

But Cummins's analysis also pointed out that little attention has been paid to analysis in discussions of scientific explanation, resulting in the easy confusion of functional analyses with causal analyses. Causal and functional analysis, for example, cannot be distinguished in terms of the structure of the theories, on which the DN theory of scientific explanation tends to concentrate. Rather, they are to be distinguished in terms of their goals, their methods, and the ontological status of their entities. Functional analyses are constrained by the physical system whose dispositions they explain, but the nature of those constraints varies according to the type of functional analysis in question.

Distinguishing functional from causal theories in this way provides us with a novel approach to the problem that explanations in terms of meanings, motives, reasons, and so on seem to be divorced from empirical evaluation, and hence require a methodology distinct from that of the natural sciences. For mentalist explanations turn out to be interpretive functional analyses. The latter have a loose, but nonetheless specified, relationship with the transition theories they explain. Minimally, the theories must be equivalent at the level of input and output.

Not only are mentalist theories not free from empirical evaluation, their relative independence from empirical evaluation does not distinguish them from natural scientific theories of the same type. Neither does the fact that the entities of mentalist theories have no precise spatiotemporal location, for neither do the entities of many functional explanations, such as, for example, the virtual governor. On this account, the strongest arguments for humanism, the fundamentally different nature of the entities of mentalist explanation, and the lack of resource to empirical evaluation, have disappeared, leaving the way open for a naturalist approach to the social sciences.

6

Knowing in a Complex World

"I'm in electric fish," she said. She had worked in fish for quite some time.
"Why?" I asked her.
"People drive you nuts," Helena replied.

—Rosaleen Love, *Where Are They?*

I have argued that all natural systems can be analyzed in terms of cause, composition, and structure, and that causal instantiation is essential for the establishment of validity. This is because it is through causal interaction that the world can be seen as a coherent whole, and through causal interaction that knowledge of the world is obtained. In addition, many systems, and in particular stable non-equilibrium structures, can be given a functional explanation. I have argued that the accounts of interpretive sociology are best seen as functional accounts of persons.

Seeing them in this way allows for the possibility of a naturalist realist metatheory of sociology, because it shows that not only are the accounts of interpretive sociology not fundamentally closed to empirical investigation, they do not differ in any fundamental sense from functional accounts in the natural sciences. Interpretive sociology does not, therefore, have to be dismissed as non-scientific in a naturalist realist metatheory, but rather has a legitimate place in sociology, provided that the mentalist entities to which it appeals can be shown to be causally instantiated in some person or persons.

The fact that interpretive explanations are a legitimate part of sociology is just one indication of the complexity of the domain of sociology. I turn now to another aspect of the complexity of sociology, arguing that the nature of the complexity of its domain has implications for the methodology of sociology. First, I argue that the natural world is a complex world. I go on to explore the ways that humans have of knowing that world. I then show how those same methods translate when applied to the social world, and derive some specific methodological prescriptions for sociology. But the resulting pluralist methodology is not without its problems for a naturalist realist, for there is a tension between a pluralist methodology and the naturalist realist aim for a unified body of knowledge.

6.1 The Complex Nature of Reality

So far, in the evolutionary naturalist realist epistemology and methodology I am developing, I have made only two claims about the nature of reality. The first is that reality exists independently of our knowledge of it. The second is that everything that exists is in principle interconnectable with everything else that exists. The connections between things are called causal connections. Causation is, in this sense, a primitive. These ontological claims do not so much constitute an ontology as form constraints on an ontology. They leave open the nature of the causally connected world.

But the concepts of evolutionary epistemology that form the basis of the notion of validity that I have developed will take us a little further. The foundation of evolutionary theory is natural selection. Organisms evolve in interaction with the environment, and their perceptual/cognitive systems are such that they maintain a passable fit between an organism and its environment—one that allows for the survival and reproduction of the organism. It follows that the nature of perceptual and cognitive mechanisms themselves (and not only human ones) carries some information about the nature of reality. If, for example, the human environment is a complex and many-layered reality, it is likely that human perceptual and cognitive mechanisms would have developed in ways that allow for the separation and recognition of any significant aspects of that environment from those that are not.

Human knowledge of the world does in fact recognize many layers of reality. It is organized into subjects that form a hierarchy according to the degree of complexity of the systems that they treat as basic. For example, studies of complex ecosystems, specific organisms, cells, molecules, atoms, and subatomic particles form a hierarchy of which ecosystems are the most complex. In the social world, studies of whole societies, sub-cultures, interest groups, families, and individuals form a similar hierarchy.

But this of itself is insufficient to claim that reality is multi-layered, because each layer may turn out to be completely reducible to the next. Reductionism, the metaphysical belief in a single-layered reality, asserts that the properties of the entities at each level are to be explained in terms of the properties of, and relationships between, the entities at the next level down on a scale of complexity. Theoretical reduction parallels ontological reduction and reduction becomes the means of unifying knowledge. To the reductionist, all observable phenomena are to be explained in terms of the ultimate entities of matter, whatever they may turn out to be.

Belief in reductionism is usually an article of faith, having the status of a First Philosophy. But the naturalist realist has no First Philosophy. Rather, apart from the general constraints on ontology that I outlined at the start of this section, theories of ontology, epistemology, and methodology are of precisely the same nature as scientific theories, and will be based on scientific knowledge. Such theories will, like all knowledge claims, be fallible and subject to revision. Humans have no other way of knowing the world. While the many successes of reductionism (its popularity stems from the successes of classical mechanics) as a research strategy have bolstered the belief in a single-layered reality, as a research method, reductionism is self-validating—a point I shall argue in chapter 7. The successes of reductionism therefore provide no empirical basis for belief in a single-layered reality. On the other hand, there is considerable evidence that supports the idea that reality is multi-layered.

One approach that is open to the naturalist realist in determining whether reality is single-layered or multi-layered is, as I have mentioned, to ask what the world must be like for humans to have knowledge of it. The naturalist realist answer will draw on a scientific account of humans as knowers. The answer will ideally be consistent with the body of scientific knowledge,[1] and will amount to an empirical claim to knowledge rather than an a priori belief.

Kai Hahlweg takes this approach, making his starting point the evolutionary biological nature of humans as knowers.[2] The mechanism of natural selection means that phylogeny bears a significant relationship to the environment. Therefore, from the nature of the human knower, one can find out something about the nature of reality by asking two questions. First, in what sort of world is evolution possible, and second, in what sort of world would the development of human perceptual and conceptual capabilities as we know them confer an advantage?

In answer to the first question, Hahlweg argues that while reductionism was, and still is, a powerful research strategy, its dominance as a metaphysics is being increasingly eroded by modern science in favor of a process metaphysics. The reductionist metaphysics conceives of a stable world in which things are aggregates of atoms. Change is conceptualized as a mere rearrangement of atoms, and time is conceptualized as non-directional. This metaphysics sits uneasily with thermodynamics and evolutionary theory. The eternal features of the universe are now seen to be but relatively stable patterns, long-lasting only with respect to the human lifespan (for example, stars), or are being analyzed into even smaller entities, as has happened with the atom. And the second law of thermodynamics demonstrates the existence of irreversible processes (for example, heat conduction and the decay of nuclear particles).[3] Evolution, too, is a one-way historical process, in which species evolve through complex interactions with the environment. Organisms both respond to the environment and act upon it, changing it. Evolution occurs in a changing world. Hahlweg, then, proposes that given the evolutionary nature of human beings and the discoveries of thermodynamics, the nature of reality is likely to be better described by a metaphysics that gives primacy to processes rather than to things.

One of the advantages of a process metaphysics over a reductionist one is that no ontological problems need arise from the recognition that changes occur at all levels of the many-layered reality and that these changes occur all at once.[4] Changes, for example, occur simultaneously at the levels of societies, families, persons, cells, and so on. Individualism, a reductionist form of sociology, does not allow that societies exist over and above the individuals who comprise them. The properties of societies must be derived from the properties of the individuals who comprise them and the relationships between them, and societal change is correctly explained only in terms of changes in the individuals and their relations. But as I showed in §1.2, structural unemployment, for example, cannot just be explained in terms of the characteristics of individuals and their relationships. While a reductionist metaphysics cannot allow the existence of relatively autonomous entities at different levels of reality in the same spatiotemporal location, this is not necessarily a problem under a process metaphysics. Under a process metaphysics, entities are conceived as relatively enduring or stable patterns in a spatiotemporal framework of processes, and it makes sense to talk of many processes occurring in the same place at the same time, which it does not with entities. A process metaphysics seems more appropriate for an evolutionary reality than does the reductionist entity metaphysics.

But my concern here is not particularly to support a process metaphysics. Perhaps there are other alternatives to a reductionist, single-layered metaphysics. Rather, my concern is to support the notion that reality is multi-layered. Apart from noting that a process metaphysics is compatible with a multi-layered reality and a reductionist metaphysics is not, I make no use of a process metaphysics in developing the MMK. I am more interested in Hahlweg's argument that the nature of human perceptual and cognitive capabilities indicates that the changing world in which humans evolved is also an extremely complex one, a many-layered reality.[5]

I shall take up this issue in the next section, where I discuss the capacities of humans to know such a many-layered reality and the ways in which they do so. The issue is of importance because the social world, at least, is very complex.[6] Indeed, the complexity of sociology is about the only point of agreement among almost all sociologists and philosophers of social science. It is its complexity that is thought to be the source of many of the epistemic problems that sociology faces, so if the natural world too can be shown to be complex, and it can be shown that humans have the ability to deal epistemically with complexity, it might be possible to get a handle on some of the epistemic problems of sociology.

6.2 Reducing Complexity in a Complex and Changing World

If the world is indeed a complex and many-layered reality, the place of reductionist methodology will be limited, and this leaves open the question of what sorts of methodology might supplement or replace it. In this section, I explore the ways in which humans can know a complex and changing world. This will serve two functions. The first is that if it can be shown that humans have evolved the perceptual and cognitive mechanisms to know a complex and changing world, we have an indirect argument that the world is indeed complex and changing. If it were not, no advantages would accrue to humans on account of those capacities. The second function this discussion will serve is that it ought to contribute to a methodology of sociology, because if humans can know a complex and changing natural world, the methods they use ought to be relevant to knowing the even more complex and changing social world.

6.2.1 Methodology in the Natural Sciences

Human perception and cognition, recall, is thoroughly theory-laden. Hahlweg explores the nature of that theory-ladenness as a basis for inferring both the nature of the world and the nature of our knowledge of it. Instead of bemoaning the fact that we cannot know the world "as it really is," he questions the validity of that very notion. What would it mean to see the world "as it really is," when stabilities depend on our perceptual frame of reference? Objects like rocks, which seem stable to us, are highly unstable from the point of view of the much longer geological time spans. A tomato plant, ephemeral from our point of view, may be stable from the point of view of the several generations of insects who are born, breed, and die on the same plant. Objects like tables that appear stable to us do not even exist at the sub-atomic level. As Hahlweg points out:

> The world is *too* rich to be captured in its entirety by any one creature. Everything is in constant flux, thus stability cannot be anything absolute but is always relative to the dimension of time and to the sensory equipment of the organism.[7]

As far as the organism is concerned, the evolutionary problem is how to sort out, in this rich and changing world, those changes that are important to the survival of the organism from those that are not.

In humans, as in other species, the very structure of the perceptual organs limits the range of sensory input. But even so, the input we do receive is highly ambiguous. One important distinction we have to learn is how to distinguish those changes that occur independently of our act of perceiving from those that are related to that act. For example, we have to learn that it is not the world, but we, who are moving when we ride on a train. Additionally, if we are to perceive change at all, we must create a stable framework against which to compare it. The most important of these for humans is the space-time framework.[8] The space-time framework and object independence are learned in early childhood. The various senses are coordinated at this time, and entities that display invariance across several of these modalities are called objects, whereas those that do not are noise resulting from the act of perception. Stability, then, is established by the coordination of various sensory frames of reference.

Vision is the most powerful of the human senses, but it is also the most indirect. While we may get direct information from the senses of touch and taste, visual perception requires interpretation. One of the more important evolutionary advances was the development of stereoscopic vision. The two eyes have slightly different projections, which, when coordinated by the brain, give the impression of depth. Again, additional information is achieved by coordinating different frames of reference.[9]

Hahlweg argues that the same principles apply to science. In investigating a particular problem, the scientist faces the same sort of problems that evolution faced in the design of the perceptual system. Reality, Hahlweg argues, is hierarchically structured (as is our knowledge) into different layers, varying in their complexity. The forces acting within each layer operate almost independently of each other. This is known, because were it not the case, were every process to interact completely with every other process, no invariant features could be detected and knowledge in our universe would be impossible.[10] The various levels of complexity, then, are relatively autonomous. But they are not completely so, and one problem scientists face is that of ensuring that changes at different levels of reality do not affect the kind of change that is being investigated—i.e., the problem of distinguishing "genuine" changes from noise, or creating a stable background against which change can be distinguished.

Noise is, as Hahlweg points out, as real as any other phenomenon, and is distinguished from "genuine" phenomena only by the intentions of the observer to investigate a particular aspect of reality. Noise is eliminated as much as possible in the physical sciences by the use of rigidly controlled experiments. One of the consequences of this approach is that reality can be investigated only one level at a time. In the historical natural sciences, for example in biology and geology, and also in the social sciences, the elimination of noise may be somewhat more problematic. Controlled experiments are not always possible, and when they are, they may not always be useful, nor ethical. Nonetheless, even the historical sciences have some equivalent to rigidly controlled experimentation, in that they use the same principles of comparison and control that underlie experimental design. These principles are, however, applied in other ways.

Sociology, for example, makes use of historical and cross-cultural comparisons.[11] The result is that the historical sciences, too, at least aim to investigate one level of reality at a time, although they are unlikely to achieve the precision of the experimental sciences.

The other major problem scientists face is that of distinguishing change internal to the experimental apparatus[12] from those external changes being studied. Just as the development of multiple perceptual frameworks allows us to distinguish those phenomena that are dependent on our acts of perception from those that are independent, Hahlweg argues that the development of multiple conceptual frameworks may enable us to distinguish those features of our experience that are robust[13] from those that are due to our involvement as perceivers.[14]

Moreover, Hahlweg argues that consistently working from within one conceptual framework, even a powerful and fruitful one like reductionism, will likely lead to error:

> Consisting of a set of mutually reinforcing theories and practices, [a powerful conceptual framework] defines what is possible and easily leads to dogmatism. Being caught within its explanatory power, we are in danger of forgetting that our framework is a construction, that the world is far too rich to be captured by any one framework alone.[15]

So although it is only by the creation of a stable conceptual framework that external changes can be perceived and regularities in the changing world can manifest themselves, Hahlweg demonstrates that "as long as we remain within that framework we might not be capable of detecting error, and all our methodologies may mislead us."[16] Multiple conceptual frameworks are as essential for establishing genuine invariance as are multiple perceptual frameworks.

6.2.2 Methodology in Sociology

The complexity that bedevils sociologists is of precisely the same nature as that faced by natural scientists. Sociologists, too, are investigating a multi-layered and changing reality. They too have to create stable backgrounds against which to investigate change. They too have the problem of distinguishing the robust features of the world they are investigating from the noise from other layers of reality and from those features that are a result of the process of investigation. They are additionally constrained by the sheer number of factors that may be operating even at a single level of analysis, and by the fact that controlled experiments are either impossible, unethical, or irrelevant.[17] But if Hahlweg is right about the way that knowledge of a complex and changing world is possible, then not only is a scientific sociology possible, but the multi-perspective nature of sociology starts to make sense.

The adoption of a particular perspective in sociology functions in much the same way as experimental controls in the physical sciences. As we saw in §1.2.3, each perspective has its own assumptions about the nature of the social world. While those assumptions do not simplify the reality to be studied, as experimental controls do, they can have a similar effect by suggesting other—conceptual—methods of control to the researcher.

Let me illustrate. The structure of society has an effect on individuals, and at the same time, the behavior of individuals affects the structure of society. Both are constantly in a state of flux. Under these conditions, how can we have knowledge of the relationships between individuals and society? We are dealing here with two distinct levels of reality. But we can investigate only one level at a time. By assuming that the social structure is stable, we can investigate what individual characteristics or behaviors are affected by position in the social structure. But individual behavior is itself affected by many other factors besides the social structure. These factors can never be eliminated as we might eliminate factors in an experimental situation, but they can be controlled to a great extent in other ways—for example, by selecting for study those individuals who are as like as possible regarding those other factors. This procedure allows the assumption that the remaining differences between the individuals are the result of the social structure.

Of course, social structure does change, and indeed it changes as a result of individual behavior. But for the purposes of investigating the effects of social structure on different individuals, it can (and indeed must) be considered relatively stable. The greater number of variables involved in sociology, and the problems of achieving control, mean that one would expect the results of sociology to be less accurate than those of the physical sciences. Nonetheless, knowledge of the social world is possible. The use of various assumptions in sociology can be seen as a way of creating stability in a complex and changing world.

Further, multiple perspectives are needed to establish the existence of genuine invariants and robust concepts in sociology. Robust concepts are those that are essentially invariant across theories. The importance of robust concepts to the unification of sociological knowledge is taken up in chapter 7. For now, I confine myself to illustrating the notion itself with respect to sociological theories. A closer look at the studies of deviance that I used as illustrations in §1.2.3 shows that the concept of deviance is reasonably robust. In Erikson's study from the consensus perspective, deviance is defined implicitly as the breaking of a norm held in common by the members of a group. Crime is usually seen as a sub-class of deviance. Pearce's study of white collar crime from the conflict perspective points out that corporate crime is the norm for those in a position to commit it. But that indicates only that it is normative for a particular group in society, not that it is normative for the wider society. Indeed, this is precisely Pearce's point. It shows the interests of capital to be in conflict with the interests of democracy in the United States.

From Goffman's symbolic interactionist perspective, the concept does not change. Again, the point is made that the norms of different groups within a wider society, particularly groups with different positions of power, can and do vary. Behavior regarded as deviant by the staff of the mental hospital was regarded as rational by the inmates (and probably by many outside observers). And in Cicourel's study, the basic concept of deviance remains the same. The question here is how some people and not others are virtually forced into deviant careers.

The concept of deviance across all of these perspectives is robust, referring to enduring patterns of relationships. But this is in contrast to the common-sense view of deviance. The common-sense view of deviance (often held by reductionists) sees the nature of deviance as absolute, as residing in particular behaviors that are intrinsically wrong, or not human—such as, for example, killing people. A little reflection will show that killing people has been approved almost universally under certain circumstances, although these circumstances vary from culture to culture and over time. The fact that a robust concept does not apply within a particular perspective is reason to suspect the perspective—or at the very least to question its usefulness—because robust concepts are required for the establishment of external consistency. This point will be elaborated both later in this chapter and, in considerably more detail, in chapter 7.

The use of multiple perspectives in sociology, then, need not be seen as a problem. It is better seen an essential part of doing sociology. The epistemic problems of sociology arise not from the existence of the different perspectives but from the way they are often viewed—i.e., as the only proper way to achieve knowledge of the social world. The structuralist perspectives, for example, point to social phenomena that cannot appear at all if the action perspectives alone are used, and vice versa. And the dichotomy between holism and individualism, reflected in the debate between the structuralists and the action theorists, disappears under a complex metaphysics that allows the existence of many relatively autonomous layers of reality, each with its own specific methods of investigation.

This can be further illustrated by looking at the multi-perspective nature of sociology from the point of view of the mapping model of knowledge. According to the mapping model of knowledge, scientific theories are essentially partial abstractions from reality. Which aspects of reality are to be described, and in what detail, are both functions of the interests of the users. The number of aspects of a particular phenomenon that can be investigated is in principle without limit. No phenomenon can ever be completely described, but the greater the number of aspects of the phenomenon in question that are in fact well described, the greater our knowledge of the phenomenon. This does not mean that every way of looking at the phenomenon in question is valid. The criteria of internal and external consistency and coherence must be met. But the meeting of these criteria is equivalent to the establishment of invariance. The establishment of internal consistency and coherence is just the establishment of invariant relations within the scope of the theory. The establishment of external consistency just establishes the possibility of invariance across theories and the establishment of external coherence is just the establishment of cross-theoretic invariance.

In the sociological examples just discussed, deviance is the aspect of social reality being investigated. The phenomenon of deviance can never be completely described, but looking at the phenomenon from various different perspectives increases our knowledge of it. But not all ways of looking at deviance are valid. The common-sense view of deviance is inconsistent with the sociological concept, and its use prevents even the possibility of establishing coherence between common-sense theories and the greater body of sociological theory. For what in all of the other perspectives is a concept of behavior relative to some cultural norm, is, in the common-sense view, an absolute concept—that certain behaviors are in themselves deviant.

Hahlweg's approach to evolutionary epistemology, then, adds to the methodology developed in chapter 4 because it explains the need for multiple perspectives in the more complex sciences in much the same way that the mapping model of knowledge does. This is not surprising. The structure of knowledge as represented by the mapping model is just what one would expect of the knowledge obtained by humans in a complex and changing world.[18] And the mapping model is an epistemology and methodology that itself takes account of the evolutionary biological and cultural nature of humans as knowers.[19] Hahlweg's approach to methodology adds a deeper understanding of why the mapping theory of knowledge is a workable methodology, and supports an argument that the methodology of sociology is essentially pluralist.

So far in this chapter, I have argued that the world is a complex, many-layered reality that is better depicted by a process metaphysics. Hahlweg's process metaphysics is compatible with the methodology of the MMK. Together, they make sense of the multi-perspective nature of sociology, and together they provide for the possibility of unifying the knowledge obtained from the diverse theoretical perspectives. The assumptions that underlie the various sociological perspectives are better seen not as ontological specifications but as methodological devices that facilitate the identification of stabilities in a complex and changing world, for it is only against a stable background that genuine invariant relations can be established. But what counts as genuine change and what counts as noise depend on the intentions of the scientist. There are many ways of viewing the world.

The fact that there are many ways of studying reality is, given human perceptual and cognitive mechanisms, a good thing. In a complex world, different perspectives make accessible different sorts of information. In addition, it is through the coordination of multiple perspectives that robust features of reality can be distinguished from those features that are merely a function of the theoretical framework used. Scientific methodology is essentially pluralist.

But the use of multiple perspectives implies a set of ontological problems that does not exist under a reductionist metaphysics and methodology. These problems create a tension within the MMK because, despite the general possibilities for unifying knowledge provided by the MMK, in practice the achievement of unification seems threatened. This raises the issue of whether knowledge obtained via the MMK methodology can as a matter of fact be unified. The rest of this chapter is concerned with the ontological implications of the MMK, the methodological prescriptions to which they give rise, and the problems for unification that they raise.

6.3 The Ontological Consequences of a Pluralist Methodology

The ontological implications of a pluralist methodology arise from the fact that both maps and theories specify their ontology. Visualize a geographic map. Geographic maps are accompanied by a key to the various symbols used on the maps. These symbols represent the various features that can be found using the maps. And the maps also contain, implicitly if not explicitly, the means for determining certain relationships between those objects. For example, a topographic map will show degrees of latitude and longitude, a grid, and grid deviation. These make it possible for the user to determine the relationship of the map to other specified maps, the position of each feature with respect to the rest of the features on the map, and to link the map with the world, respectively.

But one can determine from the map only the sort of thing that has been specified in the key. Recall that given a street directory showing a blank strip with all the streets in the vicinity terminating along it, one cannot determine why they do so. The strip may contain an open drain, a precipice, a railway, or nothing at all. It could, for example, be space left for a proposed freeway. Although one may perhaps wonder, and conduct further investigation, the map itself can tell no more.

The same point applies to theories. The ontology of theories may include entities, processes, relations, and properties. Theories, like maps, specify their ontology, although rarely explicitly. The consequence is that, like maps, theories cannot validly determine ontological features outside their scope. And as I argued in chapter 4, the scope of a theory is a function of the purposes for which the theory is designed. The fact that theories have a limited scope of valid application, and that this applies to their ontologies, is poorly recognized, which probably accounts for the fact that it is not unusual for sociologists to come to conclusions that exceed the ontological scope of the theories they use.

These points can be illustrated with reference to a sociological study by Ann Game and Rosemary Pringle. Game and Pringle, in their study of gender discrimination in the Australian work force, conclude that the sexual division of labor in Australian society is a necessary part of the capitalist economy.[20] In fact, at best, all they showed was that the sexual division of labor is functional for capital because it fragments the labor force, thus limiting the bargaining power of the latter. Even if the fragmentation of the labor force were necessary for capital accumulation (and this certainly was not established), Marxist theories of capitalism cannot by themselves explain which particular groups of people should fill the subordinate positions. Many studies have shown that in some countries particular racial groups occupy the lowest strata of the labor force. Marxist theory is sex-blind, and race-blind, too. Quite simply, such questions are beyond the validity range of Marxist theory.

Ontological errors of the sort made by Game and Pringle can easily be avoided by treating theories as maps, making their ontology explicit and specifying their scope by making explicit the sort of problems the theories were intended to solve.[21] Game and Pringle started off with two theories of Australian society, each of which was constructed with a different interest in mind (the feminist theory to remove gender inequality and the Marxist theory to remove class inequality). This can be likened to a situation in which we have two geographic maps of the same territory, a road map, say, and a map of the waterways. These geographic maps may or may not be metrically accurate, or in the same scale. Nonetheless, being maps of the same territory they will be deeply compatible and the information represented in both will be able to be combined in a more general map representing both roads and waterways. What Game and Pringle have done is to assume that one of the maps in question, the map of capitalism or class inequality, is itself the general map of which patriarchy is an essential feature—i.e., they have assumed that all social causes are ultimately economic.

Now, certainly we can have maps exhibiting certain features but not others, from which we can derive those features given certain assumptions. An example would be a map showing only contours. From such a map we could work out the waterways (although not whether they actually contained water, nor necessarily all of them, because we could not know of springs, for example). But this sort of derivation requires a theoretical link, not just a conjunction of features. This link is specified in the additional assumptions required. In this example the assumptions would include that water obeys the law of gravity and hence follows paths of steepest descent. They might also include assumptions about rainfall patterns, the geologic occurrence of springs, and so on.

A theoretical link of this sort has not been established by Game and Pringle. To establish such a link would involve showing that capitalism required for its continued existence not only a class society, but one in which each class was further divided into superior males and subordinate females. Game and Pringle have shown that gender subordination exists and that a divided working class may increase capital accumulation, but this is a far cry from showing that capitalism would cease without gender subordination.

This does not mean that there is no relationship between capitalism and patriarchy. To return to the mapping analogy, the presence of waterways will affect the siting of roads. Roads cannot be made down the middle of rivers, and the presence of rivers necessitates that roads have some way of crossing them if rivers are not to confine roads completely. So the presence of waterways will affect the way roads develop, and this will be shown on a more general map. Although roads cannot be seen as completely independent from waterways in this sense, this does not mean that waterways are necessary for roads. The analogy between waterway maps and road maps on the one hand and theories of patriarchy and capitalism on the other, is a happy one. Patriarchy certainly preceded capitalism as waterways usually precede roads, and likewise, issues concerning capitalism cannot be seen as totally independent from patriarchy. Nonetheless, Game and Pringle have given no reason to believe that a theoretical link exists such that the theory of capitalism is the general map of which patriarchy is an essential (even if unmarked) part in the same way that a contour map is the general map of which waterways are an essential (even if unmarked) part.

Not only do maps come with a specification of which entities can validly be included on the map, but the entities included must be clearly defined to a level of detail determined by the purposes of the map. In geographic maps these definitions are usually taken for granted as part of the background knowledge of the users. For example, a tourist map of some part of England may specify towns and roads by which one can locate oneself, and also places of historic interest—museums, castles, historic houses, and so on. While the symbols for these are named, rather than explicitly defined, on the map itself, their use assumes a background knowledge of these objects that makes the symbols unambiguous. Although the museums, castles and houses are all buildings of one sort or another, the definitions (functional, in this case) are sufficient to distinguish them from other buildings.

Theories, too, in order to be usable, not only have to define which entities are able to be used by the theory, but have to define those entities to an appropriate level of specificity, one that allows their unambiguous use. Biological theories of evolution, for example, define the term "species" in terms of the capacity of its members to interbreed successfully. Such a definition is precise enough to determine membership of a species unambiguously, despite great variation within a species and great similarities between members of different species. The definition itself is determined by evolutionary theory. But in the absence of the theory of evolution, it is quite possible to imagine other definitions of species, based, for example, solely on similarity of appearance. The criteria for membership of a species in a non-evolutionary theory may be quite different from those of evolutionary theory. The point here is that, although the word "species" is used in both cases, it refers to differently constituted groups. The same word in different theories does not necessarily refer to the same thing, and knowledge derived about species from one theory cannot be transported unproblematically to the other. It may turn out that, as a matter of fact, the membership of a species is the same under both theories, but whether or not that is the case is always a matter for empirical investigation. It cannot be assumed. The methodological point I wish to make here is that when the same terms are used in different theories, the ontology of each theory should not only be made explicit, it should be specified with sufficient detail to make explicit the degree of inter-theoretic coherence that might be possible.

Attention to the explicit definition of terms and their place in a broader theoretical network is essential in multi-perspective disciplines, where a common theoretical background cannot be assumed. It is particularly important in sociology, because many terms are not only used across a range of theories, they are also taken from ordinary language where they are used in quite different, although related, ways.

As in the natural sciences, the entities in sociological theory are defined by the theory in question. Marx's theory of capital, for example, specifies "class" as an entity. Classes are defined by Marxist theory as groups of people specified by their relationship to the means of production. The two major classes recognized in capitalist society are the capitalist class, who own the means of production, and the working class, who work with, but do not own, the means of production. Other societies may have different sets of relations of production and thus different classes. The number of such classes in any particular society can be objectively determined by considering the various relations of ownership to the means of production. At the time Marxist theory was formulated, the definition of class was specific enough to be useful in explaining the major economic differences that arose between groups as a result of the capitalist economic system, and allowed individuals to be objectively or unambiguously assigned to a determined class.

But the concept of class varies considerably in sociology. Weber, for example, divides the members of society into classes according to differences in their market capacity that give rise to different life chances. Although capital is one source of market capacity, it is not the only one. Skills and education are also factors. Those with essential skills in areas where supply does not satisfy demand are able to command high salaries, and become a separate class in Weber's schema. Weber identifies four major classes in capitalist society—landed property owners, entrepreneurs, the intelligentsia or professionals, and the workers. While Marx's notion of class is defined relative to the sphere of production and Weber's is defined relative to the market, both concepts of class are objective in the sense that they are determined by differences in the bases of the economic relationships that exist between the groups. While the two concepts of class have different bases and the theories are not automatically coherent, in certain circumstances coherence may be achieved. For example, in early modern capitalist societies, Weber's entrepreneurial class can been seen as identical with Marx's capitalist class. Coherence between the theories can be established and, provided that sufficient care is taken, information derived about those classes from either theoretical perspective can be unproblematically exchanged.

British sociologists in the immediate postwar period had yet another concept of class. They used the division of labor as the determinant of class. They located the major class division in British society between manual and non-manual workers, a distinction that reflected the different market capacity and life chances of the respective groups. But the market capacity of many of the more poorly paid non-manual (or white-collar) workers, for example, clerks and shop assistants, became indistinguishable from those of the more poorly paid manual workers. And skilled manual workers now often earn more than unskilled non-manual workers. The distinction was only ever between different kinds of workers, and while it may once have correlated with a difference in market capacity, that difference is no longer significant.

A more recent sociological model of the British class structure divides society into lower, middle, and upper classes, with manual workers at the bottom, followed by low-level non-manual workers, with managers, administrators, and professionals forming the upper class. This model is closest to the everyday notion of class held in Australia, but it is notoriously subjective. Class membership cannot be unambiguously determined within such a theoretical framework. And in principle, one could establish an infinite number of social classes, and the choice of any particular number and the criteria for membership of such classes could be quite arbitrary.

These problems are simply a reflection of the fact that notions of class such as the two British examples discussed above are conventional. Rather than reflecting material relationships that actually exist between groups of people, they simply reflect the way some people order their social world. As such, conventionally determined class definitions cannot be consensible, as those that reflect real relationships can be. Nor could conventionally defined classes exhibit robustness, as objectively defined classes might. I certainly do not recommend the abandonment of conventionally determined class research. The meaning that conventionally determined classes might have for people can have important causal effects. But, reverting to the analysis of chapter 5, these terms are best seen as components in a systematic interpretative analysis,[22] and as such having no one-to-one correlation with the entities of a causal analysis.

The Marxist notion of class, on the other hand, as a component in a systematic descriptive analysis, will be more closely mapped by the causal analysis. So the incorporation of such research on conventionally defined classes into a wider, scientific body of sociological knowledge must be seen as doubly problematic. For not only can one not make the assumption of inter-theoretic coherence, but if conventional definitions of class are used such coherence is impossible to achieve except at the systemic level, in this case the level of the society as a whole.

It is essential, then, to realize that theoretical terms, like the theories in which they are embedded, have a limited scope of valid application. Such terms cannot be validly transported across theories when the entities they represent are not the same. And because the words themselves are inherently ambiguous or even meaningless out of context, explicit definition becomes necessary when terms are used cross-theoretically. One of the more common errors in sociology involves the use of the word "class" unqualified, in both its Marxist and common-sense meanings, and conflating them in argument.

This problem, too, can be illustrated with Game and Pringle's study. The notion of class consciousness belongs firmly in Marxist theory. Briefly, although there is an inherent opposition between the interests of the working class and the interests of the bourgeoisie due to their respective relations to the means of production, this opposition is not necessarily recognized by the members of the classes. Recognition of this inherent opposition between the classes is referred to as class consciousness.

Although Game and Pringle purport to be attempting to map patriarchy onto Marxist theory, they speak of computer programmers as middle-class (from the everyday, rather than Marxist, notion of class) because they do not share the class consciousness of the working class. This changes the basis of class definition from relationship to the means of production to the consciousness of such a relationship. The import of such a redefintion of class on Marxist theory would be to destroy it, as not all members of the working class are aware of the inherent conflict between the working class and the capitalist class. Happily for Game and Pringle, the only inference they drew from defining programmers as middle-class was that this pointed to stratification of the workforce, which is functional for capital accumulation. They could have shown this simply by referring to the fact that programmers seemed not to share the consciousness of the working class. Nonetheless, problems can arise from such careless use of theoretical terms, showing how important it is to consider the theory dependence of ontologies.

Not only are the entities of a theory and their possible relationships specified by the theory, so too are the properties that may be ascribed to these entities. And as such, properties, too, have a limited scope of valid application. Certain properties may only be applicable to descriptions at a single layer of reality. The quantum properties of strangeness and iso-spin, for example, have no

correlates in the macro world. And as Durkheim argued forcefully in his discussion of the nature of social facts, the social world has characteristics that
cannot be ascribed to individuals nor reduced simply to the properties of individuals and their actions.[23]

Whether or not a particular domain constitutes a relatively autonomous
level of reality is contingent. It will depend on whether the complex systems
that exist at a particular level exhibit causal regularities relatively independently of the micro processes occurring within them. Rain forests, for example,
as entities, causally affect climate in a regular way despite enormous differences between them at a micro level. But when a domain does constitute a relatively autonomous layer of reality, that level will have its own specified
ontology. Only according to strict reductionism can it be assumed that all layers of reality can be adequately described in terms of the same properties, and
only the combination of Newtonian mechanics and reductionism requires that
those properties be the primary qualities.

Each theory or network of theories, then, has its own ontology, consisting of the entities, relations, properties, and processes that form part of the theory. And this ontology has a limited scope of valid application determined by
the metatheory, the parameters of which are a function of the problem the theory is intended to solve, and thus a function of interests. This holds as much for
the nature of causal connections as it does for any other aspect of the ontology
of a theory. It is for precisely this reason that I refuse to define causality as more
than connectedness. The nature of any particular causal interaction is contingent and its specification theory-dependent.

The point holds even at the level of empirical facts. This is because humans have no direct perceptual access to the nature of the world. Facts are
therefore (albeit low-level) theories. This does not mean that what exists is a
function of human interests, because theories are ultimately socially validated
through causal interaction between humans and the rest of the world. What it
does mean is that we can and should distinguish real objects from those that are
merely a function of our interests. It is precisely because they are not consensible and cannot be intertheoretically established as robust that it can be said
that some characteristics, for example, conventionally defined "classes," do not
exist except in the minds of those who create them.

The notion that all ontologies have a limited scope of valid application has
implications for research, for it becomes an empirical question whether the ontology of any theory or network of theories can be validly related to that of other
theories. The issue becomes crucial in the shift from one relatively autonomous
layer of organization to another, as is common in the social sciences. Such a
level-shift occurs in physics, too, from the classical to the quantum world.[24] In
the next section, I explore in some detail the problems associated with this shift,
as the lines of debate are more clearly drawn than is usually the case in sociology, where ideology, politics, and emotive issues cloud the debate. Moreover,

the issues involved in the shift from the classical world to the quantum world have led many to doubt the possibility of a realist theory of knowledge.

6.3.2 An Example from Modern Physics

Quantum theory, while arguably the most successful theory humans have had in terms of predictive success, has also been, since its inception, the subject of unresolved debate about its interpretation. The problem lies in the fact that quantum theoretic descriptions do not conform to the classical realist ideals of description. Mechanics attempts to describe the world in terms of the fundamental properties common to all matter. Classical mechanics works with the notion of an "ideal" closed system—one that is free from any external causal effect on its mechanical behavior. To define the mechanical state of such a system, each body within it can be characterized in terms of two state parameters, position and momentum, for each instant in time. As long as the system remains closed, such a description enables the definition of the state of the system at any future time. In any interactions between components within the system, energy and momentum will be exchanged according to well-defined principles, but the total amount of energy and momentum in the system is conserved. This is what makes it possible to define the future state of the system.[25]

The classical framework, then, supports an ideal of observation, namely a unique and exhaustive space-time description of the motions of bodies forming any system. This requires what Bohr called the "claim of causality," which enables one to define the state of a system not observed, and rests on the presupposition that physical systems change their state continuously through time.

But Bohr's quantum postulate specifically denies that physical systems change their state continuously through time. Moreover, Heisenberg's uncertainty principle, derived mathematically from the quantum theoretic representations of the atomic system, shows that the degree of determinateness with which space and time can be predicted is reciprocally related to the degree of determinateness with which energy and momentum can be predicted. Thus the classical mechanical ideal of a simultaneous causal and space-time description of a system was not attainable under the quantum theoretic representation. The classical mechanical state of a system could no longer be well-defined when applied to the objects of quantum mechanical description. Moreover, the experimental situation in the subatomic domain seemed to provide support of a kind for the uncertainty principle. The apparatus required to measure the position of a particle such as an electron precludes the simultaneous use of the equipment required to measure its momentum.

Attempts at solving the problems associated with interpreting quantum theory can be divided into two major strategies. The typical realist approach, favored by Einstein, was to reject quantum theory as either false or incomplete, seeing quantum uncertainty as a measure of ignorance. The other approach, favored by Bohr, was to reject the classical realist ideal of description and look for another conceptual framework more suitable for adequate descriptions of the quantum world. Bohr's approach has led variously to relativist, phenomenalist, and neo-Kantian theories of knowledge. A brief look at the strategies of Einstein and Bohr in attempting to provide an adequate interpretation of quantum theory will highlight this problem.

Einstein argued that quantum mechanical systems could be shown to be in a classical mechanical state, at least sometimes. This raised the question whether an experiment could be designed that would yield greater knowledge of the state of the system than the uncertainty relations would permit. If this could be done, it would show that quantum theory was incomplete. Einstein, Podolsky, and Rosen put forward just such a thought experiment, designed to show that the physical system had properties that quantum theory could not determine.

Basically, the Einstein, Podolsky, and Rosen (EPR) experiment asks us to consider a system composed of two identical microscopic particles, A and B, with zero initial total momentum or angular momentum. The particles are then separated in such a way that this total is not altered. Should the momentum of A be measured, then the momentum of B could be calculated precisely. Since the particles are well apart, the measurement on A cannot be said to affect the state of B, so B must be considered to already have that precise value for momentum.

However, it is possible that instead of measuring the momentum of A, its position could have been measured. If that were done, the position of B could be calculated precisely. Thus B must already have had a definite spatiotemporal state. Thus it seems that B can be ascribed a value for both position and momentum simultaneously, as long as one believes that measuring A will have no effect on the state of B.

But it has since been shown by Furry that this classical conception of such particles—as having definite characteristics as soon as they are separated—leads to statistical predictions for measurements that are incompatible with those of quantum mechanics.[26] This opened the way for experimental tests that could decide between the EPR type and quantum statistical predictions. Such an experiment has been performed,[27] and the results support the quantum theoretic predictions.[28] To date, it has not been possible to show that quantum mechanics is either incomplete or false, although the EPR experiment gives rise to another anomaly for quantum theory, that of action at a distance.[29]

Bohr, far from seeing quantum theory as false or incomplete, believed that it was on the right track, being developed from the quantum postulate, which he regarded as an empirically supported fact about the structure of the atom. The quantum postulate denied that physical systems change their state continuously through time. Bohr was interested in how this denial would affect the classical ideal of spatiotemporal description and the "claim of causality."

Spatiotemporal and causal dynamic descriptions could not apply simultaneously in the presence of quantum relations. No classical description of the atomic system was possible. Bohr believed that it was the classical conceptual framework, not quantum theory, that was inadequate, and worked on the development of a different conceptual framework, complementarity.

A quick and intuitive notion of what is meant by complementarity can be gained by seeing how Bohr applied it to the puzzle of wave-particle duality. Bohr argued that any experiment that allows one to detect particle-like characteristics is bound to preclude simultaneous experimental detection of wave-like characteristics. The wave and particle descriptions are complementary descriptions, i.e., they are mutually exclusive. But the implications of Bohr's doctrine of complementarity extend beyond the realm of quantum mechanics.[30] As a philosophy, it includes a new framework for viewing knowledge of the world, arguments for generalizing the classical framework to provide the new one, an epistemological lesson about the presuppositions of using concepts, and a discussion of the ontological repercussions generated by using this framework.[31]

Bohr maintained that the concepts of classical physics must be retained, as they were necessary for unambiguous communication. But he argued that there is a limit on the simultaneous applicability of certain of these classical concepts to a single situation. This is because the quantum postulate means that each experimental situation is an indivisible whole. The distinction between the observed system and the observing apparatus is therefore arbitrary. Under these circumstances, the physical conditions necessary for the correct application of the classical concepts of position and momentum cannot be jointly realized.[32]

This, in a nutshell, is Bohr's argument for complementarity. One of the key features is the "individuality" or indivisibility of the observing interaction. In the classical framework, systems are represented as changing their states continuously. Thus, a system exists in a well-defined mechanical state at all times, whether or not it is interacting with another system. At each point in an interaction, it is always possible to define separately the state of each system. In an observing interaction, it is always possible to distinguish between the observing system and the observed object. Any disturbance created by the observation can be defined and used to define the state of the system as isolated from interaction.[33] But the quantum theoretic representation of an interaction between two systems cannot define separate states for the interacting systems. The "individuality" of the whole observational interaction makes any distinction between the observing system and the observed object arbitrary. If this distinction is arbitrary, any description we give of the interaction as an observation can be referring only to a phenomenal object, defined for a particular observational interaction. The very notion of observation requires a distinction between subject and object, and yet in the atomic domain this distinction can only ever be arbitrary.

Bohr's analysis of the applicability of the classical concepts of space and time, and energy and momentum (and thus cause) to the quantum realm shows that their unambiguous use can refer only to the phenomenal objects, which themselves can be defined unambiguously only in a specific experimental interaction. Thus, the classical properties of position and momentum refer to different phenomenal objects, as the experimental situation required for the determination of one excludes the simultaneous determination of the other.

This analysis had led some to espouse a wholehearted phenomenalism, but Bohr escapes this charge. Phenomenalism is the belief that the only reality of which we can form an idea with any content is that of phenomena, and that statements about a reality underlying the phenomena are meaningless. It may appear that Bohr's insistence that the classical concepts are restricted to describing phenomena, combined with his belief that we must use these concepts, constitutes a ban on any reference to an independent reality. But according to Bohr these mutually exclusive descriptions are in fact complementary descriptions of the same underlying reality. Moreover, complementarity is erected on the quantum postulate, which entails the description of observation as an interaction between physical systems that are not phenomenal objects. Complementarity presupposes the existence of an independent reality.

But Kant, too, had to presuppose an independent reality. According to Kant, to talk of such reality was not meaningless, but there was no sense in purporting to say what that reality was like. Kant believed that the concepts of space, time, and causality could be known to apply to experienced phenomena a priori.[34] These concepts applied only to phenomenal objects and could not be used to describe an independent reality. Bohr's belief that the classical concepts are necessary for the objective description of experience and yet are applicable only to phenomenal objects is similar to Kant's position. Folse points out the many differences between Bohr's philosophy and Kant's,[35] but notwithstanding these differences, Hooker has shown that complementarity is effectively Kantian,[36] and denies the possibility of knowledge of an underlying atomic reality.

Current analyses of the quantum paradoxes have been developed from both the classical realist and Copenhagen interpretations. These analyses, even—although perhaps to a lesser extent—those that attribute the paradoxes to measurement interference, have been in a sense internal mechanical analyses of the problem. The failure of the classical realist attempts to interpret quantum theory and the persuasiveness of Bohr's analysis bode ill for realism and encourage passive acceptance of the quantum paradoxes. But an external analysis from the point of view of the mapping theory of knowledge, taking advantage of some of the insights already discussed (and commonplace, if not universally recognized, in sociology) into the nature of concepts, offers both the hope of a realist interpretation and a further research strategy.[37]

From within the MMK, I have no difficulty accepting Bohr's contention that the applicability of classical concepts to a situation depends on the relevant physical conditions obtaining in that situation. Neither need I dispute the notion that the quantum postulate means that the atomic situation and the observation system are an indivisible whole. This means that there are inherent limitations on the simultaneous applicability of classical concepts to the same atomic system under the same physical conditions. What I do not accept is that we have no choice but to use classical concepts in physics. Indeed, the idea that science be restricted to just one conceptual framework is the antithesis of the MMK, where every theory can be considered, at least initially, to have its own conceptual framework. The external validity check requires consistency and coherence with other accepted theories, but not reduction, and so there is no requirement for a single conceptual framework. The problem to be confronted by the mapping theory is rather that of unification, which I discuss in the next chapter.

Against the background of the successes of classical mechanics and the dominance of the reductionist metaphysics, the classical framework seemed unchallengeable. Einstein, at least in the context of the quantum paradoxes, did not question it. But the abandonment of the reductionist metaphysics and the adoption of the mapping model of knowledge make such a challenge the obvious starting point.

Bohr did, as we have seen, put the quantum paradoxes down to the inability of the classical concepts to provide unambiguous descriptions at the atomic level. But Bohr was convinced that we as humans had no choice but to use them. He argued that we have no other active conceptual categories of perception than those of ordinary language refined by the concepts of classical physics. Hooker has pointed out the problems of accepting such notions as this, because science does have new concepts unique to quantum theory, for example, iso-spin, strangeness, exchange-force, and many others.[38]

A Bohrian may opt for an instrumentalist/phenomenalist position, replying that these concepts are not used at the primary level of the description of experimental results, but are merely terms used within the theory. But this reply not only weakens the Bohrian position by removing content, it does not end the debate. We know from anthropology that other cultures have notions of space and time quite different from those of Western culture, and indeed quite different perceptual/conceptual frameworks. But even should it be the case that at present the classical concepts are the only way we have of unambiguously (or objectively) describing experimental results in modern science, Churchland, recall, has shown that such perceptual/conceptual frameworks are best treated as theories, to be revised or overturned if they prove inadequate.

Bohr realised that the classical conceptual scheme was not capable of describing the atomic world "in-itself," given the quantum postulate. But he thought we were stuck with using a classical perceptual/conceptual framework for objective description. However, Churchland has shown at least the possibility of changing our perceptual/conceptual framework while retaining the semantic conditions required for unambiguous description. And the MMK stresses not only the possibility, but the necessity, of using several different perceptual/conceptual frameworks in order to have knowledge of a complex reality. Given this, and the increased likelihood that different frameworks will be required for different organizational levels of reality, attempts to use classical concepts unchanged at the atomic level become surprising.

Concepts, recall, embody theories—theories about the kinds of entities, properties, relations, and processes that exist. As such, they are abstractions from a multi-dimensional reality, and have a limited scope of valid application. The classical mechanical state of a system and the entities, properties and relations used to describe it are all abstractions. The notion that physical properties are abstractions can perhaps be grasped by considering temperature as a property of contained gases. The concept of temperature abstracts from all of the features of contained gases only the translational kinetic energy of the molecules. All other information about gases is ignored. Such perceptual/conceptual categories exhibit robustness, in that they are well-defined, stable, reproducible features of reality, but only within the limits of the domain they are intended to describe. The concept of temperature as a property of contained gases, for example, is defined only when a Maxwell distribution for molecular velocity exists.

Position and momentum are robust perceptual/conceptual categories at the classical level. They are well-defined in classical mechanics as independent variables which together define the classical mechanical state of a system, itself an abstraction. At the quantum level, though, the meaning of these terms has changed. While they still appear to be robust, in the sense that the measuring procedures give stable and reproducible results, they cannot both be measured simultaneously, suggesting that they are interdependent rather than dependent properties. The interdependence of quantum variables has been shown by Hooker, and can be illustrated by the fact that the probabilities of all other quantum variables can be calculated if one is known.[39] This interdependence suggests that what is being abstracted during attempts to measure position at the quantum level is not in fact position in the classical sense but some other feature of reality—one that is related to momentum. The classical concepts of position and momentum are not well-defined at the quantum level. This is an indication that they are being used outside of their scope of valid application. A similar phenomenon seems to have occurred with the concepts of position and time in relativity theory.

This suggests a new approach to research. One could try to define different categories that better describe the quantum world. And one ought to be particularly careful in looking for ways to combine quantum mechanics with relativity theory. The EPR and other quantum paradoxes already suggest the incompatibility of nonlocality with the special theory of relativity.[40] Perhaps such incompatibility has something to do with a failure of the validity of the concepts of position, momentum, and time outside of classical mechanics. These concepts are defined within classical mechanics, and even if they should become well-defined in quantum theory and special relativity, there is no guarantee, or even likelihood, that the new definitions will converge.

While this sort of approach, based as it is on the realist mapping theory of knowledge, could remove the embarrassment to realism caused by the seeming impossibility of a realist interpretation of quantum theory, the problems associated with it should by now be apparent. For under the interpretation given here, there may be no direct way to unify quantum theory and the theory of special relativity, just as there is no direct way to unify the theories of Marx and Weber on the class structure of capitalist society.

6.4 The Fragmentation of Knowledge

I have argued that the world is a complex, many-layered reality, better depicted by a process metaphysics than a reductionist one. Together, a process metaphysics and the methodology of the MMK make sense of the pluralist nature of sociology, and together they provide for the possibility of unifying the knowledge obtained from the diverse theoretical perspectives. In a complex world, different perspectives make accessible different bodies of information. In addition, it is through the coordination of multiple perspectives that robust features of reality can be distinguished from those features of reality that are merely a function of the theoretical framework used.

I also argued that despite the general possibilities for unifying knowledge that are characteristic of a process metaphysics and the MMK, the existence of multiple perspectives has ontological implications that do not exist under a reductionist metaphysics and methodology. These ontological implications arise from the fact that each theory or interconnected network of theories specifies, either implicitly or explicitly, the sort of entities, processes, relations, and properties that the theory can validly use. The ontologies so specified have a limited scope of valid application and cannot unproblematically be transported across theories.

My discussion of this ontological implication of the MMK led me to propose several methodological prescriptions. I pointed out that errors could be avoided if the ontology of theories and their scope of valid application were made explicit. I argued further that, particularly in multi-perspective disciplines, the ontology of theories should be defined at a sufficient level of detail to make explicit the invalid nature of the automatic assumption of intertheoretic coherence. And I argued that special care should be taken in attributing properties that are clearly defined at one layer of reality to features of any other layer of reality, for there is no reason to suppose that such properties will prove robust through such a shift.

But while the ontological insights arising from the MMK ought to lead to fewer errors in scientific thought, and particularly in sociology, they raise an additional, and potentially very serious, issue—the issue of whether knowledge obtained via the MMK methodology can as a matter of fact be unified. For compared with an empiricist and reductionist epistemology, the MMK seems to be in danger of ontological overpopulation and a radical fragmentation of knowledge. The sociological concept of class is defined differently in different sociological perspectives, multiplying the number of sociological entities and limiting the extent to which research findings from different perspectives can be combined. And the external analysis of the problems involved in giving a realist interpretation of quantum mechanics suggests that the properties of position and momentum as used in quantum theory are quite different from the properties of position and momentum in classical mechanics. The possibility of achieving external coherence, one of the validity requirements of the MMK, begins to look problematic.

And when one looks at the state of the more complex sciences such as biology and psychology, there is indeed a fragmentation of knowledge. In the social sciences it is particularly marked, as Fiske has shown.[41] Along with other analysts of the social sciences, Fiske argues that the sources of the fragmentation of knowledge include the diversity of the areas being studied and the differing interests of the investigators. This diversity leads, as the mapping theory predicts, to a diversity of methods. Because much of the ontology of psychology, for example, is operationally defined, this leads in turn to ontological overpopulation. Different studies of the same phenomena may produce quite discrete parcels of knowledge.

The consequences of the fragmentation of knowledge are serious. The MMK avoids relativism only by arguing that our knowledge is unifiable because it is obtained by interaction with a single and cohesive, if complex, reality. That single reality plays a part in arbitrating between competing theories, and the assumption of a single reality underlies the validity criteria of internal and external consistency and coherence. But if a great deal of knowledge is fragmented, the relationship between different theories becomes problematic. In the face of the issues raised by the ontological implications of its methodology, the MMK requires a powerful theory of unification. While I have hinted that the notion of robustness is pivotal to the unification of knowledge, my discussion has so far been insufficient to show that it can carry the weight required. It is to the problem of unification in general, and to a further exploration of the notion of robustness in particular, that I turn in the next chapter.

7

The Unification of Knowledge

"Suppose a man saw a dog, let's say, that wasn't really there in the usual way, so to speak. Nobody else but the man can see the dog. The man feeds the dog dog food, and everyone sees the dog food eaten by the dog they can't see."

—Russell Hoban, *The Lion of Boaz-Jachin and Jachin-Boaz.*

We live in a complex world, and reliable knowledge of that world, I have argued, requires a pluralist methodology. But the knowledge thus obtained is potentially fragmented, and the ontology overpopulated, compared with knowledge obtained under the reductionist research program. The social world is even more complex than the physical world, and knowledge in the social sciences does in fact come in discrete parcels. This, and the irreducibly rich and interest-related nature of the ontology of the social sciences, has convinced many social scientists of the relativist view that the validity of theories can, at best, be assessed only from within a theoretical perspective. The possibility of the multi-perspective social sciences progressing toward a body of unified knowledge is abandoned as impossible in principle.

But the MMK, with its naturalist realist assumptions, in principle allows for the development of perspective-independent criteria for assessing the validity of theories, because the world itself plays an important part in the selection of scientific theories. Theories can be tested directly through causal interaction with the world. Recall that the prospector, in searching for gold at a location where its likely presence is indicated by a geological map, is in fact testing the map. But because theories can only be partial representations of reality, and because they cannot accurately represent all of the features in their domain, they can be tested for adequacy only with respect to the purposes for which they were designed. It is precisely the interest-based nature of knowledge, according to the MMK, that allows theories to be tested for validity.

Theories can also be tested via the application of internal and external consistency and coherence tests. But the criteria of internal and external consistency, I have argued, make sense only on the assumption of a unified reality of which knowledge can be obtained through causal interaction. And the application of those tests depends both on the assumption of the unified nature of the world and the de facto unification of our knowledge of it.

So not only is the MMK capable of unifying knowledge in principle, but it depends upon that very possibility for its criteria of validity. Nonetheless, the question remains whether, as a matter of fact, and in light of the potential of the MMK for fragmenting knowledge, unification can actually be achieved—of how, precisely, discrete parcels of knowledge, particularly those from the fragmented social sciences, might be unified. Pluralism, even the radical pluralism I develop here, does not entail a vicious relativism, but the latter might well result from the former, unless adequate methods for unifying the knowledge are available. This chapter is devoted to exploring adequate methods for unifying knowledge of a complex reality.

The potentially fragmented nature of the knowledge produced by a pluralist methodology has its source in two different but related factors, both of which were discussed in the previous chapter. The first factor is the interest-relatedness of scientific theories. Scientific theories, I argued, are constructed with interests in mind, and the validity of theories or networks of theories depends at base on how well they guide interaction with the world in respect of those interests. The unification of these interest-related theories, then, will depend on their all being related to some unique value or interest. I explore this issue in §7.1. The second factor that potentially fragments knowledge is the fact that each theory or set of theories specifies its own ontology. The validity criterion of external coherence requires a specification of the relationships between the ontologies of different theories or networks of theories. I address the issue of specifying the nature of the relationships between the ontologies of different theories in §7.2 and §7.3. In §7.4, I draw together the arguments from the previous two sections, showing how the MMK is capable of unifying knowledge of a complex reality.

7.1 Epistemic Values and the Unification of Knowledge

According to the MMK, theories are constructed with interests in mind, and are used to guide decision making and action. The relationship between the theory/map and its domain is complex. The theory/map receives input both from its domain and from the metatheoretic level. The latter is directly related to the purposes for which the theory/map was designed. The validity of a theory, then, is a function not only of the relationship between the theory and its domain but of the purposes for which it was designed. The possibility of unifying a particular set of theories, then, depends on their having, at base, an overriding common purpose.

Despite the context-dependent and interest-dependent nature of scientific theories, they do in fact have a common purpose. This point can be illustrated by analogy with geographic maps. While every geographic map is constructed with a different interest in mind, all are guides to action or decision making in the geographic world, and as such are subject to the constraints imposed by that world. Those constraints are the direct empirical constraints and the constraints of internal and external consistency and coherence. For example, while one's immediate interest may be to limit the time of overland travel between Sydney and Melbourne to four hours, this interest will not be served by placing Melbourne 200K closer to Sydney on a map and devising a means of transport that can cover the shortened distance in that time. Nor will it be served by omitting barriers to straight line travel such as mountain ranges. Rather, the best strategy will be to work with a map that is as accurate as possible in all of the relevant respects before working on a technological solution. The nature of the geographic world is an important constraint on travelling time and is ignored at one's peril. Therefore, despite the enormous variety of immediate purposes that underlie map construction, there is an overriding *common* interest in reliable knowledge of the geographic world that allows the nature of that world, manifested through our interactions with it, to act as the primary selector of geographic maps.

Similarly, the high value placed on the ability to control interaction with the physical world is the common value underlying the many different interests guiding the search for knowledge of that world, making the unification of fragmented science, and hence the application of the validity criteria of internal and external consistency and coherence, possible. The institution of science, while it may, and indeed does, have other functions, enshrines as its primary purpose the attainment of objective knowledge of the world. This purpose is manifested in the set of norms (that I shall call epistemic values) that distinguish science from other belief production and maintenance institutions. Among the preconditions of a unified science, then, is the separation of epistemic from other values and the allocation of primacy to the former.

This point has been argued from a historical perspective by Ernest Gellner.[1] In relatively stable societies, there is an affinity between the dominant means of production, the dominant ideas of a society and its methods of cognition, and the means of coercion used in that society. The precise nature of the relationships between the spheres of production, cognition, and coercion in any society is contingent. Nonetheless, these relationships are subject to some general constraints. Gellner, exploring the interplay between the various spheres of production, coercion, and cognition at various points in human history, shows that a unified science could not have developed in hunter-gatherer societies. The reason is that hunter-gatherer societies operate with multi-purpose conceptual systems. The multi-purpose conceptual systems of the hunter-gatherers results in a "multiplicity of disconnected quasi-empirical sensitivities, each deeply meshed with its set of quite *un*-referential, non-empirical, social controls."[2] The diverse conceptual senses through which the world is perceived are, as a result of their multi-purpose nature, incapable of presenting a unified picture of the world. Industrial societies, in contrast, have developed a referential perceptual system, conceptually separating the epistemic from the social, thus allowing the development of an objective science on the assumption of a unified world.[3] The success of science is due to the single-purpose nature of its theories.

The force of the distinction between single-purpose and multi-purpose conceptual systems can be seen by recalling Ziman's distinction between maps and pictures. Ziman argued that maps were more consensible than pictures, and hence could be objectively validated. Maps abstract from reality only those features that can, in principle, be agreed upon. They are able to do this because they have clearly defined epistemic purposes, underpinned by the general purpose of guiding users in their interactions with the geographic world. Pictures of some aspect of reality, on the other hand, may have multiple purposes. These may include the essentially non-epistemic aesthetic, symbolic, and emotive purposes, and may or may not include identification of some aspect of the world and its properties. The existence of multiple purposes is a part of what makes agreement over accuracy of representation unlikely, and hence makes pictures intrinsically less consensible than maps.

The products of science, scientific theories, must be consensible. And to be consensible, they must be constructed with a single overriding purpose, one which allows objective agreement to be achieved provided that the world is in fact unified. This purpose is to obtain reliable guidance in our interactions with the world. Science, Gellner argues, "is based on the assumption of an orderly, homogeneous, unified external system, endowed with no baseline fixed ontology, accessible through its fragmented manifestations, and never directly approachable as a totality."[4] But despite the fragmented and indirect nature of scientific knowledge, the procedures that make up science do work consensually and the products of science are relatively cumulative. The reliable and relatively cumulative nature of scientific knowledge is possible because of the precedence of epistemic values over other values. And the precedence of epistemic values is linked with the need to manipulate interaction with the physical world.

In contrast with the physical world, the social world, or rather some aspects of it, can be manipulated relatively independently of the possession of reliable sociological knowledge. This is because a great deal of human action is taken on the basis of beliefs that are held irrespective of their truth or falsity. In fact, false beliefs may on occasion be more functional for the cohesion of a society than true ones.[5] False beliefs may also be more functional than true beliefs for particular people or groups or classes of people in a society. The powerful in society, for example, may have a greater interest in the production of false social beliefs than in true ones, and for the very same reason that true natural scientific beliefs are favored—increased control over the world.

It is for this sort of reason that, as I pointed out in chapter 2, obscurity in social theory is often a political asset to those in power. Moreover, particular ideologies may be, and often are, supported by single-perspective views of the social world. Different ideologies have affinities with different sociological perspectives. Sociology, then, as a fragmented body of knowledge obtained via the application of different sociological perspectives, often plays a part in legitimizing domination. It is for such reasons that Gellner argues that while industrial society, in contrast to hunter-gatherer and agrarian societies, favored the development of a single-interest natural science, it has not to date favored the development of a single-interest social science.

This does not mean epistemic interests *could not* take precedence over political interests, resulting in a unified social science.[6] But it does explain, to a certain extent, the current fragmented state of sociological knowledge. For if epistemic interests are not primary, but are subordinate to other interests, the theories that arise will not be compatible. They will be like maps of imaginary countries. These maps may bear a number of similarities to real countries. Nonetheless, they will not be able to be embedded in a more general map of the world.

This situation is exemplified in the relationship between the beliefs about the origins of the physical world held by creation scientists, on the one hand, and evolutionists, on the other. The primary purpose underlying the development of creation science is not epistemic. Its main concern is consistency with a body of mysteriously revealed beliefs about the origins of the world. The primary purpose underlying evolutionary theory is epistemic. While evolutionary theory forms part of the relatively coherent body of scientific knowledge, creation science does not. Because creation science places other values before epistemic interests, it is incompatible with evolutionary theory, and the two cannot be unified.

To be scientific, then, a discipline ought to place the highest value on unified knowledge. A prerequisite of a unified sociology is that it be a single-interest sociology—one that values epistemic interests above other interests. Without this, not only will sociology itself never be a coherent body of knowledge, it will never be able to achieve coherence with the natural sciences. A unified sociology would still be pluralist. But there would be communication across the various perspectives and an attempt to unify the knowledge obtained via the various methods. The use of multiple perspectives in this way would even out the biases of the individual perspectives, at the same time ending sectarianism. It is to the extent that it is sectarian (or multi-paradigmatic), rather than to the extent that it is multi-perspective, that sociology is unscientific and incapable of unification.

7.2 Reductionism and Unification

While it is a prerequisite of a unified science, giving priority to epistemic interests is not of itself sufficient to unify a fragmented body of knowledge, because it is not the only source of fragmentation. The second factor that potentially fragments knowledge is the fact that each theory or set of theories specifies its own ontology. The relationships between the ontologies of different theories or networks of theories must be specified if the validity criterion of external coherence is to be applied.

The problem of unifying the ontologies of different layers of reality is particularly problematic, and it is to this problem that I now turn. The traditional strategy for unifying the ontologies of different layers of reality in the physical sciences is reduction. Under the sway of mechanistic materialism, the explicit goal of science during the last three centuries has been to explain the diversity and complexity of the phenomenal world in terms of the underlying stable reality of the micro world. Unification has been pursued by attempting to reduce theories accounting for the relationship between macrostates, processes, properties, and events to theories in terms of microstates, processes, properties, and events by establishing a deductive relationship between the two sets of theories.[7] Theoretical reduction, then, parallels ontological reduction.

Reductionism has been a very successful research strategy, and its successes have led to reduction being regarded as synonymous with unification. But, as I argued in chapter 6, reality is multi-layered, and the various levels of reality may be relatively autonomous. A rain forest, for example, is causally effective relatively independently of its micro composition. The relative autonomy of various layers of reality makes reduction too strong a requirement for unifying their ontologies. Moreover, the requirement of deduction in theoretical reduction shows the affinity between reductionism and the positivist epistemologies, which, recall, admitted only narrowly logistic relations between facts and theories and also between unified theories. This affinity between reductionism and positivism suggests a strategy for searching for an adequate method of unifying theories at different levels of reality. Just as earlier I searched for a model of knowledge that loosened the logical constraints on validity proposed by positivism, so now I propose to study reductionist unification strategies and their errors in the hope that the nature of those errors will lead to the discovery of adequate methods of unification.

7.2.1 Reductionist Unification Strategies

Reductionism in the more complex and historical natural sciences like biology and geology, let alone in the social sciences, never did match the success it had in the physical sciences. Nonetheless, it was for a long time paradigmatic, and is still influential—although, paradoxically perhaps, less so in the physical sciences, where the limitations of the mechanistic view of the world have been increasingly apparent.[8] I shall illustrate the nature of reductionist research strategies and some of the problems to which they give rise through a discussion of some examples from biology. This will serve several purposes. The first is that biology is among the more complex of the natural sciences, besides being historical. It thus shares many of the characteristics of sociology. A second reason is that, in discussing methodological issues that are relevant to the social sciences, it is often preferable to illustrate them, at least initially, with reference to analogous cases in the natural sciences, where emotional and political commitments are less likely to cloud the issues. A third reason is that reductive strategies in sociology lead inexorably to the reduction of social factors to biological factors, blurring the boundaries of the disciplines anyway. And a further reason is that, of late, the issue of reductionism has attracted much productive debate in biology.

Richard Dawkins's reductionist theory of the selfish gene, for example, has sparked a great deal of controversy. Life, like the rest of the world, can be organized into levels of complexity. Genes, organisms, and species are three of the major levels in biology. Within orthodox Darwinian evolutionary theory, genes mutate and are the unit of variation; organisms interact with their environment and are the unit of selection; and species change as a result of selection and are the unit of evolution. Dawkins argues that the fundamental unit of selection is not the organism but the gene, which acts merely to reproduce more copies of itself. Organisms are simply temporary homes for genes.[9]

Stephen Jay Gould argues against Dawkins's reductionist thesis on the grounds that natural selection operates at the level of the phenotype. "Selection views bodies. It favours some bodies because they are stronger, better insulated, earlier in sexual maturation, fiercer in combat, or more beautiful to behold."[10] If genes were directly responsible for those phenotypic characteristics that are acted on by natural selection—if, as Gould puts it, "bodies were unambiguous maps of their genes"—then Dawkins might be right. But they are not. Characteristics of organisms are each the result of many genes in hierarchically organized chains of action that are mediated by the environment. The organisms themselves grow, reproduce, and die as a result of those characteristics and the environment.

Gould puts the fascination of Dawkins's theory down to the dominance of an atomist, reductionist, determinist metaphysics. While reductionist metaphysics has been successful in the study of simple objects made of few parts and uninfluenced by prior history;

> . . . organisms are much more than amalgamations of genes. They have a history that matters; their parts interact in complex ways. Organisms are built by genes acting in concert, influenced by environments, translated into parts that selection sees and parts invisible to selection. Molecules that determine the properties of water are poor analogues for genes.[11]

Gould explicitly uses a many-layered model of a complex reality, with each hierarchical level relatively autonomous, but interacting with other levels. His objection to Dawkins is not that genes cannot be a unit of selection on occasion, as his discussion of Orgel and Crick's selfish DNA hypothesis shows. It is rather that they are not always the unit of selection. Let us look at Gould's argument.

Orgel and Crick put forward the selfish DNA hypothesis as an explanation of the high redundancy of middle-repetitive DNA. Middle-repetitive DNA form between fifteen and thirty percent of both the human and fruit fly genome, yet do not code for proteins. While some middle-repetitive DNA may play a regulatory role, turning other genes on and off and determining the sequence and location of expression of genes that do code for proteins, there is just too much of it, too randomly dispersed, to argue that each has been preserved because natural selection favored it in a regulatory role. It has been argued that some middle-repetitive DNA may, like the transposons in prokaryotes, be able to produce copies of themselves that can then move autonomously to other positions. Orgel and Crick argue that if this is so, an adaptive explanation of middle-repetitive DNA may not be necessary. The extra copies may persist simply because the organism has not noticed them.

Such an explanation is not satisfactory if organisms are taken as the only units of selection, as orthodox Darwinism would have it, because the selfish DNA does nothing for the organism. Certainly, selection can work only on discrete individuals with a historical lineage. But Gould argues that there is a hierarchy of such individuals with legitimate categories both above and below the organism. Although selfish DNA may do nothing for the organism, in this case the organism is the wrong level of analysis. Seen from the genetic level, transposable elements have found a way to make more surviving copies of themselves. If the effect of this repetition and transposition on the organism is not sufficient to affect the organism's chances of survival and reproduction, it will not be suppressed. But natural selection may well limit the process. Increase of selfish DNA to the point where there is a cost to the carrying organism could result in the death without reproduction of the organism and all within it.[12] On occasion, then, it may well be appropriate to consider genes as the unit of selection. But the matter is contingent. Organisms, too, are selected.

Gould also argues for units of selection above the level of the individual organism. As an example, he discusses the work of V. C. Wynne-Edwards, who argued that the social group was the appropriate unit of selection for the evolution of social behavior in animals. Wynne-Edwards considered the problem of how, if individuals struggle only for reproductive success, many species seem to maintain relatively stable populations well-matched to the available resources. The traditional explanation was in terms of external environmental controls on population growth, such as predation and the availability of food. In good times, populations rose and groups flourished. In bad times, scarcity caused hardship and could even wipe out whole groups. But Wynne-Edwards noted that many species seem to be able to read the condition of the environment and apply internal controls, regulating their reproduction accordingly. Groups from such species have a better chance of surviving both good times and bad. Yet in many such groups, individuals sacrifice their own reproduction for the group's benefit. Wynne-Edwards postulated that social organizations were the appropriate units of selection in analyzing such situations, and interpreted much animal behavior, for example, dominance hierarchies and altruistic behavior, in this light.[13]

Traditional Darwinians rejected Wynne-Edwards's thesis, pointing out that dominance behaviors could as easily be explained in terms of individual struggle. Altruism was interpreted in several ways. It was pointed out that much seemingly altruistic behavior could be seen to benefit the individual equally. For example, a warning cry given to a group might seem a risky and altruistic act, calling the attention of the group to the presence of predators but at the same time attracting the attention of the latter to the individual crier. But the swarming behavior of the alerted group may in fact be the best protection the individual has. The theory of kin selection, based on the fact that siblings share on average half their genes, was also used to explain how the altruistic behavior of an individual toward close kin, and also non-reproductive behavior, could in theory increase the chances of that individual's genes being reproduced in the offspring of kin.

Although most of the examples used to support group selection can be reinterpreted in the light of individual selection, Gould points out that most evolutionists now accept that group selection does occur under certain special circumstances.[14] Other things being equal, though, the ontologically more parsimonious explanations in terms of individual selection are preferred by biologists. My point in discussing the units of selection debate is not to come down for or against the existence of particular units of selection. Rather, it is to illustrate that reductionism as a research strategy rules out in an a priori fashion all analyses and explanations at any level but the supposedly fundamental one.

7.2.2 The Problems of Reductionism

In a single-layered reality, such an a priori assumption may not prove problematic, although the assumption itself could never be empirically supported from within a reductionist perspective. But if reality is, as I argued in chapter 6, many-layered, the reductionist assumption will lead to empirical problems. This point has been made forcefully by Levins and Lewontin in their debate with Simberloff over appropriate units of study in the related but more complex field of ecology.

Simberloff analyzes development and progress in the fields of evolutionary theory and genetics, noting similarities in their development, and associating progress in both fields with similar kinds of paradigm shifts. The paradigm shifts both involved, according to Simberloff, a change from a holistic idealism to a form of mechanistic reductionism, and a change from seeing the world in terms of deterministic cause and effect to seeing it as stochastic in principle. He argues that the same sort of progressive change is now occurring in the field of ecology, centering on the discussion of communities.

> An initial emphasis on similarity of isolated communities, replaced by concern about their differences; examination of groups of populations, largely superseded by study of individual populations; belief in deterministic succession shifting, with the widespread introduction of statistics into ecology, to realization that temporal community development is probabilistic; and a continuing struggle to focus on material, observable entities rather than ideal constructs; all [these are] parallel trends which I have described for genetics and evolution.[15]

The implications of Simberloff's approach are that ecological studies from a community perspective are not likely to enhance the progress of ecology, which should rather adopt an individual populations perspective. Holistic approaches to the community or ecosystem (and Simberloff includes Levins as a holist) are seen as idealist, as treating the ecosystem in Clementsian style as a superorganism. I shall not go into the debate in detail. Not only is it wide-ranging, but like most debates, it involves matters of claim and counter-claim over the terms of the debate, what counts as evidence, and what the authors intended as opposed to how they are interpreted. Nonetheless, the issues raised are of interest. The reduction issue is particularly important, and is familiar to sociologists in the form of the methodological individualism versus holism debates, and in the structural versus action approaches. I believe the approach of Levins and Lewontin is correct. It is certainly what one would expect from the MMK, so I shall give a brief account of it.

Levins and Lewontin, in their response to Simberloff, first point out that as long as the debate is framed in terms of a choice between "mechanistic reductionism championing materialism, and idealism representing holistic and sometimes dialectical concerns,"[16] it is likely to be fruitless. Reductionism is not to be confused with materialism.

They continue with an analysis of the reductionist approach. The reductionist approach to ecology studies the interaction between a species and its environment as a one-way relationship. The species is seen as experiencing, reacting to, and evolving in response to its environment, but the effect of the species on the environment in the interaction is neglected. It is assumed that this reciprocal effect will be picked up in studies of the other species in the environment. For example, a predator species will appear as part of the environment when the prey is being studied, and vice versa.

A number of problems arise with this sort of approach. Levins and Lewontin point out that while the reciprocal interaction of predators and prey, for example, is obvious, being almost a matter of definition, the general point that in any interaction all parties are affected is often forgotten. It is not commonly recognized, for example, that the seedling is part of the environment of the soil in that the soil undergoes lasting evolutionary changes of great magnitude as a result of the plant life it supports. More importantly, they point out that

if two species are evolving in mutual response to each other or if plant and soil are mutually changing the conditions of each other's existence, then the ensemble of species or of species and physical environment, is an object with dynamical laws that can only be expressed in a space of appropriate dimensionality.[17]

For example, the populations of predator and prey will approach an equilibrium that can be represented by a spiral path in the two-dimensional space whose axes are the abundances of the two species. From this path, given a location in the two-dimensional space at a point in time, a unique vector of change can be given for the next instant. But each of the component species oscillates in abundance, so given only the abundance of one species, one cannot predict whether it will increase or decrease at the next interval. The monotone behavior of the system is not predictable from the separate equations of each species. Levins and Lewontin point out that "the rule of behavior of the new object is not an obscurantist holism but a rule of evolution of a composite entity that is appropriate to that level of description and not to others."[18]

Note the contrast with the Clementsian concept of a superorganism, in which the community is seen as expressing some general organizing principle, some harmony of nature; or at the very least as a self-maintaining system in much the same way that Parsons sees society. In such a system, the behavior of the parts is explained solely by the way they function to maintain the whole, or otherwise realize its ends. Such explanations are correctly seen as idealist. Levins and Lewontin's point is that causal/dynamic descriptions, as well as functional descriptions, can be given at the level of community, so descriptions at the functional level are not always idealist.

Indeed, as Levins and Lewontin go on to argue, holistic idealism and mechanist reductionism share a common fault, that of recognizing "true causes" at only one level of reality and seeing phenomena at other levels as mere epiphenomena, having perhaps epistemological validity, but certainly no ontological validity. A naturalist realist materialism accepts neither of these positions, but rather equates existence with the presence of a distinctive causal dynamic. From this point of view, there are many levels of reality, the objects of which may be relatively autonomous but nonetheless may interact with objects

at other levels. The way in which the character of a particular species population affects other species populations in a community will be a function not only
of the characteristics of the other individual populations and the physical environment, but also of the structure of the community. A proper study of community phenomena requires shifting between a community perspective and an
individual population perspective, excluding neither one nor the other.

In biology, then, there are many levels of reality. Which levels of analysis are appropriate depends in any particular case on the problem in question.
In a sense, this is recognized even by reductionists. As Levins and Lewontin
point out, there is no clear stopping place in the reductionist program. Reductionists, even reductionist biologists, ought ultimately to have an interest in explaining communities at the level of some fundamental particles. Why stop at
populations, organisms, or genes? But the attribution of reality to entities at
each level is a contingent matter, and ultimately depends on whether the objects
in question form part of a causal/dynamic description at that level. Good science requires that one look not only at one level of reality, but at the interactions between levels of reality. The relative autonomy of the levels and the
complexity of the interactions both within and between levels suggests that
shifting perspective from one level to another will be a better research strategy
than either holism or reductionism. Treating all biological phenomena as
epiphenomena of a single-layer reality, whether it be the dynamic of some over-
arching whole or the relations between some fundamental individuals, is not a
good strategy for unification.

Reductionism, Sociobiology and the IQ Debate. Reductionism is perhaps
even more influential in the social sciences than it is in the biological sciences.
This is not unexpected, for given the common, though mistaken, equation of
naturalism with positivism and reductionism, it has often been assumed that the
social sciences are only scientific to the extent that they are reductionist. For
those whose aim is a scientific sociology, reductionism has often been seen as
a necessity.[19] But further, reductionist social science receives support from the
fact that its findings automatically favor the status quo. This will be illustrated
below, where I examine the typically reductionist social scientific theory of biological determinism.

Biological determinism is reductionist social science taken to extremes.
It is the thesis that both shared behavioral norms and the social and economic
differences between groups of humans are ultimately the result of innate, in-
herited characteristics. Society, in this view, is to be explained by individual
psychology, itself to be explained in terms of biology. The political utility of
such a view to those in power ought to be obvious. If the organization of society simply reflects natural differences among groups, then it makes little sense
to question it, to ask whether or not it is just, or to seek to change it. While it

may be regrettable that women are inferior to men, blacks inferior to whites, and the lower class inferior to the upper class, it is seen as an inescapable fact of nature. And strategically, it is easier to accept the status quo than to try to tamper with nature, a costly and uncertain business.

This does not mean that reductionist social scientists have a political axe to grind, although they may have. Rather, science is a social enterprise. The problems that scientists set themselves and the way they frame their questions are functions of societal values. This does not mean that science produces no valid knowledge, but it does mean that where the cultural or political significance of a topic is very high and the amount of reliable information low, the findings of science virtually reflect the dominant social values. The sectarian, nationalistic, and ethnocentric nature of sociology is better explained in this way than in terms of unscrupulous, naive, or cynical sociologists fabricating results.

But biological determinism, indeed any science, cannot be criticized simply because one finds it distasteful. Recent criticisms of biological determinism by Gould,[20] and by Rose, Lewontin, and Kamin,[21] recognize this, and while they do point out the political connections involved, their arguments against biological determinism center on the errors of thought and fact involved in much biological determinist research, on the failure of determinist research programs to adequately explain the facts in their domain, and on the inherent limitations of the reductionist view of science that both guides biological determinism as a research program and justifies it.

To illustrate these points, I shall discuss Gould's study of just one facet of the biological determinist program, the measurement of intelligence, and in particular the intelligence quotient (IQ) debate. But first I shall show the reductionist context of the IQ debate. To give a reductionist account of social stratification is to account for the various strata of society in terms of the personal attributes of the individuals in each stratum. It is a common, though highly questionable, assumption that people hold the positions they do in modern industrial societies as a result of their abilities. According to this view, political leaders, capitalists, professionals, intellectuals, and laborers, for example, have the jobs they do because their individual characteristics suit them for those positions. In modern Western societies, a high education standard is a prerequisite for most of the better rewarded jobs, and the education system is used in part to select specific people for specific jobs. Success or failure in the education system, according to reductionism, is held to be primarily a function of the characteristics of the individual, and in particular of intelligence. Intelligence, in turn, is seen as a biological characteristic. Thus, social structure becomes explicable primarily in terms of biology. While intelligence testing began with the aim of developing predictors of educational success, the reductionist strategy behind much of the research into IQ has been to isolate and quantify intelligence and to demonstrate its heritability in the biological sense, thus demonstrating the links between biology and intelligence and strengthening the claim that the social structure of modern Western societies is reducible to the biological characteristics of individuals.

Gould's[22] study of intelligence testing starts with Alfred Binet, who early this century devised a series of tests designed to identify early in schooling those children likely to do poorly at school. The intention was to provide such children with some form of special schooling to improve their chances. Binet's tests were designed to eliminate the effects of specifically learned knowledge and skills, while their range was broad enough that he hoped they would be able to abstract a child's general potential in a single score. Binet never claimed either that his tests were culturally neutral, nor that he was measuring some unitary, heritable, biological, and unchanging ability. Nonetheless, Binet's tests are the foundation of modern IQ tests, and Gould cites determinist research that suggests that modern IQ tests do make such claims. Further, the differential abilities of different race, gender, and class groups in IQ testing has been taken to indicate the naturally inferior intelligence of, for example, women, blacks, and the working class, and hence the inevitability of their generally lower social status and lack of power.

Gould traces the history of biological determinist attempts to identify and measure intelligence and to show its biological and hence supposedly fixed nature. The study shows how the whole determinist program rests on two major errors, reification and reduction. The error of reification involves the unjustified attribution of ontological existence to abstract concepts, treating them as things or entities. The error of reduction, in turn, involves the assumption that the reified object is explicable in terms of some baseline ontology. I shall examine the error of reification first.

In the present example, it is intelligence, the complex and multifaceted ability to cope with the world, that is reified. It is assumed to be a single entity, located in the brain. The assumption is then made that this entity can be measured in some objective way. Interestingly, Gould points out, these assumptions turn out to be mutually reinforcing. The positive correlation coefficients over a range of mental tests led Charles Spearman virtually to invent factor analysis, which he then used as a tool for inferring causes from correlations. Gould tells the tale:

> Since most correlation coefficients in the matrix are positive, factor analysis must yield a reasonably strong first principle component. Spearman calculated such a component indirectly in 1904 and then made the cardinal invalid inference that has plagued factor analysis ever since. He reified it as an "entity" and tried to give it an unambiguous causal interpretation. He called it *g*, or general intelligence, and imagined that he had identified a unitary quality underlying all cognitive mental activity—a

quality that could be expressed as a single number and used to rank people on a unilinear scale of intellectual worth.[23]

The range and increasing sophistication of the mathematical procedures that can be used to isolate g has led some to believe that it is a robust concept and so to attribute reality to it. But Gould's analysis shows the similarity of all of the procedures and demonstrates that g is a function of the type of mathematical tool. In the sense that g can be considered robust at all, it is a robust feature of the measurement process itself.

But it is the belief that g is a robust and relatively stable feature of the human mind that encourages the error of reduction. While ever intelligence is considered some unitary quality there is a temptation for reductionists to explain the cause of differences in intelligence genetically. Now, the possibility of a genetic explanation for differences in IQ cannot simply be assumed, any more than the existence of g. The physical and social environments are equal, if not more plausible, candidates for explaining such differences. It has been clearly demonstrated that intelligence tests are far from culturally neutral. Indeed it is hard to imagine how anyone familiar with their origins and history could imagine them otherwise. And it has also been clearly demonstrated that physical well-being, in terms of nutrition, housing, and freedom from disease, plays a part in intellectual performance. Nonetheless, many attempts have been made to show the biological basis of differences in IQ.

Gould subjects these attempts to a thorough methodological critique, making use of numerous sociological and medical studies. But he also points out the importance of advances in biology in clarifying the limits of biological explanations of social features. The notion of polygenic inheritance, for example, displaces early ideas of a one-to-one mapping between genes and characteristics, and affirms the idea that phenotypic characteristics are the result of the interaction of many genes, and of interaction with the environment. And the discovery that genetic variation between different human populations is less than that within populations has been amply demonstrated, lending support to the claim that differences between class, race, and gender groups are primarily, if not entirely, sociocultural in origin. The uniqueness of humanity lies in the human brain. The human brain has allowed the development of social organization and culture, and consequently enormous ability to manipulate the physical world. Humans both change the physical and social worlds and in turn adapt to these changes. But the primary mechanism of human change is cultural, not genetic.

Gould's study shows that the assumption of reduction is problematic. This is not to say that the possibility of reduction in any particular case should not be examined. Rather, whether reduction can be achieved is a contingent matter.

Rose, Lewontin, and Kamin take a broader look at reductionist social science rather than concentrating on one particular debate. Their exploration of reductionist fallacies ranges over the so-called scientific justifications for class,
race, and gender inequalities. They also examine the consequences of reductionist views of deviance, which, by locating the causes of deviance in the biology of individuals lead inevitably to such solutions for social unrest as
psychosurgery or "magic bullet" drugs. The entire book is an argument against
reductionist social science and reductionism generally. It is also an argument
for a pluralist methodology of science, a methodology that points the way toward an integrated understanding of the relationship between the biological and
the social.

Like Gould, Rose, Lewontin, and Kamin identify and criticize the underlying assumptions of biological determinism—reification, the assumption
that the reified "object" can be measured, and the assumption that reduction of
the reified "object" is possible—and show the part played by sociology in ex-
posing the fallacies of the IQ debate. But they leave sociologists no room for
complacency. If biological determinism is fundamentally flawed as theory and
method, so too is cultural determinism, for it, in its own way, is reductionist too.

Rose, Lewontin, and Kamin discuss two types of cultural determinism.
The first gives ontological primacy to the social over the individual. It is in this
sense the antithesis of biological determinsim.[24] The structuralist perspectives
discussed in § 1.2.3, when based on ontological beliefs and thus seen as the only
way to view the world, exemplify this type of cultural determinism. The economic determinism of vulgar Marxism, for example, holds that all forms of
consciousness, knowledge, and cultural expression are determined by the mode
of production. The corollary of this is that differences in individual ability are
to be explained solely in terms of the social structure.

The second type of cultural determinism gives primacy to the individual
over the social, but divorces the individual from the biological.[25] Such theories
see the human mind at birth as a *tabula rasa,* almost infinitely plastic, to be
shaped by early socialization processes, but hardening later. Strategies for the
cure of deviant behavior vary according to beliefs about the extent of later plasticity. If the mind is considered plastic, resocialization (or brainwashing) may
be attempted. If not, the strategies are reduced to physical control, or, somewhat
paradoxically, to the strategies of the biological determinists. This sort of approach to society leads to the assumption that a general and uniform education
system will bring about social equality. The individualist social approach shares
with biological determinism the assumption that one's role, status, and power
in society are determined by one's ability. Both ignore the influence of social
structure on the individual, instead seeing social structure as determined by the
individual.[26]

Rose, Lewontin, and Kamin's analysis does not mean, any more than
Gould's, that studies from the structuralist and individualist sociological per-

spectives should be abandoned. Rather, what needs to be abandoned is the assumption of a baseline ontology for the social world, indeed for the whole world.

The studies by Gould and by Rose, Lewontin, and Kamin into reductionist social science show that the assumption of reduction leads to empirical problems. The strategy of reduction, then, cannot be considered adequate to the task of unifying all knowledge. It remains the case, though, that reduction has sometimes been achieved in science, and that reductionism itself has been a fruitful research strategy. Rather than abandoning reduction as a research strategy, I turn in the next section to an exploration of the limits of reductionism, in the hope that an investigation of the underlying nature of the empirical problems caused by the assumption of reduction will lead to some new insights on unification.

7.2.3 The Biases of Reductionist Research Strategies and Correctives to Them

William Wimsatt has done considerable research into the nature of the empirical problems caused by reductionism, and I outline his analysis in some detail here. His work is of particular interest because in analyzing the limits of reduction it points to some non-reductionist strategies for the unification of knowledge. After arguing that, to humans as knowers, reductionism is at best an unattainable ideal, Wimsatt defines the traditional view of reduction as the

(i)   *in principle*
(ii)   *deducibility* of upper-level entities, properties, theories, and laws
(iii)   in terms of the properties, laws, and relations of *any degree of complexity* of entities at the lower level.[27]

Wimsatt points out that the claim of *in principle* translatability is usually explicated in terms of effective computability. That is, given a sufficiently powerful computer, a total state description of a micro-level system and all of the micro-level laws would be sufficient to deduce all macro-level phenomena. While others have criticized this possibility in general, Wimsatt shows that, even for the complex but completely deterministic, and thus effectively computable, game of chess, such computation is *"physically speaking, in principle impossible."*[28]

This raises the question of what can be done when the complexity of the system being analyzed exceeds the available powers of analysis. Consideration of this question led Herbert Simon to propose the principle of bounded rationality. This principle asserts that humans are generally faced with problems of such complexity that they cannot solve them accurately. But instead of abandoning the problem, they resort to various simplifying and approximating techniques.[29] These simplifying and approximating techniques are called "heuristics." It is the necessary use of heuristics that makes the reductionist ideal unachievable, irrespective of whether the world is in fact a single-layered or multi-layered reality.

The concept of a heuristic procedure plays an important part in Wimsatt's argument, because it is by analyzing the nature of reductionist heuristic procedures that the nature of the empirical problems associated with reductionism become apparent. A heuristic procedure has, according to Wimsatt, four important properties:

1. By comparison with truth-preserving algorithms or with other procedures for which they might be substituted, heuristics make no guarantees (or if they are substituted for another procedure, weaker guarantees) that they will produce a solution or the correct solution to a problem. A truth-preserving algorithm correctly applied to true premises must produce a correct conclusion. But one may correctly apply a heuristic to correct input information without getting a correct output.

2. By comparison with the procedures for which they may be substituted, heuristics are very "cost-effective" in terms of demands on memory, computation, or other resources in limited supply (this of course is why they are used).

3. The errors produced by using a heuristic are not random but systematically biased. By this I mean two things. First, the heuristic will tend to break down in certain classes of cases and not in others, but not at random. Indeed, with an understanding of how the heuristic works, it should be possible to predict the conditions under which it will fail. Second, where it is meaningful to speak of a direction of error, heuristics will tend to cause errors in a certain direction, which is again a function of the heuristic and of the kinds of problem to which it is applied.

4. The application of a heuristic to a problem yields a transformation of the problem to a nonequivalent but intuitively related problem. Most important this means that answers to the transformed problem may not be answers to the original problem.[30]

Now, there is nothing irrational in using procedures that may under certain circumstances lead to error, particularly if they are "cost-effective"[31] and/or are the only way of getting knowledge of a system. Indeed, the concept of a heuristic is fundamental, not only to human problem solving, but to evolutionary biology, because biological adaptations have the properties of heuristic procedures.[32] This suggests a functional continuity between biological evolution and cultural evolution as adaptive mechanisms, and is thus thoroughly naturalist.[33] But a rational use of a heuristic must surely explore the circumstances under which the heuristic is likely to fail. A corollary of the first and second properties of heuristics then, is that like all theories and models, heuristics are designed for use in a particular context to solve specific problems, and have a limited scope of valid application.

A corollary of the third property of heuristics is that not only can one predict its bias once a heuristic is understood, but from the observation of systematic biases one can work backward to identify the heuristic that produced them. Every heuristic, as Wimsatt puts it, leaves its own footprint.[34]

But Wimsatt's first analysis of reductionist research strategies is derived by working forward from the reductionist interest in explaining a system in terms of the interaction of its parts. From this very general assumption about reductionism, along with (1) the necessity in studying any system of distinguishing the system, however roughly, from its environment, and (2) the necessity, in studying any problem of complexity, of making simplifying assumptions, Wimsatt shows how eight specific reductionist heuristics follow.[35]

Rather than discuss all eight here, I shall confine myself to enough to bring out the significance of the reductionist approach. The first is a heuristic of conceptualization in which a relational property is described as a lower-order relatively non-relational property. If a property is a function of both system properties and environmental properties (as, for example, "fitness" is a relational property between an organism and its environment), then the simplifying procedure of keeping the environment constant will make the property appear as if it is a function only of system properties. Wimsatt notes that many context dependencies are hidden in this way.[36]

The second strategy that I shall describe operates at the level of model building and theory construction. All model building involves simplifications of both the system and its environment. When a model fails to work, the reductionist strategy is to assume that the internal structure of the system rather than the external structure needs elaborating. It is assumed, in other words, that the model failed because the internal structure was oversimplified.[37]

The last reductionist heuristic that I mention occurrs at the level of observation and experimental design. The reductionist, Wimsatt points out, having played down environmental variables, will fail to record the data necessary to detect interactional or large-scale patterns.[38]

The reductionist heuristics analyzed by Wimsatt have a generic bias—"to ignore, simplify, or otherwise underestimate the importance of the context of the system under study."[39] It was this neglect of context that both Gould and Rose, Lewontin, and Kamin associated with the problems of reductionist social science. Wimsatt illustrates and expands his analysis with a discussion of some of the facets of the units of selection debate.

This debate, recall, was over whether, under certain circumstances, groups rather than individual organisms could be the units of selection. The debate gave rise to the development of a variety of mathematical models that were designed to choose between the relative efficacy of group selection and individual selection in evolutionary theory. All of the models turned out to favor individual selection. But Michael Wade, undertaking an experimental test with flour beetles of the relative efficacy of group selection and individual selection, found that group selection was a significant force—one capable of overwhelming individual selection in the opposite direction.[40] The mathematical models all contradicted the empirical evidence.[41]

Wade became interested in why this had happened and undertook an analysis of the models in question. Despite the fact that the models each used a different set of simplifying assumptions, they had five in common. One of these was the "migrant pool assumption," the assumption that all of the migrants from any groups (the offspring of the groups) go into a common pool from which new groups are randomly drawn. Wimsatt notes that this assumption was accepted by proponents of both sides of the units of selection debate, and for two reasons. The first was the analytic simplicity afforded by the assumption. The second was that the assumption is equivalent to a "time-honored simplifying assumption of population genetics, 'panmixia,' the assumption that all members of a population have an equal probability of mating with any one member."[42] But the assumption of panmixia is just the assumption that there are no groups. It is therefore not surprising, as Wimsatt argues, that the models found little evidence of group selection. Another common simplifying heuristic, "factoring into subproblems," while valid enough under certain conditions, also, Wimsatt argues, cannot validly be used to provide a reductionist account of evolutionary dynamics, and for fundamentally the same reason. Such attempts fail in that they make illegitimate assumptions of context independence.[43]

This sort of mistake is so pervasive that the general failure to see it calls for an explanation. Wimsatt has two explanations of the phenomenon. The first is that failure to see the systematic biases in the models might lie in the fact that humans have a perceptual bias toward focusing on the individual organism rather than the group, a bias well-founded in evolution. This means humans have a tendency to perceive groups simply as collections of individuals. But in the context of the units of selection controversy such a perception assumes what is in fact open to debate, that the group is simply an aggregate of individuals. Moreover, as Wimsatt argues in detail, "The only time it is appropriate to describe it as an aggregate is when the fitness of its components are context-independent . . . or are additive. But, . . . this is a sufficient condition for their not constituting a higher-level unit of selection."[44]

The same sort of problem arises with respect to the ontological status of certain groups in sociology. Barry Hindess, for example, argues against social action theorists that some "actors" are not individual humans. He offers the following minimal concept of an actor: "An actor is a locus of decision and action, where the action is in some sense a consequence of the actor's decisions. Actors do things as a result of their decisions. We call these things actions, and the actor's decisions play a part in their explanation."[45] On this definition, many institutions, clubs, and so on, are actors. They have means of reaching decisions and acting on them. What distinguishes these actors from individual human actors is that their actions depend on the actions of others, and Hindess calls such actors "social actors." But social actors are in no sense reducible to individual actors despite the fact that their actions depend on the actions of others, because they are not constituted by those others. The actions of social actors depend on conditions that are external to any of the actors in question, conditions such as the forms and loci of decision making particular to the social actor in question.[46] The decisions of the other actors (who cannot all be presumed to be individuals anyway) are not additive.

Wimsatt's second explanation for the persistent failure to notice the nature of the reductionist bias derives from the nature of heuristics themselves. First, simplification is unavoidable, and there is, on the face of it, no way of correcting for its effects. Second, heuristics are mutually reinforcing. They reinforce, multiply, and hide the effects of their respective biases.[47] While the use of a number of models from each of a variety of heuristics should show up the artifacts of a particular heuristic, the models developed for the units of selection debate all used some reductionist strategies. Because each of these strategies or heuristics independently biases the models against the inclusion of environmental considerations, cross-checking these models against each other gives an unjustified appearance of robustness to the results. As Wimsatt puts it, " . . . different reductionistic methods hide their mutual inadequacies by covering each other's tracks."[48]

Despite the seeming intractability of the problem, Wimsatt offers two sorts of strategy for discovering and correcting for reductionist bias. The first strategy, robustness analysis, is a general one that can be applied to all heuristics, reductionist or otherwise. I have already made use of the concept of robustness, but I shall expand on it here, as well as in the next section, as it turns out to be central to the problem of unifying knowledge under the MMK.

Wimsatt borrows the notion of robustness from Richard Levins. Levins suggests that a strategy to counteract bias due to a particular model of some phenomenon would be to construct a family of models using different simplifying assumptions with respect to the phenomenon in question. Sociology, as we saw in chapter 6, has different models of social deviance, each of which makes different simplifying assumptions. Some consequences may turn out to be true across all models. These are called robust theorems because they are independent of the simplifying assumptions of any particular model.[49] The strategy of searching for robust theorems, as I shall illustrate further in the next section, means that pluralism—paradoxically for reductionists—is pivotal in the establishment of unified science.

Wimsatt notes some disadvantages of Levins's strategy of searching for robust theorems, neither of which he considers serious. The first is that there is often not even one model, let alone the two or more necessary for the comparison of results. In sociology as a whole this is not a problem. But the social organization of sociology discussed in chapter 1 indicates that access to different models may well be a problem for individual sociologists. The reorganization of the social structure of sociology to encourage the integrated use of the various perspectives is a prerequisite of the unification of sociological knowledge.

Another disadvantage of Levins's strategy is that the assumptions used in developing models are often not explicit, as we saw in the above discussion of the units of selection debate, making it difficult to establish whether or not various models are in fact independent. If models that are thought to be independent are not, then a false impression of robustness may arise. This leads to the prescription that one's underlying assumptions, or at least one's interests and the perspective from which one is working, should be stated. Sociologists are perhaps more *au fait* with this requirement of good science than are other scientists, the point having been stressed by both Durkheim and Weber as being a fundamental requirement of objective sociology.

The second strategy that Wimsatt identifies for discovering and overcoming the biases of heuristics derives from his consideration of the above problems. The analysis of the mathematical models designed to show the relative efficacy of group selection and individual selection revealed that of all possible models, the ones available were all using reductionist heuristics. It was this, recall, that led to the appearance of robustness in the results. While there is no general strategy that will prevent this problem across all heuristics, specific ones can be developed for any heuristic once its general character is known.

Wimsatt has devised a strategy that is capable of correcting the specific biases of reductionism in a way that ensures that pseudo-robust theorems do not survive. The generic nature of the reductionist bias is to ignore or oversimplify the effects of environmental variables on the system in question. Wimsatt makes the point that these are ignored or oversimplified *because* of their position outside the system. It follows that changing the boundaries of the system to include these features will help eliminate the reductionist bias.

> Thus the strategy for eliminating biases in the description and analysis of groups as collections of individuals is to build models in which groups are treated as individuals in a larger system in which they are parts and in which we focus on modeling intergroup relations. . . . The biases of the reductionistic heuristics will still apply, but because the system boundaries have changed, they will have different effects. The comparison of intragroup with intergroup models is the right comparison for testing the robustness or artifactuality of lower-level reductionistic assumptions.[50]

Wimsatt calls his strategy "multi-level reductive analysis," although the term is perhaps misleading. It is reductionist only in the sense that it uses reductionistic heuristics at a variety of levels to counteract the biases that occur from its use at a single level.

Wimsatt's approach to reductionist heuristics and their biases recognizes that reductionist research strategies, like other perspectives, have their place. They should be seen as just one kind of attempt to understand the explanatory relations between different levels of reality rather than as an unending search for foundations at a deeper level of reality.[51] But the exclusive use of reductionist research strategies results in a set of biases whose overall effect is to eliminate the context of the system in question, with the result that the research appears to provide evidence for what has in fact merely been assumed. Multi-level reductive analyses can help eliminate the pseudo-robust effects of reductionist biases. And as a general strategy, research from any perspective needs to be tempered by research from other perspectives and robust theorems sought. The strategy of searching for robust theorems both counteracts the particular biases of research strategies and is a potential unifier of knowledge obtained from different perspectives. I shall take up this point in §7.3. But in the meantime I shall explore the conditions under which microreductionist explanations are inadequate.

7.2.4 Conditions under Which Microreductionist Explanations Are Inadequate

I have just argued that the traditional strategy for unifying knowledge, reductionism, often leads to empirical problems. These problems arise because the various strategies that make up the reductionist heuristic all have the effect of ignoring or playing down the effects of the environment on the system in question, thus making it appear as if the properties of the system could be explained intrasystemically. I introduced two strategies that could help to overcome the generic bias of reductionist research, but I have said little so far about the conditions under which theoretical reduction might be expected to occur.

This problem has been addressed by Alan Garfinkel in a detailed analysis of the nature of social explanation.[52] Garfinkel's analysis revolves around three concepts—explanatory relativity, the determination of the object of explanation, and redundant causality. I shall discuss these concepts in some detail, as they are crucial to an understanding of Garfinkel's argument.

One way to get a foothold on the concept of explanatory relativity is to recall that the MMK, with its pragmatic criteria of validity, insists that every theory has a limited scope of valid application. That scope is determined by the problem that the theory was intended to solve. A theory is an adequate explanation to the extent that it addresses that problem, but it cannot be assumed to be an adequate explanation of any other problem. Garfinkel elaborates on this feature of scientific theories, showing that explanations can be seen as answers to quite specific questions, although these questions are rarely explicit.

Garfinkel is interested in specifying the relationships that exist between various explanations of some phenomena. Explanations may be mutually complementary or contradictory. They may be mutually irrelevant or they may overlap. One may even be reducible to another. But in any particular case, the nature of the relationships between a set of explanations is not always immediately obvious. The relationships between the various explanations of deviance that I outlined in §1.3, for example, are far from obvious. Garfinkel argues that such confusion arises because the dominant models of science have tended to ignore the fact that science is a problem-centred human activity that results in every theory having a limited scope of valid application. The explanatory limits of any theory can in fact be determined by an examination of the question to which the explanation provides an answer. Clarification of the limits of an explanation is a prerequisite for determining its relationship with other explanations of the same phenomenon.

The best way to illustrate these points is with a simple example. Garfinkel considers a situation in which a priest is visiting Sutton, a jailed bank robber. The priest asks Sutton why he robbed the bank. Sutton replies that that is where the money was. Although the priest and Sutton are discussing the same event, Sutton's answer bypasses the priest's question. To the priest, the problem is why Sutton robs at all, whereas to Sutton, the problem is why he robbed the bank, as opposed, say, to the service station. For an explanation to be successful it must address the question at hand.[53]

The ambiguity arises because the priest and Sutton have different objects of explanation. The fact that they do have different objects of explanation becomes apparent when one examines the context of both the question the priest wanted answered and the question that Sutton in fact answered. The context of the questions can be represented by their different contrast spaces. The contrasts the priest wants to draw are between Sutton robbing and not robbing. These two possibilities represent the contrast space of the priest's question. The contrasts that Sutton is drawing are between various places from which money can be stolen. Together, these possibilities represent the contrast space of the question Sutton is answering.

When the same event is embedded in different contrast spaces, an examination of the way their respective contrast spaces are related will show the relationship between different explanations of that event. In the case of Sutton and the priest, Sutton is answering a narrower question than the priest is asking. In fact, Sutton's answer presupposes an answer to the priest's question. It is the fact that explanations are relative to a general background of alternatives—to a contrast space—that Garfinkel refers to as explanatory relativity.

The contrast space of different explanations is a tool that can be used to compare the sorts of relationships that exist between theories. Garfinkel argues that the relationship between two explanations can be specified only if their contrast spaces line up in certain ways.[54]

Having shown that explanations are always relative to some contrast space, Garfinkel argues that the determination of the object of explanation is sometimes problematic. Again, I shall illustrate this with some simple examples from Garfinkel. Consider the following situation. I get up one morning and decide to go for a drive. On rounding a bend on a narrow road I come upon a truck that has just broken down, and, unable to stop in time, I crash into it. When I return home and relate the sorry tale to my spouse, he replies that it wouldn't have happened if I hadn't been speeding. I respond frivolously that that is not true. If I hadn't had breakfast before leaving, I would have been ahead of the truck and the accident would not have happened.

My response was frivolous because the object of my explanation was *that particular accident*. Now everything about the situation, including such irrelevancies as which shoes I was wearing at the time, were necessary conditions of that accident, since if any one of them had not occurred it would not have been *that* accident at all. To escape this absurdity, Garfinkel argues, we have to replace the object of explanation—that particular accident—with a set of perturbations that are regarded as essential to the occurrence. The real object of explanation is an equivalence class of conditions under which I would have had (or been likely to have) an accident.

An interesting question is what to include in the equivalence class. The choice is not arbitrary. It depends to a certain extent on interests. If I have a vested interest in not appearing a reckless driver, I will be interested in reducing the equivalence class. My spouse, with an interest in encouraging me to drive less recklessly, will have an interest in expanding it. But what to include also depends on the way the world is. In this case, the smaller the equivalence class, the less stable it is under perturbation. This means that the explanation cannot be as useful when generalized as a guide to future action. If the equivalence class is too small it prevents the realization that driving too fast is dangerous. Good explanations, Garfinkel argues, require relatively stable objects of explanation.

The determination of the proper object of explanation can be problematic in a different way when the explanation that is required deals with individuals related in a larger system, because some systems have structural characteristics that impose constraints on individual possibilities, while others do not. The practice of grading students according to a curve illustrates a system that imposes structural conditions on the overall distribution of grades.

When students are graded according to a curve, the overall distribution of grades is predetermined. Of a class of fifty students, say, it may have been decided that one A grade, twenty-four B grades, and twenty-five C grades will be awarded. The students' work is then ordered from best to worst. The best student gets an A. The next best twenty-four get Bs, and the last twenty-five, Cs. Such a system can be contrasted with one in which grades are awarded according to some standard of work. In the former system, the explanation of why Mary got an A grade is simply that her work was best. The grade cannot be explained in terms of any intrinsic characteristics of Mary or her work, because others in the class might also have shown those characteristics without getting an A. The object of the explanation in this case is why Mary, and not another of the fifty students, got the A. And the explanation of why Mary got an A and the rest of the class got the grades they did presupposes, but does not explain, the overall distribution of the system. The product of the contrast spaces of the individual possibilities does not equal the total possibility space of the system because certain combinations of individual contrast spaces are not possible.

Compare this with the second type of system. Here, the appropriate explanation of why Mary got an A will be in terms of the quality of her work. The object of the explanation is why Mary got an A and not a B or a C. And an explanation of why Mary got an A and the rest of the class got the grades they did will explain the overall distribution of grades. The product of the individual contrast spaces represents the possibility space of the system as a whole.

It is probably obvious that if one is grading on a curve, an explanation of the overall grade distribution cannot be reduced to an explanation in terms of the individual characteristics of the items being graded. The appropriate object of an explanation of the distribution is represented by a contrast space that includes other systems of grade assignment. When the structural conditions of a system reduce its possibility space below the product of the individual possibility spaces, an explanation of the structure will not be found in the characteristics of the individuals, and theoretical reduction is impossible. The problem is that we do not always know beforehand whether independent structural conditions exist, so we do not know whether a reduction is possible. And as we saw in the last section, to assume that a reduction is possible is to introduce a bias that hides the very possibility that structural conditions exist.

An application of the concepts of explanatory relativity and the determination of the object of explanation proves helpful in some cases. In a successful reduction, the reducing theory will be expected to explain everything that the theory to be reduced explains. This gives us a foothold on developing a precondition of a successful reduction. A reduction can only be successful if the theories concerned have the same, or in some way clearly related, objects of explanation. This means that the problem the theories are addressing must be constructed in such a way that the contrast spaces of the objects of explanation line up. If they do, then a successful reduction may be possible.[55] If grades are distributed according to some standard of work, the object of the explanation of the overall distribution will be the product of the contrast spaces that represent the objects of explanation of individual grades. The contrast spaces of the explanation of overall distribution and those of the individual grades are clearly related. Sometimes, then, an analysis of the objects of explanation of two theories may be a guide to whether one can be reduced to another.

But when the grades were distributed according to a curve, the contrast spaces of the explanation of overall distribution and those of individual grades were not so clearly related. Indeed, the object of the explanation of the distribution curve was represented by a contrast space including different methods of distribution, with no mention of individual contrast spaces. And this was only obvious because of prior knowledge of the structural conditions on the system. Without such prior knowledge, an analysis of the objects of explanation of any two theories may be impossible.

In response to this problem, Garfinkel develops another useful concept—redundant causality. Garfinkel illustrates this concept through a hypothetical example of microreduction taken from population ecology. This example shows, perhaps even more clearly than the grading example, that even if we allow that the world can be described deterministically at some microlevel, macrolevel explanations cannot thereby be dispensed with or reduced.

Garfinkel asks us to consider a simplified ecological system composed of foxes and rabbits (predator and prey). The population levels of the two species fluctuate periodically. A rough explanation of this situation is that the foxes eat the rabbits until there are too few rabbits left to sustain the level of the fox population and it starts to drop off. But with the number of foxes down, the rabbit population is able to increase. This in turn provides more food for the foxes, and their numbers increase again, and so on. The major influence on both population levels is the frequency with which foxes encounter and eat rabbits.[56]

Now, if the fox population gets high, pressure on the rabbits increases. When one of them is caught and eaten it seems reasonable to explain the cause of death in terms of the high fox population. But this is antithetical to a reductionist, as it is a macrolevel explanation of a microstate. The reductionist will want to insist that the macrolevel explanation can be eliminated in favour of a microlevel explanation. At the microlevel, the cause of the rabbit's death will be in terms of the spatiotemporal path of the rabbit intersecting with that of a fox and the fox coming out on top of the encounter.

But the explanations of the death of the rabbit at the microlevel and at the macrolevel are not explanations of the same thing. If we examine the contrast spaces of the two explanations, the microexplanation tells us why the rabbit was eaten by fox f at place p at time t and so on, in contrast to being eaten by another fox at another place at another time. The macroexplanation, on the other hand, tells us why the rabbit was eaten at all, as opposed to not being eaten.

Even if we allow that the entire system can be described deterministically at the microlevel, the macroexplanation does a different job from the microexplanation, and cannot be eliminated.[57]

Not only do the microexplanation and the macroexplanation do different jobs, but in cases like the one above, Garfinkel argues, the macroexplanation is more useful. Let us imagine that we are on the side of the rabbits. The macroexplanation tells us how to stop rabbits being eaten (reduce the fox population), whereas the microexplanation does not. The microexplanation is so specific that the death of the rabbit appears to be merely a matter of chance, in the same way that the car accident I discussed earlier could be made to appear no more than the result of the operation of chance.[58]

The notion that theories have pragmatic requirements—that they are primarily guides to action and decision making—raises again the point that what we look for in a causal explanation is not so much a complete causal specification of an event as the relevant or significant causes. We want to know how not to have car crashes and how not to get eaten. This means that an adequate explanation must have a certain amount of stability under small perturbations of its conditions.[59] The object of the microexplanation in the case of the rabbit is too specific to be stable under perturbation. But the object of the macroexplanation is stable under perturbation. By avoiding the capture space of fox f, the rabbit would likely have entered the capture space of another fox, with the result that it would still have been eaten.

The rabbit-fox system, then, has a number of mechanisms by which to achieve the same result. Such systems are said to exhibit redundant causality. Garfinkel defines these systems as follows:

> Systems which exhibit redundant causality . . . have, for every consequent Q, a bundle of antecedents (P_i) such that:
> 1. If any one of the P_i is true, so will be Q.
> 2. If one P_i should not be the case, some other will.[60]

In such systems, citing only the actual P_i that caused Q will be a defective explanation of Q, for the structure of the system is such that if it hadn't caused Q, another would have. Events within systems with redundant causality have structural conditions and require macrolevel explanations. The existence of redundant causality, then, is a good indicator that a relatively independent set of structural conditions is operating and that those conditions cannot be explained in terms of the characteristics of the individuals comprising the system. The ratio of foxes to rabbits at any one time cannot be explained in terms of how good or bad the foxes are at hunting or the rabbits at avoiding capture.

None of this means that explanations of Q in terms of the particular P_i that caused it are unimportant, for they specify the mechanism by which the structure is instantiated at the microlevel. The instantiation demonstrates the robustness of the particular P_i at both levels, thereby linking the two explanations. It is by demonstrating instantiation, rather than by theoretical reduction, that macroexplanations of the system can be unified with microexplanations.

Garfinkel's analysis shows that for a successful reduction to take place, one realm of discourse should be able to replace another while maintaining its explanatory power. For this to happen, the explanations must be addressed to the same problem or a clearly related one—i.e., the objects of the respective explanations must be the same or clearly related. But the fact that explanations are always relative to some contrast space means that while the objects of two explanations may on the face of it be the same, they often turn out after investigation to be different. For example, microexplanations and macroexplanations of the same event turn out to have different objects when the system in question is subject to a set of relatively independent structural conditions. Such explanations are therefore irreducible. Whether the system is in fact subject to relatively independent structural conditions is also not always obvious. But the existence of redundant causality is a good guide to the existence of structural conditions and hence to the irreducibility of macroexplanations and microexplanations.

As macroexplanations and microexplanations are often not reducible, reduction is not a sufficient strategy for the unification of knowledge. But the analysis of both micro- and macroexplanations of the death of the rabbit shows the distinction between reduction and instantiation. Instantiation turns out to be a key factor in unifying macro- and microexplanations, just as it is the key factor in unifying functional and causal explanations.

To summarize §7.2, while theoretical reduction cannot be regarded as the only way of unifying knowledge (and indeed results in empirical problems if pursued as such), a discussion of the problems of reductionism has brought to light a further strategy for unification—the strategy of searching for robust theorems. Instantiation is a way of demonstrating robustness. The strategy depends on showing ontological unity, but this is distinguished from theoretical reduction. The connection between ontological unity and robustness is explored further in the next section, where I discuss the various ways by which the MMK suggests strategies for unification.

7.3 The MMK and Unification

The possibility of achieving a unified body of knowledge is essential to a naturalist, realist account of validity. But the conditions for achieving successful theoretical reduction, the traditional strategy for unifying knowledge, are rarely met. Moreover, consistent use of reduction alone as a unifying strategy effectively reduces the richness of the world to a single-layered reality and results in a radically misleading, and even false, view of the world. Both in the last chapter and in this one, I have hinted that robustness analyses are adequate to the task of unifying knowledge. The time has come to expand on the concept of robustness. I shall then show how robustness analyses can be modelled by the MMK.

I argued in chapter 5 that underpinning naturalist realist claims to validity is the claim that there is a single causally connectable reality. The reality of any entity, process, property, or event could be established by showing its causal connectedness. In practice, this means that reality can be attributed to whatever features occur in valid causal descriptions or explanations, because knowing is itself a causal process. Knowledge can be unified by showing the reality of things and the ways they are connected. The precise nature of those connections will be contingent and related to the various forms of explanation I discussed in chapter 5. But *is composed of* will be a candidate, as will *is a property of,* *is a part of,* and *shares a boundary with.* The variety of possible relations between things means that the major focus of a unification strategy will be to show not only the reality but the identity of the things that appear in different theories. This was the aim of ontological reduction. The strategy failed because it was assumed that ontological identity could only be achieved by theoretical reduction. But if robustness is an indicator of the reality of an object that is relatively stable across some set of theories, then the establishment of robust entities across that set means that there is a specifiable relationship between the theories. That, according to the causal account of reality I hold, is sufficient to unify the theories in question.

Robustness is in fact taken to be an indicator of the reality of both objects and properties, at both the sensory perceptual and theoretical levels. The boundaries of an ordinary object can be detected in various sensory modalities. The boundaries of a table, for example, can be detected by visual, aural, oral, and tactile changes that roughly coincide. It is the multimodal nature of perception that establishes the table as robust—as an object—and distinguishes it from illusion. While multimodal experiences may occur in dreams and drug-induced hallucinations, robustness analysis at a higher level establishes their illusory nature. Experiences that fail to be consistent through time for a given subject, or across observers, will be regarded as illusory.[61] The coincidence of boundaries under different means of detection can be used to establish such entities as social groups. Wimsatt cites research into factors affecting the reproductive cycles of women in colleges as an example. The initially randomly timed and different length cycles of the women studied eventually became synchronized into seventeen groups, within each of which the menstrual period was in phase and of the same length. The members of each group determined in this way turned out to be just those who spent most time together. After this discovery, membership of a group could be determined in two ways, sociologically or by the reproductive cycle.[62]

The reality or otherwise of properties can also be established via robustness analysis. The distinction between primary and secondary properties can be made in terms of robustness. The primary qualities of shape and size, for example, are detectable across more than one modality, while the secondary qualities such as taste and color are not.[63] Likewise, the property of mass is regarded as real because it can be measured in a number of different ways to produce a robust result. For example, it can be measured with a spring balance, a beam balance, or by fluid displacement. These methods use quite different mechanisms but produce roughly the same result.

Robustness, then, is used as a criterion of reality, and the establishment of robustness is in principle capable of playing a substantial role in the unification of scientific knowledge. Robustness analysis is just the family of criteria and procedures based on the concept of robustness, and, according to Wimsatt, involves the following general procedures:

1. To analyze a variety of *independent* derivation, identification, or measurement processes.
2. To look for and analyze things which are *invariant* over or *identical* in the conclusion or results of these processes.
3. To determine the *scope* of the processes across which they are invariant and the *conditions* on which their invariance depends.
4. To analyze and explain any relevant *failures of invariance.*[64]

Anything that is invariant under this analysis is robust. This general specification covers a wide range of methods, a number of which are described by Wimsatt, but I do not list them here. Rather, I want to show that the mapping model of knowledge is capable of modelling the unification procedures of robustness and connectedness—in other words that it provides a set of heuristic procedures for unifying knowledge.

On a very general level, recall, all maps can be embedded in a more general map of the territory in question. The same applies to theories.[65] So maps or theories can in principle be unified if they can be shown to be embeddable in a more general map or theory. But this feature of the maps leads to no specific strategies for unification because the connectedness or otherwise of any set of theories is a contingent matter. So it is to more specific methods suggested by the MMK rather than such general principles that I turn initially in the search for unification procedures.

The first point to make is that the collection of redundant data is an important procedure in map making. Surveyors use redundant data to confirm the existence and properties of geographic features, establishing their robustness. The collection of redundant data in map making is the direct source of the method of triangulation, used for establishing robustness in the social sciences.

Features for which no redundant data are available are either not included or given conjectural status. Such features often turn out to be the results of the measurement or data-gathering processes. This fact may itself be established by the consistent appearance of the feature across different terrains but using the same type of data-collection process—in other words by establishing the robustness of instrument noise.

These points can be illustrated by considering the construction of geo-logical maps that include fault zones. Possible fault zones may initially be in-dicated by linear striations on Landsat photographs of an area. The existence of these possible fault zones must be confirmed by ground surveys that map par-ticular rock formations associated with faulting. If sufficient are found at ap-proximately the same coordinates indicated by the Landsat maps, the existence of the entire fault zone will be considered established. If nothing is found by ground surveys this does not necessarily mean the striations are a result of in-strument interference. The terrain may be impassable, the striations may repre-sent a vegetation difference unconnected with a geologic fault, and so on. But if the striations appear on other pictures using the same method, where it is known that there are no corresponding features on the ground, or if taking the pictures from a different angle changes the position of the lines on the picture, then the striations are a function of the instrument. Robustness analysis can be used both to confirm the existence of geographic features and to separate geo-graphic information from instrument noise. It can also be used to determine the relationship between different maps with a feature or set of features in common.

Figures 7.1 to 7.3 are Landsat images of the same part of the Dorrigo re-gion. Each depicts a different set of properties and has a different use. Figure 7.1 is an edge enhancement, and helps in the detection of linear crustal features. Figure 7.2 is a principal component analysis (a visual expression of a correla-tion coefficient); it correlates areas of equivalent response over the sample spectra. Figure 7.3 is a common false color image (rendered in black and white for publication) that best expresses geographic variation (surface features such as drainage and vegetation). Despite the obvious visible differences between the pictures—for example, the shading patterns are quite distinct—the pictures are obviously of the same area. The roughly circular pattern in the bottom right-hand corner is a robust feature of each. It happens to be the eroded remnant of a Tertiary volcano. Figures 4.3 to 4.6 (the Anastasia set from chapter 4) can also be known to be of the same area because of the existence of a number of features that are robust across the set. The river is probably the clearest exam-ple. Figures 7.4 and 7.5 illustrate instrument noise as a robust feature. The two are satellite pictures of adjacent areas in the Dorrigo region of New South Wales. The information in each has been processed in the same way. The ar-rows marked A point to possible fault zones and the arrows marked B to strip-ing artifacts.

FIGURE 7.1

Dorrigo Area B—East filter 5 × 5 Convolution Matrix.

Landsat MSS image processing used with the permission of the Department of Geology, University of Newcastle.

Mapping Reality

FIGURE 7.2

Dorrigo Area B—Principle Component Analysis of Bands 1, 3, & 4—RGB.

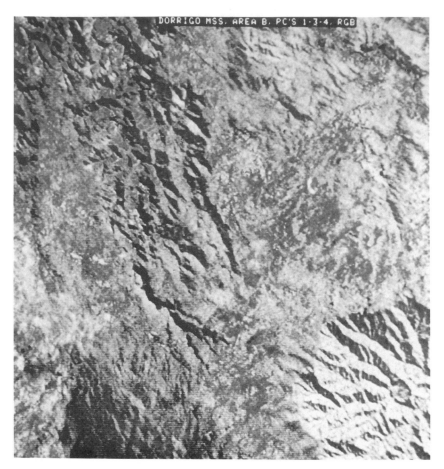

Landsat MSS image processing used with the permission of the Department of Geology, University of Newcastle.

FIGURE 7.3

Dorrigo Area B—Bands 7, 5, & 4—RGB.

Landsat MSS image processing used with the permission of the Department of Geology, University of Newcastle.

242

Mapping Reality

FIGURE 7.4

Dorrigo Area D—East filter 3 × 3 Convolution Matrix.

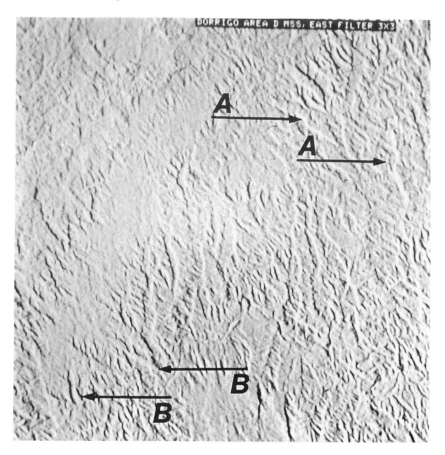

Landsat MSS image processing used with the permission of the Department of Geology,
University of Newcastle.

FIGURE 7.5

Dorrigo Area F—East filter 3 × 3 Convolution Matrix.

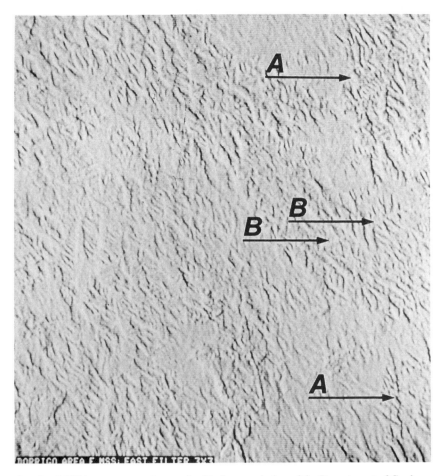

Landsat MSS image processing used with the permission of the Department of Geology, University of Newcastle.

Note that the information contained in Figures 4.3 to 4.6 of the Anastasia set is roughly additive—i.e., the information could all be combined into a more general map of the area.[66] This is because the maps are all at roughly the same level of reality and the same level of detail. But the additivity can be only rough, because there are some differences in scale, and because not all of the propositions that can be derived from a map need be true.[67] Traditionally, the ontologies of theories describing the same level of reality have been seen as sharply defined and additive, and as we saw in §7.2.4, additivity is an indication that only one level of reality is being described. But the fact that not all of the propositions that can be derived from a valid theory need be true[68] indicates that strict additivity is too strong a requirement for unification, even for theories describing the same level of reality.

Another of the ways that maps can be unified is by showing coherence across their boundaries—the robustness of cross-boundary features on two maps. This is particularly easy when the maps are of the same kind and scale. This is how we match up separate pages in a street directory. The task may be a little harder if the maps we wish to unify have no common boundary, or if they are of different kinds, or differ markedly in scale and level of detail. But it is not impossible. In the case of geographical maps, for example, we have constructed a single framework or grid system that divides the surface of the world, allowing everything on that surface to be located as precisely as need be by a grid reference. In this way, maps with no common boundary can still be located with reference to one another by their location on the grid. Likewise, a common grid reference can establish the identity of a town represented by a dot on a road map and separately by a street directory. The correlate to location on the map grid in scientific theory is spatiotemporal location. At any single level of reality, knowledge of things can be unified and identity established by location in the spatiotemporal framework.[69]

The basis of unification in both maps and theories is the fact that they refer to a single world or reality. Without the assumption of a single world, grid coordinates need not be unique and it would be conceivable that both representations could share coordinates without being in the same place. The same applies to spatiotemporal location. This assumption is itself supported by the establishment of coherence or cross-boundary robustness between maps and theories of different kinds. The routes marked as passing through a town on a road map will have correlates in the street directory of the same town.

Lack of coherence is an indication of a problem with the map in question. This can be illustrated by imagining a street map of part of a city that has been made by pasting together several pages from a street directory. If one of the pages is placed upside down, the map will be incorrect. This will be obvious. but not because of any inconsistency—given certain constraints, streets can be laid out any way. The error will appear because of the lack of relations or connections at the interface of the map segments. In assessing how good maps are, the context or environment always plays a part. Consistency checks alone are insufficient. All of these points apply to theories, too. Using the MMK forces recognition and consideration of the environment or context of any theory, contrary to reductionist heuristics, which tend to neglect such considerations.

While location on the grid is sufficient for identification and unification of features on the surface of the world, it is insufficient for the location and unification of features above or below ground. Consider a balloon floating above a field. It cannot be located *on* the grid, but its presence can become part of our knowledge of the world by locating it *relative* to the grid. Establishing its relation to the grid can be done in a number of ways. Which are used will depend on such things as the methods available, the purposes for which the knowledge is required, and so on. One way, for example, would be to establish its height above ground level using trigonometry. Or one could look from ground to balloon, trusting to the causal process of seeing. Or one could establish the material connection, such as the string holding it, if such exists. The point is, some connection must be established between the balloon and our major frame of reference if the balloon's existence and position are to be known.

But the establishment of connections is just another form of robustness analysis. Consider an example of information below the surface this time, geological cross-sections representing the rock composition of underlying units. These have very little in common with contour maps, which show, among other things, the various heights above sea level of the landform. Nonetheless, cross-section and contour maps of the same areas do have a certain feature in common. Strictly, the surface curve of the cross-section should fit neatly into a contour map of the same scale, enabling the two to be unified. This unification is realized in the three-dimensional block diagrams used in geology (see Figure 7.6).

The surface contour (e.g., AB and BC in Figure 7.6) at the precise place from which the cross-section is taken is robust across both maps. While the maps cannot be reduced to one another, they can be unified by establishing the robustness of this feature. This example is analogous to the unification of the structural and individual explanations of the rabbit's death. The structural explanation was not reducible to the individual one, but could be located relative to the individualist framework by the establishment of particular rabbits and foxes as robust features of both explanations, through unique location in the spatiotemporal framework.[70]

It is perhaps interesting to note that reduction in mapping is rare. Indeed it is hard to say what would count as a reduction between maps at all, except for a simple reduction of scale. In this case the information content of both maps is exactly the same. All that changes is ease of use. This is precisely what reductionists wish to claim about theories of higher-level entities in terms of

FIGURE 7.6

Block diagram.

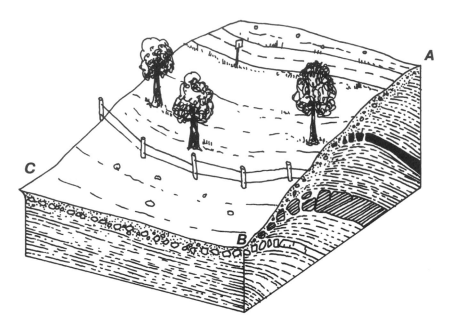

theories of lower-level entities and their properties. While not denying the use-fulness of theories in terms of higher-level entities, reductionists assert that ex-planations at higher levels of organization contain no information that cannot, in principle, be captured by explanations at the lower levels of organization. I have argued that this cannot be assumed, and that in fact successful reductions are likely to be rare. The MMK reflects this point.

The MMK, then, captures the concept of robustness, explains how ro-bustness analyses can unify knowledge, and is able to model a number of the procedures involved. In doing so, it provides guidelines for research that take account of the need for unification and show how it is likely to be obtained. And at the same time, it takes account of the criticisms of reductionism as a research strategy. The MMK, in other words, is a heuristic for the unification of knowledge.

7.4 Answering the Relativist Challenge to Realism

Whether any particular set of theories can be unified is, of course, a con-tingent matter, best handled by experts in the field in question. For this reason, I do not attempt the actual unification of any of the examples of fragmented knowledge that I have cited in this work. Nonetheless, something of the power of the MMK to unify seemingly contradictory theories can be shown

Let us look first at how different aspects of a single reality might be modelled in the MMK. Satellite imagery provides a good example of how different aspects or properties of the same part of the earth's surface can be visualized. Landsat collects information on the density of different wavelengths reflected from the earth's surface. Wavelength densities are sampled for each 80m-square pixel. Landsat images are computer-enhanced images or visually presented composites of the data on either one or some combination of the wavelengths sampled. For example, on the basis of infrared radiation emitted by plants and people, pictorial images of the earth's surface showing vegetation density or the population density of towns can be produced. Landsat images can be further interpreted, using known correlations, to provide less reliable but still useful maps of, for example, surface rock composition. Such information may be based on such facts as that, in marginal areas, basalts support more vigorous plant growth than do sandstones.

Because Landsat data is collected in a quantitative manner it can be mathematically manipulated and presented so that different features are enhanced. For example, by presenting the albedo (the amount of sunlight reflected) from the earth's surface, topographic variations are presented. The albedo data can then be further manipulated by a convolution matrix that suppresses the topographic information and instead enhances linear features such as roads, fences, or natural features such as faults or joints.[71] These manipulations can be regarded as the equivalent of the strategy in sociology of assuming some features of social reality invariant in order to study the mutual relationships of another set of variables. Figures 7.1 to 7.3 illustrate different enhancements of the same area in the Dorrigo region of New South Wales.

These images, while equally accurate,[72] are formed with different combinations of data from the same area. Those different combinations point to different properties of the area in question, none of which can be regarded as completely independent of the others. In enhancing certain aspects of the terrain, other aspects may be distorted. Thus, if each image is treated as correct in every respect, some will be mutually contradictory. But if they are treated as representing only the property of interest, they will be perfectly consistent, each showing a different aspect of the same reality. That the images are of the same reality can be known in a number of ways, ranging from the determination of robust features of the landscape to causal accounts of the position of the camera relative to the earth.

Now it would not occur to anyone to use Landsat images as if they correctly represented every aspect of the landscape. And this is just the point of using the MMK to model sociological theory and method, because within sociology, studies of different aspects of the same social feature are frequently taken to be complete. Consider studies of the mechanisms of social change. Many common approaches to history give precedence to one or other of the spheres of production, coercion, and cognition as the cause of change.[73] Those who give precedence to the organization of production in society see class struggle as the driving force of history. Vulgar Marxists, for example, hold that the realms of cognition and coercion, in their terms the ideological and political superstructure of society, are determined by the economic base. Thus, changes in the organization of production are the sole motor of historical change in society.

Those who give cognition precedence over the other spheres insist that ideas are the driving force behind social change. For example, Martin Luther's ideas against the selling of indulgences by the Church are often held to be the cause of the Reformation. The form of coercion adopted by a society is given by other theorists as the motive force behind social change. Such theorists would see Hitler's dictatorship as decisive in recent European history.

But as Gellner has shown, none of these approaches to history is adequate if treated as complete. Taken individually, all are adequate partial theories of social change. But if treated as complete, each is false. Analyses from each of these perspectives throw light on the causes of change in any historic period, but they need to be unified in some way. Gellner's strategy was to show how each was instantiated. This, I have argued, amounts to showing that each analysis could theoretically be embedded in a more general theory of the interaction between the three spheres of social life in any historic period.[74] By modelling the nature of scientific theories and the ways they can be unified, then, the MMK can act as a powerful research heuristic.

To summarize, a pluralist methodology is the essence of the MMK. As I argued in chapter 6, reliable knowledge of the complex world we live in requires a pluralist approach. But on the face of it, a pluralist methodology seems to lead inevitably to fragmented knowledge and an overpopulated ontology. This, and the fact that theories can be tested for adequacy only with respect to the problems they were designed to solve, leads many to relativism, particularly in the social sciences, where these issues are exacerbated by additional complexity.

Indeed, the fact that the MMK models these features of science may have given the impression that it is essentially relativist, despite my claims to have developed it along naturalist realist principles. This impression could be justified on the grounds that the perspective-independent criteria of validity that I developed in chapter 4, the criteria of internal and external consistency and coherence, can be applied only with respect to a unifiable body of knowledge. And it was far from clear at the end of chapter 6 that knowledge obtained from different perspectives could in fact be unified.

I established, in §7.1, that a prerequisite for unifying knowledge was to give epistemic interests priority over other interests. This, in fact, as we saw in chapter 3, is what distinguishes science from other belief-producing institutions. But in itself this is scarcely sufficient. What was needed to answer the relativist challenge were some specific strategies for unifying knowledge. My exploration of reduction, the traditional strategy for unifying knowledge, seemed initially to make the outlook for unification blacker. Reductionist research heuristics gave rise to biases whose cumulative effects were to ignore or underestimate interactions between a system and its environment, to rule out in an a priori manner the existence of relatively independent levels of reality, and to cover each other. My analysis showed, furthermore, that microreduction was impossible for systems whose structure displayed redundant causality. The scope for using reductionist strategies of unification is quite limited. The problems arising from reductionism as a position stem from the fact that the method has been generalized beyond its scope of valid application.

But in exploring the limits of reductionism and some ways in which the biases of the reductionist heuristic can be corrected for, I revealed another set of strategies for unifying knowledge—robustness analyses. Robustness analyses unify knowledge by establishing the reality of entities, properties, processes, and the connections between them. The reality of some entity, property, or process is held to be established when it appears invariant across at least two (and preferably more) independent theories. A pluralist approach, therefore, is essential to robustness analysis and hence to the possibility of unifying knowledge.

Sociology uses multiple perspectives. But the biases inherent in each perspective, if not corrected for, lead to the acceptance of a partial and approximate view of the world as a complete and accurate one. It is this that has led to the appearance within sociology of so many apparently inconsistent theories about the nature of the social world. But once theories and perspectives are recognized as partial, inaccurate, and involving an inherent bias, the number of apparent contradictions in sociology can be reduced significantly. Within the framework of the MMK, even seemingly contradictory theories are candidates for unification.

IV

THE CONCLUSION

8

The MMK and the Metatheory of Sociology

What is a map? There is only one place, and that place is time.

—Russell Hoban, *The Lion of Boaz-Jachin and Jachin-Boaz*

Crisis literature abounds in sociology.[1] While the issues remain much the same as they were when sociology emerged as a discipline late in the nineteenth century, the appearance in 1970 of *The Structure of Scientific Revolutions* by Thomas Kuhn gave the debates added urgency, for two reasons. First, the nature of the problems that sociology faces could be put down to the fact that, on Kuhn's account, it is pre-scientific because it is multi-paradigmatic. The corollary is that nothing need be done to solve the problems of sociology. One simply awaits the arrival of a Newton or a Darwin with a new theory that would unify sociological knowledge. Second, and at the same time, Kuhn's schema provided the hope that this event would not be too long in the coming, because of the constant state of crisis brought about by the diverse nature of the discipline.

These interpretations of the diversity of sociology are, I believe, wrong. While I leave open for the moment the question of whether sociology is a science or not, and while I do not take issue, at least here, with Kuhn's notion that to be multi-paradigmatic is to be pre-scientific,[2] I do not see diversity of theory and method as in themselves sufficient to establish multi-paradigmicity. As I see it, to be multi-paradigmatic requires two additional features. The first is that the knowledge obtained from the diverse perspectives is not unifiable, and the second is a general lack of communication across the perspectives.

Be that as it may, the popularity of these interpretations of Kuhn makes the diversity of sociology itself problematic for the discipline. For in times when the status given to scientific knowledge is high, and funding for non-scientific research is increasingly limited, the importance of scientific status to a discipline cannot be overstressed.

This problem is compounded by the nationalistic and sectarian nature of the diversity of sociology, which, together with the fact that the different sects are supportive of different political structures, has led to a picture of sociology as pure ideology and raises problems about the ethics of sociological research.

As well as these practical and ethical problems, the discontinuous, sectarian nature of sociology leads to conceptual problems. These include the production of conflicting truth-claims and the conflicting nature of the assumptions that underlie the views of society and persons held by the various perspectives. These conflicting assumptions each lead to a different methodology. But, as Mills demonstrated in his analysis of the "grand theorists" and the "abstracted empiricists," each methodology, if regarded as the single correct way to do sociology, can be criticized at the very least for gross inadequacy. This raises for sociologists the rather strange problem that whichever methodology they use, they will be wrong.

Sociology as a discipline, then, faces a number of serious problems, all of which center on the question of whether sociology is, or can be, scientific. This question was taken up in chapter 2, where I examined the major metatheoretical approaches to sociology. The fundamental parameters of the question are simple. To determine whether sociology is, or can be, scientific, one must first know what it is to be scientific and what it is to be sociological, and then compare the two. On the assumption that if anything is scientific, the natural sciences are, the issue is usually resolved into a comparison of sociology (or the social sciences in general) with the natural sciences, to ascertain whether there are any fundamental differences between them.

There are two possible solutions to this issue. The naturalist position is that, while there may be, and indeed are, differences between sociology and the natural sciences, these differences are not fundamental. Sociology, provided it adheres to the methods of the natural sciences (and I leave open for the moment what these might be), can indeed be scientific. The humanist position, on the other hand, is that the differences between sociology and the natural sciences are so fundamental as to require a quite different set of methodological principles. The humanist position, then, is incapable in principle of solving—and indeed explicitly rejects solving—the problems that sociology faces either by attributing to it scientific status or by making the methodology of the natural sciences available to sociology as a successful model.

It was crucial to examine the arguments for humanism to see if they were sound. Runciman, recall, argued that at a general level, humanist positions are usually based on one or more of the following premises:

 . . . first, that human actions cannot be explained in terms of law-like relations of cause and effect; secondly, that to grasp the meaning which human actions have to those performing them requires a different method from any known to, or required by, practitioners of natural science; and thirdly, that the social scientist's moral, political and/or aesthetic values necessarily enter into his conclusions in a way that those of the natural scientist do not.[3]

To these premises I added a fourth, that the human sciences were distinguishable from the natural sciences on the grounds that research in the former had consequences for social and moral practice, while the latter did not. I was able to argue in §2.2 that the third and fourth premises were false. But the first and second premises presented a real challenge to a naturalist realist account of the social sciences. In order to show even the possibility of a naturalist realist metatheory of sociology, one had to be able to show (a) that explanations of human action in terms of reasons could be related to causal explanations in some way, and (b) that the methods of interpretive sociology had some parallel with methods in use in the natural sciences. These issues would obviously have to be covered, so I added them to the budget of problems to be solved, and deferred the answering of them to chapter 5.

But any answer to them would obviously have to address the second parameter of the question whether sociology could be a science—the nature of the natural sciences. This brought me to a consideration of the other great metatheoretical debate—the debate between realism and relativism, both of which are best seen, in the present context, as post-positivist. Realism, recall,[4] is the thesis that there is a real world existing independently of our attempts to know it; that we as humans can have knowledge of that world; and that the validity of our knowledge claims is, at least in part, determined by the way the world is. In response to the theory-ladenness of facts and the failure of logic to guarantee certainty, the realist adopts a fallibilist approach to science and denies that it is rational to accept only what one is forced to. Nonetheless, the realist wishes to maintain some sort of objective criteria for deciding whether a theory is good or bad. The realist, then, has to develop a quite different notion of rationality from the logic of the positivists, and a quite different notion of objectivity from the incorrigibility of observation. In other words, the realist has to develop a new methodology for science.

The relativist agrees with the realist on the theory-laden nature of observation, and, following Kuhn and Feyerabend,[5] the paradigm and/or cultural specificity of methodology. As a consequence, relativism, like naturalist realism, embraces fallibilism. But the relativist, in contrast to the realist, having denied the incorrigibility of observation and the adequacy of formal logics to account for scientific methodology, believes that there can be no grounds for objectivity. Contemporary relativists do not usually take this to entail a retreat to solipsism. Rather, they focus on the sociocultural frames of reference that shape the way that everybody sees the world. Different sociocultural groups have been found to have different sets of values, and different ways of categorizing the world. Within each culture or interest group, it is held, common values and theories as to the nature of the world may ensure objective knowledge, but there can be no way of judging between the theories of different groups. Relativism is therefore, like humanism, incapable in principle of solving the problems of sociology, but for different reasons. To the relativist, no particular status ought to attach to science, because scientific knowledge is merely a social construction.

Science is better seen, particularly according to postmodernist and poststructuralist versions of relativism, as a literary enterprise than as a way of gaining knowledge of reality. So although one might decide to call sociology a science, and piggyback on its status, to do so would simply be a matter of convenience. As for the epistemic problems faced by sociology, to model sociology on the methods of science would not help resolve competing truth-claims or disputes between conflicting perspectives, because the socially constructed nature of scientific knowledge means that there are no value-neutral ways of resolving such issues.

While agreeing with the relativists that social values are embedded in scientific theory, I argued against the notion that there could therefore be no culture- or perspective-neutral ways of arbitrating between competing theories—on the grounds that our causal interactions with the world could, under certain conditions, constitute an effective arbiter.

Nonetheless, it remained the case that while naturalist realism is a well-worked-out philosophical position, and while many natural scientists and sociologists have worked consciously within a naturalist realist framework, there was a lack of a generalized naturalist realist methodology of science that specified a set of criteria for the establishment of validity. While strongly developed as an anti-empiricist metaphysics and epistemology, the only comprehensive naturalist methodology available was positivism. And positivism is not only a totally inadequate methodology of the social sciences, as the humanists have pointed out, it is also inadequate as a methodology of the natural sciences.

Indeed, it is arguably the inadequacy of positivism that lies behind the present demonization of realism by postmodernism and poststructuralism. Demonization of the intellectual opposition is a time-honored practice among scholars but is no less reprehensible for that.[6] Stephen Jay Gould laments the frequency with which scholars rip apart "the nonexistent caricatures of each other's ideas."[7] Postmodernists and poststructuralists are masters of this practice, persistently setting up positivist strawmen, beating them mercilessly, and regarding their argument with realism as therefore settled.[8]

It is worth diverting briefly to look at just how this is done, not least because one of the easiest ways to do so is by using textual analysis, the paradigmatically postmodernist/poststructuralist method. It would be wrong to characterize poststructuralist, and, more particularly, postmodernist positions as a single, coherent intellectual movement. Historically, poststructuralism developed from methodological positions in linguistics and anthropology, while postmodernism developed in opposition to modernism, and has at least three major strands. But at the level of generality required here, the various positions can be dealt with together, and I shall use "postmodernism" as a generic term to cover them.[9]

Like naturalist relativists, postmodernists adopt a radical skepticism. If one cannot be certain of knowledge, then there is no knowledge, except locally. Truth is a matter of consensus, and is thus at the very least culturally defined, if not idiosyncratically, and locally determined. But interestingly, while most postmodernists make no distinction between the natural and the social sciences (and hence could be thought to be naturalist), the position is fundamentally humanist.[10] The creation and interpretation of meaning, which is supposed to be distinctly human, is seen as radically indeterminate and culturally constructed. Hence, the human sciences are based not on some external reality but on the shifting sands of meaning. But science, too, is a meaning system. The natural sciences collapse into the social sciences rather than the other way around. Lyotard, and Latour and Woolgar, are examples of those who hold this position.[11]

As this brief sketch shows, there are, and always have been, solid issues to debate between realist and postmodernist positions. These debates were rehearsed in my arguments against relativism, and have been taken up in their postmodernist context by, e.g., Norris, and Freadman and Miller.[12] My concern here is rather with how postmodernists avoid debate by setting up a positivist straw man in lieu of realist positions. And part of the answer, I found, lies in the way "dirty words" are constructed in postmodernist texts. I scanned the literature to which I had easy access for words that were repeatedly used in a pejorative sense, a sense that assumed that debate was *passé*. I then traced these words back in the postmodernist literature, identifying where possible any background arguments that might support such pejorative usage. This is my list of "dirty words," grouped for convenient discussion:

Group 1:   positivist, empiricist
Group 2:   modernist, evolutionist, enlightenment, metaphysics, foundationalist
Group 3:   universalize, totalize
Group 4:   grand narrative, grand theory, metanarrative, metatheory, metadiscourse
Group 5:   truth, ideology, reason
Group 6:   objective, reality, realist
Group 7:   naturalize, naturalism
Group 8:   Anglo-American

The Group 1 words, *positivist* and *empiricist,* are used pejoratively by almost everyone these days when referring to contemporary practitioners because they refer to a model of scientific knowledge that is not only flawed, but outmoded. Current adherents to positivism and empiricism are considered ignorant and behind the times. But the French postmodernist critique of evolutionism, positivism, and physicalism is itself notoriously underdeveloped.[13] *Positivism* and *empiricism,* then, as dirty words, have probably been borrowed from Anglo-American critiques.

The Group 2 words, *modernist, enlightenment, evolutionist, foundationalist,* and *metaphysics,* require a little more explanation. Modernist radical social science claims to have achieved a decisive break with speculative or metaphysical accounts of the social world. Both Marx and Durkheim, for example, argue that social structures and processes form an autonomous level of reality that could be studied scientifically in terms of its own patterns of causality. The discovery of these principles of scientific understanding of society coincided with the massive social transformations that gave rise to modern societies. Historical materialism and Durkheimian sociology are both modernist projects in that they claim privileged access to the formative principles of modernity. They are radical in the sense that, because of the link between theory and practice, each can claim to be the instrument through which the potential of modernity can be achieved.[14]

The postmodernist critique of modernism is often based on the argument that modernism has not in fact broken from metaphysics. It is as well to note that "metaphysics" in this sense is quite narrowly construed to mean something like "speculative metaphysics," or the metaphysical thought that preceded positive thought in Comte's law of the three stages of social development. It refers, that is, to foundationalism, the attempt to guarantee the validity of inquiry by a priori principles. Marx and Durkheim both attacked foundationalist social theories that attempted to move from epistemological or ontological principles to privileged and speculative accounts of social reality. The postmodernist critique is that "Marx and Durkheim do not simply practice science, they produce programs which load their sciences with metaphysical significance. . . . Moreover, historical materialism and sociology are both the subject of foundationalist guarantees: both establish what social reality is like, and how it is to be known, prior to inquiry itself."[15] The values with which modernist theory is imbued are thoroughly humanist (in the sense in which postmodernists use the word), i.e., they are linked to the enlightenment values of truth and reason.

While I would defend Durkheim and Marx against the charge of foundationalism, for the purposes of this discussion, I will allow postmodernism its points against modernism, because the issue I really want to address is whether these criticisms are true of contemporary realisms. And as I have shown in chapter 2, naturalist realisms are definitely not open to this charge. For one thing, knowledge claims are not guaranteed at all. All knowledge is seen as fallible. Scientific method is not determined a priori, but is derived from our best practice. It is extremely varied, and always open to criticism and change. For another, its metaphysics, at the level of specific ontologies, is derived from knowledge and practice. In the hierarchical system of ways in which we know the world, for example, epistemology is both derived from, and prescriptive of, the ways we do science. Every level of knowledge is qualified by the levels below and above, the whole being fallible.

The last dirty word in this group is *evolutionist.* Some interpretations of Marx and Durkheim (including most postmodernist ones) insist that they each hold teleological views of social development, society necessarily passing through a series of stages towards some predetermined end. These interpretations can, of course, be challenged, but the point here is to give the context in which the word *evolutionist* becomes a dirty word. But there are no teleological implications in the way that naturalist realists use the word, so its use against contemporary realisms in general is inappropriate.

The Group 3 words, *universalize* and *totalize,* like the last set, relate to the nature of modernist social theory. In this postmodern world, not only has the object (society) of modernist social science changed sufficiently to render modernist analyses inappropriate, but the whole idea of such totalizing (or universalizing) social theory is questioned, harking back, as it does, to speculative metaphysics. What is being said here is that it is, and always was, inappropriate to base one's theory and practice on values, e.g., equality, that are only assumed to be universally valid. With the "humanizing of the natural sciences"[16] that postmodernists indulge in—most often through a linguistic or cultural turn that sees science as just a linguistic or cultural product, denying it any reference to a real world—*universalizing* and *totalizing* are dirty words applicable to any claim to universality for laws or theories of any kind. While agreeing in part with this critique,[17] I stress that in most forms of naturalist realism there is no claim for absolute universality in any area, from the laws of physics to the realms of ethics.

Of the Group 4 words, *grand narrative, grand theory, metanarrative, metadiscourse,* and *metatheory,* the first four, at least, seem virtually interchangeable, referring to the specific totalizing social theories of various modernists. I can illustrate this best with some extracts from the work of Lyotard, one of the founders of postmodernist thought. Modernism, according to Lyotard, "legitimates itself with reference to a meta-discourse . . . making an explicit appeal to some grand narrative."[18] Lyotard distinguishes two such grand narratives, according to whether the hero is presented as cognitive or practical, "a hero of knowledge or a hero of liberty."[19] To Lyotard, "modernism remains metaphysical because it seeks a foundation in the image of history as the working out of a purpose (enlightenment or emancipation)."[20] Lyotard sees postmodernism as moving beyond this foundationalist teleology, defining itself in terms of "an incredulity towards metanarratives."[21] Marxism and the like are dismissed as delusory metanarrative creeds. *Metanarrative, metadiscourse,* and *grand narrative* are certainly dirty words. While I have come across *grand theory* and *metatheory* in the literature, I have yet to find their use as dirty words explained, but imagine the arguments are similar to those of the rest of the group.

Do these criticisms of metanarrative and the like apply to realism as they do to modernism? While most contemporary versions of realism steer clear of totalizing theories, realists certainly talk about (and do) metatheory, metaphilosophy, metascience, and so on. My problem here is that, while I can see that specific metanarratives or metatheories might be challenged, I cannot see how a global challenge, i.e., a challenge to all meta- activities or objects, might work. Perhaps the idea is that the postmodernist critique is supposed to work against metanarrative and the like in the same way that it worked against metaphysics. The idea might be that if one can move beyond metaphysics, one can perhaps move beyond metanarratives. That, I think, is the postmodernist claim.

But to claim such is to do violence to language. *Meta-* is a prefix, meaning beyond, or above, or about. Metascience, for example, is the study of science. One cannot just rule out of court everything that has the prefix *meta-* by association with speculative metaphysics. To do so would be rather like the positivist attempt to rule meaningless terms that could not be grounded in observation. That rule itself could not be so grounded, and therefore would have to be judged meaningless and hence unjustifiable. Despite denials from within, positivism was shown to have a metaphilosophy.[22] Similarly, postmodernism can be shown to have a metaphysics. Stephen Crook has argued persuasively that postmodernisms are foundationalist, monistic, and reductionist, although the foundations themselves vary according to the variety of postmodernism. Jamieson, for example, relies on a species of economic reductionism, while Lyotard, in trying to differentiate an antiformalist postmodernism from a formalist modernism, does so in a manner that is definitively formalist, and can be done clearly only through the resources of modernism.[23] And Derrida, Freadman and Miller argue, is committed to an "undifferentiated linguisticised monism."[24] Monism, even if implicit, is still a metaphysics.

Group 5 contains the words *truth, ideology* and *reason*. Truth and reason form part of the modernist grand narrative, and the word *ideology* (like *false consciousness*) depends on some non-consensus version of truth for its meaning. So *ideology* is a dirty word because *truth* and *reason*, in any realist sense, are dirty words. To the postmodernist, the fallibility of knowledge is sufficient reason to abandon the possibility of truth. Now, all contemporary versions of realism have, to my knowledge, discussed the relationship between notions of truth and the fallibility of knowledge. Most come up with something like a statement that, while absolute truth is an unattainable ideal, more workable versions of the correspondence theory of truth are not incompatible with the fallibility of knowledge. In the MMK I prefer to substitute *validity,* in the sense of well-foundedness, while Bhaskar prefers his representational theory of truth to a correspondence theory of truth. But all agree that the inevitable fallibility of knowledge does not imply either the abandonment of the ideal of truth or the adoption of a consensus model of truth, but merely the abandonment of positivist criteria of truth. *Reason* is a dirty word because it is equated with the truth-preserving logics of positivism. But contemporary realisms have no such a priori notions of reason. While the pejorative use of these words might make its mark on a positivist, it is misplaced when used against contemporary realists.

The Group 6 words, *objective, reality,* and *realist,* are used pejoratively for similar reasons. For knowledge to be objective, under positivism, it also has to be true in some absolute sense, having been acquired according to the scientific method of gathering objective observations and combining them under truth-preserving logic to make scientific theory. The word *reality* is problematic for a related reason. According to both positivism and its relativist critics, we know that there is a reality external to us as knowers only because of our knowledge of it. But, the relativist argues, our knowledge is theory- and culture-laden, and therefore we cannot be certain that there is indeed anything out there. At one level, the denial of reality hinges on the belief that knowledge must be certain to be useful, and certainty is out of the question, so knowledge of external reality (if indeed there is one) is impossible. Reality is simply a social construction. Extreme linguistic versions, as shown, for example, in Lyotard's extreme nominalism or Derrida's linguisticized monism, go one step further in insisting that words have no reference outside of the discourse of speculative reason.

Postmodernism takes for granted the collapse of all realist or representational paradigms.[25] It does this in two ways. First, through a Lyotardian focus on the (Kantian) sublime—that which cannot be represented, e.g., the realm of ethics and values. Lyotard adheres to a rather extreme form of the fact/value distinction, but insists that just about everything that is meaningful is value-laden and therefore in the territory of the sublime, so disputes cannot be solved by reference to the facts.[26]

The other way that postmodernism (and poststructuralism in particular) takes the collapse of realist or representational paradigms for granted seems to be via the structuralist position of Saussure with respect to the study of language. Saussure, in setting up his studies of language as a system, decided for heuristic reasons to put aside any question of the relationship of terms to the real world, and to concentrate instead on the relationship between terms within the system, looking at the ways in which oppositions and differences contribute to meaning. But, as Norris points out,

> there is no warrant whatsoever in Saussure for extending this strictly heuristic principle to the point where any mention of the referent—any appeal beyond the self-enclosed domain of signification—is regarded as

a lapse into naive ("positivist" or "metaphysical") ways of thought, to be dismissed briefly with a sigh.

What such ideas amount to is a form of specular misrecognition, a confinement to the structural-linguistic imaginary which mistakes its own theoretical preconceptions for the limits of language, thought, and experience in general.[27]

Indeed. Nonetheless, the move seems not uncommon. Textbooks on critical and cultural theory often include a discussion of Saussure and structuralism as part of the development of poststructuralist theory, and while the texts I have seen are faithful to Saussure, his heuristic strategy is not recalled as such in later sections.[28] Rather, it is assumed that Saussure has proven that the differences between meanings within a linguistic system depend entirely upon the conventionally defined differences between words. By extension, no cultural meaning system can have reference to an external reality.

It is relatively easy to see how the Group 7 words, *naturalize* and *naturalism*, have become dirty words. Postmodernists tend to make a clear distinction between the natural and the sociocultural. Indeed, the distinction, while not, I believe, fundamental, can be extremely useful. To naturalize something, in postmodernist discourse, is to attribute to nature a bundle of causal factors that are better seen as sociocultural. For example, a person's health is far more a product of sociocultural factors than of purely genetic factors. To picture this relationship the other way around—to say that health is more a product of genetics than sociocultural factors—is to naturalize the issue, and is bad. I have no argument with this usage. Slightly different is the way in which *naturalistic* is used as synonymous with *realist* in literary theory, to convey the notion of art trying to portray itself as reality, as natural, rather than calling attention to itself as art.[29] Because, according to the postmodernist, representations of reality must necessarily be false, as well as culturally bound and interest-laden, any pretense at realistic representation is deliberately deceptive, and therefore bad. Knowledge shows on television that purport to represent knowledge of reality, for example, misrepresent the nature of knowledge. Though my views are not as extreme as the postmodernists—I think that we can and do have reliable knowledge of reality—I too have problems with the ways that knowledge is presented in the mass media. But this is not the issue. I am simply investigating the ways that *naturalize* and *naturalistic* have been constructed as dirty words by postmodernists. And the problem seems to be that these are the only uses of the words known to many postmodernists. But these senses of *naturalize* and *naturalism* are quite different from the senses in which they are used in descriptions of naturalist realisms, where the word *naturalize* simply means to bring into some unified system of nature. For example, to search for a naturalistic ethics is to search for an ethics that does not rely on revelation from God, or on some other a priori principle, but is something developed by humans within human culture. The unfortunate connotations of the first sense are thoughtlessly applied to all senses, by association.

The last group, Group 7, contains only one word, *Anglo-American.* Roughly, the postmodernist translation of this term is "behind the times" and "ignorant." It probably owes this usage to the dominance in the U.S. for quite some time of positivist and empiricist philosophies of science, and the cognate behaviorist psychologies and empiricist sociologies. The term also implies an ignorance of European critical theory and of the points that it makes. Anglo-American thought is primitive, and it is very, very bad. One finds discussions of theory in various fields that start with Anglo American straw men later trounced by European theorists. Communication theory is one field in which this seems to happen.[30] To admit that one's thought has been largely influenced by Anglo-American scholars is to be taken to mean that one is dated, and ignorant, or worse dismissive, of European theory.

But it simply is not the case that Anglo-American philosophy of science and sociology is ignorant of European thought, or even European critical thought. Indeed, if one goes back in the history of ideas, one finds that both schools of thought rely on many of the same great thinkers. While the Anglo-American/European distinction might serve some intellectual purpose, it is simply not the case that there has been no, or even very little, cross-fertilization of ideas between the schools.

My own experiences in working within a postmodernist perspective, and my attempts to analyze these, has led me to believe, rather, that postmodernists show a profound ignorance of contemporary realisms and a reluctance to engage in serious debate. My analysis of the postmodernist construction of dirty words indicates that postmodernism is systematically depicting caricatures of positivism and modernism and then falsely attributing the characteristics of these caricatures to realisms of any kind. "Mischaracterisation," according to Gould, "lies at the core of nearly every academic debate."[31] And "the root of this lamentable behavior can only lie in careless habits of reading and thinking (or, worse, in our willingness to argue without reading at all)."[32] Perhaps. Gross and Levitt argue forcefully that poor scholarship underlies much of the postmodernist characterization of science.[33] More charitably, perhaps the reason for such systematic misrepresentation is the lack of a well-articulated naturalist realist alternative to the positivist methodology, the task of this book.

To return to my summary of chapter 2, then, I was able to argue that the development of a naturalist realist metatheory of sociology was in principle the only strategy capable of solving all of the problems faced by sociology. But the discussion of the debates with humanism and relativism revealed that for such a strategy to be successful, a naturalist realist metatheory of sociology had to meet two criteria. First, an adequate naturalist realist metatheory had to be able to incorporate explanations of human action in terms of reasons. Second, a methodology that incorporated perspective-neutral criteria for the establishment of the validity of theories had to be developed.

It was the second of these issues, the development of a generalized methodology of science from within a naturalist realist perspective, that I tackled in Part II. Chapter 3 was devoted primarily to exploring the processes by which humans come to have knowledge of the world. The fundamentally naturalist premise was that humans are products of biological evolution. Such knowledge as we have must have its source in biologically evolved perceptual and cognitive mechanisms. Studies in the psychology of perception have shown that observation is thoroughly theory-laden. The burning issue, then, as Rubinstein, Laughlin, and McManus point out, is to discover "the processes people use to keep their views and understandings of how the world is in some passably accurate relationship to how the world actually is."[34]

The major function of the human brain is to model reality, and the distinction between the real world (the operational environment) and our models of it (the cognized environment) is fundamental to any attempt to understand how we know what we know. Humans interact with the operational environment, and it is that interaction that determines their survival and well-being or otherwise. But the models of that environment that guide their interactions are necessarily partial, inaccurate, interest driven, and often culturally specific. Nonetheless, there is a constraint on the modelling process, because the construction of knowledge is a biological process, and thus open to selection. Natural selection would not have left us with grossly misleading perceptual and cognitive mechanisms.

At base, then, it is through our interactions with the environment that we select from among competing cognitive models. The ultimate test of validity is practice. However, even at a perceptual level, humans are notoriously prone to error. While natural selection has validated the general operation of the perceptual system for middle-sized physical objects and boundary acts, individual perceptual foundationalism is not justified. But as both Rubinstein et al. and Campbell argue, perceptual beliefs are revised so that they become coherent with the bulk of our other perceptions. And as Campbell points out, the overall reliability of the human perceptual system comes from the social cross-validation of beliefs—the social establishment of robustness.

This does not, Campbell argues, lead to cultural solipsism, for the very reason that reality plays a part in editing our beliefs. Valid beliefs, therefore, are achieved as a result of social processes rather than despite them. And the basis of objectivity lies in intersubjective, and even cross-cultural, agreement at the level of middle-distance objects and boundary acts.

But human models of the world extend beyond middle-distance objects to include invisible theoretical entities such as the Easter Bunny or the electron. And there are many social institutions besides science whose business includes the production and maintenance of beliefs about such entities. What distinguishes science from these other belief-producing institutions? Campbell argues that science differs from other belief production and maintenance systems in two major ways. First, science is one of the belief production and maintenance institutions that opens a window on the world through which nature can speak. Second, and unique to science, its norms function to channel consensus in a way that maximizes the opportunity for reality to influence that consensus. These norms, or epistemic values, include a questioning attitude to tradition that leads to openness to innovation, a less authoritarian attitude that makes science open to change, and the notion that contribution to truth should be the only criterion of status in science.

The result of this exploration into the way humans practice science is the emergence of a new criterion of what it is to be scientific. To be scientific is not to be free of error, nor to follow some particular method. Rather, what it is to be scientific is tied up with the nature of the structure and the norms of the institution of science, for it is these that distinguish science from other belief production and maintenance institutions.

This notion of the scientific did not make the search for a generalized methodology of science redundant, because the institutional features of science are simply preconditions for the objective operation of a methodology. And I was looking for some general criteria that might guide the assessment of the validity of scientific theories. Specifically, I was looking for an easily conceptualizable (and hence easy to use) model of scientific knowledge. I turned to Ziman's social model of science because it held the promise of a methodology and was thoroughly consistent with both Campbell's model of socially validated perceptual foundationalism and Rubinstein, Laughlin, and McManus's cognitive model of sciencing as a fallible human activity. Ziman saw science as consisting of a body of scientists, a set of consensible beliefs, and a set of consensual beliefs—and he showed that a characterization of scientific theories as maps took full account of that social model.

In chapter 4, I extended Ziman's model, using insights from Harré and Toulmin, to develop a generalized methodology of science. I explored the way in which the validity of theories is both relative to the interests that guide theory creation and a function of the reality that they represent. It turned out that theories, like maps, are valid insofar as they are reliable guides to action and decision making. Explanatory and predictive success and the criteria of internal and external consistency and coherence are guides to the reliability of theories, and hence to their validity.

The fact that theories are relative to guiding interests has the effect of limiting their scope of valid application, but does not mean that they cannot be assessed in a perspective-neutral way, provided that those interests are made explicit. Indeed, it is the very fact that science is ultimately a guide to action and decision making and is guided by interests that allows it to be assessed practically—by how well it facilitates understanding of and control over nature. It is in precisely this way that science "opens a window on Nature, allowing her to speak." But it is precisely because of the interest-related nature of science that relativists argue that there can be no perspective-neutral way to assess theories. Hence, the MMK provides an answer to relativist arguments against the possibility of a naturalist realist metatheory of science.

The mapping model of knowledge (MMK) is not only descriptive, in the sense that it is based on how humans in their social setting can and do know; it is prescriptive, in that it provides criteria for the paradigm-neutral assessment of validity. And more, it has the advantage, as did the positivist model of science, of being easy to use, because mapping is so nearly intuitive. The nature of validity and the criteria for its determination are the same for maps and scientific theories. This means that the MMK can act as a powerful heuristic.

The development of the MMK showed that a naturalist realist metatheory of science was possible. But it did not show how a naturalist realist metatheory of sociology might be achieved. An adequate metatheory of sociology, recall, still had to show how explanations of social action that were given in terms of reasons could be accommodated. This issue, along with other metatheoretical issues, was taken up in Part III.

Chapter 5 was devoted primarily to showing how explanations of social action in terms of reasons could be accommodated within the MMK. I started by showing how the MMK models the naturalist realist assumptions of a single, and in principle interconnectable, reality. The realist assumption of the in-principle interconnectedness of the world, particularly with humans as knowers, makes causal analysis the basis of validity. This is reflected in the MMK, where interaction with reality underpins the validity criterion of predictive success, and where it is the assumption of a unified reality that underlies those general criteria of validity: internal and external consistency, and coherence.

But causal explanation is not the only sort of scientific explanation. Explanations in terms of composition, structure, and function are just as much part of science. The validity of these types of explanation, however, depends on their being shown to be connected to a causal explanation. It is therefore important to be able to distinguish causal explanations from other types of explanation.

Cummins, in his analysis of scientific explanation, distinguishes causal explanation from all other types of explanation, which he calls collectively *analysis.* He points out that little attention has been paid to analysis in discussions of scientific explanation, resulting in many functional analyses being confused with causal analyses. One of the reasons for this confusion is that causal and functional analyses cannot be distinguished in terms of the structure of the theories, on which the dominant DN model of scientific explanation tends to concentrate. Rather, they are to be distinguished in terms of their goals, their methods, and the ontological status of their entities.

Functional theories aim to explain dispositions, whereas causal theories aim to explain transitions. The method of causal theories is subsumption, whereas the method of functional theories is systems analysis followed by instantiation. The entities of causal theories have specific spatiotemporal coordinates, whereas the entities of functional theories have no spatiotemporal location that can be defined closer than the system as a whole. Moreover, while functional analyses are constrained by the physical system whose dispositions they explain, the nature of those constraints varies according to the type of functional analysis in question, and may in fact be quite loose.

On all of these counts, mentalist theories are clearly functional theories. They aim to explain dispositions rather than transitions; they use the methods of analysis and instantiation; and the entities of mentalist theories (reasons, motives, and intentions) have no spatiotemporal location other than the person as a whole.

Distinguishing functional from causal theories in this way provided me with a novel approach to the problem that explanations in terms of meanings, motives, reasons, and so on seem to be divorced from empirical evaluation, and hence require a methodology distinct from that of the natural sciences. For mentalist explanations turn out to be interpretive functional analyses. The latter have a loose, but nonetheless specified, relationship with the transition theories they explain. Minimally, the theories must be equivalent at the level of input and output. Both causal and functional theories and the relationships between them can be modelled in the MMK. One has only to think of a functional map of the processes of a power station compared with a causal/descriptive map, which would be based on the actual floor plan.

Not only are mentalist theories not free from empirical evaluation, their relative independence from empirical evaluation does not distinguish them from natural scientific theories of the same type. Neither does the fact that the entities of mentalist theories have no precise spatiotemporal location, for neither do the entities of many functional explanations, such as, for example, the virtual governor. On this account, the strongest arguments for humanism—the fundamentally different nature of the entities of mentalist explanation and the lack of resource to empirical evaluation—disappear, leaving the way open for a naturalist approach to the social sciences.

But removing the fundamental dualism between the natural and the social sciences in no sense diminishes the diversity of sociology. And this diversity, recall, had itself has been used to argue that sociology is not scientific. I addressed this problem in chapter 6. Here, I argued that reality is complex, and that knowing a complex reality actually demands the use of multiple perspectives. In a complex world, different perspectives make accessible different bodies of information. The assumptions underlying the various perspectives are best seen, not as competing ontologies or epistemologies, but as methodological devices for establishing stabilities in a complex and changing world. Sociology is among the more complex sciences, and hence actually requires the use of many different perspectives.

But according to the MMK, the use of different perspectives has ontological implications that arise from the fact that each theory or interconnected network of theories specifies—either implicitly or explicitly—the sorts of entities, processes, relations, and properties that the theory can validly use. The ontologies so specified have a limited scope of valid application and cannot unproblematically be transported across theories.

My discussion of the ontological implications of the MMK led to several methodological prescriptions. I pointed out that errors could be avoided if both the ontology of theories and their scope of valid application was made explicit. I argued further that, particularly in multi-perspective disciplines, the ontology of theories should be defined at a sufficient level of detail to make explicit the invalid nature of the automatic assumption of intertheoretic coherence. And I argued that special care should be taken in attributing properties that are clearly defined at one layer of reality to features of any other layer of reality, for there is no reason to suppose that such properties will prove robust through such a shift.

But while the ontological insights arising from the MMK ought to lead to fewer errors in scientific thought, and particularly in sociology, they raise an additional, and potentially very serious, issue—the issue of whether knowledge obtained via the MMK methodology can as a matter of fact be unified. For compared with an empiricist and reductionist epistemology, the MMK seems to be in danger of ontological overpopulation and a radical fragmentation of knowledge.

The issue is important. It raises the question of whether the complex sciences can produce valid knowledge at all, as it is a theory's relationship to a unified body of knowledge as much as to the world itself that underpins validity within the MMK. If knowledge is fragmented, it becomes a very real question how consistency and coherency can be established. The fragmented nature of sociological knowledge and doubts about the possibility of unifying it lead many supporters of pluralism to espouse relativism.

The unification of science is the subject of chapter 7. A prerequisite of the unification of knowledge, I argued, is that epistemic values must be given priority over other values. This, recall, was one of the features that distinguished science from other belief production and maintenance institutions. But it is also a function of the nature of theories themselves that they are constructed with interests in mind, and are used as guides to decision making and action. The validity of a theory, then, not only lies in its relationship to the world and the body of established theory, but is also a function of the purposes the theory is meant to serve. In the natural sciences, there is a common interest in obtaining understanding of and/or control over the natural world, and this leads to a congruence between the purposes for which the theory was constructed and its relationship with reality. The prerequisite of unification—that epistemic values take priority over other values—is automatically met.

The case is somewhat different in sociology. The social world, in contrast to the natural world, can be manipulated independently of reliable sociological knowledge, and epistemic values are not necessarily primary. If sociological knowledge is to be unified, the institutional structure of sociology must be consciously manipulated so that it mirrors the institutional structure of the natural sciences, hence making sure that epistemic values are in fact given primacy. Attempts must be made to overcome the present nationalistic, ethnocentric, and sectarian nature of sociology. The formation of the International Sociological Association with its four-yearly World Congress of Sociology and its journal, *Current Sociology,* represent such attempts, albeit so far with limited success.

But strategies like this are by themselves not sufficient for the unification of knowledge in the complex sciences. Some specific strategies for unifying knowledge are required if the relativist challenge is to be met. The first step in my search for specific strategies for unifying knowledge involved an analysis of reduction, the traditional strategy for unifying knowledge. Initially, this analysis made the outlook for unification seem bleak. Reductionist strategies in the complex sciences such as biology, ecology, and sociology lead to empirical problems. These arise because reductionist research heuristics give rise to biases whose cumulative effects are to ignore or underestimate interactions between a system and its environment, to rule out in an a priori manner the existence of relatively independent levels of reality, and to cover for each other. My analysis showed, furthermore, that microreduction is impossible for systems whose structures displayed redundant causality. The scope for using reductionist strategies of unification is quite limited. The problems arising from reductionism as a position stem from the fact that the method has been generalized beyond its scope of valid application.

But in exploring the limits of reductionism and some ways in which the biases of the reductionist heuristic can be corrected for, I revealed another set of strategies for unifying knowledge—robustness analyses. Robustness analyses unify knowledge by establishing the reality of entities, properties, processes, and the connections between them. The reality of some entity, property, or process is held to be established when it appears invariant across at least two (and preferably more) independent theories. A pluralist approach, therefore, is essential—not only to acquiring knowledge of a complex reality, but to robustness analysis, and hence to the possibility of unifying knowledge.

Sociology uses multiple perspectives. But the biases inherent in each perspective, if not corrected for, lead to a partial and approximate view of the world being accepted as a complete and accurate one. It is this that has led to the appearance within sociology of so many apparently inconsistent theories about the nature of the social world. But once theories and perspectives are recognized as partial, inaccurate, and involving an inherent bias, the number of apparent contradictions in sociology can be reduced significantly. Within the framework of the MMK, even seemingly contradictory theories and truth-claims are candidates for unification.

Take, for example, the contradictory truth-claims that I discussed in §1.1. Gareau, recall, demonstrated a nationalistic bias in the description of the Falklands/Malvinas conflict. Some sociologists and political scientists described the conflict as a territorial war while others described it as a colonial war. There is a sense in which any war can be described as a war over territory, but nonetheless there is a distinction between territorial war and colonial war. Territorial war in this context is war to protect one's own territory or property. This is the way the British tended to see the Falklands/Malvinas conflict. Colonial war, on the other hand, is initiated specifically to gain control and ownership over other people's land and labor, and this is how the Argentine social scientists saw the conflict—as resistance against colonization.

But if these contradictory claims are placed in a temporal framework, the contradiction resolves into a dispute about the length of time of occupation that is required to change what was other people's land into one's own. While I do not deny that this issue would be hotly disputed, it is no longer a contradiction. Moreover, to frame the issue in this way has the practical consequence of providing a basis for negotiation, which the straightforwardly contradictory views did not. For no one, I think, could view the latter formulation of the problem as non-negotiable. To do so would be either to hold that current ownership ought to be based on prehistoric ownership, or to hold that ownership is simply to be equated with possession. Neither of these extreme views is held by the international community.

If the unification strategies that I have suggested are applied, and the necessity for a pluralist sociology is realized, then the sectarian, as opposed to multi-perspective, nature of sociology should disappear. This would leave sociology less open to the charge that it is mere ideology, because the realization of the pluralist, yet in principle unifiable, nature of sociological knowledge would be reflected in the institutional structure of sociology.

But as individuals affect social structure, so too does the structure affect individuals, and strategies for achieving a scientific sociology can take place on two fronts. Not only is there the strategy of making practitioners aware of the nature of sociological knowledge and the importance of epistemic values—there is also the strategy of changing the institutional structure of sociology directly. Donald Campbell has already suggested such changes—for example, the change from sectarian or perspective-oriented journals and conferences to issues-based journals and conferences.[35] Indeed, it seems that such changes are already happening, with issues-based conferences and journals on topics such as feminism, racism, unemployment, and criminology ignoring not only sectarian boundaries, but also traditional disciplinary boundaries. Unfortunately, the opposite tendency is also apparent in the increasing institutional dominance of postmodernism, not only in the humanities and the social sciences but also in science education, through the Cultural Studies movement.[36]

It is clear that further research needs to be done, not only on the present nature of the institutional structure of sociology and the barriers it presents to unification, but on more specific strategies for changing that structure to conform to the best institutional practices of the natural sciences. But sociologists of science have given little attention to functional studies of the structure and norms of science of late. Most recent work focuses on the study of the microprocesses involved in the creation of scientific knowledge, to show how it is socially constructed, or on the specific content of scientific theories, to show how content is affected by social factors. Studies such as Robert Merton's, of the norms and institutional structure of science,[37] have been neglected since the realization that individual scientists do not necessarily give priority to epistemic values, but are influenced by other factors, including funding, career prospects, and so on. But recent studies have shown that, while scientists do indeed break epistemic norms, those norms are well recognized, regarded as essential to science, and play a large part in scientists' judgment of the work of their peers.[38] Further work in this area could benefit the natural sciences as well as the social sciences.

More needs to be done, too, on changing the beliefs of individual practitioners about the nature of scientific theory in general, and of sociological theory in particular. This book, I hope, will make some contribution to this task. Huxley long ago pointed out that scientific knowledge had a limited scope of valid application.

> The great danger which besets all men of large speculative faculty, is the temptation to deal with the accepted statements of fact in natural science, as if they were not only correct, but exhaustive; as if they might be dealt with deductively, in the same way as the propositions in Euclid may be dealt with. In reality, every such statement, however true it may be, is true only relatively to the means of observation and the point of view of those who have enunciated it. So far it may be depended upon. But whether it will bear every speculative conclusion that may be logically deduced from it, is quite another question.[39]

The model of science developed here reflects this view of the natural sciences. By basing the naturalist realist metatheory of sociology on a realistic model of science, I hope to have made the nature of sociological knowledge explicit and to have made a substantial contribution to the methodology of sociology, in particular by modelling validity criteria and unification strategies in an easily used heuristic, the mapping model of knowledge.

I hope also to have opened the way for more meaningful interchange between humanists and naturalists, realists and relativists. No adequate social science can ignore the ways that humans invest the world with meaning and use culture as a guide to action and interaction. And no adequate science can ignore the fact that science itself is part of culture, a human artifact. Nonetheless, scientific knowledge is not merely convention, but a powerful representation of reality, a guide to action and decision making, and one that can always be improved.

These issues cannot be dismissed as just some obscure epistemological debate. The ethical implications are enormous. If no distinction can be made between knowledge and ideology, it is difficult to see how one can be made between education and indoctrination. The idea that education might serve to instil a capacity for critical thought becomes illusion.[40] The well-documented failure of contemporary intellectuals to criticize political, economic, and social issues that affect the existence and quality of life of millions[41] might well be a reflection of the increasing popularity in the academy of relativist epistemologies. Failure to recognize any distinction between knowledge and ideology gives implicit support to the powerful, particularly those with influence on the mass media. At the same time, it leaves the less powerful with no rational means to criticize the system, and no justification—beyond personal commitment— to do so. Of course, many of relativist persuasion do have a deep personal commitment to support the causes of the less powerful, often just on the grounds that everybody has the right to "a voice." But aside from the fact that that too is a principle in need of justification, the problem with such a position is that it would have to give equal support to the demands of the disempowered Australian Aboriginal minority for adequate health care, say, and the demands of an equally small minority that the magical properties of crystals be taught to health workers and that crystals be available through the health care system.

To define truth conventionally is to give implicit support to the powerful, to equate truth with political success. The ideals of truth and reason as modelled in positivism were clearly inadequate. But it is not the ideals that should be abandoned, but the positivist models. The MMK redefines truth as reliable knowledge, retains realist criteria for establishing the validity of knowledge claims, and sees formalizable logics as just one small part of the rationality of science, much of which uses analogical or metaphorical reasoning. Moreover, it sees much of the rationality of science as vested in social decision-making procedures that are little understood at present, but that have something to do with the institutional structure of science and the way it enshrines the norms of truth, honesty, and reason. While avoiding the ethical pitfalls of extreme skepticism, this model, with its recognition of the profoundly social and interest-related nature of science, removes its mystique, and opens the way for healthy criticism—of its content, its methods, and the interests it serves.

Notes

Introduction

1. The reasons are discussed in chapter 1.

2. Shweder and Fiske 1986. See also Bhaskar 1979, 1986, and 1989 and Sayer 1984.

3. Ritzer 1992a.

4. Shweder and Fiske 1986.

5. Norris 1993, Windschuttle 1994.

6. Trigger 1993.

7. Lodahl and Gordon 1972.

8. Gareau 1985.

9. See, for example, Legge 1990.

10. See, for example, Filippov 1993.

11. Mills 1959a.

12. See, for example, Baldus 1990.

13. See, for example, analyses by Norris 1993 and Windschuttle 1994.

14. Sayer (1984) provides an excellent discussion of many methodological issues from a realist perspective, but provides no model for a methodology. One would have to remember the book, as it were, to use it consistently, because it comes with no heuristic.

1. Sociology Today

1. Kuhn 1970.

2. Lodahl and Gordon 1972.

3. See, e.g., Giddens 1986; Giddens 1993; Cuff and Payne 1984; Cuff, Sharrock and Francis 1990; Najman and Western 1993; Jagtenberg and D'Alton 1989; Worsley 1992.

4. Gareau 1985.

5. The structural functionalist and Marxist perspectives will be described in §1.2.2 and §1.2.3.

6. Gareau 1985: 27.

7. Although Soviet bloc sociology is more unified than North American sociology, there are differences between the Rumanian and Soviet approaches, and Polish sociology has a marked Western influence. (Gareau 1985:27)

8. These perspectives and the relationship between them and methodology will be explained in §1.2.2 and §1.2.3.

9. Gareau 1985: Ch.2.

10. Gareau 1985: Ch.5.

11. The breakdown of the Soviet bloc following perestroika in the U.S.S.R., the Solidarity successes in Poland, and the fall of the Berlin Wall in East Germany, have weakened Gareau's argument with respect to the second world, but the situation in the third world remains the same.

12. Gareau 1985:33.

13. Gareau 1985:34–35.

14. Gareau 1985:37.

15. Popper, quoted in Gareau 1985:38.

16. Gareau 1985:38.

17. Gareau 1985:38.

18. Gareau 1985:43.

19. Gareau 1985:45.

20. Gareau 1985:48–53.

21. See §1.2.2 and §1.2.3.

22. Gareau 1985:55–58.

23. Gareau 1985:82–89.

24. Roy 1977.

25. Mills 1959a.

26. Mills 1959a:12–13.

27. The "grand theorists" are more commonly discussed now under the structural functionalist school, but I will stay with Mills's terminology here as his criticisms do not apply to all forms of functionalism.

28. Cuff and Payne 1984:41.

29. Mills 1959a:34–50.

30. Parsons, quoted in Mills 1959a:52.

31. Parsons, quoted in Mills 1959a:52.

32. Mills 1959a.53.

33. Mills 1959a:57.

34. Mills 1959a:58.

35. Mills 1959a:60.

36. Mills 1959a:63.

37. Mills 1959a:64.

38. Mills 1959a:66.

39. Regardless of the various developments, and accompanying name changes, I shall refer in future discussion to those epistemologies adhering to the general principles above as positivism, except where I wish to distinguish between the variants.

40. These links, for the early positivists such as Comte, were, as for Hume, of psychological association. Later, the logical positivists and logical empiricists formulated these links in terms of logic.

41. Andreski 1974:20.

42. Some positivists and later empiricists, although definitely not Comte or Durkheim, extend the idea of the unity of science to include the notion that each branch of science is reducible to the next most general branch, and ultimately to physics.

43. Although many natural scientists may have given lip service to the positivist model of the scientific method, many did not. Mills quotes Nobel Prize-winning physicist Polykarp Kusch as saying there is no "scientific method." Percy Bridgman, another Nobel Prize-winning physicist, wrote: "There is no scientific method as such, but the vital feature of the scientist's procedure has been merely to do his utmost with his mind, *no holds barred.*" (Mills 1959a:69) Whatever individual scientists may have thought or done, historians of science have demonstrated clearly that had the "scientific method" actually been followed, science could not have progressed as it has.

44. Lazarsfeld, quoted in Mills 1959a:72.

45. Lazarsfeld, quoted in Mills 1959a:72.

46. Lazarsfeld, quoted in Mills 1959a:72.

47. As opposed to the later falsificationist version. Falsification uses deductive logic, rather than inductive logic, but the underlying assumptions of both are positivist.

48. Chalmers 1982:4. I shall not go into the problem of induction here, or the problems associated with specifying these conditions. Those unfamiliar with these problems could refer to Chalmers for an excellent introduction.

49. Lazarsfeld, quoted in Mills 1959a:72.

50. Mills 1959a:73.

51. Mills 1959a:84.

52. Mills 1959a:83.

53. Mills 1959a:83.

54. Mills 1959a:86.

55. Baldus 1990.

56. These sociological perspectives will all be discussed later in the book, at least insofar as they are relevant to my argument.

57. The "external" features of a science are those non-epistemic features that contribute to it, e.g., political and economic features, whereas the "internal" features are more clearly epistemic in nature, in that they provide a warrant for the relationship between the content of a science and the world. The distinction is one that, I believe, cannot ultimately be sustained, but it can serve a practical purpose.

58. Cuff, Sharrock, and Francis 1990: Ch 1. This approach has also been used by Cuff et al. to distinguish various ways of knowing the world, e.g., literary versus scientific. Their approach is consistent with the view of science I develop in later chapters.

59. See Cuff, Sharrock, and Francis 1990, Brown 1979, and Giddens 1989, in that order, for examples of the above.

60. This point is developed in chapter 4.

61. Debate over whether structure or agency should be given priority in sociological explanations is the sociological equivalent of the holist/individualist debate in philosophy.

62. In recent times, major schools within the consensus perspective have been referred to as functionalists, or structural functionalists, as well as consensus theorists.

63. Durkheim 1982:52.

64. By "representations," Durkheim means states of consciousness. Or at least by individual representations he means individual states of consciousness. I think now that we do not require representations to be conscious, and that the definition can be broadened to "mental state" without altering Durkheim's argument. Indeed, inasmuch as Durkheim considers some social facts are not transparent, but can be recognized only by their *generality* (in addition to their externality) rather than by any apparent constraint, he too must go beyond the notion of consciousness. This he does anyway in his talk of the "collective consciousness," for he is quite clear that in using this concept he is not proposing the existence of some sort of giant conscious mind. Rather, he has in mind norms and values that are held intersubjectively.

65. Durkheim 1982:39.

66. Durkheim 1982:39.

67. Durkheim 1982:39.

68. Durkheim 1982:123.

69. Durkheim 1982:94.

70. Durkheim,1982:121–122.

71. Durkheim 1982:123.

72. See Erikson 1962 and Erikson 1966.

73. Erikson 1962:310–311.

74. Genovese 1971:381.

75. Marx quoted in Carver, 1982:22.

76. Roxborough 1979:4.

77. See particularly chapters 2 and 3.

78. Pearce 1976.

79. President's Commission on Law Enforcement 1967. Quoted in Pearce 1976:78.

80. Weber 1978a:4.

81. Weber 1978a:13.

82. Cuff and Payne 1984, Worsley 1987.

83. Goffman 1961.

84. Garfinkel 1967:78.

85. Cicourel 1976.

86. Becker 1953 and Becker 1955.

87. Mills 1959b:8–9.

88. Mills 1959b:49.

89. Andreski 1972: Ch. 5 & 6.

90. Andreski 1972:102–103.

91. Weber, for example, although defining sociology in terms of the interpretive understanding of individual human action, made effective use of the essentially collective notions of class and status group.

92. See Levine 1965, and particularly Levine 1974.

2. Issues in the Metatheory of Sociology

1. Although I am faithful to my understanding of the theorists in question, it scarcely matters whether I have *the* correct interpretation, if indeed there is such. The construction of the ideal-typical naturalist, humanist, positivist, etc., would serve my purposes equally but for the fact that I can assume some familiarity on the part of the reader with classic theorists such as Durkheim and Weber.

2. Baldus 1990.

3. Such confusion is apparent, e.g., in Frankel 1986, and most postmodernists and poststructuralists seem unaware of the distinction. See Norris 1993 for a detailed analysis.

4. Hooker 1987a: Ch. 3.

5. Hooker 1987a: Ch. 2.

6. Hooker 1987a: Ch. 3.

7. Hooker 1987a:65.

8. Hooker 1987a:73.

9. See, e.g., Hanson 1958 and Kuhn 1970.

10. See, e.g., Feyerabend 1962 and Kuhn 1970.

11. These are just a few of the many widely discussed criticisms of empiricism. A full discussion of the issues involved is beyond the scope of this book, but for a brief review of these criticisms, see e.g., Chalmers 1982. The position is no longer dominant in philosophy of science.

12. See Popper 1979. See Feyerabend (1978: Ch. 15) for a criticism of this methodology.

13. "Metaphysical" is used here in the sense that Comte used it, and contrasts with scientific or "positive."

14. Popper 1983:127.

15. Popper 1983:128.

16. Hooker 1987a:79.

17. Hooker 1987a: 68, 75, and 83.

18. Hooker 1987a: 68, 75, and 83.

19. Hooker 1987a: 68 and 75.

20. Hooker 1987a: 82.

21. Hooker 1987a: 68, 75, and 83.

22. Hooker 1987a: 68, 76, and 84.

23. Hooker 1987a: 76.

24. Hooker 1987a: 84.

25. Hooker 1987a: 68, 75, and 83.

26. Much of Hooker (1987a) is devoted to criticisms of positivism and the parallel development of a naturalist realist position.

27. Hooker 1987a: 88.

28. Hooker 1987a:88.

29. Hooker 1987a:88–89.

30. Hooker 1987a:89–90.

31. Hooker 1987a:90.

32. Hooker 1987a:92.

33. Hooker 1987a:92.

34. Hooker 1987a:92.

35. Hooker 1987a:92.

36. Hindess (1988) refers to such institutions as "social actors." It may turn out that the institution of science can be regarded as a social actor.

37. Hooker 1987a:93.

38. Hooker 1987a:93.

39. Hooker 1987a:94.

40. Hooker 1987a:94.

41. Berkeley is an example.

42. Berger and Luckmann 1967.

43. Marx and Engels 1978:144.

44. I shall discuss Durkheim's naturalism and realism in the next section. In this chapter, I avoid as much as possible using Marx to illustrate the positions I discuss, because his work has been interpreted in so many ways that to do so might be more confusing than illuminating. For example, although I see Marx as a naturalist and a realist, in the 1950s Marxism developed into two opposing camps, the structuralist Marxists (who were naturalist and realist) and the critical theorists (who were humanist). See Bottomore (1978) for an analysis of these developments.

45. Runciman 1978:65–66.

46. Gadamer 1975:5.

47. The adoption of a different model of the natural sciences that can also adequately model the social sciences was, of course, the fourth position open to those developing the social sciences. The naturalist realist model presented earlier is one such model. It is arguable that Marx adopted this strategy, as a study of his scattered writings on methodology from a naturalist realist perspective reveals. (See Marx 1975 for a collection edited by T. Carver). It is also arguable that Durkheim was rather less positivist and more naturalist realist than is commonly held. (See next section).

48. Weber 1978a:4.

49. Weber is rather vague about what it is for behavior to be meaningful, but his discussions suggest a link between meaningful behavior and purposiveness. Despite the vagueness, it is clear enough that "meaning", for Weber, can be equated with intentionality, and explanations of meaningful behavior, or "action," are in terms of reasons or motives.

50. "Social actions," the object of sociological study to Weber, form a sub-class of "actions," defined in Weber's definition of sociology. As it is arguable that all "actions" are social, in the sense that they are meaningful and belong to a symbolic world, I shall not dwell on the distinction.

51. Freund 1968: Ch. 2.

52. Freund 1968:104–107.

53. Weber 1978a:8.

54. Weber 1978a:8.

55. Weber 1978a:5.

56. Weber 1978a:5.

57. Weber 1978a:5–6.

58. Weber 1978a:12.

59. Weber 1978b:99.

60. Runciman 1978:65.

61. Runciman 1978:65.

62. Runciman 1978:66.

63. This position is held, for example, by Kenneth Gergen (1986).

64. Gergen 1986.

65. Habermas, for example, can be seen as taking some such position. Although he attempts to justify the critical, rather than the hermeneutic, social sciences in this way, both the hermeneutic and the natural sciences are justified by the critical sciences, at least according to his position in *Knowledge and Human Interests* (1972).

66. Radnitsky 1970.

67. Wardell and Turner 1986.

68. For an elaboration of this claim, see, e.g., Hooker 1982.

69. Radnitsky 1970.

70. Andreski 1972.

71. Rosenthal and Jacobsen 1968.

72. There are some notable exceptions. Durkheim's studies of the functions of religion for society, for example, are precisely not historically and culturally specific. See Durkheim 1976.

73. Converse 1986:44.

74. Converse 1986:52.

75. Feyerabend 1978.

76. I use "external" here to indicate factors excluded by positivist philosophies from the scientific process, i.e., to mean all factors apart from supposed value-free facts and logic. I do not actually believe all such factors to be irrelevant epistemically, although some, e.g., coercive politics, are. The terms "internal" and "external" are still used in post-positivist philosophy of science, particularly in the debate between sociologists of knowledge and critical rationalists. Sociologists of knowledge argue that both the process of scientific discovery and the content of scientific theories are to be explained in terms of social factors, whereas critical rationalists argue that such factors are

"external" to the scientific process and should be invoked only when the history of science cannot be explained in terms of rational or "internal" factors.

77. Realism, as developed in the last fifteen years or so, goes under a variety of names; viz. scientific realism (Hooker), naturalist realism (Hooker), transcendental realism and critical realism (Bhaskar), theoretical realism (Keat and Urry). While the authors mentioned develop different aspects of realism, and differ in some of the details, there is remarkable consistency in modern realist positions at the level of generality at which I discuss them here. I prefer the term "naturalist realism," as it emphasizes that aspect of realism that most concerns me in the development of a metatheory of sociology, and I use it as representative of all of the above versions.

78. The rationalists (e.g., Descartes, Spinoza, and Leibniz) believed the general nature of the world could be established by wholly non-empirical reasoning. Rationalism has also been traditionally opposed to realism.

79. Although their position was internally inconsistent, the logical positivists and the later logical empiricists held (the latter in a weakened version) to a verification theory of meaning, whereby any proposition that was not empirically verifiable was meaningless. Thus, to these empiricists at any rate, epistemology was the only philosophy worth discussing. That the statement of the verification principle was itself not verifiable seemed not to be of major concern.

80. For a comprehensive and systematic account of scientific realism, see Hooker 1987a.

81. This was Popper's great contribution to the philosophy of science. See Popper 1979.

82. Among sociologists, Marx, and the contemporary Marxist sociologists, Jessop and Urry, are good examples.

83. See Kuhn 1970 and Feyerabend 1978. Postmodernist and poststructuralist positions have their origins in European philosophy and rarely refer to Kuhn and Feyerabend, but at this level of analysis their positions neatly fit the relativist model described here.

84. For example, Dilthey and Mannheim.

85. I use the term "validity" here in the more general sense of "well-foundedness," rather than in the logical sense in which the premises imply the conclusion. The sense in which I use the term is the more common, outside of analytical philosophy.

86. Most contemporary realists hold some version of benign relativism. Bhaskar, e.g., calls his version "epistemic relativism," which he combines with ontological realism.

87. Many of the issues in this debate are put forward by their proponents in a collection edited by J. R. Brown (1984), which includes contributions from Laudan and

from Bloor and Barnes. The debate is also prominent in the journals *Philosophy of the Social Sciences* and *Social Studies of Science.*

88. The term "critical rationalists" in contemporary philosophy usually refers to philosophers who recognize that no single specifiable set of methodological rules can adequately account for the progress of science, yet wish to retain from positivism the notion that science is a rational process and that in some sense its progress is to be explained by its rationality. Feyerabend, for example, calls Lakatos a critical rationalist in the light of the latter's attempts to demarcate good from bad scientific research programs in the light of whether they are progressive or degenerating. While this may well be an important distinction in science, it cannot be used as a normative principle, as whether a program is progressive or degenerating can only be decided over an extremely long time frame. See Lakatos and Musgrave (1970) and Feyerabend (1978) for thorough discussion of these issues. Critical rationalists in this sense may well also be realists.

89. Many philosophers of science distinguish the "context of discovery" from the "context of justification," reserving rationality for the *post facto* justification of scientific theories while denying the applicability of rationality for scientific discovery, citing imagination, creativity, and numerous other factors including social ones as responsible in some unknown way for scientific discovery.

90. Barnes 1984: 120.

91. Nicholas 1984:267.

92. Mulkay 1979:3.

93. Latour and Woolgar 1979.

94. Latour and Woolgar 1979:106.

95. The methodological presuppositions and details of this method are clearly set out in the first chapter of *Laboratory Life.* I shall not go into the details here, except to say that they are based on the notion of treating the object of study (in this case, scientific processes) as a literary fiction and analyzing its construction. The method is common to postmodernists and poststructuralists, and is not unrelated to the ethnomethodology I described in §1.2.3. The realist is not necessarily opposed to its use as methodology—a point I develop in chapter 6.

96. Instrumentation includes the laboratory apparatus, but also, in the sense that I use it here, the scientists themselves, and hence could include psychological dispositions.

97. Latour and Woolgar 1979:180.

98. This point will be taken up in detail in chapter 7.

99. Latour and Woolgar 1979:181–182.

100. Latour and Woolgar 1979.

101. Woolgar 1986.

102. Radford 1985.

103. Berger and Luckmann 1967.

104. As social theory their work has been much criticized, along with that of other phenomenological sociologists, for being based on a priori assumptions, for being purely descriptive and trivial, for neglecting social structure, and for having little empirical application. (Abercrombie, Hill, and Turner 1984:158) I shall not take up these criticisms here, as it would take me too far afield.

105. Radford 1985:17.

106. Radford 1985:15.

107. Radford 1985:15n.

108. Radford 1985:16.

109. Radford 1979:19.

110. Radford 1985:20–21.

111. Unless, like Berkeley, one invokes a God to do the work. But then for the social constructivists it would have to be a special kind of God, quite unlike Berkeley's, that gave reality only to the social rather than to everything external.

112. Collins 1985.

113. Collins 1985:148.

114. Hesse 1986:717–718.

115. Hesse 1986:718.

116. Collins 1985:165.

117. Note that this notion of rationality is the same as the positivist one.

118. But see McMullin 1984, for a much better distinction between epistemic and non-epistemic factors which does not follow the rational/social distinction.

119. Gareau (1985) and Andreski (1974) show this. See chapter 1 §1.2 and chapter 2 §2.1.

120. Many such studies have been done by historians of science. I mention here only the delightful examples by Stephen J. Gould in his books on topics in evolutionary theory. See bibliography.

121. The Edinburgh School agree with the realists here, using their (inductively arrived at) belief in the efficacy of science as justification for their causal approach to

the sociological study of science, while admitting that this belief, like all others, is in some sense socially determined. See Barnes 1984:122.

122. Such a "bootstrapping" view of science and of norms fits well with many evolutionary epistemologies. See chapter 3 for a discussion of these. I believe there is a sense in which a naturalist realist epistemology leads automatically to some form of evolutionary epistemology, but this is not argued here.

123. Much recent discussion of the realist/relativist debate shows that much hinges on the definitions of realism and relativism that are used. It also shows that in many cases there is no inconsistency between specific realist and relativist positions, although the history of the debate, dating to as early as Protagoras, has led to the names themselves acting as red rags to a bull. The crucial point is that realism offers the hope of distinguishing good from bad science while *radical* relativism does not. The same applies in the area of ethics. See Margolis (1988), Jordan (1989), and Nicholas (1984) for some of the discussion on varieties of relativism and how they are placed in the debate with realism.

124. "Social facts" were, for Durkheim, on account of their reality, to be treated as "thing-like." Although he starts from the positivist position that the basis of knowledge is incorrigible sensory perception or observation, and that the proper objects of science are therefore phenomena, he moves quickly to the position that some social "facts" cannot be directly observed but are known through their effects. He does not, however, wish to call collective representations or norms material objects. The word "fact," for Durkheim, both signifies reality and is a move away from "phenomena," while being noncommittal with regard to materiality.

125. Durkheim 1982: 33.

126. Durkheim 1982:33n.

127. Durkheim 1982:32.

128. Durkheim 1982:159.

129. Durkheim 1982:176–177.

130. Durkheim 1982:178.

131. Durkheim laid the foundations of the functionalist method in sociology and produced several substantive studies that are still relevant today, e.g., Durkheim (1976) (1933) (1951). But his definition of sociology excludes the study of social action and hence much of sociology.

132. Keat and Urry 1982.

133. See Urry (1981) and Jessop (1982) for just two contemporary Marxist theorists who take a naturalist realist perspective.

134. Hesse 1986:725.

3. Theories as Maps of the World

1. Hooker 1989a:101.

2. Campbell 1974.

3. Lorenz 1982.

4. The word "sciencing" is taken from Rubinstein, Laughlin, and McManus (1984). I use it, as they do, to convey the notion of science as an activity as opposed to science as a body of knowledge.

5. See Carrithers (1990b) for a discussion of how sociality could have been selected for, and for the consequences of this for the applicability of evolutionary theory to the evolution of culture.

6. See Munz, 1989. The units of selection controversy generally is dealt with in some detail in chapter 7. I do not intend to discuss here either this or the many other controversies associated with the various positions in evolutionary epistemology. To do so would take me too far from my goal, which is merely to show how evolutionary epistemologies accommodate the theory-ladenness of observation and the sociocultural factors that affect science, and yet retain the idea that scientific theories are reliable. Many of the controversies are raised and argued in Hahlweg and Hooker (1989a). Reader (1988) discusses many of the anthropological studies that show how particular forms of social organization and the belief systems that support them are adapted to local environments.

7. Rubinstein, Laughlin, and McManus 1984.

8. Rubinstein et al. 1984:xx.

9. Rubinstein et al. 1984:22.

10. Rubinstein et al. 1984:25.

11. Munz 1989.

12. Gould 1987b.

13. Rubinstein et al. 1984:27.

14. Rubinstein et al. 1984:27.

15. Kinsbourne in Rieber (1983:158).

16. We shall see later that the notion of collaborative epistemic development is crucial to science. For example, one of the means by which we justify the acceptance of a scientific theory is that it has achieved intersubjective agreement in the self-critical scientific community.

17. Rubinstein et al. 1984:32.

18. Donald Campbell has been in large part responsible for the emergence of, and continuing interest in, evolutionary epistemology, and has written extensively on the subject. See the bibliography for a small selection of his works.

19. Campbell 1974:422–423.

20. Campbell and Paller 1989:236.

21. Campbell and Paller 1989:234.

22. These would include most of the sociologists of knowledge I discussed in chapter 2. The possible exceptions are Barnes and Bloor in their more recent works.

23. Campbell 1973:1050.

24. Berlin 1973:260.

25. Berlin 1973 and Berlin, Breedlove, and Raven 1966.

26. Berlin 1973:269.

27. Berlin, Breedlove, and Raven 1966:274.

28. Bulmer and Tyler 1968.

29. Bulmer and Tyler 1968:334–335.

30. Bulmer and Tyler 1968:352.

31. Campbell and Paller 1989:240.

32. Campbell 1974.

33. Campbell and Paller 1989:232–233.

34. Campbell 1979:183–184.

35. Campbell 1979:184.

36. Campbell and Paller 1989:248.

37. Campbell 1979:197.

38. Campbell 1979:198.

39. Campbell 1979:198.

40. Latour and Woolgar 1979.

41. Campbell 1979:198.

42. Campbell 1979:185.

43. Campbell 1979.

44. Campbell 1979:192.

45. Campbell 1979:193.

46. Campbell 1979:194.

47. Campbell 1979:194.

48. Campbell 1979:194.

49. Hull 1988.

50. Campbell 1979:193.

51. Campbell and Paller 1989:248.

52. But see Bhaskar's "expressive theory of truth" for a happier alternative. "Expression (as representation or description) is not identity and only metaphorically correspondence. Speaking of 'expression' reminds us that there are different (and better and worse) ways of expressing something—i.e. it reminds us of the connections between ontological realism, epistemic relativity and judgemental rationality." (Bhaskar 1986:100)

53. These points will be expanded in chapter 4.

54. Rorty 1979.

55. Rorty 1979.

56. See, for example, Toulmin (1953) and Ziman (1978). I have drawn heavily on both of these books in developing my model. But others, such as Samuel (1985) and (1990), use the metaphor explicitly to argue particular points about the nature of scientific theories.

57. Ziman 1978:6.

58. Ziman 1978:77.

59. Theories must be compatible at some deep level, as must maps. This will be discussed in chapters 4 and 7.

60. Toulmin 1953:111–112.

61. Ziman 1978:82.

62. Toulmin 1953:110, and Ziman 1978:82.

63. This issue will be discussed in detail in chapter 4.

64. Toulmin 1953:127.

65. Global theories (Hooker's term) are the most radical examples of map making. This matter is discussed in Hooker (1975).

4. The Nature of Validity

1. It is arguable that science, conceived positivistically, can be used to support the status quo, whatever that may be. See Bhaskar 1986:Ch. 3. So another possible function of science would be the maintenance of social cohesion.

2. "To take a decision is to choose between branching paths into the future, in the light of their imagined or calculated end points." (Ziman 1978:107)

3. For example, the 1:100 000 scale topographic maps produced by the Central Mapping Authority of NSW.

4. The Oxford Atlas 1951.

5. Perhaps it cannot even be arrived at inductively. I tend toward a position that denies that metatheory (or any theory) is arrived at solely by the use of deductive and inductive logic. Indeed, I believe that the process is not formalizable. But to argue that metatheory is not arrived at inductively is to go well beyond the bounds of my thesis, and is in any case irrelevant to it.

6. There is no reason, in principle, for any upper limit on this cognitive hierarchy.

7. This concept of objectivity was discussed in chapter 3.

8. Ziman 1978:86.

9. A "picture" in this context means either a painting (or a drawing, etc.) *or* an ordinary photograph. The latter is also the view of a particular person in a particular place at a particular time.

10. Many, including myself, who have not personally seen Red Square in Moscow, have seen enough representations from a variety of perspectives to be able to agree that some newly perceived representation was also of Red Square. Such vicarious judgments at this level of abstraction rely on there being no trickery and on certain well-known features and relations being present.

11. I am indebted to C. A. Hooker for clarification of these points, and for the term "deep compatibility."

12. See Hooker (1987a:Ch. 7) and Harré (1983).

13. See Laudan (1979) and Shapere (1984).

14. Laudan (1979:13) defines the functions of a theory as " . . . to resolve ambiguity, to reduce irregularity to uniformity, to show that what happens is somehow intelligible and predictable . . . " It is in this sense that he refers to theories as solutions to problems. While in general agreement with Laudan that these are epistemic problems, I would not wish to say that all theories must address all of these, and nor do I consider

the list complete. Indeed, I do not know how one might say of any such list that it was complete.

15. This does not necessarily mean that one must reject a correspondence theory of truth, as I showed in chapter 3. The additional requirements that a valid theory, like a valid map, exhibit internal and external consistency and coherence and have explanatory value, together differentiate my position from the pragmatists.

16. Toulmin 1953: 26 and 32–33. Harré and Ziman make this point as well, although Harré specifically wishes to exclude mathematical models from his use of the word "model" (Harré 1970:37). He is a little confusing on the issue, as he wishes also to exclude sentential models from his scheme. Yet in his own analysis of Darwin's theory of natural selection he uses sentences for the model rather than a diagram. Indeed, it is hard to see how a diagram could be used in this case. Harré need not reject mathematical and sentential models, for he could regard them as higher-order models in the way Rubinstein et al. do. I use the word "model" to include all the forms mentioned here.

17. See, e.g., Harré (1970, 1979, 1983, 1985). The first edition of Harré (1983) was published in 1960.

18. Shapere 1984: Ch. 13.

19. Shapere 1984.

20. See Gould (1981) for details of the debate and an argument that all such attempts are in vain. Although head measuring failed to provide a basis for the belief in white superiority, the attempt to provide some such criteria for distinguishing racial groups according to intelligence has not been abandoned. The latest attempts simply substitute IQ for brain size.

21. Ziman 1978:85.

22. Harré 1970.

23. Functional explanation will be discussed in detail in the next chapter.

24. Harré 1970:45.

25. What counts as a single-source science? Intuitively, Harré says we can understand single sciences as those which are not explicable in terms of each other, e.g., mechanics and electrodynamics (p.45). He says we can strengthen this notion by asking of two individuals, one defined in terms of one science, the other in terms of the other science, whether they can occupy the same place at the same time, and the one not be a part of the other. If so, they are different sciences as sources for paramorphs.

26. The analogy depends on the fact that living lampreys bear a marked resemblance, both in brain structure and in having a jawless, sucker-type mouth, to the extinct proto-fish found in the fossil record and believed to be the evolutionary predecessors of fish, and to the fact that they are not usually regarded as "proper" fish.

27. I can find no brief way to describe these, but a lengthy description is inappropriate here. See Harré (1970:50–52).

28. Toulmin 1953.

29. Hempel expanded his notion of explanation to include inductive-statistical (I-S) explanation, but this need not be discussed here, as the principle involved is the same. I-S explanation is used where we have less than total evidence.

30. Hooker 1980:285.

31. Hooker 1980:286.

32. Hooker 1980:287.

33. Ziman 1978:33.

34. Ziman 1978:34.

35. Cartwright 1983.

36. Harré 1970:52.

37. Harré notes that this example needs refinement, and uses it only for illustrative purposes.

38. Harré 1970:53. Harré's modal transforms correspond with what I call property theories. I deal with these, and with their place in explanation, in chapter 5.

39. "Picture" meaning "model," but see note 16.

40. Toulmin 1953:38. Harré believes a theory should prompt consideration of four types of question: 1) Existential questions. With reference to the kinetic theory of gases, "Are there molecules?"; 2) Descriptions of the model or hypothetical mechanism, e.g., "Are molecules in motion?"; 3) Questions about the power of the hypothetical mechanism to produce the phenomena e.g., "Is gas pressure caused by the impact of molecules?"; 4) Questions that invite us to consider modal transforms, e.g., "Is gas temperature really only another way of looking at the mean kinetic energy of the molecules?" (Harré 1970:55).

41. This account of fruitfulness is merely a suggestion, as I have not gone into the matter in any depth. Intuitively, theories that are fruitful in this way will lead to, or at least offer the opportunity of, progress in science, via increased causal understanding.

42. Laudan notes that "cosmologists and geologists are often prepared to attach much less significance to seemingly large discrepancies between predicted and observed results than is, say, a physical chemist or a spectroscopist. These differences in precision tolerance in the various disciplines do not mean that these tolerance limits are arbitrary. To the contrary, they usually reflect the subtle instrumental and mathematical constraints on the field, as well as the complexity of the process under investigation." (Laudan 1979:39).

43. Such limitations are mainly matters of specialization in education and training, but much scientific knowledge is restricted, at least initially, by the institutions that develop it, often for reasons of security or economic advantage.

44. There is no reason, in principle, for any upper limit on this cognitive hierarchy. In fact, it is always more complex than I have represented it here. Part of the reason for this is that any theory that explains a domain may itself become the domain of a more general theory. I limit myself to talking about three levels here because my aim is only to show how the question of validity cannot be limited to relations between a theory and its domain. See Hooker (1989b) for a list of the broad cognitive hierarchies applicable to physics.

45. Both theories and maps are defined functionally. This means that, to the extent that they are functionally equivalent, maps are just special kinds of theories and theories just special kinds of maps.

46. See chapter 5 for a detailed discussion of this issue.

47. Toulmin 1953:21.

48. The metaphysical basis for this claim is the realist assumption that there is a single reality. Further discussion of this assumption is deferred to the next chapter.

49. I deal with some of the problems associated with establishing consistency in chapter 7.

50. Feyerabend 1978.

51. Ziman 1978:82.

52. Ziman 1978:84.

53. Laudan 1979:55.

54. Laudan 1979:59.

55. Toulmin 1953:48.

56. Toulmin 1953:31.

57. Toulmin 1953:59.

5. Validity and Reality in the Social Sciences

1. Aristotle 1961:Δii, Aiii.

2. Hahlweg 1983:91–92.

3. Hahlweg 1983:92. The status of the laws of thermodynamics as causal is controversial within physics, but this point need not concern us here.

4. Hahlweg 1983:95–96.

5. The degree of precision required will, as I argued for precision in general in chapter 4, be relative to the problem that the theory addresses.

6. See, for example, Harris (1988) and Dawkins (1988), for a part of that debate as it appeared in *New Scientist*. The hypothesis of formative causation was first outlined in *A New Science of Life* (1987), and later expanded in *The Presence of the Past* (1988).

7. Azevedo 1988.

8. See §1.2.2.

9. See Abercrombie, Hill, and Turner (1984:92–93) for a brief account.

10. See §1.2.3.

11. See Chambliss (1975) and Gordon (1973).

12. Cummins 1983.

13. Cummins 1983:2. Cummins notes here that subsumptions under non-causal laws may be considered explanations, but of a different sort, for they are merely summaries of our reasons for believing the change would occur, or justifications of our expectations.

14. Cummins 1983:2.

15. Cummins regards the fact that DN explanation is still considered paradigmatic as due to the fact that no suitable alternative has been developed. Cf. the sort of criticisms of DN explanation made in chapter 4.

16. Cummins 1983:2–5

17. See chapter 6 for a brief discussion of some of the problems of quantum theory.

18. Cummins 1983:13–14.

19. Cummins 1983:28.

20. Cummins 1983:6.

21. Cummins 1983:7–8.

22. This figure was adapted from Hooker:1987b.

23. Cummins does not equate instantiation with the reduction of all properties to the properties of physics. Indeed, he argues that many of the problems of reductionism could be avoided if the language of reduction were replaced with the language of instantiation. See Cummins 1983:22–25. In this I agree with Cummins. The point is taken up in chapter 7.

24. Cummins 1983:26.

25. Cummins 1983:28. By "programmed," Cummins means organized in a way that could be specified in a program or flow chart.

26. Cummins 1983:29.

27. Cummins 1983:29–30.

28. Cummins 1983:31.

29. Cummins 1983:31–32.

30. Cummins 1983:32.

31. Cummins 1983:33–34.

32. Hooker 1981b.

33. Hooker 1981b:508–509.

34. Hooker 1981b:509.

35. See, e.g., Putnam (1960). I argue this point in §5.5.

36. Cummins 1983:34.

37. See Bhaskar 1979, Bhaskar 1986, Bhaskar 1989.

38. I do not believe that the open/closed system distinction serves to distinguish the social sciences from the natural sciences, as my earlier discussion of open and closed systems showed. Nor do I believe that predictive success has no place as a criterion of validity in the social sciences, but certainly it cannot be the only criterion.

39. Weber 1930.

40. An ideal type is ideal in the sense that it is an idealization, formed by abstracting salient and identifying features from reality. One would not expect to find any person, set of ideas, etc. in reality that would exactly match the ideal type, just as one would not expect any animal to reflect exactly all of the features used to identify its species.

41. Cummins 1983:14. See also Bhaskar 1979.

42. Gergen 1986.

43. Gergen 1986:147.

44. Gergen 1986:147.

45. Gergen 1986:151.

46. Gergen 1986:159.

47. Sociologists of knowledge such as Berger and Luckmann and Latour and Woolgar take this view of the whole of science, as we saw in §2.3, raising the question of self-reference.

48. Carrithers 1990a.

49. Firth, quoted in Carrithers 1990a:266.

50. Carrithers 1990a:266.

51. Carrithers 1990a:266.

52. Carrithers 1990a:268.

53. Firth, quoted in Carrithers 1990a:268.

54. Carrithers 1990a:269.

55. Carrithers 1990a:270.

56. Churchland 1979.

57. Churchland 1979:21.

58. Churchland 1984:64.

59. Churchland 1984:64.

60. Churchland 1984:64.

61. Churchland also shows that, as an empirical theory, folk psychology is totally inadequate, and can be expected to be so. But this point need not concern us here, because Churchland makes this assessment in terms of causal theories and the stricter correspondence with reality that is required of them.

62. Hooker 1981a. See also §7.4.

63. Carrithers 1990a:270.

64. Carrithers 1990a:271.

65. Carrithers 1990a:271.

66. Carrithers 1990a:271.

67. Carrithers 1990a:271.

68. Carrithers 1990a:271.

69. I expand on the concept of robustness and its importance in chapters 6 and 7.

70. Weber 1978a:9.

71. Hindess 1988.

72. Hindess 1988:48.

73. Hindess 1988:86.

74. Hindess 1988:86–87.

6. Knowing in a Complex World

1. Whether it is in fact consistent with the body of scientific knowledge will obviously be contingent, depending on such things as the cohesiveness of the scientific account of humans with the rest of scientific knowledge, the sophistication of the latter, and so on.

2. Hahlweg 1983.

3. Prigogine and Stengers 1984.

4. Hahlweg 1983:30.

5. Hahlweg 1983: Ch. 1 and Ch. 3.

6. See Ziman (1978), Fiske (1986), Richter (1986), and Wimsatt (1986) for discussions on various aspects of complexity in the social sciences.

7. Hahlweg 1983:38.

8. All humans have a space-time framework, but the nature of that framework may differ from culture to culture.

9. See also the discussion in Hahlweg 1983:40–43.

10. Hahlweg 1983:112.

11. Weber's *The Protestant Ethic and the Spirit of Capitalism,* discussed in chapter 5, is a classic example of the use of cross-cultural comparison.

12. Hahlweg, himself a chemist, primarily uses examples from chemistry to explicate his position. The equivalent to "apparatus" could, in sociology, be the cultural background of the researcher, for example.

13. "Robustness" can be defined as cross-situational invariance, a concept I exploited in chapter 4 in developing the MMK. The concept is crucial to the theory of unification that I develop in chapter 7, and will be discussed further there. Here I preempt that discussion by noting that robust and causally instantiated objects can be attributed reality, at whatever level is appropriate.

14. Noise is discussed further in chapter 7, where Figures 7.4 and 7.5 illustrate instrument noise.

15. Hahlweg 1983:57.

16. Hahlweg 1983:60.

17. The irrelevance of much experimentation in the social sciences stems from the fact that human systems are open systems. Laboratory conditions are so simplified that any results have no relevance outside the laboratory situation. See, for example, discussions in Vickers (1983), Campbell (1986), and Ziman (1978).

18. In fact, Hahlweg recognizes that maps are a more appropriate analogue for theories than mirrors, although he does not develop the point. His thesis is more concerned with metaphysics, and epistemology at a more general level than my treatment, which is more at the level of methodology.

19. See chapter 3.

20. Game and Pringle 1983.

21. I argue this in detail in the Azevedo 1989.

22. See chapter 5.

23. See §1.2.3 and also Mandelbaum (1973).

24. Polkinghorne 1984:68.

25. Folse 1985:57–59. Hooker (personal communication) disagrees with this claim, but this does not, I believe, detract from the argument here.

26. Hooker 1989c:8.

27. The Wu-Shakanov experiment. See Hooker (1972:125–128).

28. Although siding with the quantum theoretic predictions, Hooker points out that it falsifies an EPR-type reality assumption only against the background of the remainder of quantum mechanical method. (Hooker 1972:127)

29. See Hooker (1989c) for a recent discussion of this argument.

30. See Hooker (1972) and Folse (1985).

31. Folse 1985:29.

32. Hooker 1972:134.

33. Folse 1985:69.

34. For Kant, space and time were the a priori forms of intuition without which perception would be impossible. Cause, on the other hand, was an a priori concept, a category necessary for our understanding of experience. The differences need not bother us in this context.

35. Folse 1985.

36. Hooker 1972.

37. I am not a physicist and so cannot contribute to the internal analyses. But the issues I raise arise as a result of the epistemology and methodology I have developed, and apply equally to all subject areas. Whether they turn out to be significant in particular areas is a contingent matter.

38. Hooker 1972:197.

39. Hooker 1989c.

40. Simpson 1987.

41. Fiske 1986.

7. The Unification of Knowledge

1. Gellner 1988.

2. Gellner 1988:197.

3. Gellner demonstrates how unlikely this development was, showing the number of contingent factors it depended upon. While he sees the ecological changes of human societies from hunter-gatherer to agrarian and from agrarian to industrial as evolutionary, unlike the social Darwinists, Gellner sees no inevitability in the change. Rather, he notes that both changes were improbable, the second more so than the first. Many cultures made the transition from hunter-gatherer to agrarian, but only one spontaneously made the transition from agrarian to industrial.

4. Gellner 1988:196.

5. Munz 1989.

6. One might speculate, as Gellner does, that the methods of coercion, of cooperation, in developed societies, are stretched to their limits, and that the resulting crises, for example the world environmental crises, will make clear the need for a unified social science.

7. Reduction need not necessarily be from macrostates to microstates, although the dominance of mechanistic atomism has made this the more usual form. Reduction to a field theory merely requires that phenomenal states, processes, etc., be reduced to some single set of underlying states, processes, etc. The force of atomistic reduction is to reduce change to spatiotemporal rearrangement, so bringing it under geometry.

8. The importance of taking account of the irreversibility of time was a crucial factor in undermining the mechanistic world view. See Prigogine and Stengers 1984.

9. Dawkins 1976.

10. Gould 1980:76.

11. Gould 1980:77–78.

12. Gould 1983:166–176.

13. Gould 1980:73–75.

14. Gould 1980:75.

15. Simberloff 1980:13.

16. Levins and Lewontin 1980:47.

17. Levins and Lewontin 1980:49.

18. Levins and Lewontin 1980:50.

19. Humanists have also often taken a reductionist approach to society, although for different reasons. Historically, the foundations of humanism lie in the belief that humans are fundamentally different from material objects inasmuch as they have minds, are intentional, have free will. Society is treated as an aggregate of individuals, and social phenomena as the aggregate of individual social actions. But for humanists there is a natural stopping place in reduction: the individual human. The immaterial nature of minds and ideas prevents further reduction to any material category.

20. Gould 1981.

21. Rose, Lewontin, and Kamin 1984.

22. Gould 1981.

23. Gould 1981:251.

24. Rose, Lewontin, and Kamin 1984:75.

25. See footnote 19.

26. Rose, Lewontin, and Kamin 1984:80.

27. Wimsatt 1980:215.

28. Wimsatt 1980:219.

29. Simon's work on bounded rationality has also been used to effect by Barry Hindess (1988). Hindess uses the distinction between maximizing rationality, which is not an option for humans, and satisficing rationality, involving the use of simplifying and approximating techniques (or heuristics). Different interests and/or cultural perspectives lead to the use of different heuristics. This is a selection process. Hindess argues that because different standards of adequate satisficing may be adopted, there are different forms of rationality. This becomes part of his argument against even the most sophisticated of rational choice theories being adequate for the description of the individually rational, let alone the socially rational.

30. Wimsatt 1986:295.

31. The considerations of time and monetary cost as well as computational complexity that are included in the term "cost-effective" are real problems for scientists—problems largely ignored by traditional philosophy of science.

32. Wimsatt 1980:221.

33. Wimsatt (1980:221) also points out that the concept of a heuristic is pivotal in evolutionary epistemology. I believe that a thoroughgoing naturalism does in fact require the use of some form of evolutionary epistemology to explain scientific progress, but this point is outside the scope of this book, which is not concerned with scientific progress *per se* so much as with modelling validity. Nonetheless, this work is founded on the evolutionary biological nature of humans.

34. Wimsatt 1986.

35. Wimsatt 1986:299–300.

36. Wimsatt 1986:301.

37. Wimsatt 1986:302.

38. Wimsatt 1986:302.

39. Wimsatt 1986:299.

40. See references in Wimsatt 1980.

41. Wimsatt 1986:303.

42. Wimsatt 1986:304.

43. Wimsatt 1980:230.

44. Wimsatt 1980:249.

45. Hindess 1988:44–45.

46. Hindess 1988: 103–104.

47. Wimsatt 1980:233–234.

48. Wimsatt 1986:306.

49. Wimsatt 1980:251.

50. Wimsatt 1986:309.

51. Wimsatt 1980:252.

52. Garfinkel 1981.

53. Garfinkel 1981:21.

54. Garfinkel 1981:27.

55. The reduction is not necessarily possible, because, for example, two contradictory theories may have the same object of explanation.

56. Garfinkel 1981:53.

57. Garfinkel 1981:56.

58. Indeed, our use of the term "accident" to describe such events says much about our attitude towards them. Very few car crashes are properly accidents in the sense of happenings without apparent cause.

59. Garfinkel 1981:57.

60. Garfinkel 1981:58.

61. Wimsatt 1981:144,

62. Wimsatt 1981:145.

63. Wimsatt 1981:146.

64. Wimsatt 1981:126.

65. This was argued in chapter 4.

66. Note, though, that to actually do this would be to defeat the whole purpose of the maps, which is precisely to extract useful information from the total. The more one combines maps, the closer one gets to a replica, and the studying of complete replicas offers little if any advantage over studying the world as a whole.

67. This point was argued in chapter 4.

68. This point was argued in chapter 4.

69. I am not suggesting that the space-time framework is just a human construct in the way that the map grid is. I am merely saying that it functions for us in the same way.

70. Note that the individualist explanation fits more easily into the spatiotemporal framework than the structuralist one. Wimsatt explains the persistence of reductionism on this feature.

71. Drury 1987:Ch.5.

72. Inaccuracies are due to the underdetermination of the data, which itself can be regarded as accurate.

73. Gellner 1988.

74. Gellner 1988.

8. The MMK and the Metatheory of Sociology

1. Shweder and Fiske 1986, Bhaskar 1979, Ritzer 1992b.

2. Dudley Shapere (1986) has attacked Kuhn's globalism, and I am inclined to agree with him, but I have not given a great deal of attention to the issue. Nonetheless, Kuhn is so popular among social scientists that I believe it is useful to argue from within his framework here.

3. Runciman 1978:65.

4. See §1.2.2.

5. See Kuhn (1970) and Feyerabend (1978).

6. Gould 1993.

7. Gould 1993:125.

8. Norris 1993.

9. This seemed to be the best solution. While the terms "new idealism" and "new orthodoxy" have been used to describe these positions, and even "cultural studies" (which reflects the name given to the burgeoning degrees, academic departments, and so on that are developing on the basis of these perspectives), these terms seem to me either too abstract or too capable of being used derogatively to be of use here.

10. The use of the word *humanism* here differs from the way the word is usually used in postmodernist debates, where humanism is closely related to the ideals of the enlightenment, and hence to *modernist*, as opposed to *postmodernist*, ideals or goals.

11. See Latour and Woolgar 1979 and Lyotard 1984.

12. See Norris 1993 and Freadman and Miller 1992.

13. Crook 1990.

14. Crook 1990:48.

15. Crook 1990:51–52.

16. A rather inelegant phrase I use to convey the reverse of "naturalizing the human sciences."

17. Though I do not agree with the existence, or even the possibility, of completely universal laws, I have reservations about the ethical issues raised by denying, e.g., the presumption of equality. I take up some of the ethical problems associated with relativism later in the chapter.

18. Lyotard 1984: xxiii.

19. Lyotard 1984: 31.

20. Crook 1990: 53.

21. Lyotard 1984: xxiv.

22. Hooker 1987.

23. Crook 1990:53–58.

24. Freadman and Miller 1992:125.

25. Norris 1993:23; Freadman and Miller 1992.

26. Norris 1993:16.

27. Norris, 1993:26.

28. c.f., e.g., Easthope and McGowan 1992.

29. Docker 1982:75.

30. cf Turner 1993.

31. Gould 1993:125.

32. Gould 1993:125.

33. Gross and Levitt 1994.

34. Rubinstein et al. 1984:xx.

35. Campbell 1986.

36. Gross and Levitt 1994; Windschuttle 1993; Trigger 1993.

37. Merton 1973.

38. Bridgstock 1994.

39. T. H. Huxley, quoted in Darwin 1887:347.

40. Slezak 1994.

41. Chomsky 1969 and Norris 1993.

BIBLIOGRAPHY

Abercrombie, N., Hill, S., and Turner, B. S. 1984. *The Penguin Dictionary of Sociology*. Penguin, Harmondsworth.

Andreski, S. 1972. *Social Sciences as Sorcery*. André Deutsch, London.

Andreski, S. 1974. *The Essential Comte*. Trans. M. Clarke. Croom Helm, London.

Aristotle. 1961. *Metaphysics*. Trans. John Warrington. Dent, London.

Azevedo, Jane. 1988. A Backwards Approach to Science; a review of *The Presence of the Past*, by Rupert Sheldrake. *Newcastle Herald*, 1 October.

Azevedo, Jane. 1989. Marxism, Feminism and Epistemology: A Mapping Model of Knowledge Applied to a Feminist Case Study. *Dialectic* 32: 1–9.

Baldus, Bernd. 1990. Positivism's Twilight? *Canadian Journal of Sociology* 15 (2): 149–163.

Barnes, Barry. 1984. Problems of Intelligibility and Paradigm Instances. In *Scientific Rationality: the Sociological Turn*. Ed. J. R. Brown. D. Reidel, Dordrecht.

Becker, Howard S. 1953. Becoming a Marihuana User. *American Journal of Sociology* 59: 235–242.

Becker, Howard S. 1955. Marihuana Users and Social Control. *Social Problems* 3, 34–44.

Benton, T. 1977. *Philosophical Foundations of the Three Sociologies*. Routledge and Kegan Paul, London.

Berger, P. L. and Luckmann, T. 1967. *The Social Construction of Reality*. Allen Lane The Penguin Press, London.

Berlin, B., Breedlove, C., and Raven, P. H. 1966. *Principles of Tzeltal Plant Classification; an Introduction to the Botanical Ethnography of a Mayan-Speaking People of Highland Chiapas*. Academic Press, New York.

Berlin, Brent. 1973. Folk Systematics in Relation to Biological Classification and Nomenclature. *Annual Review of Ecology and Systematics* 4: 259–271.

Bhaskar, Roy. 1978. *A Realist Theory of Science, 2nd ed.* Harvester, Brighton.

Bhaskar, Roy. 1979. *The Possibility of Naturalism*. Harvester, Brighton.

Bhaskar, Roy. 1986. *Scientific Realism and Human Emancipation.* Verso, London.

Bhaskar, Roy. 1989. *Reclaiming Reality: A Critical Introduction to Contemporary Philosophy.* Verso, London.

Bottomore, T. 1978. Marxism and Sociology. In *A History of Sociological Analysis.* Eds. T. Bottomore and R. A. Nisbet. Heinemann, London.

Bradie, Michael. 1986. Assessing Evolutionary Epistemology. *Biology and Philosophy* 1: 401–459.

Bridgstock, Martin. 1994. How Do Scientists Think About Scientific Misconduct? Paper presented at the Australasian Association for the History, Philosophy and Social Studies of Science Annual Conference, Griffith University, Brisbane.

Brown, C. H. 1979. *Understanding Society; an Introduction to Sociological Theory.* John Murray, London.

Brown, J. R., ed. 1984. *Scientific Rationality: the Sociological Turn,* D. Reidel, Dordrecht.

Bulmer, R. N. H. and Tyler, M. J. 1968. Karam Classification of Frogs. *Journal of the Polynesian Society* 77: 333–385.

Campbell, Donald T. 1973. Ostensive Instances and Entitativity in Language Learning. In *Unity Through Diversity: A Festschrift for Ludwig von Bertalanffy.* Eds. W. Gray & N. D. Rizzo. Gordon and Breach, New York.

Campbell, Donald T. 1974. Evolutionary Epistemology. In *The Philosophy of Karl Popper.* Ed. P. A. Schilpp. Open Court Publishing, La Salle.

Campbell, Donald T. 1979. A Tribal Model of the Social System Vehicle Carrying Scientific Knowledge. *Knowledge: Creation, Diffusion, Utilization,* 1(2): 181–201.

Campbell, Donald T. 1986. Science's Social System of Validity-Enhancing Collective Belief Change and the Problems of the Social Sciences. In *Metatheory in Social Science; Pluralisms and Subjectivities.* Eds. Donald W. Fiske and Richard A. Shweder. University of Chicago Press, Chicago.

Campbell, Donald T. and Paller, Bonnie T. 1989. Extending Evolutionary Epistemology to "Justifying" Scientific Beliefs (A Sociological Rapprochement with a Fallibilist Perceptual Foundationalism?). In *Issues in Evolutionary Epistemology.* Eds. Kai Hahlweg & C. A. Hooker. State University of New York Press, Albany.

Carrithers, Michael. 1990a. Is Anthropology Art or Science?. *Current Anthropology* 31 (3): 263–282.

Carrithers, Michael. 1990b. Why Humans Have Cultures. *Man (N.S.)* 25: 189–206.

Cartwright, Nancy. 1983. *How the Laws of Physics Lie.* Clarendon, Oxford.

Carver, T. 1982. *Marx's Social Theory*. Oxford University Press, Oxford.

Chalmers, A. F. 1982. *What Is This Thing Called Science? An Assessment of the Nature of Science and its Methods, 2nd ed.* University of Queensland Press, St Lucia.

Chambliss, W. J. 1975. Towards a Political Economy of Crime. *Theory and Society* 2: 149–170.

Chomsky, Noam. 1969. *American Power and the New Mandarins*. Pelican, Harmondsworth.

Churchland, Paul M. 1979. *Scientific Realism and the Plasticity of the Mind*. Cambridge University Press, Cambridge.

Churchland, Paul M. 1984. *Matter and Consciousness*. M.I.T. Press, Cambridge, Massachusetts.

Cicourel, A. 1976. *The Social Organization of Juvenile Justice*. Heinemann, London.

Collins, H. M. 1985. *Changing Order: Replication and Induction in Scientific Practice*. Sage, London.

Converse, Philip E. 1986. Generalization and the Social Psychology of Other Worlds. In *Metatheory in Social Science; Pluralisms and Subjectivities. Eds. Donald W. Fiske & Richard A. Shweder.* University of Chicago Press, Chicago.

Crook, Stephen 1990. "The End of Radical Social Theory? Radicalism, Modernism and Postmodernism." In *Postmodernism and Society*. Eds. Boyne, Roy and Rattansi, Ali. Macmillan, Basingstoke.

Cuff, E. C. and Payne, G. C. F., eds. 1984. *Perspectives in Sociology, 2nd ed.* Allen & Unwin, London.

Cuff, E. C., Sharrock, W. W., and Francis, D. W. 1990. *Perspectives in Sociology,* 3rd edition. Unwin Hyman, London.

Cummins, Robert. 1983. *The Nature of Psychological Explanation*. M.I.T Press, Cambridge, Massachusetts.

Darwin, Charles. 1887. *The Life and Letters of Charles Darwin, including an Autobiographical Chapter.* Ed. Francis Darwin. John Murray, London.

Dawkins, Richard. 1976. *The Selfish Gene*. Oxford University Press, New York.

Dawkins, Richard. 1988. Letter. *New Scientist,* 8 October.

Docker, John. 1982. "In Defence of Popular Culture." *Arena* 60: 72–87.

Drury S. A. 1987. *Image Interpretation in Geology*. Allen and Unwin, London.

Durkheim, Emile. 1933. *The Division of Labour in Society*. Trans. George Simpson. Macmillan, New York.

Durkheim, Emile. 1951. *Suicide: A Study in Sociology.* Trans. J. Spaulding and George Simpson. Free Press, Glencoe.

Durkheim, Emile. 1976. *The Elementary Forms of Religious Life.* Trans. J. W. Swain. Allen and Unwin, London.

Durkheim, Emile. 1982. *The Rules of Sociological Method and Selected Texts on Sociology and its Method.* Edited with an introduction by Steven Lukes. Trans. W. D. Halls. Macmillan, London.

Erikson, Kai T. 1962. Notes on the Sociology of Deviance. *Social Problems* 9: 307–314.

Erikson, Kai T. 1966. *Wayward Puritans.* Wiley, New York.

Feyerabend P. K. 1962. Explanation, Reduction and Empiricism. In *Minnesota Studies in the Philosophy of Science, Vol. III. Scientific Explanation, Space and Time.* Eds. H. Feigl and G. Maxwell. University of Minnesota Press, Minneapolis.

Feyerabend P. K. 1978. *Against Method: Outline of an Anarchistic Theory of Knowledge.* Verso, London.

Filippov, Alexander F. 1993. A Final Look Back at Soviet Sociology. *International Sociology* 8, 3 (September): 355–373.

Fiske, Donald W. 1986. Specificity of Method and Knowledge in Social Science. In *Metatheory in Social Science; Pluralisms and Subjectivities.* Eds. Donald W. Fiske and Richard A. Shweder. University of Chicago Press, Chicago.

Fiske, Donald W. and Shweder, Richard A., eds. 1986. *Metatheory in Social Science; Pluralisms and Subjectivities.* University of Chicago Press, Chicago.

Folse, Henry J. 1985. *The Philosophy of Niels Bohr: the Framework of Complementarity.* North-Holland Physics.

Frankel, Barbara. 1986. Two Extremes on the Social Science Commitment Continuum. In *Metatheory in Social Science; Pluralisms and Subjectivities.* Eds. Donald W. Fiske and Richard A. Shweder. University of Chicago Press, Chicago.

Fraser, S. J., Gabell, A. R., Green, A. A., and Huntington, J. F. 1986. Targeting Epithermal Alteration and Gossans in Weathered and Vegetated Terrains Using Aircraft Scanners: Successful Australian Case Histories. In *Remote Sensing for Exploration Geology: Proceedings of the Fifth Thematic Mapper Conference.* Reno, Nevada, 29 September–2 October 1986.

Freadman, Richard and Miller, Seumas. 1992. *Re-thinking Theory: a Critique of Contemporary Literary Theory and an Alternative Account.* Cambridge University Press, Cambridge.

Freund, J. 1968. *The Sociology of Max Weber.* Trans. Mary Ilford. Allen Lane, London.

Gadamer, Hans-Georg. 1975. *Truth and Method.* Sheed and Ward, London.

Game, A. and Pringle, R. 1983. *Gender at Work*. Allen and Unwin, Sydney.

Gareau, Frederick H. 1985. The Multinational Version of Social Science.*Current Sociology* 33 (3): 1–169.

Garfinkel, Alan 1981. *Forms of Explanation: Rethinking the Questions in Social Theory*. Yale University Press, New Haven.

Garfinkel H. 1967. *Studies in Ethnomethodology*. Prentice-Hall, New Jersey.

Gellner, Ernest. 1988. *Plough, Sword and Book; the Structure of Human History*. Collins Harvill, London.

Genovese, E. 1971. *In Red and Black*. Vintage, New York.

Gergen, Kenneth J. 1986. Correspondence Versus Autonomy in the Language of Understanding Human Action. *Metatheory in Social Science*. Eds. Donald W. Fiske & Richard A. Shweder. University of Chicago Press, Chicago.

Giddens, Anthony 1971. *Capitalism and Modern Social Theory*. Cambridge University Press, Cambridge.

Giddens, Anthony. 1986. *Sociology; a Brief but Critical Introduction, 2nd ed*. Macmillan, London.

Giddens, Anthony. 1989. *Sociology*. Polity, Cambridge.

Giddens, Anthony. 1993. *Sociology,* 2nd ed. Polity, Cambridge.

Goffman, Erving. 1961. *Asylums*. Penguin, Harmondsworth.

Gordon D. M. 1973. Capitalism, Class, and Crime in America. *Crime and Delinquency* (April 1973): 163–186.

Gould, Stephen Jay. 1977. *Ever Since Darwin; Reflections in Natural History*. Penguin, Harmondsworth.

Gould, Stephen Jay. 1980. *The Panda's Thumb; More Reflections in Natural History*. Penguin, Harmondsworth.

Gould, Stephen Jay. 1981. *The Mismeasure of Man*. Penguin, London.

Gould, Stephen Jay. 1983. *Hen's Teeth and Horse's Toes; Further Reflections in Natural History*. Penguin, Harmondsworth.

Gould, Stephen Jay. 1985. *The Flamingo's Smile; Reflections in Natural History*. Norton, New York.

Gould, Stephen Jay. 1987a. *Time's Arrow, Time's Cycle; Myth and Metaphor in the Discovery of Geological Time*. Harvard University Press, Cambridge.

Gould, Stephen Jay. 1987b. *An Urchin in the Storm: Essays about Books and Ideas*. Penguin, Harmondsworth.

Gould, Stephen Jay. 1989. *Wonderful Life: The Burgess Shale and the Nature of History.* Penguin, Harmondsworth.

Gould, Stephen Jay. 1991. *Bully for Brontosaurus: Further Reflections in Natural History.* Penguin, Harmondsworth.

Gould, Stephen Jay. 1993. *Eight Little Piggies: Reflections in Natural History.* Penguin, Harmondsworth.

Gross, Paul R. and Levitt, Norman. 1994. *Higher Superstition: the Academic Left and Its Quarrels with Science.* Johns Hopkins University Press, Baltimore.

Gurney, Patrick J. 1981. Historical Origins of Ideological Denial: the Case of Marx in American Sociology. *The American Sociologist* 16: 196–201.

Habermas J. 1972. *Knowledge and Human Interests.* Trans. J. J. Shapiro. Heinemann, London.

Hahlweg, Kai. 1983. *The Evolution of Science: A Systems Approach.* Ph. D thesis. The University of Western Ontario, unpbl.

Hahlweg, Kai and Hooker, C. A., eds. 1989a. *Issues in Evolutionary Epistemology.* State University of New York Press, Albany.

Hahlweg, Kai and Hooker, C. A. 1989b. Evolutionary Epistemology and Philosophy of Science. In *Issues in Evolutionary Epistemology.* Eds. Kai Hahlweg, Kai and C.A. Hooker. State University of New York Press, Albany.

Hanson, N. R. 1958. *Patterns of Discovery.* Cambridge University Press, Cambridge.

Harré, Rom. 1970. *The Principles of Scientific Thinking.* Macmillan, London.

Harré, Rom. 1979. *Social Being: A Theory for Social Psychology.* Basil Blackwell, Oxford.

Harré, Rom. 1983. *An Introduction to the Logic of the Sciences, 2nd ed.* Macmillan, London.

Harré, Rom. 1985. *The Philosophies of Science, 2nd ed.* Oxford University Press, Oxford.

Harris, Jack. 1988. Defenders of the Faith. *New Scientist,* 22 September.

Hesse, Mary. 1986. Changing Concepts and Stable Order. *Social Studies of Science* 16: 714–726.

Hindess, Barry. 1988. *Choice, Rationality, and Social Theory.* Unwin Hyman, London.

Hoban, Russell. 1973. *The Lion of Boaz-Jachin and Jachin-Boaz.* Pan, London.

Hoban, Russell. 1974. *Kleinzeit.* Pan, London.

Hooker C. A. 1972. The Nature of Quantum Mechanical Reality: Einstein versus Bohr. In *Paradigms and Paradoxes*. Ed. R. G. Colodny. University of Pittsburgh Press, Pittsburgh.

Hooker, C. A. 1975. Global Theories. *Philosophy of Science* 42: 152–179.

Hooker, C. A. 1980. Explanation, Generality and Understanding. *Australian Journal of Philosophy* 58 (3): 284–290.

Hooker, C. A. 1981a. Towards a General Theory of Reduction, Part I, Historical Framework. *Dialogue* XX: 38–59.

Hooker, C. A. 1981b. Towards a General Theory of Reduction, Part III, Cross-Categorial Reduction. *Dialogue* XX: 496–529.

Hooker, C. A. 1982. Understanding and Control. *Man-Environment Systems* 12 (4): 121–160.

Hooker, C. A. 1987a. *A Realistic Theory of Science*. State University of New York Press, Albany.

Hooker, C. A. 1987b. Review of "The Nature of Psychological Explanation" by Robert Cummins. *Philosophical Reviews*: 223–228.

Hooker, C. A. 1989a. Evolutionary Epistemology and Naturalist Realism. Part IV of Evolutionary Epistemology and Philosophy of Science, by Kai Hahlweg and C. A. Hooker. In *Issues in Evolutionary Epistemology*. Eds. Kai Hahlweg and C. A. Hooker. State University of New York Press, Albany.

Hooker, C. A. 1989b. Understanding Quantum Mechanics. *Dialectic* 32: 15–37.

Hooker, C. A. 1989c. Projection, Physical Intelligibility, Objectivity and Completeness: The Divergent Ideals of Bohr and Einstein. Typescript.

Hull, David L. 1988. A Mechanism and its Metaphysics: An Evolutionary Account of the Social and Conceptual Development of Science. *Biology and Philosophy* 3 (2).

Jagtenberg, Tom and D'Alton, Phillip. 1989. *Four Dimensional Social Space; Class, Gender, Ethnicity and Nature*. Harper and Row, Sydney.

Jessop, Bob. 1982. *The Capitalist State; Marxist Theories and Methods*. Martin Robertson, Oxford.

Jordan, Tim. 1989. Review of "Relativism and Realism in Science." Ed. Robert Nola. *Metascience* 7 (1): 21.

Kassof, Allen. 1965. American Sociology Through Soviet Eyes. *American Sociological Review* 30 (1).

Keat, R. and Urry, J. 1982. *Social Theory as Science, 2nd ed.* Routledge and Kegan Paul, London.

Kuhn, Thomas. 1970. *The Structure of Scientific Revolutions, 2nd ed.* University of Chicago Press, Chicago.

Lakatos, Imre and Musgrave, Alan, eds. 1970. *Criticism and the Growth of Knowledge.* Cambridge University Press, Cambridge.

Latour, Bruno and Woolgar, Steve. 1979. *Laboratory Life: the Social Construction of Scientific Facts.* Sage, Beverly Hills.

Laudan, Larry. 1979. *Progress and its Problems; Towards a Theory of Scientific Growth.* University of California Press, Berkeley.

Legge, Varoe. 1990. Sociology for One World: Selected Abstracts from the XIIth World Congress of Sociology Newsletter. *Nexus* 2 (3): 2–4.

Levine, Donald N. 1965. *Wax and Gold: Tradition and Innovation in Ethiopian Culture.* University of Chicago Press, Chicago.

Levine, Donald N. 1974. *Greater Ethiopia: The Evolution of a Multiethnic Society.* University of Chicago Press, Chicago.

Levins, Richard and Lewontin, Richard. 1980. Dialectics and Reductionism in Ecology. *Synthese* 43: 47–78.

Lodahl, Janice Beyer and Gordon, Gerald. 1972. The Structure of Scientific Fields and the Functioning of University Graduate Departments. *American Sociological Review* 37: 57–72.

Lorenz, Konrad. 1982. Kant's Doctrine of the A Priori in the Light of Contemporary Biology. In *Learning, Development and Culture: Essays in Evolutionary Epistemology.* Ed. H. C. Plotkin. Wiley, New York.

Love, Rosaleen. 1989. *The Total Devotion Machine and Other Stories.* Women's Press, London.

Lyotard, J. -F. 1984. *The Postmodern Condition.* Manchester University Press, Manchester.

MacPherson, C. B. 1977. Do We Need a Theory of the State? *Archives Europiennes de Sociologie* 18 (2): 223–244.

Mandelbaum, M. 1973. Societal Facts. In *The Philosophy of Social Explanation.* Ed. Alan Ryan. Oxford University Press, Oxford.

Margolis, Joseph. 1988. In Defense of Relativism. *Social Epistemology* 2 (3): 201–226.

Marx, Karl. 1975. *Karl Marx; Texts on Method.* Trans. and ed. Terrell Carver. Basil Blackwell, Oxford.

Marx, Karl and Engels, Frederick. 1978. *The Marx-Engels Reader, 2nd ed.* Ed. Robert C. Tucker. Norton, New York.

McMullin, Ernan. 1984. The Rational and the Social in the History of Science. In *Scientific Rationality: the Sociological Turn.* Ed. J. R. Brown. D. Reidel, Dordrecht.

Merton, Robert K. 1973. *The Sociology of Science: Theoretical and Empirical Investigations.* University of Chicago Press, Chicago.

Mills, C. Wright. 1959a. *The Sociological Imagination.* Penguin, Harmondsworth.

Mills, C. Wright. 1959b. *The Sociological Imagination,* Oxford University Press, London.

Mulkay, Michael. 1979. *Science and the Sociology of Knowledge.* Allen and Unwin, London.

Munz, Peter 1989. Taking Darwin Even More Seriously. In *Issues in Evolutionary Epistemology* Eds. Kai Hahlweg and C. A. Hooker. State University of New York Press, Albany.

Najman, Jake M. and Western, John S., eds. 1993. *A Sociology of Australian Society; Introductory Readings,* 2nd ed. Macmillan, South Melbourne.

Newton-Smith, W. H. 1981. *The Rationality of Science.* Routledge and Kegan Paul, London.

Nicholas, John M. 1984. Scientific and Other Interests. In *Scientific Rationality: the Sociological Turn.* Ed. J. R. Brown. D. Reidel, Dordrecht.

Norris, Christopher. 1993. *The Truth About Postmodernism.* Blackwell, Oxford.

The Oxford Atlas 1951. Eds. Clinton Lewis and J. D. Blackmore, with the assistance of D. P. Bickmore and K. R. Cook. Oxford University Press, Oxford.

Pearce, Frank. 1976. Corporate Crime and American Society. *Crimes of the Powerful Part 2 (77–109). Pluto, London.*

Polkinghorne, J. C. 1984. The Quantum World. Penguin, Harmondsworth.

Popper, K. R. 1979. *Objective Knowledge: An Evolutionary Approach.* 2nd ed. Clarendon, Oxford.

Popper, K. R. 1983. *A Pocket Popper.* Ed. D. Miller. Fontana, Oxford.

Prigogine, Ilya and Stengers, Isabelle. 1984. *Order Out of Chaos: Man's New Dialogue with Nature.* Bantam, Toronto.

Putnam, Hilary. 1960. Minds and Machines. In *Dimensions of Mind: a Symposium.* Ed. Sidney Hook. New York University Press, New York.

Quine, W. V. 1960. *Word and Object.* M.I.T. Press, Cambridge.

Radford, Colin. 1985. Must Knowledge—or "Knowledge"—be Socially Constructed. *Philosophy of the Social Sciences* 15: 15–33.

Radnitsky, G. 1970. *Contemporary Schools of Metascience, 2nd rev. ed.* Scandinavian University Books, Goteberg.

Reader, John. 1988. *Man on Earth.* Harper & Row, New York.

Reynolds, Paul Davidson. 1970. *A Primer in Theory Construction.* Bobbs-Merrill, Indianapolis.

Richter, Frank M. 1986. Non-Linear Behaviour. In *Metatheory in Social Science; Pluralisms and Subjectivities. Eds. Donald W. Fiske and Richard A. Schweder.* University of Chicago Press, Chicago.

Rieber, R. W., ed. 1983. *Dialogues on the Psychology of Language and Thought.* Plenum, New York.

Ritzer, George. 1992a. Metatheorizing in Sociology: Explaining the Coming of Age. In *Metatheorizing.* Ed. George Ritzer. Sage, Newbury Park.

Ritzer, George, ed. 1992b. *Metatheorizing.* Sage, Newbury Park.

Rorty, R. 1979. *Philosophy and the Mirror of Nature.* Princeton University Press, Princeton.

Rose, S., Lewontin, R. C., and Kamin, L. J. 1984. *Not in Our Genes: Biology, Ideology and Human Nature.* Penguin, Harmondsworth.

Rosenthal, R. and Jacobsen, L. 1968. *Pygmalion in the Classroom.* Holt, Rinehart and Winston, New York.

Roxborough, I. 1979. *Theories of Underdevelopment.* Macmillan, London.

Roy, Ramasray. 1977. Social Science Cooperation in Asia. In *Inter-regional Cooperation in the Social Sciences.* UNESCO, Paris.

Rubinstein, R. A., Laughlin, C. D., and McManus J. 1984. *Science as Cognitive Process; Towards an Empirical Philosophy of Science.* University of Pennsylvania Press, Philadelphia.

Runciman, W. G. 1978. Introduction to Part 2. In *Max Weber; Selections in Translation.* Ed. W. G. Runciman Cambridge University Press, Cambridge.

Samuel, Geoffrey. 1985. Science, Anthropology and Margaret Mead: a Galilean Dialogue. *Search* 16, # 9–12: 251–259.

Samuel, Geoffrey. 1990. *Mind, Body and Culture: Anthropology and the Biological Interface.* Cambridge University Press, Cambridge.

Sayer, Andrew. 1984. *Method in Social Science: A Realist Approach.* Hutchinson, London.

Shapere, D. 1984. *Reason and the Search for Knowledge: Investigations in the Philosophy of Science.* D. Reidel, Dordrecht.

Sheldrake, Rupert. 1987. *A New Science of Life; The Hypothesis of Formative Causation, New ed.* Paladin, London.

Sheldrake, Rupert. 1988. *The Presence of the Past; Morphic Resonance and the Habits of Nature.* Collins, London.

Sherwood, S., Smith, P., and Alexander, J. 1993. The British Are Coming . . . Again! The Hidden Agenda of "Cultural Studies." *Contemporary Sociology* 22, 2: 370–375.

Shweder, Richard A. and Fiske, Donald W. 1986. Introduction: Uneasy Social Science. In *Metatheory in Social Science: Pluralisms and Subjectivities. Eds. Donald W. Fiske and Richard A. Schweder.* University of Chicago Press, Chicago.

Simberloff, Daniel. 1980. A Succession of Paradigms in Ecology: Essentialism to Materialism and Probabalism. *Synthese* 43. 3–39.

Simpson, Michael K. 1987. *Realism, Bell's Theorem and Locality.* Ph.D thesis, University of Newcastle, NSW, unpbl.

Slezak, Peter. 1994. *Ethics and the Sociology of Science.* Paper presented at the Australasian Association for the History, Philosophy and Social Studies of Science Annual Conference, Griffith University, Brisbane.

Stich, S. 1983. *From Folk Psychology to Cognitive Science; the Case Against Belief.* M.I.T Press, Cambridge.

Toulmin, S. 1953. *The Philosophy of Science.* Arrow, London.

Turner, Graeme. 1993. "Media Texts and Messages." In *The Media in Australia.* Eds. S. Cunningham and G. Turner. Allen & Unwin, Sydney.

Trigger, David S. 1993. Review Article. Australian Cultural Studies: Radical Critique or Vacuous Posturing? *Anthropological Forum* 6, 4.

Urry, John. 1981. *The Anatomy of Capitalist Societies; the Economy, Civil Society and the State.* Macmillan, London.

Vickers, Geoffrey. 1983. *Human Systems are Different.* Harper and Row, London.

Wardell, Mark L. and Turner, Stephen P. 1986. Introduction: Dissolution of the Classical Project. In *Sociological Theory in Transition.* Eds. Mark L. Wardell & Stephen P. Turner. Allen and Unwin, Boston.

Weber, Max. 1930. *The Protestant Ethic and the Spirit of Capitalism.* Trans. T. Parsons. Allen and Unwin, London.

Weber, Max. 1978a. *Economy and Society; an Outline of Interpretive Sociology.* Eds. Guenther Roth and Claus Wittich. University of California Press, Berkeley.

Weber, Max. 1978b. *Max Weber; Selections in Translation.* Ed. W. G. Runciman. Trans. E. Matthews. Cambridge University Press, Cambridge.

Wimsatt, William C. 1980. Reductionist Research Strategies and their Biases in the Units of Selection Controversy. In *Scientific Discovery: Case Studies*. Ed. T. Nickles. D. Reidel, Dordrecht.

Wimsatt, William C. 1981. Robustness, Reliability, and Overdetermination. In *Scientific Inquiry and the Social Sciences: A Volume in Honor of Donald T. Campbell*. Eds. Marilynn B. Brewer and Barry E. Collins. Jossey-Bass, San Francisco.

Wimsatt, William C. 1986. Heuristics and the Study of Human Behaviour. In *Metatheory in Social Science; Pluralisms and Subjectivities*. Eds. Donald W. Fiske and Richard A. Shweder. University of Chicago Press, Chicago.

Windschuttle, Keith. 1994. *The Killing of History: How a Discipline is being Murdered by Literary Critics and Social Theorists*. Macleay, Sydney.

Woolgar, Steve. 1986. On the Alleged Distinction Between Discourse and Praxis. *Social Studies of Science* 16, 309–317.

Worsley, Peter, ed. 1987. *The New Introducing Sociology*. Penguin, Harmondsworth.

Ziman, J. 1978. *Reliable Knowledge: an Exploration of the Grounds for Belief in Science*. Cambridge University Press, Cambridge.

INDEX